Africa's Changing Markets for Health and Veterinary Services

Africa's Changing Markets for Health and Veterinary Services

The New Institutional Issues

Edited by

David K. Leonard
Dean of International and Area Studies
University of California, Berkeley
USA

First published in Great Britain 2000 by
MACMILLAN PRESS LTD
Houndmills, Basingstoke, Hampshire RG21 6XS and London
Companies and representatives throughout the world

A catalogue record for this book is available from the British Library.

ISBN 0–333–76284–3 hardcover
ISBN 0–333–76285–1 paperback

First published in the United States of America 2000 by
ST. MARTIN'S PRESS, INC.,
Scholarly and Reference Division,
175 Fifth Avenue, New York, N.Y. 10010

ISBN 0–312–23266–7 (cloth)
ISBN 0–312–23267–5 (paperback)

Library of Congress Cataloging-in-Publication Data
Africa's changing markets for health and veterinary services : the new institutional issues / edited by David K. Leonard.
p. cm.
Includes bibliographical references and index.
ISBN 0–312–23266–7 (cloth) — ISBN 0–312–23267–5 (pbk.)
1. Medical economics—Africa, Sub-Saharan. 2. Veterinary services—Economic aspects—Africa, Sub-Saharan. I. Leonard, David K.
RA410.55.A357 A357 2000
338.4'73621'0967—dc21

99–088269

This book is printed on paper suitable for recycling and made from fully managed and sustained forest sources.

10 9 8 7 6 5 4 3 2 1
09 08 07 06 05 04 03 02 01 00

Printed and bound in Great Britain by
Antony Rowe Ltd, Chippenham, Wiltshire

Contents

List of Figures

List of Tables

Abbreviations

AHC	Animal Management and Health Center (Zimbabwe)
AHI	Animal Health Inspectors (agriculturale diplomates, Zimbabwe)
AI	Artificial Insemination
ANVS	Association Nationale des Vétérinaires Sénégalais
ATE	Agents des Travaux d'Èlevage; low level technicians in Senegal
CBPP	Contagious Bovine Pleuropneumonia
CMBT	Christian Medical Board of Tanzania
CSSC	Christian Social Services Commission
DMO	District Medical Officer (Tanzania)
DVM	Doctors of Veterinary Medicine (Senegal)
ECF	East Coast Fever
ELCT	Evangelical Lutheran Church of Tanzania
FLT	First-level Transformation (Senegal)
FMD	Foot and Mouth Disease
GVO	Government Veterinary Office (Zimbabwe)
GVP	Government Veterinary Practitioner (Senegal)
HH	Head of Household
IOE	International Office for Epizootics
ITE	Ingénieurs des Travaux d'Èlevage; middle level paraprofessionals in Senegal
MD	Medical Doctor
MF	Master Farmer
NGO	Nongovernmental organization
NR	Natural Region (Zimbabwe)
PNVA	Programme Nationale de Vulgarisation Agricole (Senegal)
PVO	Provincial Veterinary Office (Zimbabwe)
PVP	Private Veterinary Practioner (Senegal)
RC	Roman Catholic
SDA	Seventh-Day Adventist
SEM	Standard Error of the Mean

SERAS	Société d'Exploitation des Ressources Animales du Sénégal
SLT	Second-level Transformation (Senegal)
TRA	Traditional System (Senegal)
VLT	Veterinary Livestock Technician (Zimbabwe)
VLU	Veterinary Livestock Units (Senegal)
VVP	Village Veterinary Pharmacies (Senegal)
WHO	World Health Organization

Biographical Notes

Damen Haile Mariam: MD (Addis Ababa University, 1987), MPH (Addis Ababa University, 1989), Ph.D. (Health Policy, University of California, Berkeley, 1996); Assistant Professor, Department of Community Health, Medical Faculty, Addis Ababa University, Ethiopia.

Lee M.P.K. Koma: BVM (Makerere, 1980), M.Phil. (Edinburgh, 1984); Chair and Senior Lecturer, Department of Veterinary Surgery and Reproduction, Faculty of Veterinary Medicine, Makerere University, Kampala, Uganda.

David K. Leonard: BA (Haverford, 1963), Ph.D. (Political Science, University of Chicago, 1974); Dean of International and Area Studies and Professor, Department of Political Science, University of California, Berkeley, USA.

Kenneth L. Leonard: BA (Swarthmore, 1989), Ph.D. (Agricultural and Resource Economics, University of California, Berkeley, 1997); Assistant Professor, Department of Economics, Columbia University, New York, USA.

Cheikh Ly: DVM (EISMV - Dakar), MSc. (Agricultural Economics, Michigan State University); Professeur agrégé au Service d'Economie Rurale et Gestion de l'Ecole Inter-Etats des Sciences et Médecine Vétérinaires (E.I.S.M.V.) de Dakar.

Gilbert R. Mliga: MD (University of Dar es Salaam, 1978), MPH (Royal Tropical Institute, Amsterdam, 1983), MHPEd. (University of New South Wales, 1989); Director, Human Resources Development, Ministry of Health, Tanzania.

Sylvester Ndeso-Atanga: RN (SUNY-Albany, 1974), BSc. (CCNY, 1978), MPH (Yale, 1980), Ph.D. Candidate (London School of Hygiene & Tropical Medicine); Lecturer in Epidemiology and Public Health, Faculty of Health Sciences, University of Buea, Cameroon.

Pamela S.A. Woods: BVSc. (University of Zimbabwe, 1987), Residency in Clinical Veterinary Studies (University of Zimbabwe, 1989), MSc. (Large Animal Clinical Sciences, Michigan State University, 1992); Ph.D. Candidate (Epidemiology, University of Utrecht); Lecturer, Clinical Veterinary Studies Department, Faculty of Veterinary Science, University of Zimbabwe.

Abstracts

1. David K. Leonard, **The New Institutional Economics and the Restructuring of Animal Health Services in Africa.**

The chapter establishes the theoretical framework for the research conducted for the book, on both animal and human health services. Using the New Institutional Economics, it reviews a number of critical issues in the structural reform of animal health services in Africa and highlights several problems that others concerned with the privatization of this service area have tended to neglect. Most notably, it calls attention to (1) the need to retain a central role for paraprofessionals in any new delivery system, (2) the important and problematic relationship between the veterinary and paraveterinary professions, (3) the importance of developing state contracting procedures for assisting the private delivery of animal health services that will minimize the problems of local monopoly, and (4) the central role that professionalism will have to play in this area if collective goods and the public interest are to be served. The chapter's larger purpose is to demonstrate that the New Institutional Economics offers an array of tools that improve the ability of policymakers and scholars to anticipate and think through the fundamental challenges posed by the privatization of professional services in Africa. It sets the agenda for the research projects that comprise this volume.

2. Damen Haile Mariam. **Traditional Insurance Mechanisms and the Choice of Health Care Providers in Ethiopia.**

In most Sub-Saharan African countries, governments can no longer afford to finance health care services for the same reasons that the African state is claimed to be failing more generally. International assistance for health services is also falling. The adoption of cost sharing and the institution of service charges in government facilities are among the alternatives that are prescribed to these states for alleviating such difficulties. However, such polices require the presence of well-established formal insurance schemes that are nonexistent in these countries (unless one considers government financing of health services as national insurance).

Only traditional arrangements to help victims of catastrophic events deal with financial burdens are pervasive in most of these countries.

This chapter uses household survey data to examine the determinants of choice of health care providers in rural Ethiopia. It also investigates how traditional forms of social insurance work in the context of health care provision among the study population so as to determine their role in possible community financing schemes. The results show that age, severity of illness, and support from extended families significantly affect the choice of health care providers that either were geographically distant (involving time and travel cost) or that charge higher prices (monetary cost). Further analysis shows that potential assistance by relatives and friends acts as an insurance mechanism.

3. Pamela S.A. Woods, **The Importance of Gender, Proximity and Transport Availability as Transaction Costs in the Utilization of Veterinary Services in Zimbabwe**.

The productivity of livestock owned by subsistence farmers could be increased by veterinary intervention in the form of disease prevention and treatment, and extension about management techniques. In 1987, the Government of Zimbabwe introduced Veterinary Livestock Technicians (VLTs) to supply grassroots veterinary services. However, two sets of transaction costs may reduce the full utilization and efficacy of these services. The transaction costs identified in this chapter are those of geographical and social distance between veterinary personnel and the subsistence farmers. A paired sample design of eight matched pairs of female and male VLTs was employed. Eight enumerators delivered a questionnaire about livestock owned, household characteristics, and the previous use of the veterinary services to 768 farmers whose farms were located away from the AHC in three selected distance zones (0–2 km, 5–7 km and 10–12 km). The farmers included male head of households, widows, and female managers whose husbands were elsewhere.

This survey did not find that women VLT interactions with women farmers were more effective than those of male VLTs. There was a gender bias in the demand for veterinary services, with male farmers less likely to request the services of women VLTs. However, women VLTs were generally as effective as their male counterparts, and the farmer's use of veterinary services increased after attending VLT-held training sessions. Forty-five per cent of both cattle and goat owners reported having had a sick animal in the past, but fully 30 per cent of cattle owners asked the VLT for assistance, compared with only 17 per cent of goat owners. The VLTs serve large areas, often without motorized transport, and the farmers travel long distances to call the VLT for assistance. This greatly affects both the demand and the supply of all the veterinary services. VLTs who either owned a motorbike or were provided with one by the government tended toward the provision of curative services at the cost of preventive services, especially routine disease surveillance.

4. Kenneth L. Leonard, **Incentives and Rural Health Care Delivery: Cameroon I.**

Patients seek quality care but cannot purchase it directly on the market. They must instead choose the practitioner they believe is appropriate from a limited list of possible practitioners. To learn about the important elements of quality, we observe patient behavior in choosing between government health centers and hospitals, mission health centers and hospitals, and traditional healers in rural Cameroon. Quality clearly is related to the incentives that practitioners have to exert effort on the behalf of the patient. Since mission facilities are more likely to punish practitioners who do not provide high levels of effort, we observe that patients who seek these facilities believe high levels of effort are necessary in order to cure their condition. Furthermore, it appears as if the institution of traditional medicine is designed to insure patients that practitioners have the appropriate incentives to cure their condition.

Structural estimation is then used to examine the effect of asymmetric information on different groups and to test the effect of different pricing and management policies on those groups. It is clear that the current lack of quality has caused great losses to the poor. The government has a responsibility to increase the incentives that practitioners have to deliver quality health care by increasing the supervision of medical quality. A government policy that addresses this concern will have a very large benefit to the population and will not require additional outlays from the government.

5. Sylvester Ndeso-Atanga, **Health Care Quality and the Choice of Care Providers: Cameroon II.**

The factors affecting choice of providers of curative and maternity services are examined and compared for one area of rural Cameroon. Patient income, service price, and distance all influence selections, but much less than had been believed. Considerations of service quality and disease severity dominate choice. The reasons patients give for choosing a particular health provider are the best predictor of their decisions. These reasons do not represent invariant values of preference functions for the patient, however. We show that the subjective reasons or preferences given can be predicted from the objective nature of the symptoms from which the patient is suffering. When a disease dictates quality treatment, this factor dominates the choice made and the reason given for it. When a condition is less sensitive to quality of treatment, decisions and reasons then reflect considerations of price, distance, and income.

The pattern for maternity services appears at first to be quite different. Although income once again has only a modest effect on choice, selections overwhelmingly favor the lower cost and easier to reach facilities; quality concerns are not immediately evident. We argue that this contrasts with the pattern for curative services for two reasons: (a) the very widespread use of health centers for prenatal examinations allows women to know if birth complications are likely and therefore whether or not a facility's quality is important; and (b) the payment system for maternity cases includes strong incentives in favor of superior medical effort. This makes their claims of high quality prenatal care more credible than similar claims for curative interventions that are not buttressed by a similar payment incentive structure. We therefore conclude that medical quality and the incentives that help to assure it are central to health care, even in rural Africa.

6. Lee M.P.K. Koma, **Can Private Veterinarians Survive in Uganda?**

This chapter examines animal health priorities and patterns of consumption for livestock producers in two representative districts of southern Uganda and contrasts producer priorities with the priorities and work patterns of the veterinary service community. It concludes that no significant damage to livestock production in Uganda is likely to result from privatization, because producers and veterinarians have very similar priorities for animal health. However, full veterinarians will need to adapt their practices to the new realities of privatization if they are to survive in competition with paraprofessional animal health practitioners because producers will pay extra only for what practitioners actually do, not for their level of training.

7. Cheikh Ly, **Veterinary Professionals in Senegal: Allocation of Priorities and Working Behavior**.

This chapter evaluates the structure of Senegal's veterinary services market. It analyzes the results of two cross-sectional descriptive surveys, conducted in 1995, that explored the priorities and behavior of livestock herders and veterinary practitioners. The path to privatization has been slow, and inputs such as services delivery, working behavior, and priorities are not yet clearly differentiated. Private practitioners do give somewhat greater weight to curative interventions and grant less importance to public health regulation than do their government counterparts, but the differences are not as great as market pressures might have led one to expect. Signs of a set of common professional veterinary values are evident across all levels of training.

Animal health providers have different and more appropriate service priorities than herders do, indicating the importance of professionalism. Also, fully trained veterinarians are facing a 'lemons' market in which their superior skills, compared with those of paraprofessionals, are not visible to herders and therefore are not competitive. To strengthen the process toward an efficient market, avoid veterinary monopolies and limit unnecessary competition with paraprofessionals and auxiliaries, this chapter concludes that Senegal's veterinary self-regulatory board must become an organizational entrepreneur that promotes and maintains more stringent veterinary standards.

8. Gilbert R. Mliga, **Decentralization and the Quality of Health Care in Tanzania**.

The relative performance of 51 mission and government hospitals and health centers in the Arusha and Iringa regions of Tanzania is analyzed and related to the ways in which the facilities are managed. Quality is evaluated on several dimensions and is based on the direct observation of 749 clinical consultations by a team of medical experts. The study concludes that decentralization improves the quality of health care. Local control of personnel, along with staff salaries linked to facility revenues, give health providers the incentive to provide quality service and to attract clients. Decentralization in the management of material resources is usually closely linked with staff decentralization and is a less powerful contributor to quality. The presence of an MD at the facility contributes to quality both directly through higher professional standards and indirectly by increasing resource decentralization.

9. Cheikh Ly, **Management and the Impact of Auxiliaries on Pastoral Production in Senegal.**

In the Senegalese pastoral area of the Ferlo, providers of livestock services at the herder level are diverse and are characterized by the presence of village veterinary pharmacies (VVP), auxiliaries, government veterinary paraprofessionals, and private formal and informal sellers of drugs and vaccines. This chapter reports on field research that was con-ducted in 1995 on 32 pharmacies, 63 auxiliaries and 348 pastoralists chosen from 12 randomly selected water boreholes to represent three types of veterinary service delivery system. Survey results show that herder attitudes toward animal health providers are better in the NGO VVP system, where auxiliaries are under better supervision and management.

10. David K. Leonard, **Lessons from the New Institutional Economics for the Structuural Reform of Human Health Services in Africa.**

Curative medical care in Africa has become increasingly commercialized. By and large, however, the market has not yet worked any miracles. Instead, the expansion of markets has exposed the absence or weakness of the institutions required for their efficient operation. Among the important institutional issues that need to be addressed are three on which the New Institutional Economics and the research presented in this book cast considerable light. (i) An institutional mechanism for providing some kind of insurance against catastrophic medical expenses must be crafted. In the context of economies dominated by the informal sector and peasant agriculture, our research suggests that the extended family is the most viable base for such an insurance system. (ii) The organizations providing curative care need to be restructured so that the increasing fees and charges paid by patients unlock improved supply rather than simply reduce demand. Our work suggests the benefits of extending the role of decentralized nongovernmental organizations (NGOs) that manage their own resources and depend on them for their survival. (iii) Mechanisms that reduce the serious imperfect information problems in medical transactions must be found if markets are to prosper and patients are to find quality care. Our research leads us to give particular attention to two institutional solutions that are particularly important in contemporary Africa: the contingent contract and missions.

Preface

In the wake of the 'Great African Depression' of the 1980s and 90s and the consequent fiscal collapse of most of the continent's states, international donors have sponsored a massive attempt to restructure African economies. Led by the World Bank, donors have sought to move services wherever possible from the public to the private sectors. And for those services that they judged it impossible or inappropriate to privatize, donors have encouraged user fees to check consumer demand, increase revenues and reduce the pressures on the national treasury.

The implicit theories that have underlain these endeavors have been quite simple. They are, as argued initially in the Bank's Berg Report: (1) the limited implementation capacity of the African state has been seriously overextended; and (2) in most domains any form of private enterprise is likely to outperform the public sector. Admittedly, the Bank's staff do believe that the privatization of economic enterprises is more important than that of social services (World Bank 1981). Hence there has been more pressure to privatize government corporations (parastatals) that direct services to citizens and a greater reduction in government's role in animal health (as an economic service) than in human medicine (as a welfare one). Beyond that, however, to judge by the Bank's actual practice, the theory appears to be that (3) any form of privatization or fee recovery to which African political leaders will consent is economically and socially desirable.

The third 'theory' alerts us to danger, for it really is no more than an assumption and a poorly grounded one at that. In the phrase of Johnston and Clark (1982, pp. 15–16), 'if we can't always get what we want, we also should not always want what we can get.' The dynamics of political action are such that the policies that are offered first in response to crisis or pressure can often be perversely inappropriate.

Similarly the proposition about relative efficiencies of states and markets is rooted in theoretical work done before 1975[1] and does not take

---

1. We choose this as the watershed year because it corresponds with the publication of a

advantage of the major contributions of the last 20 years in the New Institutional Economics, the theory of collective action, and organization theory. Thus, these endeavors at structural reform have been lacking in the subtlety and sophistication that they could possess. The World Bank itself has been rethinking its approach to structural adjustment and sees a more significant role for the state than it did a decade ago (World Bank 1997). But when we look at specific sectors and services, important structures and policies have still received insufficient examination. This is very much the case for veterinary medicine and human health care in Africa.

WHY HUMAN AND ANIMAL HEALTH SERVICES?

In this volume, we probe and challenge the assumptions that implicitly underlie the restructuring of services providing human and animal health care in Africa. Government health services have featured prominently in debates about structural adjustment because of their obvious welfare implications. And within the livestock sector, veterinary services have received considerable attention as well (for example, FAO 1997b). We submit that parallel consideration of experience in both these services is remarkably productive for a variety of reasons.

At the level of economic theory, customers (patients or herders) of both these services the have considerably less knowledge and information than the providers (clinicians or veterinarians), who also have made a considerable sunk investment in their training. Neoclassical economics assumes that individuals always maximize their welfare, have full information and knowledge about how to do so, are able to contract and enforce the terms of exchanges costlessly, and have an unrestricted ability to reinvest assets in more attractive opportunities (North 1990, pp. 17–26). With these premises, economics assumes a world in which incentives are unfettered and work to their maximum effect. Human and animal health care do not neatly fit these assumptions. Seller and buyer are unequal in their information and the seller has a considerable sunk investment in his or her 'human capital' (an example of what Williamson, 1975, calls 'asset specificity'). In this way, these two services challenge us to examine the limits of the assumptions that neoclassical economics

founding work of the New Institutional Economics, Williamson's *Markets and Hierarchies* (1975).

uses in making its policy prescriptions and take us into the world of the 'New Institutionalism' in economics, sociology, and political science.

What, other than empirical realities that diverge in common from the esoteric assumptions underlying economic theory, would lead us to examine human and animal health services together? Do policymakers in each of these two domains have anything at all to learn from looking at the other? We can start with the obvious: the biological science that undergirds human and veterinary medicine is the same; in fact, a great deal of the medical research on which the treatment of humans depends is actually veterinary research, for it is conducted on an array of animals. Although the various species of mammals do have important differences in their responses to disease and treatment, there are significant physiological parallels and many diseases—and cures—pass back and forth across the human/animal divide (Schwabe 1984). Physicians and vets also receive similar training, work in professions that are structured much like one another, and oversee analogous hierarchies of paraprofessionals and auxiliaries. We have already observed that both professions enjoy an information advantage over their clients.

To be sure, there are important differences between human health and veterinary services as well. Specialization is not as extensive among veterinarians as it is among physicians, and hospitals do not play the role in the treatment of animals that they do for humans. Distance in Africa is an even more serious constraint on realizing professional care for sick animals than it is for humans. The 'bottom line,' when further expenditure on care is no longer warranted, is much clearer for ruminants, which have an identifiable economic value, than it is for humans, who have an intangible moral worth. And the two professions have different histories and thus different conventions. As an illustration, it is usually considered unethical for private physicians to act as their own pharmacists, while most private veterinarians make over half their income from the sale to their clients of the medications they prescribe. As will become clear in the studies reported in this volume, these differences do shape the ways in which human and animal health care are provided. In our experience, however, the two professions are close enough that these very differences help each to look at its own structures and operations in new and illuminating ways. Each assists us in asking 'unthinkable' questions about the other. For example, the very fact that curative veterinary services are now effectively privatized in a large number of African countries enables us to see more clearly the issues that soon will trouble a human health system that is more and more marketized each day yet remains dominated by a discourse over user fees.

THEORY AND POLICY RELEVANCE

What can a policymaker hope to gain from reading these studies? Much more, we hope, than simple lessons about the specific systems studied, for we have paid attention to the theoretical implications of our work in a way that leads to generalizability. Anything with the word 'theory' attached to it is usually and appropriately anathema to policymakers. We contend, however, that the magnitude of the shifts that are occurring as Africa's economies are restructured is so great that policymakers in practice are relying heavily on theory. Proposed changes often lie beyond the experience of African states, and the number of dimensions along which reforms are being made is so large that the permutations and interaction effects defy evaluation through simple experiment and observation. Restructuring of the scope proposed and implemented in Africa in the last 20 years has to be based on theory, for theory alone condenses other human experiences in a way that permits policymakers to step into terrain that has never been explored in their country or by their neighbors.

When we speak of theory here, we do not mean obtuse verbal treatises or complex mathematical formulae. Instead we mean the simple, often intuitive, models that policymakers use when they try to guess how a reform might work in their country. It is easier to see that those with whom one disagrees are guided by theoretical assumptions than it is to see the same in oneself. Most African policymakers are all too aware of the neoliberal assumptions driving the World Bank, just as some donors think their African counterparts are captured by old statist approaches. Some of the models and theories that guide policymakers are simple and unconscious; at other times they are complex or explicitly articulated. Either way, they shape the way policymakers evaluate and choose among alternatives.

The studies that follow in this volume will challenge many of the theoretical assumptions of both neoliberal and statist policymakers. It is reasonable to expect that they point to features of African societies and markets that transcend national frontiers. As such, they have very real policy consequences beyond the boundaries of the individual countries in which the studies were made. We are modest in providing detailed policy prescriptions, however, and for an excellent reason: we ourselves do not know all the implications of what we have found. We find that African social systems and markets handle human and animal health care in different ways than others have assumed. Our findings will lead, we hope, to new theories—new mental models guiding the policymaker. These theories or models have to be integrated with others that we did not study—ones about other aspects of the health systems, about political dynamics, and so on. And all these models have to be combined with country and situationally specific facts. This is a task that policymakers have to perform for themselves in their own highly particular circumstances.

VALUE PREMISES

Our findings would lead policymakers to experiment further with market structures for the delivery of services traditionally provided by governments in Africa. In contrast to neoliberals, however, we stress that such experiments will turn out well only if, in contrast to World Bank analyses to date, closer attention is paid to the deep institutional context within which these markets are operating.

Nonetheless, given that we do often find ourselves on the 'market' side of the policy debate in Africa, we would like to make clear that we are not advocating a reduction in government expenditures on human or animal health for the continent. Veterinary services contribute directly to the productivity of livestock and, in most African countries, herders have received much less attention from their governments than have those in other sectors of the economy. Human health services add to the welfare of African peoples, and their formation of human capital fosters economic development. And there is a direct link between the human health and veterinary economies: the improved food products generated by superior veterinary services improve human health as well. The levels of expenditure by African governments in these health domains is not high at present. For example, African public expenditures on human health have not been above those of the Newly Industrializing Countries (NICs) of East Asia when the NICs had comparable levels of gross national product per capita in the early 1960s (World Bank 1994, p. 38). And African expenditure levels do not even approach adequacy for the health and veterinary needs of Africa's peoples.

Still, when the public sector is the sole provider of human and animal health care in the Africa of today, it leaves a huge volume of unmet demands. Furthermore, as we will show in this book, governments in Africa have difficulty in delivering certain kinds of health products that people want. Our position is that (1) people who want a service the government is unable to provide should be able to purchase it in the market if they can afford to do so; (2) government should provide services and regulate markets in such a way as to facilitate, not hinder, such private transactions; and (3) both government and private services should be organized in such a way that people are able to gain from them the maximum degree of benefit per unit of expenditure. Thus we do not advocate markets over the state for their own sake or to reduce government expenditures but as instruments that can help people get more of the kinds of human and animal health care they deserve and than would be provided otherwise.

THEMES

The empirical studies in this volume have a rich array of theoretical and policy implications. To whet the readers appetite, we will discuss those that revise human understanding of the nature of demand for these services, that call our attention to the importance of a variety of non-price costs in shaping demand, that point to the critical importance of the ways in which incentive structures shape the services that are being offered, and that illustrate the need for new institutions to support the emerging markets for these services, particularly insurance and professionalism.

Demand

Most studies of the impact of restructured health services in Africa have focused narrowly on possibly discriminatory impacts of price changes on the volume of demand. Our research suggests that this focus has been too circumscribed. We do not deny that price rises will lead to a drop in the quantity of demand for a particular service. Indeed, Cheikh Ly reports for Senegal that government animal health providers do double the volume of preventive and curative cases— as do their more expensive private counterparts— and Lee Koma finds that the propensity to seek veterinary in Uganda care drops as the expected cost of the treatment rises.

On the other hand, Ndeso Atanga shows that in Cameroon there are startlingly high levels of use of more expensive health providers, even among those who cite a concern with price as one of the determinants of their choice, and Damen Haille Mariam confirms this pattern in Ethiopia. As they and Kenneth Leonard demonstrate, clients are seeking first the quality of care that they feel is dictated by their particular condition and give only secondary consideration to price. If they have a condition that may not be treated well in the least expensive facility, they will seek out more costly ones that are appropriate. Thus there is a strong market for quality in Africa and people are prepared to pay for it when it is needed.

The quality clients are seeking has more to do with the effort providers are making than with formal qualifications. Lee Koma finds in Uganda that herders are prepared to pay full vets (DVMs) extra for the procedures that only they can perform, but they are not willing to pay more to have a DVM do a task that can be performed by a competent paraprofessional. He and Cheikh Ly (Senegal) report that DVMs rarely perform diagnostic procedures and therefore are not using the superior training and capacity for which herders might otherwise be prepared to pay. Rather, that training has earned them a credential— DVM— and that credential is a pre-requisite for entering the lucrative pharmaceuticals market. Kenneth Leonard demonstrates that clients are most concerned not with formal competence or capacity but with the exertion of the medical effort that is appropriate to their condition. Those institutions that can provide assurance that such effort will be made will attract the custom of those clients who need it. We discuss these types of institutions further when we look at incentive structures below.

When appropriately analyzed, price turns out not to have as much discriminatory effect as others have suggested. Kenneth Leonard and Ndeso Atanga find no evidence of differential treatment in Cameroon along gender or age lines once they control for the needs associated with the conditions from which the patients suffer. Damen Haile Mariam also observes no gender discrimination in Ethiopia when disease is taken into account. He does find that the young are treated more often and in less expensive facilities, but this is explained by the differences between childhood and adult diseases.

Income effects are weaker and different than expected. Lee Koma reports that the effects of herder income and wealth on the demand for animal health services are so weak as to lack statistical significance in a sample of reasonable size. Ndeso Atanga shows that differences in the structure of demand between top and bottom income quartiles are quite modest. Damen Haile Mariam proves that, in Ethiopia, the material resource constraint that shapes demand is not that of the individual or the nuclear family but of the extended family. The Cameroon study confirms this result.

A different question about demand concerns not its quantity but the appropriateness of its structure. There has been concern that African clients might not make full use of appropriate disease prevention measures, either because they were too short-sighted or because they wanted to 'free ride' on paying for services that have collective (or public) benefits, rather than just private ones. In this regard, there has been a fear that private health providers will give less attention to 'public goods,' dictating the retention of preventive services in government. Our studies looked at these questions most thoroughly with regard to animal health. It may well be that professionals are more sensitive to the long term benefits of prevention than herders are. Cheikh Ly found that animal health providers give much higher priority to vaccinations against rinderpest and contagious bovine pleuro-pneumonia than herders do in Senegal. The two diseases are extremely dangerous and are present elsewhere in Africa but haven't been seen in Senegal for many years. On the other hand, in Uganda, where epizooties (the animal equivalent of epidemics) are more threatening, herders give as high a priority as vets do to such preventive measures of a 'mixed public/private good' nature.

The market therefore does not threaten the provision of these services, for they offer adequate, visible benefits to the herder. On the other hand, meat inspection and disease control, which are pure 'public goods', are viewed quite negatively by Ugandan herders no matter who pays for them, and private practitioners in Senegal also give them a much lower priority. Because these measures provide little direct private return to herders— despite their strong collective benefit— even their provision by the state is threatened by corrupt evasion. These observations lead Koma to suggest that the categorical thinking promoted by the 'public' v. 'private goods' distinction is not helpful. Externalities (or the presence of benefits external to the direct consumer of a service) is a more useful concept, as it leads one to quantify both private and societal benefits and to see that in some circumstances private ones may be sufficient to assure demand (even when 'public' ones also are present). Payment by oneself or by a collectivity does not seem to affect the way in which herders evaluate services. They calculate only in terms of benefit to themselves, without too much reference to cost. 'Public goods' that have negative private benefits together with positive externalities are much more difficult to provide than ones that have externalities and weak private benefits. In fact, they are so difficult that even their public provision is called into question.

Transaction Costs

Not all the costs of a service are revealed by its price. Other factors may intervene to make the transaction between the provider and the consumer of health care inefficient, so that some of the value that one party to a 'sale' surrenders is not fully captured by the other. The literature refers to these as 'transaction costs.' Such inefficiencies are 'dead losses,' in that neither party derives any benefit from them and both buyer and seller stand to gain if they can be reduced. If a health delivery system were structured in such a way that its explicit prices were very low but its transaction costs were high, it would be providing illusory savings to the consumer.

The most prominent transaction cost in African health care is that of distance. It matters most for veterinary services, because it is extremely difficult for a smallholder to transport for a large animal, so the animal health practitioner has to travel to the animal. This imposes a double cost on the herder; he must pay in time and money to get to the practitioner to announce his need for service and then he must pay again for the latter's trip out to his farm. In Uganda and Zimbabwe, Lee Koma and Pamela Woods establish that greater distance to health providers noticeably reduces demand for veterinary services. In an unpublished study that was conducted as a part of this project, George Njiru found in central Kenya that over half the business of private animal health providers came from requests for service by farmers once the vet had come into a neighborhood on call for another farmer, a further confirmation of the importance of this transaction cost. More needs to be done to explore the tradeoffs between the transaction costs of transport and the transaction costs of administering a system whereby animal health personnel travel a route to treat sick animals at fixed times and places.

The greater transaction costs of travel in animal health are probably the major reason why northern hemisphere vets consider it ethical to sell directly to the farmer the drugs they prescribe. Inadequate attention to these costs has created a very inefficient drug system in the communal areas of Zimbabwe. Veterinary technicians (paraprofessionals) are not allowed to carry drugs for sale, thus adding onto the herder the transaction costs of yet another round trip to the Animal Health Center. This is a pure efficiency loss.

In human health care, people are much more able and willing to travel long distances for the services they need, bypassing other, cheaper facilities en route, as is clearly evident in our Cameroonian and Ethiopian studies. Distance matters more for maternal and child health care, however, than for adult curative care. The needs of the former two populations are much more time sensitive. The appropriateness of the World Health Organization's emphasis on maternal and child health care for primary health facilities is reaffirmed by these studies.

The fact that people are willing to travel long distances in search of appropriate care does not change the fact that it is costly to do so and that these transaction costs represent 'dead losses.' Damen Haile Mariam argues that the extended families of rural Ethiopians would be willing to pay more for care for sick adults if the income were kept by local facilities to raise their quality to a level that made health trips to the capital unnecessary.

Finally, Pamela Woods raises the issue of another class of transaction costs: those associated with gender stereotyping. She shows that herders demand fewer curative services of women veterinary paraprofessionals, even though the women are quite responsive when called. She also shows that the reluctance of some of these female paraprofessionals to use bicycles reduces their ability to do their jobs. Both of these efficiency losses are transaction costs from cultural prejudices.

Incentives

The most important implications of our studies come when we turn from the structure of demand to that of supply. Elementary economic theory tells us that, if other things are equal, an increase in prices will reduce demand and increase supply. Only rarely does the literature on African health systems acknowledge the latter fundamental. Even when it does, it focuses on the effects of increased user fees on relaxing *government* budget constraints that are affecting quality service (Litwack and Bodart 1993). Our research indicates that the effects of market transactions on health care go far beyond relief of resource constraints; they change its fundamental character by shifting the incentive structure.

Gilbert Mliga compares the performance of a number of different mission (church) and government health facilities in Tanzania and concludes that those that use fee income to gain more decentralized control over staff and material resources provide better quality care. Decentralized control over *material* resources is associated with the presence of an MD in the facility, which is an even stronger predictor of quality. But decentralized control over the *personnel* system remains the most important variable. It shows the importance of high powered incentives in creating facility quality. For Ethiopia, Damen Haile Mariam was accordingly led to conclude that decentralization of facility finance and management is necessary in order to capture potential revenue increases locally and use them to create improvements in quality.

Of equal interest is the contrast between the curative and maternity services of Cameroonian government health centers. Kenneth Leonard demonstrates that government facilities there have little incentive to provide medical *effort* for curative care, thereby wasting much of their technical *capacity* and leading consumers to judge them inferior in quality to mission facilities and traditional healers. Ndeso Atanga points out, however, that government facilities are dominant with regard to births; clearly in this domain they are judged to be of good quality. The reason is that the incentive system surrounding maternal services in government health centers is radically different from that for curative services. The success of the delivery is known at the time that the mother and child leave the facility and it is customary to pay a significant 'appreciation' for a good delivery. Thus the incentive system here is high powered and more like that used by traditional healers and Tanzania's decentralized mission services.

The effects of incentive systems go well beyond the creation of quality; they in turn indirectly affect the shape of demand itself. Kenneth Leonard establishes that the nature of the demand for a particular health facility is shaped by the fit between the characteristics of the disease the patient has and the facility's incentive system. Some systems are good at inducing effort on the part of the practitioner, some at combining such effort with medical skill, and some at stimulating effort from the patient, while others deliver a product of indifferent quality. Patients choose between these facilities on the basis of the requirements of the disease they have.

Of course not all incentive effects are positive. Gilbert Mliga reports that more decentralized health facilities were more likely to over-prescribe in order to increase their income, albeit in ways he thinks are not dangerous and can be regulated. Cheikh Ly observes that private Senegalese DVMs devote a good deal of time to the commercial supply of drugs, therefore exploiting their state-granted monopoly here at the expense of using their technical comparative advantage.

These incentive issues provide a bridge to a discussion of institutions. Which institutions, we may ask, currently provide incentives to produce medical effort? We have already noted the payment of 'appreciation' when healthy babies are delivered in Cameroon. In medicine, there is a severe asymmetry (or inequality) in the information possessed by the client and the health provider— what the literature calls a principal/agent problem. Patients and livestock owners have no way of knowing for certain if the professionals they employ are exerting maximum effort. What they can know is whether or not the health provider had an incentive to provide that effort. If payment is made only if there is a successful birth outcome, such an incentive exists and clients therefore know that they are purchasing effort. A similar incentive system exists for traditional healers, who collect most of their fees in 'appreciation' long after the outcome of the treatment is known.

Modern (or, more properly, science-based) human health providers cannot charge for their curative charges in the same way as traditional healers do because their patients do not believe they will be punished by the supernatural if they do not pay. On the other hand, George Njiru found credit to be important in animal health care in Kenya, where it enables the herder to see the success of the treatment before he pays for it, creates an incentive to effort for the provider, and provides the herder with an assurance which makes him more willing to purchase the service. This practice is feasible in veterinary medicine while it is not in modern human health care precisely because of the distance problems we noted earlier. If the provider enjoys an effective local monopoly, the herder is forced eventually to return to the same animal health provider and confront the 'rightness' of his non-payment. On the other hand, where, as Ly finds for drugs (but not service) in Senegal's Ferlo, there is a good deal of effective local competition, credit will lead to mounting non-payment and liquidity problems. (Incidentally, we might note here that David Leonard and Jean-Germain Gros found in Kenya and Cameroon that these local veterinary monopolies permit the existence of 'price discrimination' whereby the poor are charged much less than the rich for the same service (Leonard 1987; Gros 1993.)

Missing Institutions

The preceding discussion of incentive structures points to the importance of institutions (both formal and informal) that work to sustain optimal transactions in the health sectors. One of the reasons structural adjustment has faced such difficulties in Africa is that markets are not easy to create; their effectiveness depends on the presence of institutions that all too often do not yet exist.

One important such institution is insurance. Charles Griffin (1989) has observed that a privately financed hospital system depends on the existence of a health insurance system. Otherwise the patient is faced with sudden, bulky costs at precisely the time that her earning capacity is lowest. Private, formal health insurance is impossible for anyone other than elites in Africa. The transaction costs are too high and the adverse selection and moral hazard problems (whereby only those who know themselves to be sick buy insurance) too great.

Damen Haile Mariam's research in Ethiopia establishes what should have been obvious to those who know Africa well but the implications of which have been neglected in health policy: extended family support is a form of social insurance in Africa. It is the resources of the extended family, not of the nuclear one, that determine the ability of patients to access more expensive health care. This assistance is insurance, not informal credit, for its availability increases with age and is not limited to the patient's productive years— when the prospects of assistance's being repaid with another favor later on are best. Damen Haile Mariam discusses circumstances in which burial societies, which are prevalent in Ethiopia and enlarge the insurance system of the extended family, are also used to provide assistance with health care. Through burial societies it may be possible to tap into the informal insurance networks of Ethiopian society and provide additional resources to improve the quality and effectiveness of local health facilities.

The other missing institution we want to examine is the professions, as associations that regulate their own members and assure the quality of their work. We noted above that, in medical matters, clients have an information disadvantage relative to health providers. In such a principal/agent relationship the clients lack the expertise needed to evaluate the quality of the effort the practitioner is providing. Cheikh Ly points out, following Akerloff (1970), that if the buyer is unable to tell if the product being offered for sale is inferior, the price she is willing to offer will fall to the value of the poorest quality product on the market, so that we will have a 'market for lemons.' In such a situation, the charges the best physicians and vets are able to make will fall to the level of those of the worst. Lee Koma confirms that this has occurred in Ugandan animal health practice, where DVM charges are no higher than those of paraprofessionals for the same complaints. The principal/agent literature predicts that in this situation the higher quality practitioners have an interest in establishing a self-regulatory mechanism that would assure the client of the high quality of their service and thereby enable them to charge a higher price (Pratt and Zeckhauser 1985).

An active professional organization would provide such a self-regulatory mechanism, solving the principle/agent quality problem. But as Cheikh Ly illustrates for Senegal, the professional bodies established to govern the health providers of Africa have not been assuming this role. It appears that the principle/agent theorists underestimated the 'collective action problem' in creating such formal self-regulatory organizations from nothing. Although there are benefits to the collectivity of health professionals in such self-regulation, any individual professional would lose income if he diverted his energies toward getting the joint effort underway.

Instead, Africa has evolved its own distinctive institutional mechanisms to solve the problem of regulating for professional quality: the nongovernmental organization (NGO) and most especially the church mission. Gilbert Mliga emphasises the high powered incentives that exist in Tanzanian mission facilities, especially in comparison with government facility incentive structures. In the mission facilities, profit incentives are tempered by a strongly institutionalized set of values. The latter could be said to be substituting for systemwide organized, professional self-regulation, which currently is weak in the private sector. These mission systems may therefore be Africa's most appropriate vehicle of privatization in the health sectors, for they provide a crucially required framework of professional controls. They also provide a vehicle for charity to the poor, which is certain to remain necessary. Cheikh Ly's observation in Senegal that mission management of animal health auxiliaries is superior to government use of the same supports Mliga's finding. He also finds that herders are willing to purchase at least double the quantity of preventive services from mission veterinary auxiliaries that they buy from government ones that are similarly trained and provisioned. The mission's assurance of professional quality increases the size of the market.

There are other points that might be drawn from the following chapters, but this should be enough to stimulate the reader to draw out the implications of the seemingly isolated research results that are reported here. Many of them will be elaborated further in Chapters 1 and 10, the first of which focuses on bringing the insights of the New Institutional Economics and our research program to veterinary care and the second on doing the same for human curative health services, both in Africa. Neither of these chapters— nor any other in the volume— seeks to address all the relevant issues for these two policy domains. That has not been our purpose. Instead, we explore in great detail certain issues that are critical to forming larger sets of policy prescriptions for specific countries, and we challenge the conventional wisdoms of both by policymakers and economists.

THE PROJECT'S HISTORY

In an important sense this project began early in 1982 when I was working as a Management Advisor to Kenya's Ministry of Livestock Development. As the 'Great African Depression' hit Kenya, all of its ministries were asked to reduce their expenditures significantly. Ishmael Muriithi, Director of Livestock Development, and Leonard Kibingi, the Ministry's Permanent Secretary, asked me to propose ways in which essential veterinary services could continue to be offered despite the drastic cuts in budgetary provision (Leonard 1983). Thus began my effort to understand the market for animal health care in Africa and to find theoretical tools that could help African policymakers navigate the previously unexplored shoals of user fees and privatization. At the invitation of Stephen Sandford of the International Livestock Center for Africa, I visited 10 African countries in 1990 to explore these issues further and developed a collaborative research proposal to address them, although ILCA financing turned out to be possible for only a portion of the project (Gros 1993).

In 1992, however, through an international essay competition, the Dutch Ministry of Foreign Affairs identified the proposal as a promising one. It then asked me to organize a group of junior African scholars to conduct a series of empirical case studies on the ways in which the rapidly evolving markets for human and animal health care in Africa were operating. This initiative was financed by the Government of the Netherlands, with smaller contributions from the U.S. National Science Foundation and the University of California at Berkeley, and was brilliantly administered by Dr. Osita Ogbu of the (Canadian) International Development Research Centre in Nairobi, with assistance from the Berkeley-Stanford Joint Center for African Studies. A group of 13 African scholars were selected in an internationally advertised competition and met at Berkeley in July 1993 for a month-long seminar on the theoretical issues underlying the inquiry. They were assisted in this seminar by Jean-Germain Gros, Kenneth Leonard and myself. My article on 'Structural Reform of the Veterinary Profession in Africa and the New Institutional Economics' (1993) provided the framework for the seminar. The following chapter draws on this chapter, which was largely written at the Institute of Development Studies at the University of Sussex (U.K.) in 1991. The seminar participants prepared research proposals, and an international panel selected six of them for funding by the Government of the Netherlands. Damen Haile Mariam and Kenneth

Leonard subsequently won a grant from the U.S. National Science Foundation (Award No. 9422768) and joined the group. During the early stages of their research, I visited all the scholars at their field sites. Kenneth Leonard and I provided extensive support to the scholars on the statistical analysis and interpretation of their data. David Stuligross, assisted by Elizabeth Penn and Peter Houtzager, provided the final editing of this book. The studies contained in this volume were presented to a conference of African policymakers— both veterinary and human health, government and professional— in Nairobi, Kenya in July 1997. To all of the many institutions and individuals who have assisted us in this grand endeavor, we offer our deep thanks.

David K. Leonard
Berkeley, California
February 1999

1 The New Institutional Economics and the Restructuring of Animal Health Services in Africa

David K. Leonard

A profound change has overtaken veterinary medicine in Africa during the last two decades. The colonial state had been the primary provider of veterinary services for African animals. In the rapid expansion of the state in the first two decades of independence, private veterinarians (save for a small number dealing with urban pets) all but disappeared from the countries north of Zimbabwe and south of the Sahara. In this era it was considerably easier to find a physician than a vet practicing outside of government. The 'Great African Depression' and the fiscal crisis of the state changed all that. Today, the vast majority of animal health practitioners in the same region are engaged, either formally or informally, in private practice. Within a decade African veterinary care moved from being more statist than its human health care counterpart to being considerably more privatized. The theories that drove the donor community to orchestrate this profound change largely were simple neo-liberal ones, derived from neoclassical economics. International experts did make a valiant effort to protect state provision of veterinary regulation and the prevention of the most virulent epizootic diseases (de Haan and Bekure 1989; Umali *et al.* 1992; FAO 1997a). (Epizootic is the animal equivalent of epidemic.) By and large, however, curative animal health care was thrown into a laissez-faire market. Policymakers implicitly (and perhaps unintentionally) overestimated the quality of information that buyers and sellers of veterinary services had about one another and underestimated the importance of the large number of institutional structures that make animal health markets function well in northern, capitalist economies. Not surprisingly, African veterinary markets have not operated as well as they were expected to and further attention to the institutions that frame their transactions is needed.

Institutions matter! As we come to accept this reality, we are driven beyond neoclassical economics into the insights of organization theory and sociology that have nurtured the exciting recent advances of New Institutional Economics.

What, then, can we learn from the New Institutional Economics (NIE) that might help us with the restructuring of health services in Africa? This question set the agenda for the research in this volume from its outset. Prior to examining the chapters on the discrete pieces of research we have done, it is useful to place them in a larger theoretical and policy context. This chapter presents a number of key issues that arise in restructuring veterinary services that can be illuminated by the NIE. Rather than presenting the NIE in the abstract, I hope to elucidate its key concepts and demonstrate its analytic power by applying the theory to a number of concrete policy dilemmas. I begin with a very brief description of what the NIE is and then develop it further as we consider issues in animal health.

Most of these veterinary issues apply to human medicine in Africa as well, and the theoretical tools I develop in this chapter will be useful to the later chapters that probe human health services. Indeed they guided the research. In order to keep the presentation manageable, however, the focus in this chapter is on animal health and issues in human health care are reserved for this volume's concluding chapter. In each chapter, research on the 'other' health service is incorporated only to the extent that it illuminates the policy issues for the service under active consideration. In this opening chapter on African veterinary care, we also will bring out the differences in the way we conceptualized issues at the start of the project and what we learned from our research itself.

The New Institutional Economics

Sometimes it is difficult to know what to call the broad range of efforts by economists to analyze institutional and organizational questions.[1] These approaches have tended to adopt different labels for the new institutional movement as a whole, and in choosing one or another name one may give the impression that one has accepted the corresponding viewpoint of that school. In what follows I seek to be quite catholic in my approach, but I have accepted the label for the movement advocated by Oliver Williamson because it seems to have the widest currency (Moe

1. Portions of this article are based on Leonard (1993), which it seeks to update, and are reprinted by permission of the publisher.

1984; Zald 1987).

The NIE is centrally concerned with the ways in which incentives affect social systems. This focus is obscured in much of the NIE by the insistence of some leading analysts that they are concerned with transaction costs instead (North 1990, pp. 27–35; Williamson 1985, pp. 24–7). This twist derives directly from the fact that the NIE comes out of economics. Unlike the rest of the social sciences, neoclassical economics starts with demonstrably false assumptions about human behavior (North 17–26).[2] By assuming that individuals always optimize their welfare, have full information and knowledge about how to do so, are able to contract and enforce the terms of exchange costlessly, and have an unrestricted ability to reinvest assets, the economists assume a world in which incentives are unfettered and work at their maximum effect. Thus, whereas most social scientists seek theories that explain what enhances incentives, economists need ones that explain how they can be distorted or diminished. The concept of transaction costs serves this function. In Williamson's words (1985, p. 19), 'Transaction costs are the economic equivalent of friction in physical systems.' They are the costs in the exchange that do not benefit either of the parties to the transaction; they simply make it more difficult and less attractive. They are one way to reintroduce more realistic assumptions about human behavior and thereby explain why incentives do not work perfectly.[3] As John Toye (1995, p. 56) points out, economists have methodological

---

2. We do not wish to derogate economics for having made these simplifying assumptions. The accomplishments of the discipline testify to their having been useful. But many economists feel that more realistic assumptions are now a prerequisite for new theoretical breakthroughs.

3. Our preferred behavioral assumptions for theory building are that: people satisfice rather than optimize, are opportunistic and risk averse; information is incomplete and costly; and there are barriers to the free movement of capital assets in the market (that is, there is asset specificity so that monopoly is a problem). These assumption derive from the March and Simon view of the world. (For example, see March and Olsen 1989.) The several schools of the New Institutional Economics vary in their acceptance of these more realistic assumptions. North comes closest (1990, F 3). Williamson insists on asset specificity, opportunism, and bounded rationality but he still accepts maximization and risk neutrality (pp. 30-32, 43-63,388-89). The Agency school still holds to the unbounded rationality assumption [Williamson, pp. 30-31]. These schools adopt assumptions not out of ignorance or perversity but because of their fit with the particular set of analytic tools that they have found to be powerful. As our theoretical treatment is not mathematical, we are not as constrained as some of these analysts are. We will attempt to incorporate their insights in an eclectic manner, while remaining sensitive to the distortions that their various assumptions could introduce.

reasons for believing that it is easier to measure obstacles to incentives (and hence transaction costs) than to measure incentives themselves. From our point of view, however, the important point is that the NIE is compatible with an incentives approach to behavior; in fact, the less dominant but still important Property Rights and Agency branches of the NIE use the language of incentives, not transaction costs.

Transaction cost economics becomes an institutional economics when it is used to examine how social structures that can be used to overcome barriers to the high powered incentives assumed to operate in the neoclassical market. In this way we begin to see that the market must be embedded in an appropriate set of institutions if it is to operate at its assumed level of allocative efficiency. And there are situations in which the market simply cannot be made to work efficiently and alternative institutional arrangements are needed. The NIE therefore is built on the premise that 'institutions matter.'

The Veterinary Policy Problem

The state of human medical systems features quite prominently in debates about the consequences of structural adjustment for Africa and therefore is a natural choice for an analysis of changing markets (for example, Van der Gaag and Barham 1998). But why veterinary medicine? One reason is that animal and human health services both employ professionals and therefore pose more complicated set of issues than do more 'pure' business domains. If we can succeed in developing a theory for animal health services, we will have made a major step toward developing one for other professional services— not only for human medicine, which is quite similar in science and organizational structure, but also for areas such as education.

However, we have not selected veterinary medicine randomly from among the professions. It is an important and particularly interesting case in its own right. Animal health, obviously, is one of several inputs to a livestock production system. As such it would attract little attention in most developed economies. The picture in Africa is quite different. First of all, agriculture makes a significant contribution to most African economies and is the major employer of most of its labor force, on average about 70 per cent (World Bank 1989, p. 277). Second, within agriculture livestock represents about half of the value of production, particularly if we include the contribution of animal traction. (De Haan and Bekure

1989, p. 1).[4] Livestock has the kind of critical importance for African economies that steel might have for an industrialized one. Third, animal health services are the most important purchased input in most African livestock systems. Labor generally comes from family members, feeds come from the farm or range, and as yet little investment is made in the improvement of grazing. Thus animal health services loom large within a sector that itself looms large within the economy of Africa.

Until the mid-1970s, African governments assumed virtually complete responsibility for all animal health care matters for small producers. At first these services were confined to preventive and disease control measures, that is, injections against a variety of epizootic diseases supplemented by quarantines and the regulation of livestock movements. Initially these 'services' were introduced by colonial governments largely as a way of protecting European-owned cattle from the reservoirs of disease in African herds. However, as African producers were encouraged to enter the formal markets and began to respond, the range of veterinary services increased. The number of preventive measures were augmented (often including tick and tse-tse abatement), curative (or clinical) services often were added, extension advice on production management was offered, and even artificial insemination to upgrade the quality of stock was occasionally provided. This period of expansion coincided with the first decade or two of independence, when African states were subsidizing a wide variety of new services for their citizens. In this period there was fairly wide consensus as to the ideal service system model, toward which most countries were trying to move. A full range of heavily subsidized services would be brought within walking distance of the producer and the quality of personnel would gradually be upgraded toward the professional levels found in Europe. Simply put, the state would provide as wide a range of services, with as many staff, with as high a level of training, as it could.

Then financial crisis broke on Africa and these traditional veterinary systems began to experience severe difficulties. Funds dried up first for the West African Sahelian states, but by the 1980s problems in continuing with the traditional model were felt virtually everywhere on the continent. As budgets failed to keep pace with costs, most states found it easier to make cuts in operating expenses than in the number of service

4. In some countries, such as Botswana and Somalia, the importance of livestock is considerably greater than this. In others it is less. In most African countries, however, there are important groups that rely on livestock as their primary source of subsistence and still more groups that use them as a supplement to subsistence and as a store of value.

providers. It is generally accepted that a veterinary service in Africa will be ineffective if staff salaries represent more than 60 per cent of its budget, leaving less than 40 per cent for veterinary supplies and transport (IEMVT 1988, pp. 8–9). By the 1980s, the personnel item in the budget reached 90 per cent in some African states and in most it exceeded the target maximum (Antenah 1984). In the worst cases, state-provided veterinary services effectively ceased to exist and in most they fell far below the level needed and expected by producers. The widespread reappearance of the deadly Rinderpest in Africa in the 1980s was but the most visible sign of the crisis.

In response, African states engaged in interesting and commendable experimentation, hoping to find new models for animal health systems that would be better adapted to contemporary financial reality. Not infrequently, these innovations were undertaken after considerable prodding from donors. The World Bank, the European Economic Community, and West Germany have been particularly vigorous proponents of privatization initiatives (De Haan and Bekure 1989, Annex 2), notwithstanding or perhaps because these same donors earlier had financed the ill-fated expansion of subsidized state services. As a result of these innovations, there now is a wide variety of experimental structures where once there was relative uniformity.

THE NEW INSTITUTIONAL ECONOMICS AND THE PERFORMANCE OF THE AFRICAN STATE

The State of the State

One of the key assumptions underlying structural adjustment efforts in sub-Saharan Africa is that the implementation capacity of the continent's states is limited and has been overextended. Although donor arguments in the 1980s for the market and privatization were presented with a universal logic (World Bank 1981), they were a poor fit for Japan, Korea, and Taiwan, which are at least as interventionist as any African state (Johnson 1982; Wade 1990). The World Bank recently has qualified its negative views on the state. But it is still pressing privatization for most sectors of African economies (World Bank 1997). Obviously, donors believe that there is something different about states in East Asia and Africa, and indeed there is.

The larger number of African states are confronted with most of the following: corruption (Gould 1980; Gould and Amaoro-Reyes 1983;

Klitgaard 1990); patronage (Joseph 1987); inflated public payrolls; severe fiscal scarcity and a consequent 'budgeting by cash-flow' (Caiden and Wildavsky 1974); constant shortages of critical inputs (Moris 1977, pp. 78–83); weak performance rewards for public servants, due both to erosion of their value by inflation and the failure to use them to support organizational objectives (Montgomery 1987); and political authorities who are insecure, indecisive, arbitrary, and interventionist (Moris 1977; Jackson and Rosberg 1982). There are controversies in the literature about whether to ascribe the roots of these problems primarily to collective action problems, the logic of patronage politics, or the dynamics created by village and kinship loyalties— although in fact they all are closely related (Bates 1981; Hyden 1980 and 1983). But there is little disagreement that the problems themselves are pervasive, although not universal, and that they imply a reduced role for the state in Africa (relative both to its own recent past and to Asia's). It is evident that these problems create a set of incentives for civil servants that are variously perverse, negative, or weak, thereby creating lower levels of public sector performance in Africa than in many other parts of the world.

It will be useful to analyze these problems in terms of the New Institutional Economics (NIE). Doing so will serve to introduce these theories to us and thereby lay the groundwork for the analysis of institutional design and change which is to follow.

Colonial Provision and Collective Goods.

Following Oliver Williamson (1975), we first need to explain why colonial African states undertook to provide veterinary services in the first place. Under the purest assumptions of neoclassical economics, the market works so well that individual private entrepreneurs should have undertaken to provide veterinary services themselves, and intervention by either the state or large corporations should have been unnecessary.

Veterinary services were first introduced in Africa in order to deal with epizootic diseases, initially through stringent movement controls (quarantines) and later through mass inoculation campaigns. For a long period of time these were the only veterinary services for indigenous African livestock that could pass an economic benefit/cost test, and this is still true in some parts of Africa (Sere 1979).

From a market point of view, the problem with movement controls and, to a lesser extent, inoculations is that they are public goods. The economics literature has long made a distinction between what it refers to as public and private goods. Services are private goods when the individual who consumes them captures their full benefit. Public goods exist when the benefits of a service 'spill over' to other members of the community. Economists hold that goods are 'public' whenever the 'exclusion' and the 'rival' principles are not operative. Exclusion applies when it is relatively easy to deny access to a service to those who have not paid for it. The rival principle operates when two consumers cannot both enjoy a specific benefit at the same time. Pure public goods are those to which neither principle applies. A classic example of such a public good is a radio broadcast on improved methods of keeping livestock. An additional listener subtracts nothing from the benefit of those already listening and it is very difficult to prevent people from hearing the broadcast who have not paid for it (Samuelson 1954). A pure private good exists when both the exclusion and rival principles are at work. A perfect example is a clinical farm call by a veterinarian. The livestock owner captures the full benefit of the veterinarian's services during the call and no one else can benefit from the veterinarian at that time.

Any time exclusion is not possible, a 'collective good' exists (as opposed to a 'pure' public good). Economists call such a condition a market failure because there is a 'free rider' problem. The latter simply means that those who have paid for the service cannot prevent those who have not paid for it from benefiting as well (Olson 1965). In such a situation, it often is difficult to get anyone to take the initiative and pay for the service because everyone wants to wait and be a 'free rider.' The state then frequently and appropriately intervenes to provide the service and may use its powers of taxation to force all beneficiaries to pay for it.

Thus there is a tendency for collective goods to be provided by the state. But there is no necessary relationship between a good's being public, collective, or private and its being provided by the state or the private sector. Many services with private goods attributes are provided by the state, as curative veterinary services have been in many African countries. Describing a good as 'private' signifies only that an *economically* optimal provision would result from its delivery by the private sector. Similarly, collective and public goods can be provided by private actors; the terms signify only that economically optimal provision of these goods is not straightforward under market conditions (Coase 1974).

Movement control is very much a public good; the farmers that benefit are those whose animals are outside the quarantine area and thereby spared exposure to an epizooty. The fact that movement control brings no benefit to the owner whose herd is quarantined and indeed denies access to markets with better prices means that enforcement generally requires coercion. This combination of public good and coercion makes it very difficult for any collectivity other than the state to execute movement control. The state holds a monopoly on the legitimate exercise of force in society (Weber 1978, p. 56) and the transaction costs in gaining access to this coercive force would be lower if the executing agent were the state itself.

Inoculations against epizooties also have a collective goods aspect to them (Umali *et al.* 1992, pp. 12–16). The epidemiological principle of 'herd immunity' holds that if a certain percentage of a population is immunized against a disease,[5] an epidemic will be unable to spread in it and even the unimmunized members will be relatively safe. Since there are always potentially negative side effects from an immunization as well as the costs of administering it, there is a 'free rider' problem; it pays for the individual herder not to immunize much of his stock as long as others are immunizing theirs. However, if enough herders reason in this way a serious epizootic outbreak can occur fairly easily. Some method of assuring collective action is always needed— or so it seemed to us at first.

The categorical reasoning dictated by the public-private goods distinction proves too blunt an instrument for the fine art of making veterinary policy, although it is useful for grasping the issues involved. An alternative way of discussing public goods is to speak of externalities (Umali *et al.* 1992, pp. 12–16). An externalities approach contrasts the costs and benefits incurred by the immediate parties to a transaction with those who are affected by it only indirectly and therefore are external to it. The 'internal' and 'external' benefits each can be either positive or negative. Koma's research with Ugandan herders (Chapter 6) strongly suggests that the externality method of conceptualizing these issues is preferable to my initial public-private goods formulation. First, it lends itself more readily to degrees of difference; the public v. private goods language is categorical and handles mixed types awkwardly. Second, the externality method leads one to do a better job in evaluating the adequacy of private demand, for it quantifies rather than categorizes both internal and external benefits. Where the unit of consumption is 'bulky,' so that the private purchaser decides not how *much* but *whether* to buy, it is perfectly possible for private consumption decisions to be socially optimal as well. Koma found that Ugandan herders considered immunizations against prevalent epizooties so valuable at the market price that

5. The necessary percentage depends on the degree of contagiousness and the life cycle of the disease.

they needed no public subsidies to buy them. On the other hand, the private 'benefits' of quarantine are so negative that no amount of public subsidy (short of purchase of the sick animal at its healthy price) would induce herders to comply voluntarily. Koma found that collective purchase by a cooperative would not have changed the shape of demand for either immunizations or quarantines, contrary to the implication one would derive at first from the public v. private goods method of analysis (Chapter 6).

In addition to the externalities aspect of disease prevention, African herders in the colonial period discounted the future heavily (paid more attention to present benefit than to future risk) and lacked the knowledge that would enable them to appreciate the scientific basis of the proposed measures. The latter violation of the rationality assumptions of economic action and the veterinary profession's smaller discounting of the future also argued for the state as the agent of service delivery at that time. This historical argument has less force today. Where the threat of killer diseases, such as rinderpest, is acute, livestock producers as different as owners of improved stock in Uganda and pastoralists in the Central African Republic have been eager to buy immunizations (Chapter 6; Tacher 1986). On the other hand, Ly found that in situations such as Senegal's, where there have been no recent outbreaks, veterinarians give much higher priority to the immunizations than herders do (Chapter 7).

Finally, given the modest demand for veterinary services when they were first introduced and the tremendous distances that were involved, any private animal health practitioners have had a local, geographically-based monopoly in any given area. This would have distorted their incentives to provide services at a marginal cost price, creating yet another argument for replacing the market with a hierarchy—in this case the state. Veterinary medicine in Africa continues to have high transaction costs associated with distance, despite the great improvements in transportation that have taken place. Woods finds a clear distance gradient in the use of animal health services in Zimbabwe (Chapter 3). Animals, especially large ones, do not have access to the buses and taxis that carry human patients over considerable distances in their search for appropriate medical care. Thus, local monopoly remains a distinguishing characteristic of most African veterinary medicine. On the other hand, it does not affect every aspect of veterinary services. Ly points out (Chapter 9) that regional price differentials for veterinary pharmaceutical products, which *are* easy to transport, are competed away in Senegal.

Transaction Costs and the Current Decline

Many animal health departments seek to provide more than just preventive services today and herder knowledge of veterinary medicine has improved dramatically since the colonial era. As we just noted, however, many of the other factors that initially favored the state as a veterinary provider remain. Furthermore, governments were judged to be quite effective at this function in the first years after independence (for example, see Leonard 1991 Chap. 7). Why then should animal health departments have become a major focus for privatization initiatives?

The answer is that there has been a significant increase in the transaction costs involved in state activity in Africa since independence, with corresponding diminishment and distortions to incentives. As states have become overextended through taking on increased responsibilities despite stagnant economies, budgetary provisions and access to foreign exchange have become unpredictable and less adequate. Veterinarians often are lacking supplies that are critical to their work. Even when they have access to these supplies, veterinarians have had to devote considerably more time and energy to their acquisition. In similar vein, the hiring and promotion of staff along patronage or ethnic lines diminishes the performance incentives for staff at every level and makes the supervision of subordinates more difficult for senior officials who are committed to their work. Finally, corruption and the decline in real income of civil servants, separately and in combination, diminish the relative force of official incentives and increase the power of those that subvert formal duties. The transaction costs of government activity have increased, the incentives supporting formal organizational purposes have diminished, and African governments simply can not do as much as effectively as they did a quarter century ago. This is not to say that all African states have experienced these kinds of changes in transaction costs relative to animal health care. For example, the state veterinary departments of Zimbabwe and Botswana appear to function relatively well, although the former has adopted policies that threaten eventually to overextend its finances. Our picture, however, is the modal one.

THE IMPLICIT ECONOMIC THEORIES UNDERLYING PRIVATIZATION

The proposition that the modal contemporary African state is weak and overextended is sound. But the current argument for privatization depends as well on the theory that the market can outperform the state in virtually any circumstance. How sound are the empirical grounds for such an assumption for animal health?

The Miracle of the Market

Unlike the relatively recent political and administrative contributions we have just examined, the economic theories implicitly guiding all but the newest efforts at structural reform have older roots. In the tradition of Hayek (1966) and Friedman (1962), the argument is that markets outperform hierarchies and thus that the private sector is more effective than the public. By decentralizing decisions to the point where the relevant information about demand exists and giving those who make the decisions a strong personal incentive to make them efficiently, markets are vastly simpler to administer and thus generally more effective than hierarchies (Hayek 1945; Stinchecombe 1968, pp. 165–68).

Originally, the appeal of the private sector was constrained by the acknowledged existence of market failures in a wide variety of circumstances, such as the presence of natural monopolies and the need for collective goods (Olson 1965; Friedman 1962, p. 128). Government action was held to be appropriate in such situations. During the 1960s, even this limitation on the 'miracle of the market' was undercut from two directions. First, some economists began to suspect that even an imperfect market could outperform governments (Coase 1964, p. 195). They argue that private firms have greater incentives to keep their labor forces small and to contain wage rates, and that state regulation can force these firms to return their labor savings to consumers and not simply retain them in the form of monopoly profits. This argument gained credence, for example, from the fact that the Bell Telephone/International Telephone and Telegraph private monopoly in the United States was much more effective than its public counterparts in Europe.

The second thrust against government presence in imperfect markets was the argument that social efficiency could be achieved even under conditions of natural monopoly. If several firms competed for the right to the monopoly, they would bid away their monopoly advantages and yield an economically optimal outcome (Demsetz 1968; Stigler 1968; Posner 1972). Williamson (1985 Chap. 13) has shown that the reasoning in this argument is defective and that in many situations the case ultimately depends on effective government regulation, throwing us back onto the immediately preceding set of arguments for the private sector.

Until very recently, World Bank attempts to promote privatization in Africa suggest an oversight or willingness to ignore the issue of regulation under imperfect market conditions. The implicit World Bank theory instead was that the market was nearly always superior due to the force and clarity with which it transmits incentives. This theory has guided governmental and nongovernmental approaches to development well beyond the African continent. As current events in Eastern Europe and Latin America attest, government-supported privatization has considerable political power at present.

Regulation

What indeed are the conditions under which the supervisory powers of the state— either as contractor to the private sector for collective goods or as regulator— are likely to be exercised effectively? American political scientists have directed considerable attention to this question. In general, this literature is pessimistic about the effectiveness of regulation (Wilson 1980). It notes that usually there is a considerable imbalance between the intense interest that a regulated industry has in favorable terms of regulation and the diffuse interest that consumers have in better prices or quality. As a consequence, producers are much more likely to organize than consumers, particularly since their smaller numbers make organization easier. It follows that even though consumers have the advantage in votes, the organizational advantages of the regulated usually lead to their interest groups' capturing their corresponding regulatory agencies. There are circumstances in which these advantages are reversed in the United States but the preceding is the more common case (Wilson 1980).

It could be argued that this theory of regulation is too pessimistic. As the Bell Telephone/ITT example suggests, it may be that private production under an albeit captured regulatory control still produces greater benefits for consumers than provision by a purely public enterprise does. This would imply that the political advantages of the regulated in the regulatory game, although real enough, are outweighed by the efficiency advantages of private over public production. This might be the case in the United States, where voters and public interest groups are strong (relative to those in many other countries), which makes it more difficult for U.S. regulated businesses to fully capture their regulators.

However, conditions favorable to regulatory effectiveness are rare in Africa. The mass of voters are barely organized and the state itself has already demonstrated a weak capacity for implementation. Far from assuming that regulation can be used to compensate for any untoward consequences of the market, thereby permitting indiscriminate privatization, we find that organizational and institutional design will have to solve problems in Africa that often can be slighted in the U.S. and Europe. These are questions to which the New Institutional Economics has been particularly attentive.

MAKING PRIVATIZATION EFFECTIVE: EFFICIENCY, PROFESSIONALISM AND MONOPOLY

A strong consensus has emerged that certain animal health functions could be privatized relatively easily, especially clinical diagnosis and treatment and drug production and distribution (Umali *et al.* 1992; FAO 1997a). Government provision of goods and services at subsidized rates would be effective policy in only two cases: (1) the government provides a sufficient volume to satisfy the demands of all animal owners; or (2) the government effectively directs its subsidized programs to those who genuinely cannot afford the service otherwise and the needs of more wealthy owners are met by private suppliers. In fact, neither of these cases occurs in Africa today and the existence of subsidized programs actually reduces the potential for both wealthy and poor livestock owners to be served to the extent they desire and can afford. There are three reasons for this: (a) for political and social reasons, subsidized services tend to go to wealthy rather than poor farmers; (b) government regulations prohibit private entry or make private provision sufficiently unprofitable that it is not offered; or (c) a subsidized government service may cause private service to be much more expensive by reducing the volume of remaining demand and thus losing economies of scale (Leonard 1987; 1977, Chap. 9; Leonard and Marshall 1982, Chap. 1.)

Nonetheless, because of the more bounded rationality of herders, who underestimate distant but catastrophic risks, and because of the tendency of producers to underprovide for goods with externalities, a completely privatized, fee-for-service system would lead to the neglect of certain functions that veterinary medicine assures us have great social importance. It might be thought that the externality problem between herders would be solved if groups of herders were to purchase veterinary services collectively. Koma's work in Uganda casts doubt on this proposition, however (Chapter 6). Even if local collective action did work for some services, certain society-wide and professional issues in animal health, such as food inspection and disease quarantines, would receive inadequate attention. Thus, although many animal health functions could be turned over to a free market, it seems inevitable and desirable that the state will retain an interest in other aspects. There may even be functions that in principle could be privatized but in which state involvement will continue in order to assure that needy groups are able to retain access to them. However, the retention of an interest in a matter by the state and its direct provision by the government are not necessarily the same; the state could contract the delivery of selected services to private parties. Furthermore, due to economies of transport, government contracting for public goods services with high externalities could positively affect the distribution and price of other services purchased privately from the same contractors. (FAO 1997a.)

Efficiencies

Establishing that particular inputs and services should be candidates for full privatization and others for public sector contracting under certain conditions is only the first step in specifying the appropriate shape of service provision. Issues of structure, quality, and price remain. To simplify the matter, we will discuss these with particular reference to preventive and curative inputs and services.

The extent to which privatized preventive and curative services are actually used by producers will depend on their price and availability both in time and in space. In Chapter 3, Woods finds a definite decrease in the demand for curative services as the distance— and hence the cost in terms of time and effort to reach the veterinary supply— increased. She also shows that the supply of curative services to the more distant farmers increased greatly when the veterinary service providers had access to motorbikes. Thus, the development of economies in service provision is absolutely central even though donors have given the issue little attention in the privatization debate. Making services available on market days, at gazetted dipping times, and along pre-set routes that animal health providers travel at regular, established intervals are all ways of reducing the time and money involved in travel and thereby the unit cost of service.

The professional level of animal health providers is another important component of the cost issue. The more highly trained the provider, the larger the income he (or she) demands and the greater the cost of transport is going to be, for increased professionalization tends to carry with it reduced numbers, urban residence, and greater comfort in travel. From an economic point of view, one would argue that the appropriate level of training for providers would be determined by making the following calculation for the alternative levels and choosing the result with the highest total:

The average value of the animals served[6]
[multiplied by] The reduction in the probability of death resulting from service at a particular level of training
[less] The average unit cost of providing that service

The foregoing calculation is almost certain to demonstrate that on-call service by full veterinary doctors in the European/American mode is not economic in Africa save for commercial herds of high value animals (Umali *et al.* 1992, pp. 46–49; Sere 1979; Leonard 1983). New veterinary graduates are finding their way into viable private practice in Central Kenya, where smallholders with exotic animals are part of a strong dairy industry (Wamukoya *et al.* 1995). The more general pattern, however, is reflected in the work of Koma and Ly in Uganda and Senegal, which demonstrates that such vets are now under great competitive pressure (Chapters 6 & 7). A more economical structure of practice will be necessary if these fully trained vets are going to prosper. At the start of our research I had argued that a private sector role for veterinarians was likely to be found only if they achieved substantial economies both by operating on something like a route system and by supervising paraprofessionals to do the bulk of the actual work (Leonard 1993). With the former, the veterinarians travel set routes at regular, established intervals. They either treat animals gathered at roadside crushes or at dips, go to the farms of those who have left messages in roadside boxes, or meet their auxiliaries to discuss and/or treat difficult cases and to provide them with pharmaceuticals (that is, drugs, sera, vaccines, etc., which we will often refer to simply as drugs). In fact, however, we have not seen such patterns of service emerging in our research. Vets do not travel routes and the assistants they employ tend to be untrained ones.

6. The animals served would include those that benefit indirectly through the provision to other animals of services with significant externalities (that is, collective goods).

In most of Africa, where exotic dairy animals are rare, smallholder practices by full veterinarians would have to be supplemented by other sources of income. This was effectively recognized by the regulations that controlled the work of government veterinarians in many countries during the colonial period (and in a very few, such as Zimbabwe and Botswana, still do). These veterinarians have their basic living costs covered by their government salary in compensation for providing a range of public services. They then are permitted to engage in private, fee-for-service practice to the extent that it does not interfere with their public duties. The price that the producer has to offer such veterinarians to induce them to provide a service then has to be sufficient only to cover the value to them of the leisure they lose and does not have to cover the average cost of their standard of living. This system provides an incentive to veterinarians to work longer hours and to remain in the rural areas, while still keeping their prices within the reach of less-commercialized producers. An alternative mechanism that could achieve much of the same effect would have the state contract private veterinarians to provide certain public functions in an area, again leaving them free to provide private care on the side. This system is used in Sweden (Hellberg 1990).

Both of the preceding systems effectively provide a state subsidy for the existence of a private curative practice in a community. On paper this would appear to be no different than a government's providing these services itself for a set fee. The operational superiority of the mixed public-private alternatives over the government one derives from the quite different sets of incentives at work. Under the quasi-private systems the veterinarian has a direct, personal incentive to increase the volume of his (or her) work and consequently both works longer hours and requires less supervision. Since the pharmaceutical supplies being handled are also private in these systems, the state is spared the substantial problems of managing their provision, including the prevention of corruption. Thus, because their transaction costs are lower, the quasi-private systems are likely to be much more efficient than their public alternatives and to be able to offer a much larger volume of service for the same combined level of private fees and public subsidies.

The major fear that directors of veterinary services express about these mixed government/market systems of care is that the personal commercial incentives to provide private goods are going to be so great that the collective goods the state is paying for will receive scant attention. Such a tradeoff need not occur. If the increase in commercial incentives simply leads the vet to work longer hours to meet the demand for private goods and there is no change in the time devoted to collective goods, the same amount of collective goods would still be provided. Indeed, because the transaction costs from travel are so large in African veterinary medicine, there is likely to be considerable synergy between the two types of service, with vets using the travel they do on private functions to provide such public services as management advice to producers they otherwise would not reach, and similarly to provide curative services to those whom they meet on immunization campaigns. George Njiru reports that as much as half of the requests for curative care received by vets in Central Kenya come after the vet is already in the locality on other business (private communication).

We would expect that the degree to which provision of public goods was protected in these mixed systems would be a function of (a) the extent of professionalization and (b) the volume of private demand. The deeper the vets' commitment to the core values of veterinary medicine and state service, the more they will resist incursions on their public goods functions and the greater the degree to which their response to private incentives will be only an increase in the total amount of time worked. The extent of the steps taken by the veterinary professional association to encourage and regulate adherence to these values thus becomes an important variable, as we will argue later.

On the demand side, as the clamor for private services increases, vets will reach a point at which they no longer have any leisure that they are willing to surrender, for the marginal value of their time will have grown and they will begin to increase the prices they charge for their care. This dynamic will cause the prices of these mixed-duty vets to come closer and closer to those that a purely private vet would charge. This gradually lays the groundwork for an independent private practice to come into existence. But if for some artificial reason (such as state regulations) private vets fail to appear *or* if the mixed vets' commitment to their public function is weak, the incentives to allow private practice to eat into the government-sponsored, collective goods portion of their work day will become irresistible.

The problem of public commitment is nearly identical for 100 per cent government vets as it is for private ones, however, for various pressures and inducements to provide private services may similarly tempt them to give inadequate attention to collective goods. These problems are well illustrated by the dynamics of government-provided care for smallholders in Zimbabwe. Veterinary paraprofessionals who are provided with motorbikes increase their attention to curative care and reduce the amount of time they devote to their preventive duties at the dips (Chapter 3). We do not know if the amount of preventive care is thereby deficient. But it is clear that the fact that the government stipulates the same fixed fee for the slow response of a paraprofessional on bus or bike and the more rapid response of a motorized one stimulates increased demand for the latter. If the price charged were able to move up in response to the increased demand for the more valuable service, the pressure to move away from prevention would be less or increased revenues for a full private system would be created. It is interesting that the same tradeoffs exist in both public and private service delivery systems.

Pharmaceutical Supply

Veterinarians' economic survival also would be enhanced if they were vendors of drugs (themselves and through auxiliaries) and used the greater capital and transport available to them to supply drugs that need to be controlled or require a cold chain.[7] Cheikh Ly did observe such a pattern in Senegal (Chapter 7), as have I in Kenya. The profitability of these sales are based on the legal right of vets to sell pharmaceutical products, a right not granted in these countries to non-professionals. How should we think about the distribution of drugs?

The first issue is the one posed by current practice— should the state control supply of pharmaceuticals? The very high transaction costs that we have shown to be associated with the operations of the contemporary African state make it highly likely that other bodies will handle this function more efficiently. Goods such as drugs that have a high value-to-size ratio, require refrigeration, and have expiry dates are difficult to manage and are particularly susceptible to corrupt exchanges. When service providers own and sell these drugs themselves, they have a stronger incentive to manage them well and the possibilities for corruption are reduced. As most of the cost of drugs is in their development, their marginal costs of production are low, leading manufacturers to be particularly willing to pay kickbacks to purchasing agents who make wholesale orders for the state. Thus privatization can reduce the transaction costs in trying to reduce corruption, and/or through competition, assure that wholesaler discounts are passed on to consumers, not retained by purchasing agents. Even where the state has the capacity to control

7. That is, must be kept refrigerated continuously between manufacture and use.

corruption, the necessary bureaucratic structures may prevent the optimal distribution of drugs. Woods (Chapter 3) has found in Zimbabwe that the regulated quantities in which government-supplied drugs have to be sold reduce farmer demand and that the paperwork requirements for receipts and stock control discourage paraprofessionals from making sales, since they derive no compensating financial benefit.

If veterinary pharmaceuticals are to be handled on the private market, however, does there need to be any control over their distribution? Two issues are at stake here: permission for a product to be distributed in a country at all, and control over to whom and when it may be sold. The first is highly technical and quite susceptible to improper influence by drug companies. Most African states lack the necessary combination of institutionalized competence and assured integrity to perform it well. To do the task of drug evaluation properly is extremely expensive. Thus there is every reason for countries that are similar in their economies and ecologies to pool the costs of this task. Delegation of the function to an international body that had the resources to sustain the integrity of the needed technical skills as well as to evaluate appropriateness to African conditions would be both effective and efficient. A possible candidate would be the International Laboratory for Research on Animal Disease (ILRAD) in Nairobi, Kenya. The ideal evaluative function would include assessments of the levels of technical training that are needed to employ the drug properly and of the cost-effectiveness of the treatments in African production conditions, so that certain drugs were labeled as 'essential' and others as 'esoteric.'

As far as retail sales are concerned, it would seem appropriate for the state to retain some control over consumer access to pharmaceuticals where: (a) improper dosage could create drug resistance; (b) misuse is dangerous; (c) a cold chain needs to be maintained; or (d) there is a risk of confusing symptoms of mild and serious infections, so the advice of those competent to tell the difference needs to be assured. The first of these conditions is an externalities issue and appears to be a less serious problem in Africa than usually believed.[8] The latter three involve

8. Burrows *et al.* (1995.) found that E. coli isolates from Zimbabwe typically were more sensitive to most antimicrobials tested than were isolates from Australia or the U.S. There were few consistent differences between isolates from the U.S. and Australia. The study suggests that antibiotic use in animals under Zimbabwe on conditions is not particularly problematic. With more under-dosing due to economic and delivery constraints but less total usage, E. coli are still relatively more susceptible to antibiotics than in the U.S. and Australia, which have different usage patterns, intensity of usage, and more total usage per

bounded rationality. Most other veterinary pharmaceuticals should be uncontrolled and available widely. The production benefits that follow from the lowered transaction costs of easy accessibility would outweigh the costs of misuse for this large category of drugs.

Should pharmaceuticals then be sold by rural shops, as is now being done in Madagascar, or by vet practitioners? Shops give wider, quicker distribution but break the link with advice on their use and put drugs into the hands of those who have little incentive to maintain quality and ensure appropriate use. As veterinary drugs are a small percentage of the inventory of the shops in which they are sold, the consumer is less likely to engage in a patronage boycott if a drug were to fail. Unification of diagnosis, prescription, and sale in the hands of the practitioners heightens their incentives, for they are then responsible for a larger portion of the possible causes of failed treatment and therefore more likely to be subject to client sanctions. The implications of these considerations are that, for non-controlled drugs, the advantages of enabling ordinary shopkeepers to distribute probably outweigh those of specialized advice, but that for the controlled ones the linking of advice to sale most likely outweighs the benefits of broad distribution. Sale of even non-controlled drugs exclusively by trained personnel would be feasible and attractive if, but only if, there were an extensive network of animal health paraprofessionals who could combine wide sales with advice— as long as some regular mechanism for assuring their competence were provided.

There are two further advantages to keeping at least controlled drugs in the hands of animal health practitioners. One is that there is then no need to regulate shopkeepers in this domain— a notoriously difficult undertaking for a weak state— while the practitioners need to be regulated anyway. The other is that a monopoly on controlled pharmaceuticals helps practitioners in their quest for financial survival. If, as we have argued, veterinary advice is useful and in the public interest, even if the bounded rationality of herders devalues it, then measures such as these which keep their services available are appropriate. Even in industrialized countries where competing pharmacies exist, veterinarians make a substantial portion of their income from drug sales. All these arguments depend, however, on the maintenance of professional standards in sales by veterinary professionals. This cannot be taken for granted. It is reasonable to assume that vets are more responsible in their management of drugs than generalist shopkeepers are, for their retail income depends

animal.

more on their reputations in this specific area. But we have observed vets employing untrained and unsupervised sales clerks in their pharmacies in Kenya and Senegal. This observation reinforces the importance of professional regulation, to which we will turn later.

Paraprofessionals

Earlier we implicitly assumed that only vets are engaged in the private market, and this is true of southern African countries such as Zimbabwe. But paraprofessionals often unofficially engage in subsidized private practice, as employees of the state, elsewhere in Africa (Leonard 1987; Gros 1992) and are legally in fully private practice places such as Senegal. How are we to evaluate the issues posed by paraprofessional involvement in the provision of veterinary services?

By far the largest number of practitioners in Africa are *not* veterinarians but paraprofessionals with non-degree training ranging from a few months to three years. In a majority of countries, veterinarians in state employ have served more as supervisors of these paraprofessional cadres than as direct practitioners (Gros 1993). In one way or another, privatization radically alters this structure of service. Are only the professional veterinarians to be allowed in private practice? Or are paraprofessionals going to be privatized as auxiliaries operating under the control of full vets? Or are the professionals and paraprofessionals to compete against one another in the open market?

The industrialized west has suppressed paraprofessionals and given full vets a monopoly on animal health care. However, this 'solution' raises the cost of care to the level necessary to compensate a university graduate and tends to make it financially accessible only to fully commercialized producers, leaving the mass of quasi-subsistence herders outside the net of protection. This is a 'solution' of professional purity at the expense of social and economic benefit, and hardly seems acceptable.

A system in which paraprofessionals were to concentrate on preventive and promotive functions, and were allowed to perform curative functions only under the physical oversight of a professional, would capture many of the economies that lower paraprofessional cost offers while minimizing the areas in which their lesser skill and weaker professional commitment might lead to harm. Paraprofessionals could be prevented from illegally practicing curative medicine when out of the sight of the full vet if— but probably only if— the vets retained physical charge of the supply of controlled drugs. Still greater economies would be captured if all paraprofessional work could be supervised at a distance, but this would raise more acutely the supervisory problem that the public sector has failed to solve: personnel who are responsible to both their clients and their hierarchical superiors while out of sight of the latter. However there is evidence that small, simple, informal hierarchies are more effective at some tasks than their larger, formal counterparts (Mintzberg 1979, pp. 466–67 and passim). Thus, this alternative is worthy of experimentation in those countries, such as Zimbabwe, that have been successful in restricting formal and informal private practice to full vets. In most of Africa, however, paravets are already operating privately outside of professional supervision.

Another use of paraprofessionals would keep them in the public sector and effectively turn them into extension agents rather than direct service providers. Such paravets would train livestock producers to make simple diagnoses and treatments themselves. Where the most important diseases do not involve drugs that have to be controlled or refrigerated, this extension-type of system provides an attractive benefit/ cost ratio in most pastoralist production systems. Such a system is already in place in the Central African Republic and is being encouraged in the 'communal' areas of Zimbabwe (Tacher 1986, pp. 43–44). Full veterinarians then play a supervisory and training role and only provide care themselves when exceptionally challenging animal health problems are confronted. Pastoralists are particularly appropriate for paravet-led training in herder-provided care because the travel costs in reaching their animals are so great and herders handle so many animals that short courses on animal health would be worth their time. Self-treatment probably will be appropriate for sedentary, mixed-farm producers only for common, simple maladies such as worms. Particularly if these farmers are densely settled, the costs of reaching them are less and the smaller number of their animals makes it less likely that they will have remembered the relevant skills when the need to treat an infrequent problem arises.

All of the preceding alternatives leave the full veterinarians in monopoly control over most aspects of animal health care—a position that they might exploit by restricting their numbers and forcing up the prices for their services. The free market solution to the paraprofessional issue calls for unrestricted competition of the various cadres against one another. My research in Kenya and that of Koma and Ly in Uganda and Senegal indicates that, at the moment, herders have difficulty distinguishing the relative qualifications of the various cadres of practitioners who are serving them. Most livestock owners therefore are unwilling to pay a premium for the diagnostic services of a full professional, although they willingly pay extra for procedures that only the latter can provide. Full vets therefore are under considerable competitive pressure at the moment, although they do appear to be surviving in Kenya, Senegal, and Uganda (Wamukoya *et al.* 1995; Chapters 6 & 7). A response within the logic of the market would be for a country's veterinary professional association to educate the public as to the value of the full vet, whom it would certify and differentiate. This response is insufficient, however, for it fails to acknowledge several additional benefits the professional vet is expected to provide to society but which are unlikely to be adequately compensated by a free market. When professionals are granted a monopoly they can charge for the attention to goods with externalities which they are socialized to provide. But in a fully free market their ability to charge for these externalities would be competed away.

Full vets not only possess additional skills but also are intended to be a link to the future and to the collective good through their membership in their professional association. We will return to the role of professional associations in the next section, but two attributes of their functions must be remarked upon here. First, the formal and informal socialization and sanction of the association provide a greater assurance of attention to externalities in animal health practice, aspects that will not be fully compensated by the market precisely because they address collective rather than private goods. Indeed, if vets imposed all quarantines on animals, herders might even *avoid* their services. Second, the professional association provides a way for vets to be integrated into the ongoing and international developments of their field, giving some assurance against the danger that they will be completely outdated within a decade of earning their degrees. Unless they are connected to these two aspects of the profession, paraprofessionals will rapidly become isolated from the collective good and changing aspects of their field. No matter how appropriate their training and intentions are at the point that they set up in private practice, it seems inevitable that paravets would become quacks over time.

The foregoing considerations suggest that four steps *should* be taken if the market is to be allowed to freely determine the demand for various types of animal health personnel.

(1) It is necessary to decide which levels of animal health personnel have sufficient training to be able in principle to operate outside the supervision of full veterinarians, to provide for the externalities that attend the services they sell, and to be capable of the periodic updating needed for them to perform these particular functions adequately far into the future.

Cadres who lack these qualifications should be prohibited from working independently and could be employed for animal health work only by the government or private veterinarians. It is already clear that countries will not make the same decisions on this matter, in good part because of the differences in the character of their livestock systems. It also is clear that the informal reality in some countries lies outside these parameters.

(2) Those cadres who function privately and independent of full veterinarians should have their own professional association (comparable, for example, to that of nurses). This association needs to be responsible for regulating its membership, assuring their attention to externalities, providing the required regular training that is necessary to keep them abreast with the latest international practices, and representing their interests in dealings with veterinarians and the state. To the best of our knowledge, only Senegal has such a paraprofessional association and, so far, it is performing only the last of these functions (Chapter 7).

(3) The tasks that this cadre is permitted to perform and the drugs it is able to sell have to be clearly specified and differentiated from those that presumably are reserved to full veterinarians. For restricted functions and controlled drugs, they would have to arrange a link with a full veterinarian. This step seems much less problematic than the first two and in practice may be the vehicle for achieving them. In Kenya and Senegal, but not in Uganda, paravets seem to rely largely on vets for their drug supplies, partly because of legal restrictions that are easier to enforce for wholesale than retail transactions and partly because of lack of capital. Even in Uganda there are clear functions, such as surgery, that paravets do not attempt (Chapters 6 & 7). These links between professionals and paraprofessionals could be encouraged and used as a means to guide and regulate the activities of the latter. We shall return to this point below.

(4) Private paraprofessionals need to be subject to the oversight of the veterinarian in their area whom the state has appointed—either by hire or contract—to assure attention to the collective goods essential to animal health. Such a contract would offset the failure of the market to fully compensate those who provide goods with large externalities. Presumably this regulation would be more stringent than the norm because the paraprofessionals would be the vets' competitors.

Such a set of institutions should assure the minimum necessary professionalization while providing veterinarians with competition for most of the animal health functions that herders regularly use. It would stimulate private vets to hire paraprofessionals and auxiliaries into their practices and to economize in their service delivery systems—the second alternative discussed above. And it would permit the market to determine just what mix of skills is economical at this stage of development.

Monopoly

The structure of an animal health care delivery system— the level of the providers' training and the extent to which economical structures are achieved— is a critical determinant of the price that these services will cost the producer. But it is not the only one. Another is competition, which offers the most effective mechanism for assuring the lowest economic price for a good or service. Unfortunately, however, competition often is imperfect in the animal health sector. The low density of producers and hence of effective demand (especially in the pastoralist areas), combined with the importance of distance in determining timely access, often creates effective local monopolies for animal health service providers. In other words, although there may be many comparable providers in existence, only one is within reasonable reach of a particular livestock owner. Of the 768 farmers Woods interviewed in Zimbabwe, only two went to an alternative government paraprofessional. In these circumstances the market cannot work properly and monopoly profits may be extracted from the producer.

The dangers of local monopoly are likely to be exacerbated if, as was argued above, private veterinarians are contracted to provide selected collective-good services in each locality, as is done in Sweden and as is planned for Uganda. The capture of this part of the market would provide a vet with a sound financial base that would make it very difficult for other veterinarians to find a profitable niche in competition with them in the less-commercialized, rural markets.

As difficult as these problems are, the New Institutional Economics suggest ways in which they could be resolved. We noted above that many neoclassical economists believe that if several firms competed for the right to the monopoly, they would bid away their monopoly advantages and yield an economically optimal outcome. Oliver Williamson (1985, p. 41 and Chap. 13) has shown that this reasoning is defective in several respects. Some mechanism has to be found to arbitrate the differences over the contract that will inevitably arise because of unforeseen circumstances and to enforce the terms of both the original contract and its amendments. Except in special circumstances, such arrangements are tantamount to regulation, which is what competitive bidding was supposed to avert in the first place. Nonetheless, these special circumstances can be created for veterinary practices.

Williamson suggests that competitive bidding will avert the local monopoly problem if, but only if, (1) the contract is subject to rebidding at relatively short intervals, and (2) neither party has significant sunk assets invested in the agreement at the time of rebidding. To these points we might add a third which Williamson takes for granted, that (3) the party making the contract with the bidder to provide the services is genuinely acting on behalf of the clients who are going to be served.

With regard to the first point, Williamson (1985, p. 339) suggests that,

> A leading advantage of recurrent short term contracting over long-term contracting is that short term contracts facilitate adaptive, sequential decision-making. The requirements that contingencies be comprehensively described and appropriate adaptations to each worked out in advance are thereby avoided...
>
> Additionally, under the assumption that competition at the contract renewal interval is efficacious, the hazards of contractual incompleteness that beset incomplete long-term contracts are avoided. Failure to define contractual terms appropriately gives rise, at most, to malperformance the duration of the current short term contract. Indeed, recognizing that a bidding competition will be held in the near future, winning bidders may be more inclined to cooperate with the franchising authority, if specific contractual deficiencies are noted, rather than use such occasions to realize temporary bargaining advantages. Opportunism is thereby curbed as well.

This short term contract condition seems feasible in veterinary medicine. Every two to five years, say, there could be open competitive bidding among veterinarians for the various geographically defined practices. Their bids could specify the range of services they would contract to offer, the prices at which they would be offered, and the level of government subsidy they would require. The request for tenders could indicate a minimum range of services that had to be offered, maximum prices that could be charged for particular services, and the maximum subsidies that government would be willing to provide, with a tradeoff function specified between prices and subsidies. One advantage to such an arrangement is that marginal cost consideration would incline the bidding toward the minimum prices and maximal subsidies in the poorer areas, while for the wealthier regions prices would be bid closer to the upper limit and the subsidy element might well be eventually competed away. A proposal much like this actually was made by the Kenya Ministry of Livestock Development to an official Working Party on Government

Expenditure in 1982 (Republic of Kenya 1982).

Nonetheless, Williamson (1985, p. 339) cautions that, 'The efficacy of recurrent short term contracting depends crucially ... on the assumption that parity among bidders at the contract renewal interval is realized.' This is turn requires that there be what Williamson (1985, pp. 74–5) refers to as no specificity in the assets that are up for bidding. By this he means that there be no sunk investments in human or physical capital that had been developed specifically for this transaction and that could not be used to trade with another partner if the first transaction relationship were discontinued. Williamson argues that asset specificity is quite common and is what explains both the frequent replacement of free-trading market relationships by hierarchical firms and the difficulty in doing without regulatory institutions.

Still, Williamson (1985, p. 351) concedes that

> This is not ... to suggest that franchise bidding for goods or services supplied under decreasing cost conditions is never feasible or to imply that extant regulation or public ownership can never be supplanted by franchise bidding with net gains... .[Where] physical assets can be redeployed [easily], ... deregulation would appear to have merit. Franchise bidding might also be warranted for ... situations in which] the winning bidder ... can be displaced without posing serious asset valuation problems, since the base plant ... can be owned by the government, and other asset ... will have an active secondhand market.

By and large, precisely these conditions apply to veterinary practices. Medical instruments, pharmaceutical supplies, laboratory equipment, refrigerators, and vehicles all would have a ready secondhand market. The surgery and staff houses for the practice might well be difficult to re-let for other purposes in rural markets, but they could easily be owned by the government and made available to whichever group won the contract. The problem is with the human capital that the owner of the practice had invested in learning how to operate it, building up a reputation with clients, and finding and training assistants in whom he or she had confidence. Most of these could be carried to a bid on the contract for another practice or access to them sold to a successor. Vets who were unable to win another contract could still seek employment as another's assistant in order to recoup the investment they had made in their own training.

In fact, the biggest barrier to competitive entry in most of Africa is simply access to capital on the part of vets who would like to bid for contracts. In the initial stages this might be overcome by generous, guaranteed loan schemes such as the veterinary association itself is providing in Mali and a donor is financing in, at least, Burkina Faso, Kenya, Senegal, and Zimbabwe. In the long run, vets would probably accumulate startup capital by working as assistants in other practices for a number of years. None of these problems seems insurmountable.

To my mind, the most troublesome issue is the one not explicitly stated by Williamson, that is, the extent to which the party negotiating the contract for the prospective practice with the various competing vets is in fact acting in the interests of the clients (Moe [1990] begins to deal with this type of issue). Given the conditions that prevail in many parts of Africa, agents of the state may be bribed or influenced to give or renew a contract for a practice to someone who will exploit its monopoly position. In other words, the agents may bid away the clients' interests in favor of their own. It seems to me that this problem is best averted by some sort of client involvement in the selection process. A decision by a local authority or cooperative with a *de facto* local monopoly over animal health services would not do, for the process then simply would be political at another level, with all the problems associated with the state itself.

Three mechanisms for client involvement in the award of the contract seem possible. The first two would emphasize what Albert Hirschman (1970) referred to as the consumer's 'exit' option at the expense of some economies of contiguity. The third relies upon what he called 'voice' and preserve the advantages of geographical compactness. All three alternatives would require that local participation in the bidding took place only after the state, the veterinary association, or the like had certified a list of candidates who met minimal standards of technical proficiency and society's collective interests in animal health. Of course this judgement is a regulatory one. It seems less likely to be fatally tainted by corruption since it only permits competition and does not assure success. Nonetheless, for reasons that we will explore in the next section, a professional veterinary body is more likely to fulfill this function effectively than is a government ministry.

In the first alternative, livestock producers would choose between competing veterinary practices they had contracted with the state to provide services to those on their 'list' at a pre-negotiated range of prices and per-herder subsidies.[9] This option preserves the producer's freedom

9. I favor a subsidy per herder rather than per animal, although it may seem counter-intuitive. First, it averts the common reluctance of herders to report the number of their

of choice at all times and permits a continuous transmission of the larger part of the relevant market signals.

In the second option, herders would join animal health or livestock producers' cooperatives with which vets would contract to provide services. The state subsidy would be based on the number of members, the fees negotiated by the vet with the coop might either be for discrete services, or an insurance premium for treatment of all problems. The latter method would increase the incentives to vets to stress preventive and promotive health practices, although they would incline lightly in the opposite direction for the producer. The payments could be deducted from coop payouts if it is engaged in marketing. Under this alternative the consumer also would retain the option to 'exit' an unsatisfactory service, although probably at less frequent intervals than the first alternative would offer. Added to the power of 'exit' would be that of the 'voice' of the coop leadership, who would be able to negotiate the details of the vet's service package and monitor its delivery. This alternative would be unacceptable if the coop had an effective monopoly for some service that the producer needed and the contract were negotiated by the coop leadership, for then the 'exit' option would be removed and the herder could easily be exploited by the leaders.

Because both of the first two alternatives preserve the ability of individual producers to take their custom elsewhere if they are dissatisfied with the services offered, they lose the advantages of geographical contiguity. In order for the right of choice to be meaningful, at least two vet practices or animal health coops must operate in the area. The overlap in service areas means that travel to service clients would not be as efficient, and in sparsely populated areas these economic costs could be considerable. Furthermore, if there were a disease outbreak or contaminated meat incident in an area, it would be harder to pin the responsibility on a particular practice.

The third alternative captures all the advantages of geographical compactness, but in order to do so has to substitute 'voice' for 'exit.' Under this mechanism all producers would vote periodically to determine who among the approved bidders would receive the contract.

Each of these potential arrangements has pros and cons that might make them more attractive for some production conditions than others.

---

livestock and the even greater difficulty that the state would have in auditing these numbers. Second, the mechanism would bias service toward the smaller herders, a useful counter to the other pressures that bias service in the opposite direction.

The third alternative is more likely to be appropriate to pastoral areas and the first feasible only for areas where there is a dense demand for veterinary services. The second generally would depend on the strength of the traditions of cooperative action in an area. But all three are mechanisms whereby the economic disadvantages of local monopoly probably can be countered and the interests of both livestock producers and society at large can be protected.

PRINCIPAL/AGENT THEORY AND THE VETERINARY PROFESSION

Patients and physicians are frequently cited as a quintessential principal/agent relationship (Pratt and Zeckhauser 1985, p. 2; Arrow 1985, p. 38).[10] And if human patients are principals and physicians their agents in caring for them, then animal owners also are principals and veterinarians their agents. This therefore is an another excellent place to explore the New Institutional Economics for clues as to the appropriate ways to design the privatization of professional services.

In an agency relationship,

> The individual taking the action is called the *agent*. The affected party is the *principle*.... The challenge in the agency relationship arises whenever—which is almost always—the principal cannot perfectly and costlessly monitor the agent's action and information. The problems of inducement and enforcement then come to the fore.... [G]iven information asymmetries—agents typically know more about their tasks than principals do, though principals know more about what they want accomplished—we cannot expect any ... business institution to function as well as it would if all information were costlessly shared or if the incentives of principal and agent(s) could be costlessly aligned. The shortfall is sometimes called the *agency loss* or *agency costs*. The challenge in structuring an agency relationship is to minimize it (Pratt and Zeckhauser 1985, pp. 2–3).

How is the herder (the client and the principal) to monitor the veterinarian (the agent) and provide appropriate incentives for his or her behavior, when the herder cannot effectively observe the vet's actions—

10. In an extended discussion of the agency issue in health care, Robert G. Evans (1984, pp. 69–81, esp. footnote 15) asserts that the patient-doctor relationship should *not* be seen as a principal/agent one. His final position closely parallels the one I take later in this section, although I see my position as a more complicated version of the agency relationship.

because he or she lacks the knowledge to do so— and when the outcome of the animal's health is only partly a function of the actions the vet takes? (This is known technically as a hidden action or moral hazard problem [Arrow 1985, pp. 37–8].)

The agency literature is helpful at a number of points in dealing with this dilemma. The first is that *both* herders and veterinarians benefit if the former are more effective in monitoring and motivating the latter.

> The benefits of any reductions in agency loss will be shared between principal and agent in most market situations, including competition and monopoly. Therefore ... [t]he principal and agent have a common interest in defining a monitoring-and-incentive structure that produces outcomes as close as possible to ones that would be produced if information monitoring were costless (Pratt and Zeckhauser 1985, p. 6).

When the market is unable to distinguish between high- and low-quality agents, principals will pay a price that represents the agents' average value. This poor product differentiation causes a loss of efficiency. However the primary losers are not the principals (herders) but the better vets (agents) who are being confounded with the worse ones and therefore are being paid less than their services are truly worth. Agency theory refers to this as a hidden information or adverse selection problem, because the better agents will try to exit this particular market for one in which their superiority can be recognized and therefore compensated. Akerloff (1970), referring to the difficulties in getting a good price for the sale of a used car on the open market, called this a 'market for lemons.'

The agency literature suggests there would be some redistributive effects in moving from one, already established, set of monitoring relationships to another (Pratt and Zeckhauser 1985, p. 19). But all parties lose from the agency costs that are created by the weak and distorted incentives governing animal health practice in Africa today, and the market would distribute benefits to all concerned from the increase in economic efficiency that would result from reform.

Second, long-term associations increase the value to agents of their relationships with principals. This makes limited monitoring by the principal more effective, for it increases the value of the threat to sever future connections if something is found to be wrong. Thus both high-quality vets and herders would benefit if they can develop extended, personal relationships. Such relationships would enable herders to make more discriminating judgments of the quality of service over a long period and to bestow their custom accordingly.

Third, a large stock of value that could be lost through bad behavior—such as reputation or assets subject to suit—is a strong incentive for good behavior. If the penalty is a large fine and is paid by the faulty vet to the aggrieved herder, as in a malpractice suit, the latter has considerable incentive to collect it and the transaction is economically conservative (in the sense that little value is lost in the transfer). However if, as is more common, the penalty is a revocation of the right to practice, the transaction is 'nonconservative,' since the vet loses value but the herder gains none from it and the penalty therefore is an economic dead loss. The fact that, because of its size, the penalty would be invoked rarely makes it economically more efficient, since it is 'nonconservative' when used (Pratt and Zeckhauser 1985, pp. 6, 12–13).

Both types of penalties for agent misperformance have institutional implications. Malpractice suits depend on the existence of courts that are both effective and accessible. The ability of an African smallholder to use a court successfully against a member of the educated elite is chancy and therefore a weak protection. Revocation, since it is 'nonconservative,' carries weak incentives for the aggrieved herder and generally would involve action by state institutions that, in Africa, are even more likely to be corrupt or ineffective than the courts. As Douglass North (1990, p. 33) remarks, 'one cannot take enforcement for granted. It is (and always has been) the critical obstacle to increasing specialization and division of labor.'

This leads to the importance of instituting some third party method of enforcement, a party beyond the client and the state who has an interest in the quality of service. Who or what might this be? We noted earlier that the professionals, and especially the better ones, lose as agents when a hidden information problem leads to ineffective monitoring by principals (clients). It is precisely this dynamic that frequently leads professional groups, which tend to be dominated by their better practitioners, to try to regulate themselves, differentiate themselves from lesser competitors, and improve their market position (Pratt and Zeckhauser 1985, pp. 19, 29; Arrow 1985, pp. 38, 40).

Nonetheless, say Pratt and Zeckhauser (1985, p. 29),

> It is worth observing that policing or self-policing can only work (assuming that the major penalty is banishment) if there is some prize to be lost. The competitive market system does not generate prizes, how-

> ever. The ability to enforce good behavior on the part of agents thus may require that there be some element of monopoly profit.

Hence professional association self-policing is likely to be most effective when the state has delegated licensing authority to it. This is not a matter of 'making criminals responsible for policing crime,' as long as there is a market element in the setting of prices for professional services and as long as the professional association is dominated by its better practitioners. Under these conditions, the association then would have an incentive for enforcing higher standards and thereby gaining a greater market differentiation from those offering competing services. In fact, a greater danger lies in the opposite direction: the professional association may use its licensing powers to force out of the market lesser quality and lower priced services which consumers legitimately desire. Both types of problems become severe when a professional association gains a complete monopoly over a particular type of service and has no effective competition. If one were concerned with veterinary professionals only as agents of individual principals, the herders, one would wish to confine licensing to the function of labeling (or product differentiating), not to limiting access to the market.

However, there is an element to the veterinarian's function that is not captured by simple agency theory, the claims of some of its protagonists to the contrary not withstanding. And this other set of functions also is directly relevant to the role of the professional association. When introducing agency theory we noted that it is based on the assumption that the function of the agent is to do what the principal would want if the latter knew everything the former does. In fact, this frequently is not the case for professionals, who are assigned certain responsibilities by *society* in addition to those they have contracted with the individual client (Clark 1985; Zald, p. 707). The dual nature of this responsibility is captured by the classic remark that, 'The quack is the man who continues through time to please his customers but not his colleagues.' (Hughes 1958, as cited in Wilensky 1964, p. 154).

Partly what is involved here is the responsibility of veterinarians to take the risk of disease more seriously and to discount the future less heavily than most herders do. Generally, societal welfare and economic growth are better served by longer time horizons than those on which most of the poor act. Thus, vets should urge various disease prevention and health promotion measures that clients would generally neglect if they knew the associated probabilities. Vets also should be expected to decline to administer certain cures the scientific status of which is doubtful, even when the client requests them 'just in case.' These differences in perception and the dissimilarities in incentives that follow from them are important to the way the herder and the vet relate. However, all of this can properly be said to be part of an agency relationship in which the agent possesses superior knowledge to the principal. It was apparently considerations such as these which started Kenneth Arrow (1963) on his path toward agency theory in his reflection on health care.

Much more important, and outside of a simple understanding of the agency relationship, is the obligation of the veterinarian to pursue selected collective goods on behalf of the larger community even when they have a negative benefit/cost ratio for the herder. Thus the vet is obliged to impose a quarantine on cattle diagnosed with foot and mouth disease and to prevent public consumption of diseased meat, even though these acts cause a great loss to the herder who might have requested the vet's presence. Similarly, the vet must strive to bring inoculations against epizooties to the 'herd immunity' level for the whole community even when individual herders feel their livestock are not worth the product of the cost multiplied by the probability of disease or want to 'free ride' on the inoculations of their neighbors' herds. One could, and most agency analysts probably would, argue that these responsibilities demonstrate that the vet as agent is serving two principals: the individual herder and society. This is all very well, but it reinforces the necessity for some body to represent this societal principal and reshape incentives on society's behalf. This body would be some combination of the professional association and the state.

The public standing and licensing authority that society and the state grant to a professional association are really one side of a bargain in which the profession commits itself to maintain standards and protect the public interest in return. The terms of this bargain can be, and frequently are, contested, particularly once the profession has gained monopoly powers. It then may be tempted to extract much benefit and to provide little regulatory service in return (Freidson 1970). The formal and informal organizational attributes of the profession thus are of great importance, particularly in African societies where the government has difficulty effectively representing the public interest.

Society's interests in a profession are not served solely by its regulating the technical standards of its members and differentiating its product from other service providers. 'The professional ... adheres to a set of professional norms.' (Wilensky 1964, p. 138.) These involve 'a collectivity or service orientation' (Goode 1960, p. 903) and are what R.K. Merton

(1982) calls 'institutionalized altruism.'[11] Where do these come from and how are they sustained?

Professionals in the ethical sense are not produced and certainly are not sustained simply through the exposure of individuals to professional training. The mastery of technique *and* the socialization in professional norms that are provided through this training *are* of critical importance. But training and socialization alone will not sustain the candidate professional in the face of strong contrary pressures in the environment. Only when the potential professional has other professionals as an important reference group in his or her work life will he or she be transformed into a true professional. The group of peers provide the social structure that permits the professional to resist the otherwise powerful pressures to fall short of professional norms. In the extreme case, the professional assoation formally sanctions or bars someone who violates professional standards. But even short of formal sanctions, the existence of informal criticism from a group of people whom one respects and identifies with is a powerful social sanction. Furthermore that professional *community* and its norms provide the strength to actually bar the deviant member when the public interest is betrayed. (On norms in economic behavior, see Elster 1989.)

Is there any reason to expect a professional association to be able to protect a societal collective good when most national interests in Africa are subordinated to ethnic and local ones? I think that the answer is 'yes,' but only with nurturing. At the beginning of this research project I thought that professional associations would emerge to perform the role of self-regulation in Africa. Ly's research in Senegal suggests that I probably was mistaken; the *Ordre Vétérinaire* has not been aggressive in taking on the regulatory functions in the way the Principal/Agent literature would lead us to expect, and the organization of paraprofessionals has done nothing along these lines (Chapter 7). I want first to indicate the reasons I thought that professional associations *would* begin to do meaningful self-regulation, then why it appears they are not doing so, and finally another way of thinking about professional self-regulation that may guide the creation of a more promising institutional framework.

First of all, I expected meaningful self-regulation by veterinary associations because a profession has certain advantages over most other nonethnic African groups in organizing for its collective interest. Its

11. Goode, in contrast to some others, sees these first two attributes alone as the basic defining ones for a profession.

members are highly educated and have a clear occupational identity and self-consciousness. In addition, the African professions are small, and Mancur Olson (1965) has suggested that small organizations, which maintain face-to-face relationships or control critical services for their members, are most likely to be successful at producing collective goods or at organizing to get the state to provide them. Russell Hardin (1982, p. 102) has demonstrated that the logic of collective action is actually slightly different than this. A collective good will be provided once an individual or a cohesive *subgroup* finds that the benefits to itself of the good are greater than the costs to itself of creating the collective good for the whole group by itself. The likelihood of such a subgroup's existing (what the literature calls a *k*-subgroup) increases with the inequality of the benefit that will be derived from the collective good (that is, the asymmetry in demand). The more unequally distributed the potential benefits, the smaller the subgroup needed to reach the critical point at which benefits outweigh costs; and the smaller the subgroup, the more likely it will achieve the cohesion necessary for collective action.

Because the professions in most African countries not only are relatively small but also have members with unequal skills and less-trained nonmembers claiming similar skills, I thought the probability was high that at least some members would find it in their interests to organize so as to promote standards and product differentiation and capture a better price on the market when professional services are privatized. I found evidence for this proposition both in Kenya, where the Kenya Veterinary Association lobbied vigorously and successfully for experimental privatization, and in Mali, where the employed veterinarians agreed to tax themselves to provide the loan capital to set up other veterinarians in private practice.

The preceding line of reasoning was overly optimistic, as Ly's research shows. The return that the Principal/Agent literature posits for professional self-regulation is still valid. To gain these returns through formal regulatory procedures, however, the profession must overcome the collective action problem: a small group of individuals have to be willing to undertake the personal costs of organizing enforcing regulation mechanisms. I recognized and correctly specified this problem but was wrong about its magnitude: I misjudged how easy it would be to overcome organizational hurdles when sanctions against one's colleagues rather than simple economic gains for everyone in the profession are involved. The existence of associational self-regulation in many societies must be seen much more as the result of a hard bargain driven by the state in return for professional privileges, rather than an internally motivated strategy to capture benefits from overcoming the 'market for lemons' problem.

We are now beginning to see that professions in the northern hemisphere create self-regulation in a much more informal and decentralized way. Professionals tend to monitor and steer one another to higher standards of performance through networks of day-to-day interactions as they work together, what Deborah Savage calls 'professional coproduction' (1997; Savage and Robertson, forthcoming). Better professionals make higher incomes than the inferior ones because other good professionals recognize their skills and both are willing to work with these colleagues and give their patients referrals to them (Friedson 1970).

The problems then with self-regulation among health professionals in Africa are:

1. Most professionals work in isolation. They are only rarely involved in 'professional coproduction.' This is especially true for animal health but tru also in human health, for multi-physician hospitals are not as common in Africa as they are in the north.
2. When 'coproduction' does take place, it tends to involve paraprofessionals under the supervision of a professional and the hierarchical nature of the relationship interferes with mutual regulation.
3. Referrals are rare in these systems.

This line of theoretical reasoning would suggest that, rather than mutual exclusion, the combination of encouraging cooperative relationships between professionals and paraprofessionals as peers and developing referral networks between them is the best way for quality differentiation to emerge in the conditions of African veterinary markets. The Ugandan evidence that full vets cannot collect a price premium for the performance of procedures that paravets usually provide, but that paravets do recognize that they would risk sacrificing their reputations with their clients if they attempted advanced procedures that only full vets can perform effectively. Koma did not find referral networks in existence in Uganda yet, but these informal vet/paravet recognitions lay the groundwork for them (Chapter 6). In this context, the reliance of paravets on full vets for the pharmaceutical products they resell to their herder clients (which has currently broken down in Uganda) creates a very important context for professional-paraprofessional interaction and the development of networks and informal regulation of quality. In Senegal, Ly did observe such a network between a full vet and paravets created by a mission in the Ferlo. The result of the quality assurances that come from a well-functioning referral network was at least a doubling in herder purchases of preventive treatments from paravets (Chapter 9). Our work thus leads us to see referral networks as central to the maintenance of quality in African veterinary medicine.

CONCLUSION

This chapter has reviewed a number of critical issues in the structural reform of animal health services in Africa. Using the New Institutional Economics, it has highlighted several problems that others concerned with the privatization of this service area have tended to neglect. Most notably, it has called attention to (1) the need to retain a central role for paraprofessionals in the new delivery system; (2) the centrality of the relationship between the veterinary and paraveterinary professions; (3) the importance of developing state contracting procedures for assisting the private delivery of veterinary services that have externalities in ways that will avoid the problems of local monopoly; and (4) the central role that strengthened professionalism has to play in this area if collective goods and the public interest are to be served.

This chapter has not addressed all the important issues that will affect restructuring of animal health services in Africa. (For others, see Umali *et al.* 1992.) Instead, its larger purpose has been to demonstrate that some of the newer economic literatures on organization have a great deal to contribute to the older precepts of neoclassical economics in anticipating and thinking through the issues posed by fundamental changes in the structure of service delivery. Hopefully what has been done has been sufficient to demonstrate that theories do indeed exist that permit powerful deductive propositions to be generated about professional domains like animal health in Africa. We now turn to the pieces of empirical research that this line of theoretical enquiry stimulated. As our discusssions have already demonstrated, that research confirms the utility of these theories but also leads to reformulating some of them.

2 Traditional Insurance Mechanisms and the Choice of Health Care Providers in Ethiopia

Damen Haile Mariam

Among the greatest challenges developing countries face in today's context of severe financial crises is sustaining the delivery of social services. Even though many countries are attempting to improve their health services, particularly by designing health programs to achieve the goals of the Alma Ata declaration of 'Health for All,' they are confronted by increased health care needs even as inefficient service delivery and scarce resources limit their capacity to act. The attempt to service foreign debt accumulated in the past has created formidable balance of payments deficits; the inevitable devaluation of local currencies has increased the cost of debt servicing in national terms and strained government budgets still further. Some governments have diverted their revenue away from the social sector to projects that promise short term economic gains. For all these reasons, the health sector has often found itself with a budget that has declined substantially in real terms (Abel-Smith 1991; Alubo 1990; Hoare 1987). In Ethiopia, as in most developing countries, health services are provided primarily by publicly owned institutions. These institutions have a low geographic coverage of the population and their performance is inefficient, resulting reduced public use. With very limited resources that can be devoted to the social sector, achieving optimal health care will be very difficult with exclusive reliance on the public sector (Mills and Lee 1993).

These and other problems have forced policy makers to consider alternative sources of funding for health activities, one of which is cost recovery from community financing (or user charges). Establishing service charges for health services in poor countries is still controversial. One of the reasons for this is the inadequacy of empirical studies in the developing world regarding the demand for health care, particularly studies that can guide the consideration of alternatives in financing mechanisms (Waddington and Enyimayew 1989; Gertler and Van der Gaag 1990; McPake *et al.* 1993).

Ethiopia's health policy reflects the Primary Health Care approach and emphasizes health promotion and disease prevention. The Ethiopian government also expresses commitment to the decentralization of health care delivery, including cost recovery measures and private and non-governmental involvement in the financing and provision of health care (Ethiopian Office of the Council of Ministers 1993; Transitional Government of Ethiopia 1995). The government's allocation to health care has remained at less than 4 per cent of the national budget for each of the past ten years, and 60–65 per cent of the health care budget goes toward personnel salaries. Health care workers have to function in poorly equipped facilities and face constant shortages of drugs. As of 1990, more than 70 per cent of the hospitals were concentrated in a few urban centers, and around 60 per cent of the physicians and 46 per cent of the nurses were located in the capital. In addition, the system has few performance incentives and as a result health professionals' performance is suboptimal (Ethiopian Ministry of Health 1992).

Private health services, in contrast, are flourishing in the urban centers of Ethiopia. Health professionals are giving more attention to part time private practices where the incentives for hard work in the public sector are weak, and a growing number of people are seeking medical attention at private institutions because of their disenchantment with public sector inefficiency. This trend has, on the one hand, raised fears that these mainly urban institutions may divert resources away from the public sector, especially by drawing professionals away from under-served rural areas. On the other hand, there is an expectation that it may help relieve the public services from patient overload, even though only people who can afford the higher fees use private services. To identify which components of health care can be better handled by the private sector more needs to be known about the factors that influence health care demand. Ethiopia in particular is under-studied (Buschkens and Slikkerveer 1982; Slikkerveer 1990).

This study of health care demand in Ethiopia analyzes the relationship between the choice of health care providers, the attributes of the maladies, and the attributes of the providers. It seeks to contribute to the debate on how best to reformulate health policy objectives in light of the health care financing crisis in developing countries. The study draws on Grossman's human capital model and Andersen's behavior model to identify the effects of disease characteristics, sociodemography, economic factors, and epidemiology on people's choices of health providers. Particular attention is given to the impact of health care financing on provider choice because developing alternative mechanisms of health care financing is the single most important factor determining the feasibility of private sector involvement in health services provision, particularly in the area of in-patient hospital care (Griffin 1989).

Among the study's most important findings is the strong effect that extended family systems have on the choice of health care providers. Traditional families ensure that responsibility for economic survival does not fall on the individual alone; they function as a form of social insurance. One possible health care financing alternative is the development of risk sharing mechanisms among the consumer population. However, formal risk sharing mechanisms, in the form of health insurance, are less evolved in the developing countries. The findings of this study show that extended families should to be taken into account in developing such new financing arrangements. Among the main limitations of the present study is recall bias because interviews were conducted between April and August only. This problem is mitigated because we used a six-month recall period to address the seasonality problem.

THE CONCEPTUAL FRAMEWORK AND PROPOSED ESTIMATION

The two theoretical models most commonly used to analyze demand for medical care are Grossman's human capital and Andersen's behavioral models (Feldstein 1993). The central proposition of the Grossman model is that health can be viewed as a durable capital stock that produces an output of healthy time. The model assumes that individuals inherit an initial stock of health that depreciates with age and that can be increased by investment. In this framework, the 'shadow price' of health depends on many other variables besides the price of medical care. The shadow price rises with age if the depreciation rate on the stock of health rises over the life cycle, and falls with education if more educated people are more efficient producers of health (Grossman 1972). Andersen's behavioral model defines three categories of determinants of demand for medical care services: predisposing factors, enabling factors, and the need for care. According to this model, it is the interaction of these determinants that result in an individual's demand for a particular service (Andersen 1968).

In both models, several independent variables besides illness influence the demand for medical care. Even though different forms of interaction of these factors are envisaged, the models use similar individual variables, including monetary price of care, time price (this includes the cost of travel to a health institution and the time spent before getting services at a facility), age as a proxy for health status, education, and income (Fuchs 1968; Selden 1993; Newhouse 1981; Newhouse 1985).

While a good deal is known about the factors that affect demand for medical care in developed countries, there is little information about whether or not these same variables can account for differential demand on the health services in developing countries (Benyoussef and Wessen 1974; Akin *et al.* 1986). In addition, the information we have on health care demand in developing countries is based on the strictly individualistic assumptions of neoclassical economics theory, which limits an individual's budget constraint to his or her own income (Lavy and Quigley 1993). Most of the health care demand studies assume that individuals seek to maximize their own health input, using their household health production function and subject to their budget constraint.

Such considerations, however, do not account for other factors in traditional social systems that may play important roles in dealing with disease and other catastrophic conditions in developing countries. It is argued here that an individual's budget constraint may be relaxed when she gets remittances from other family members. It is reasonable to suspect that this relaxation of the individual's budget constraint affects the amount of health input one consumes, depending on the types of conditions that are subsidized by such risk sharing systems.

The conceptual basis for the present analysis is Andersen's behavioral model, which has been modified by adding 'support by relatives' as one of the enabling factors. The modified model is represented in Figure 2.1. Evidence in Africa indicates the transitory nature of most affordability problems for the individual patient (McPake *et al.* 1993). This suggests that for most common uses of health services, adequate cash is potentially available within the extended family, which raises the transitory income of the individual and therefore affects her demand. Thus, there is a need for an analysis that incorporates culturally specific socioeconomic factors that may play a role in determining demand.

If the extended family support variable is found to be significant, we want to know whether it acts as a credit or as an insurance system, and its consequences for those family members who are covered and those who are not. If the extended family system works as a source of credit

Figure 2.1. Modification of Andersen's Behavioral Model

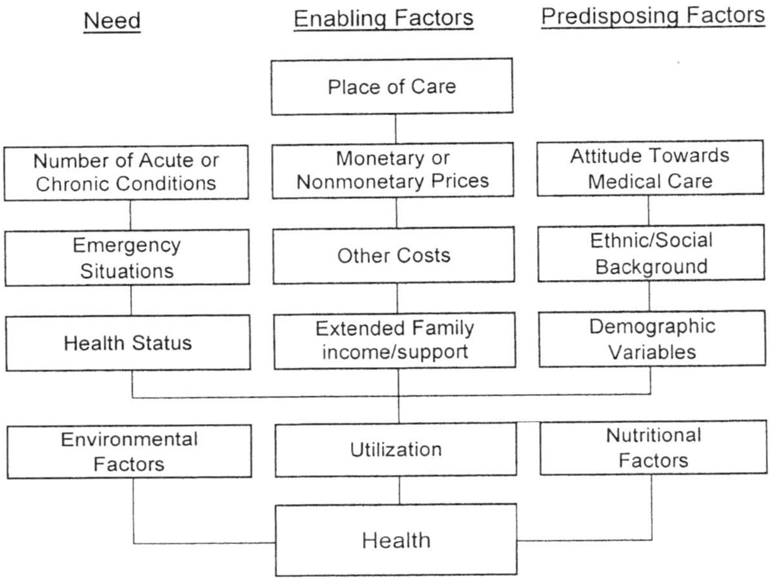

based on eventual ability to pay, it is rational to assume that it will more likely pay for immediate life threatening situations in working adults than for non-working chronic patients. On the other hand, if it acts as insurance, there will be little difference in the willingness to pay based on disease type or occupational status. Furthermore, this increases the size of the insurance unit for an individual and reduces the problem of adverse selection.

The econometric estimation methods used in the study involve limited dependent variables. The analysis is concerned with a behavior that is observed only as a binary indicator, that is, whether or not someone seeks outside medical help when she gets sick. While it is possible to use dummy variables as dependent variables to see such a dichotomous choice, ordinary least squares regression is not appropriate in such circumstances for several econometric reasons. Nonlinear estimation techniques have been developed to overcome some of the major statistical problems. Two techniques most commonly used in this instance are the probit and the logit analyses. The probit uses the cumulative normal function while using the logistic function creates the logit model. While both use the maximum likelihood estimation method, the logistic function involves less computational cost (Kennedy 1992, Greene 1993).

Once one decides to seek outside medical help, an individual's health seeking behavior is manifested as multiple responses to a condition (an actual disease or perceived threat). Such responses are best expressed in ordinal or categorical variables for which simple logistic regression is not usually an appropriate analytic technique. In these cases, estimation is undertaken by means of multinomial logit or multinomial probit models. Again, the great advantage of multinomial logit is its computational ease. The likelihood of an individual's choosing a given alternative is easily expressed and a likelihood function can be formed and maximized in a straightforward fashion (Madala 1983; McKelvey and Zavonya 1975; Duan *et al.* 1983).

The multinomial logit model allows an arbitrary number of responses and continuous right hand side variables to provide an extension of the linear logit model in relation to consumer demand theory (Theil 1969). One can specify a set of relationships that describe the way in which each of the probabilities of the multiple responses depend on certain determining factors. Schmidt and Strauss have applied this model to the prediction of occupation (type of job) for individuals, based on certain personal characteristics (Schmidt & Strauss 1975). For this particular analysis, simple logistic regression was used initially to assess the factors affecting utilization of any kind of health care. Then, extending the multinomial logit estimation model, the probability of a person's demanding a health service among various types of providers can be expressed as follows:

$$P1 + P2 + P3 + P4 = 1$$

$$LOGe(P2/P1) = a2 + b22\ NEED + b23\ ENABLING\ FACTORS + b24\ PREDISPOSING\ FACTORS + E2$$

$$LOGe(P3/P1) = a3 + b32\ NEED + b33\ ENABLING\ FACTORS + b34\ PREDISPOSING\ FACTORS + E3$$

$$LOGe(P4/P1) = a4 + b42\ NEED + b43\ ENABLING\ FACTORS + b44\ PREDISPOSING\ FACTORS + E4$$

Where P is the probability of seeking treatment from:

P1 = local health stations
P2 = traditional healers and local vendors
P3 = public health centers and hospitals
P4 = private and mission facilities

There may be more than one enabling factor in an equation (need, enabling, and predisposing factors). Based on the coefficients of the independent variables from the above model, one can discern the effect of the various factors in seeking health services from different kinds of providers, and the types of health conditions for which these factors may significantly affect health care demand. In addition, one can use our model (unlike the standard Anderson model) to determine the effect of extended family support as an enabling factor.

Family expenditures for health services and quantities of medical care consumed are the main measures typically used for estimating health care demand. However, both of these measures have shortcomings (Andersen 1968). Expenditure is not an adequate measure of family use because of the variation found in the price per unit of service. If there is sliding scale pricing or price discrimination by income in the area, then expenditures will be positively biased for high-income families and negatively biased for low-income families. Furthermore, families living in areas with the highest prices for medical care will appear to consume more services than may actually be the case. On the other hand, the major weakness of using quantities of medical care services is the absence of a common denominator for the various kinds of health care services that are consumed by families.

In the case of the present study, the dependent variable 'choice of health units' has a strong service quality characteristic (even though it also embodies monetary and travel time prices). In Ethiopia, health services are provided at a standard nominal fee, which is usually lower than marginal cost to the government health units. The fees are lowest at health stations and health centers. Even though hospital fees are higher, it is usually the travel cost and the waiting time that makes hospital care more expensive. The monetary price charged across similar health units tends to be uniform, which gives us reasonable justification for using 'choice of health units' as a dependent variable for the present estimation. On the other hand, using this measure also assumes uniformity of services across similar types of health institutions (for example, all health stations are treated as giving the same quality of service), an assumption which may not always be accurate.

DATA AND METHODS

We carried out a cross-sectional descriptive study in which a random sample of 1000 individuals was surveyed. The source population was drawn from the central region of Ethiopia, previously called the Shoa administrative region. This region was selected because, compared to other regions, its population has access to at least the basic level of health services, and has a composition that nearly approximates that of the nation as a whole. In addition, Shoa includes the capital Addis Ababa. After selecting the region, we undertook a multistage systematic sampling. Using a sampling frame prepared by the Central Statistics Office, a sample of 25 *waradas* (townships) were chosen from the over 600 in the region. A village was then chosen at random within each *warada* and within each village 40 households were selected by systematic random sampling (CSA 1991). At the household level, a slight modification of the Kish procedure was used to select respondents (Kish 1965, pp. 398–401). Appropriate weighing procedures have been used to produce unbiased population estimates in the following analyses.

The survey was conducted from the beginning of April to the end of August 1995. From the 1000 households interviewed, a total of 822 interviews were analyzable (178 interviews were aborted because no one had been sick in the reporting period). Each interview followed a structured questionnaire that had 163 question items, which were entered as variables. In addition, focus group discussions were conducted in four villages selected at the end of the survey. These were transcribed and used for the purpose of validating the quantitative results.

Table 2.1 illustrates some of the sociodemographic characteristics of the sample population. About 66 per cent of interviewees aged ten and above were illiterate, and only about nine per cent had at least secondary education. Eliciting information regarding individual or household income was the most difficult part of the survey. When we weighted our 807 responses, the average annual household income was Birr 2430 (about US$386) with a range of 45 to 75,000 birr. Number of cattle per household was also used as a proxy for additional household income information. The weighted average reported from 616 responses was 4.37 with a range of 0 to 37. Both estimates may be low, as it is customary to underreport both household income and cattle in the country in general. In each of these respects, the demographic makeup of our sample corresponds closely with that of the population in the survey area.

The average number of episodes of illness within the six month recall period (for those who reported being sick) was 1.8 with a range of 1 to 9 in each household, which leads us to assume 3.6 episodes of illness per household, per year. From this we deduce a probability that an *individual*

Table 2.1 Percentage Distribution of Respondents by Selected Characteristics, Central Ethiopia, 1995 (n = 822, weighted for Kish* selection procedure)

Characteristic	Percentage	Characteristic	Percentage
Gender		Religion	
Female	60.58	Orthodox Christian	72.77
Male	39.42	Muslim	18.82
		Age	
Education		0–4	16.82
(older than ten years)		5–9	9.08
Illiterate	68.94	10–14	8.62
Read & write	14.04	15–19	9.27
Elementary	7.60	20–24	6.91
Secondary	8.17	25–29	6.34
College & up	1.25	30–34	7.06
		35–39	10.05
		40–44	6.77
		45 +	19.10

*Kish (1965), 398–401

would get sick at 0.26, and that each individual is likely to generate 0.21[1] new contacts with health facilities each year. The fact that this figure is higher than the 0.14 utilization ratio calculated in the Eastern Harrarghe study (Slikkerveer 1990) can be explained by the time difference between the two studies (almost 20 years) and by the fact that the Eastern Harrarghe study was done in a single village. On the other hand, the present figure is close to the 0.27 contacts per year that was estimated earlier by the World Health Organization for the whole country (WHO 1993). This is especially noteworthy in view of the possibility of recall bias since we used a six-month recall period for the study.

The average time needed to reach the nearest conventional health facility by walking was 1.37 hours, while for those who used a vehicle it was about three quarters of an hour. The facility visited was a health station in 78 per cent of cases (of these 41 per cent were staffed with

1. The annual episodes of illness per household (3.6) was multiplied by the number of households reporting sick family members during the recall period (822) and the product (2,959) was divided by the total population of interviewed households (5,463). The quotient (0.5417) was again multiplied by the proportion of the sick who went to government facilities (0.39). The final product was 0.2113 = Annual new contacts to government facilities.

health assistants and 37 per cent by at least one nurse), a health center in 19 per cent of the cases, and a hospital in only 3 per cent of the cases.

The interviewee's choice of health care provider during their last illness is shown in Table 2.2. We can place these choices into three major categories: 27 per cent stayed at home or were assisted by relatives, 14 per cent went to traditional or transitional healers, and 59 per cent went to modern health services. A World Bank health care demand study found that in rural areas of the Ivory Coast 10 per cent of the patients consulted traditional healers, 69 per cent were seen by nurses, and 17 per cent were seen by doctors (Dor and Van der Gaag 1987). If we attempt to generate corresponding figures for the present study, we find a similar pattern except for the nurse alternative (eight per cent went to traditional healers, six per cent went to transitional healers, about 38 per cent went to nurses, and about 18 per cent were treated by doctors). In addition, these findings are similar to those reported by Mwabu *et al.* (1993) on the choice of medical treatment in Kenya. They found that among their adult sample, 39 per cent treated themselves or went to traditional healers, 36 per cent went to government facilities, 20 per cent went to private clinics, and six per cent went to mission facilities. The corresponding figures from the present study would be 41 per cent for self-treatment and traditional care, 40 per cent for government facilities, 15 per cent for private clinics, and five per cent for mission facilities.

The average total cost of a visit to a health provider was 70.00 birr (US$11.11) with a range of 0–9000 birr. When the outlier value for total cost (9000 birr) is approximated to the next lower value (1500 birr), the average total cost would be 62.33 birr (about US$10). 9.3 per cent of the respondents paid nothing (weighted n = 1019), and 80.6 per cent of the respondents had a total cost below the average (0–75 birr). The breakdown of the total cost by medical and nonmedical (for example, travel or lodging) expenses was very difficult for most of respondents. Among those for whom the breakdown was possible (weighted n = 951), the reported average medical cost was 41.20 birr (US$6.54) with a range of 0–6000 birr while that of the nonmedical cost was 31.33 birr (US$4.97) with a range of 0–3000 birr. Approximating the value of the outlier to the next lower value, the average medical cost would be 37.21 birr (range 0–1000) while the average nonmedical cost would be 27.10 birr (range 0–750). Those who had expenditures below the average treatment cost (0–46 birr) were 83.7 per cent of the respondents (weighted n = 951).

Table 2.2 Choice of Health Care Providers and Reasons for Choice. Central Ethiopia, 1995 (n = 822, weighted for the sampling procedures)

Choice of Provider	Percentage
Did nothing	21.31
Self-treatment	5.35
Friend/Neighbor	0.64
Traditional Healer	7.48
Local vendor	6.49
Non-MD clinic	8.13
MD clinic	3.06
Health post	0.07
Public health station	20.60
Mission health station	1.92
Public health center	9.91
Mission health center	2.35
Public hospital	8.41
Mission hospital	0.86
Other	3.42
Main reasons for choosing provider	
Distance	49.22
Believe provider is efficacious for condition	25.44
Monetary price	8.22
Less crowded	4.70
Main reasons for not taking action	
Lack of money	40.93
Assumed disease was self limiting	37.21
Other reasons	21.86

EFFECTS OF DETERMINANTS

This section assesses the effects of the three types of demand determinants suggested by the modified version of Andersen's model on the choice of health care providers. Table 2.3 summarizes the variables for each of the determinants— need, predisposing, and enabling factors— and the characteristics of the health care providers.

Need Factors

The study categorized reported symptoms according to their severity and created a new variable called severity. The lowest severity rating (1) implies that the condition is self-limiting and one would not get any benefit by going to a health unit. On the other hand, a severity of 10 implies the problem is life threatening unless one reaches a hospital or a higher-level health unit with in-patient facilities. In this scoring, therefore, a disease that can be dealt with at a local health station would have a lower severity rating and a complicated case that needs admission and intervention by specialists at a referral hospital would get the highest severity score. Disease epidemiology and the capacity of the health units at various levels to deal with the conditions were taken into consideration in making these ratings. If we take a mental problem, for instance, even if the condition is severe enough to warrant a visit to a higher level institution, mental health services are so scarce in the country that a patient might be better off seeking holy water or some other form of traditional treatment. (The severity scores were compiled from respondents' reports of symptoms by the author, an Ethiopian MD with rural clinical experience.)

The severity variable was positive and significant in the decision to seek outside medical help when someone becomes sick. It was also positive across the choice of higher level facilities and statistically significant in the choice of government hospitals and health centers. This indicates that people were acting rationally in choosing institutions, which are appropriate to their condition. The choices significantly correlate with what one would rationally choose given disease epidemiology and the organization and structure of health facilities. It is likely that this pattern was observed because most of the diseases were endemic and people would know where to go from their past experiences. A related explanation may be that the local government health stations were known to be relatively more focused on the pediatric conditions that were more prevalent in the present study.

Severity was statistically significant in the choice of government hospitals because these are the appropriate units for severe and life threatening conditions, and where one would get specialized tertiary level care. The finding that traditional healers and local vendors were also preferred over the local health stations for more severe conditions might be explained by the fact that the local vendors were more likely to have drugs and injections than the local health stations, which frequently run out of drugs (Table 2.5). In addition, these might also be the types of cases for which these categories of providers were perceived to be the best alternatives. This is particularly true in the case of traditional healers, which are usually considered to have potent remedies for diseases that do not seem amenable to modern medical practices.

Table 2.3 Characteristics of Health Units, Central Ethiopia, 1995

Choice of Health Care Provider
0 = Local government health stations
1 = Drug vendors or traditional healers
2 = Government health centers or hospitals
3 = Private or mission facilities (health stations, centers, hospitals)

Need Factors
SEVERITY = Scoring of symptoms based on the benefit to skill and capacity of the available health institutions (Categorical 1–10)

Predisposing Factors
AGE = Age of the interviewee in years
GENDER = 1 if male, 0 otherwise
AMHARA = 1 if ethnic group is Amhara, 0 otherwise
HOSAN = 1 if ethnic group is either Kembata or Hadia, 0 otherwise
RELIGION = 1 if Christian, 0 otherwise
EDUCATION = Educational status of the interviewee (Categorical 1–5)

Enabling Factors
TIME = Walking distance to the nearest health unit (in minutes)
ADDIS = 1 if the village was in Addis Ababa (the capital)
RELATIVE ASSISTANCE = 1 if relatives were potentially supportive

	Providers
Health Posts	Run by community to coordinate primary health care activities. Can deal with normal delivery, minor and first aid like problems; staffed by a community health agent and/or a trained traditional birth attendant
Health stations	Front line units usually staffed by Health Assistants or Nurses. Designed for health promotive and preventive programs, as well as childhood care and locally endemic conditions.
Health centers	Coordinate all health activities at district level. Staffed with physicians (one or two), nurses, sanitarians and health assistants; perform all preventive and curative activities and perform minor operations; may have up to ten beds for maternity and emergency conditions.
Hospitals	Depending on their size are staffed with all types of health personnel. Perform all preventive, curative, rehabilitative and training activities; handle referral cases, perform operations, and admit patients.

Table 2.4 Logistic Regression of Seeking Medical Help, Central Ethiopia, 1995 (Dependent variable No Visit = 0; Any Visit = 1)

Variable	Estimate	Standard Error
CONSTANT	0.744	0.283(-)***
AGE	0.0123 (-)	0.00407(-)***
AMHARA	0.422	0.207(-)**
SEVERITY	0.156	0.0414(-)***
TIME	0.00597 (-)	0.00115(-)***
RELATIVE ASSISTANCE	0.324	0.175(-)*

* p < 0.10 ** p < 0.05 *** p < 0.01; Criteria for assessing model fitness Log-Likelihood –405.214; Chi-squared 72.863 (p < 0.0000)

Table 2.5 Multinomial Logit Estimation of Choice of Different Levels of Providers. Central Ethiopia, 1995 (local health stations are the default group)

Patient Choice	Estimate	Standard Error
Choice 1 Drug vendors and traditional healers		
Constant	1.529 (-)	0.528(-)***
Age	0.0139	0.00641(-)**
Religion	0.194	0.314(-)
Hosan	2.000	0.554(-)***
Severity	0.0887	0.655(-)
Addis	1.021	0.555(-)*
Education	0.303 (-)	0.182(-)*
Relative assistance	0.693	0.257(-)***
Choice 2 Government health centers and hospitals		
Constant	3.599 (-)	0.566(-)***
Age	0.0355	0.00681(-)***
Religion	0.0380 (-)	0.340(-)
Hosan	0.899	0.651(-)
Severity	0.135	0.0671(-)**
Addis	3.736	0.470(-)***
Education	0.237	0.144(-)
Relative assistance	1.145	0.279(-)***
Choice 3 Private and mission facilities		
Constant	3.282 (-)	0.538(-)***
Age	0.0168	0.00628(-)***
Religion	0.860	0.337(-)**
Hosan	1.944	0.580)***
Severity	0.0752	0.0616(-)
Addis	1.364	0.498(-)***
Education	0.330	0.129(-)**
Relative assistance	1.623	0.256(-)***

*p < 0.1 **p < 0.05 ***p < 0.01

Log-Likelihood -678.164 Chi-Squared 302.696 (p = 0.0000)

Predisposing Factors

Among the predisposing factors, age stands out in the present study as affecting people's behavior in seeking medical care as well as in choosing the type of provider where medical help is sought. When older people were sick, they were more likely than the young to stay at home rather than seek outside medical attention. On the other hand, as people got older they were more likely to visit distant and higher level facilities than the local health station. In contrast, children were more likely to be treated and to be taken to local facilities (see Tables 2.4 and 2.5). Dor and Van der Gaag's study (1987) of the Ivory Coast shows that adults obtained the largest share of medical care in the household, which they interpret as reflecting that age group's control of household expenditures. But this interpretation is inconsistent with the greater propensity to seek care for children. It seems more probable (and medically sound) that children are more likely to be treated when they have minor illnesses. Moreover, it is likely that the local health stations in Ethiopia were better prepared to handle childhood conditions. Local units provide mainly primary health care, usually free of charge, and target diseases of children and childbearing women.

Dor and Van der Gaag (1987) also show the income elasticity of the nurse choice to be smaller than the income elasticity of the doctor choice. They suggest that this difference reflects the fact that nurses provide children's services at no charge and that, in the extended family structure, at least one family member is typically available to take children to health units. These explanations are plausible for the present study as well. In addition, diseases that affect children tend to be more frequently recurring than those affecting adults.

Therefore, from an economic point of view, it makes more sense to take children to the local centers as often as they become sick. Children who are sick also tend to deteriorate more rapidly than adults do. Therefore, time would be a more critical factor in seeking care for children than it is for adults. It would be very reasonable to take a sick child to a nearby facility as soon as possible and deal with the condition before it becomes life threatening. On the other hand, the illness threshold for seeking outside medical action might be higher in older people and thus most of the conditions affecting adults would allow the patient relatively more time for choosing an appropriate health unit. Dor and Van der Gaag's findings support our suggestion that old people would be less likely to seek treatment initially than younger people and children.

Household size and gender did not appear to have a significant effect on either the decision to seek medical care or on the types of providers chosen. In the Ivory Coast study, the gender effect (of being a male) was negative and insignificant in the nurse choice, while being positive and significant in the case of doctor visits, indicating that males were more likely to obtain higher quality health care (Dor and Van der Gaag 1987). In Mwabu's study of Kenya, on the other hand, men were less constrained by distance and user fees than women, and women were more likely to consult all the three types of providers other than self treatment compared to men. Two possible explanations given for the latter were that there were more women than men in the rural population, women would be more prone to illness due to obstetrics needs that are peculiar to them; and that women would be more likely to accompany children to health units and thereby seek treatment for themselves at the same time (Mwabu *et al.* 1993). However, most of these factors are associated with severity of illness, for which we controlled in the present study. Our results show clearly that gender *per se* does not affect the choice of provider; the malady and total available financial resources are the most important variables (Table 2.4).

Among the other predisposing factors, religion seemed to have an effect on the choice of health care provider. The statistically significant effect in this regard is that Christians were more likely to use the missionary and the private facilities. One possible reason for this might be that the mission and private facilities were located in the predominantly Christian areas. But it is also possible that Christians are more comfortable than Muslims with using Christian missions. Those belonging to the Amhara ethnic group also seemed more likely to seek outside medical attention than stay at home once they become sick. On the other hand, those belonging to the Hadia and Kembata ethnic groups were more likely to visit the traditional/local vendor and the mission/private facilities than the other ethnic groups. It is likely that the observed effects of religion and ethnic group primarily reflect the effect of the location of health units. Historically, the mission health facilities were relatively more active in the Kembata and Hadia areas where there were fewer government facilities compared to other areas of Shoa.

Furthermore, in most Ethiopian towns people would be more likely to identify with the Amhara ethnic group than would people in the rural areas. Health care facilities also tend to concentrate in the towns. Therefore, it is not surprising that the Amhara were significantly more likely to seek health care from health facilities than the other ethnic groups; this is a surrogate indicator for urban propensity to consume health care. An earlier study in Eastern Ethiopia has also shown the Amhara households as reporting significantly higher utilization of modern medical care in comparison to the Oromo. This variation was proved to be directly linked with the physical proximity of a cosmopolitan clinic to the former ethnic group in the study area (Slikkerveer 1982, 1990).

Education does not appear to have any significant effect on the amount of outside medical help sought, but it does correlate strongly with choice of service provider. Patients at higher level private and mission facilities tend to be more educated than the population in general; those who choose traditional healers tend to be less educated. This finding appears to confirm the hypothesis that the more educated favor modern over traditional medical care.

Enabling Factors: The Cost of Care and Traditional Social Insurance

The findings reveal that extended family systems are a significant enabling factor. Extended families and other traditional risk-sharing systems help shift the individual budget constraint in the demand for health care in poor rural communities. Given the importance of health care financing to both care seekers choice of provider and to current debates on health care reform, this section undertakes a detailed analysis of the issue. Among other enabling factors the study examined, travel time to the nearest modern health facility had a significant and negative impact on the decision to seek medical care. This is logical and in line with the results of most earlier studies of the demand for medical care (Buschkens and Slikkerveer 1982; Dor and Van der Gaag 1987; Slikkerveer 1990). In the multinomial provider choice model, Addis (being in Addis Ababa) was used as a surrogate measure for distance since the other quantity would create an endogeneity problem in this regression. The Addis variable was found to be positive and significant across all the higher level facilities over local health stations. This again makes sense because most of the nation's hospitals are located in Addis Ababa and almost all the health stations in the city were recently upgraded to health centers. Most of the private medical practices also are in Addis Ababa. We have already argued that the presence of ethnic identifiers in the choice equations is also an indicator of the physical proximity of facilities. Thus, properly speaking they should be seen as enabling rather than predisposing factors.

The effect of household income was never statistically significant in any part of the present analysis. More household income appeared to correlate positively with the choice to seek outside medical help rather than to self treat. It also correlated with the choice to seek private or mission alternatives rather than government clinics, government hospitals, or traditional healers. But, again, none of these effects were statistically significant. Why not? On the one hand, it is customary for people to get free hospital care by claiming they are poor once they are able to reach and find lodging close to these medical facilities. However, hospitals tend to be located in areas farther from these patients' homes and there is usually a long waiting period before being attended. Transport and finding a place to stay are limiting costs to patients. It is customary, however, for relatives to assist in covering transport, food and lodging costs while the patient is being seen as an outpatient, and in purchasing drugs from outside pharmacies. Private and mission centers usually charge higher fees regardless of one's economic status. But better off families help here too. In general therefore, household income does not seem to have any consistent and significant effect on health seeking behavior or on the choice of health care providers.

Support from relatives. Potential support by relatives seems to be the real budget constraint. This shows that attempts to determine health care demand in Ethiopia (as elsewhere; see Lavy and Quigley 1993) by assuming household income as the only rate-limiting factor would miss the most important contributing factor: potential assistance by relatives. This latter variable, as an enabling factor, was found to be positive and significant both in the decision to seek outside medical care and in the choice of all levels of higher level providers over local health stations. Potential support was determined by asking the respondents if they had relatives who would provide assistance in the event of medical necessity. Regarding the handling of cost, 14.19 per cent of the respondents (weighted n = 1019) were free patients during the last illness and thus did not have to pay anything for medical expenses (Table 2.6). 70.94 per cent paid the expenses themselves, and in 14.88 per cent of the cases the expenses were paid by relatives. There was no statistically significant difference in reported household income between those who got 'free patient' status and those who did not report getting that privilege during the last illness ($p < 0.1$). When we exclude the free patients from the sample, 17.29 per cent of the respondents received family help in medical costs (weighted n = 874). In addition, in 32.94 per cent of cases the non-medical cost was covered by relatives (n = 252).

Table 2.6 Payment Method during the Last Visit to Health Care Providers, Central Ethiopia, 1995

	Medical Cost		Non-Medical Cost	
	(N)	Percentage	(N)	Percentage
Free patients (government)	145	14.2	----	----
Paid themselves	725	70.9	287	67.0
Assisted by relatives	152	14.9	141	33.0
Total	1 022	100.0	428	100.0

There were 62 reported cases (weighted) of hospital admissions with an average length of stay of 14.27 days. The average reported total cost of hospitalization was 241.09 birr (US$38.27) with a range of 0–2160 birr. Of this group, 39.41 per cent were free patients, 40.72 per cent paid by themselves, and in 19.86 per cent of the cases relatives covered the cost. Again, the reported household income for those who were free patients did not show any statistically significant difference from those who were in the other categories ($p < 0.1$).

Regarding one's place of stay when being treated at a distant facility (Table 2.7), 50.78 per cent of the cases in this category (weighted n = 193) had stayed at the home of their relatives, while 40.41 per cent stayed at a hotel. The estimated average cost of such a stay was 76.48 birr (US$12.14) with a range of 1.5–450 birr.

Extended family systems and Eders: The critical feature of the extended family is the presence of a group of adults, male and female, who are siblings or siblings-in-law, who act as the centers of economic activity, decision making, and care for children and dependents. Members of extended families recognize obligations for mutual aid in job hunting, housing, and

Table 2.7 Where did Patients Stay During Their Visit to a Distant Facility? Central Ethiopia, 1995

Place to Stay	Number
At a hotel	78
At the facility's compound	13
At relatives	98
Other places (unspecified)	4
Total	193

the care of children and the ailing (Shimkin *et al.* 1978). Even in the developed world, microeconomic studies using an altruism model have shown that the extended family is the basic economic decision-making unit. According to such studies, altruism can lead a group of individuals to act as if it is maximizing a single preference function subject to the group's joint budget constraint (Joseph *et al.* 1989). Anthropological studies particularly emphasize the central role played by extended families and kinsmen in the management of illness and therapy in Africa (Janzen 1978). Such kinsmen or their advocates constitute what the author calls the 'therapy managing group,' which exercises a brokerage function between the sufferer and the specialist for all types of ailments and treatment procedures. It is the persistence of these groups, Janzen claims, that gives continuity to modern medical treatment in the central Africa. Slikkerveer (1990) has also reported that the Gossa, an extended kinship group among the Oromo of Eastern Ethiopia, plays an important social function by collectively providing the necessary funds for health care when serious illness affects one of its members.

The other principal form of traditional social insurance in Ethiopia is the burial association (which is locally called *Eder* or *Shengo*). These voluntary associations, established for the purpose of mutual aid in matters of burial and other community concerns, are found in most urban and rural areas. Households either pay the associations when a household member dies, or through fixed monthly contributions. Eders have been found to be very effective in mobilizing community members for various sorts of activity, be it cooperative or political, implying they possess both techniques of enforcement and incentives for applying them.

To assess the presence of potential support by relatives, those interviewed were asked to list their relatives living in or out of the area and to describe each relative's socioeconomic status. After making such a list, they were also asked which relatives would potentially assist them in times of health problems. Of the total survey respondents, 92.16 per cent reported participating in an *Eder* (burial association), and the average annual contribution to these associations was 69.47 birr (US$11.03). Most important, however, 20.72 per cent of the *Eders* were reported to give some kind of assistance (financial or otherwise) when a household member gets sick. This assistance includes monetary loans, food, chat, or coffee to the patient, carrying the patient to a health institution, and covering the work of the patient. In one particular case, the *Eder* reportedly paid half of the expenses of members, or their family members, who required hospitalization. Fifty-four per cent of the reported relatives were

Table 2.8 Potentially Supportive Relatives, Central Ethiopia, 1995

	Potential Assistance				
Relative	No	Yes	Percentage	Total	Percentage
Brother	317	400	55.8	717	30.1
Sister	196	221	53.0	417	17.5
Uncle	192	178	48.0	370	15.6
Aunt	126	89	41.4	215	9.0
Cousin	88	88	50.0	176	7.4
Son	35	97	73.5	132	5.6
Father	8	70	89.7	78	3.3
Mother	11	67	85.9	78	3.3
Nephew	45	32	41.6	77	3.2
Daughter	16	13	44.8	29	1.2
Total	1 093	1 283		2 376	100.0

willing and able to assist the respondents if the latter faced problems in financing their health care consumption. In addition, 58 per cent of the respondents had at least one relative on whom they could rely in times of health care financing need. Table 2.8 shows the most frequently reported potentially supportive relatives and their characteristics. The list does not include all the relatives of the respondents since there was a tendency to list only the few that they could think of at the moment. It also does not contain an exhaustive list of the relatives mentioned by the respondents during the interview.

The most frequently reported relatives who assisted in defraying costs were brothers, sisters, uncles, aunts, and cousins (Table 2.8). Mothers, fathers, sons, and daughters were mentioned in the smaller percentage of cases because some respondents might have thought that the question referred also to nuclear family members. The small number of cases in which the latter were listed as extended family members should be cases where heads of the households would have living parents or children who have established their own families. (The typical family in the area is composed of a father, a mother, and children.) Table 2.9 shows that extended families are more likely to be called upon for assistance in cases of higher than average costs. Extended families are also more likely to help if they have higher reported socioeconomic status (Table 2.10). The above findings indicate that the extended family system functions by selectively covering higher cost care and that cosmopolitan and more affluent relatives are more likely to be involved in assisting their kin. This

Table 2.9 The Odds Ratio of Health Care Cost Being Covered by Relatives, Central Ethiopia, 1995

If Cost Was Above	Odds Ratio	95% CI	CHI sq	P-Value
Average (medical)	11.11	(6.48, 19.09)	106.64	0.00000
Average (nonmedical)	2.22	(1.22, 4.03)	7.36	0.00666
Above 75% (hospital)	3.28	(1.28, 8.49)	6.64	0.00994

Table 2.10 The Odds Ratio of Being of Potential Help During Health Problem for Relatives, Central Ethiopia, 1995

If a Relative	Odds Ratio	95% CI	CHI sq.	P-Value
Owns a TV set	10.40	(5.23, 21.30)	72.98	0.0000
Owns a house	1.27	(1.01, 1.59)	4.22	0.0400
Owns a car	3.69	(2.39, 5.72)	42.11	0.0000
Middle or high income	2.70	(2.24, 3.24)	121.45	0.0000
Resides in the area	0.88	(0.74, 1.04)	2.49	0.1142

Table 2.11 Variables Used in Regression, Central Ethiopia, 1995

CHOICE	0, if 'low level:' nearby health posts, stations, drug vendors, or traditional healers 1, if 'high level:' distant government centers and hospitals; all private or mission health facilities
AGE	Age of interviewee
AGE2	Age–15, if age >= 15 years, otherwise 0
AGE3	Age–55, if age >= 55 years, otherwise 0
SEVERITY	Disease severity scored from symptoms
HELP	1, if family support for medical expanses
WORK	1, if interviewee is active salary earner
FARM	1, if interviewee is either a peasant or shepherd
GENDER	1, if male, 0 if female
EDUC	Educational status of interviewee
ADDIS	1, if village is within the capital
EMERG	1, if condition was labeled an emergency
RELAST	1, if relatives were potentially supportive
INCOME	Reported annual income of interviewee
HINC	Reported household income in Birr ($1 = 6.3 Birr)

suggests the presence of enabling factors that favor the establishment of user charges for higher level urban services.

To assess the effect of extended family support on the demand for medical care, a regression of the choice of providers was run on various independent variables, which include the potential support one could get from one's relatives if one were sick. The various health providers visited

Table 2.12 Logistic Regression of Provider Choice, Central Ethiopia, 1995
(Dependent Variable is Choosing Higher Level Institutions)

Variable	Estimate	Standard Error
CONSTANT	-2.392	(0.360)***
AGE	0.189E-01	(0.469E-02)***
SEVERITY	0.571E-01	(0.472E-01)
EDUCATION	0.378	(0.109)***
HOUSEHOLD INCOME	0.319E-04	(0.307E-04)
RELATIVE ASSISTANCE	1.124	(0.194)***

* $p < 0.10$ ** $p < 0.05$ *** $p < 0.01$
Criteria for assessing model fitness, Log likelihood – 332.499
Chi-squared 169.114 ($p = 0.0000$)

by the interviewed when they were last sick were grouped by cost into two major categories which together comprise a dichotomous dependent variable (Table 2.11).

According to the results shown in Table 2.12, potential assistance by relatives as an enabling factor is found to significantly affect the choice of higher level health institutions over the local health stations. The odds ratio of choosing a higher level over a lower level institution when someone has a potentially supporting relative was 3.45 (95 per cent confidence interval 2.10, 4.50).

To test whether the support factor acts as insurance or credit, some of the relevant variables were also regressed on the variable for actually getting family support (Table 2.12). All the coefficients except the intercept were statistically insignificant, a fact that is noteworthy and that favors the insurance argument over the credit hypothesis. If relatives received assistance on the basis of their ability to give return assistance in the future, as implied by the credit argument, we would expect men, those in cash employment, and those of working age to be favored. Table 2.13 shows that there is no evidence to support this claim. Table 2.13 also indicates that those 55 and older get more, not less assistance than those of working age, the opposite of what the credit hypothesis would lead one to expect. The fact that extended family support seems to act more as an insurance than credit is also corroborated by the practice of the Eders, which in some areas provide health insurance. As mentioned above about 21 per cent of the Eders in the surveyed area were found to be giving assistance (financial or otherwise) when an Eder member or a family member got sick.

Table 2.13 Logistic Regression of Receiving Family Support, Central Ethiopia, 1995

Variable	Estimate	Standard Error
INTERCPT	-1.779	(0.758)**
AGE	0.003	(0.011)
MALE	0.498	(0.437)
EMERG	-0.338	(0.607)
ADDIS	-0.414	(0.555)
WORK	0.082	(0.572)
FARM	-0.216	(0.531)
EDUC	0.175	(0.211)
INCOME	-0.00005 .	(0.0001)

* $p < 0.10$ ** $p < 0.05$ *** $p < 0.01$
Criteria for assessing model fitness, -2 LOG L 165.995
Chi square 4.056 with 8 DF ($p = 0.8521$)

Table 2.14 Logistic Regression of Receiving Family Support on Age, Central Ethiopia, 1995

Variable	Estimate	Standard Error
INTERCPT	-1.556	(0.603)***
AGE	0.013	(0.005)**

* $p < 0.10$ ** $p < 0.05$ *** $p < 0.01$
Criteria for Assessing Model Fit -2 LOG L 494.871
Chi square 5.950 with 1 DF ($p = 0.0147$)

Table 2.15 Logistic Regression of Receiving Family Support on Age (with Spline Function), Central Ethiopia, 1995

Variable	Estimate	Standard Error
INTERCPT	-2.740	(0.430)***
AGE < 15	0.111	(0.035)***
AGE 15–54	-0.123	(0.041)***
AGE> 55	0.055	(0.031)*

* $p < 0.10$ ** $p < 0.05$ *** $p < 0.01$
Criteria for Assessing Model Fit
-2 LOG L 485.094 Chi square 15.728 with 3 DF ($p = 0.0013$)

The age variable alone was significant in the regression and the effect increased from infancy to age 15 years (Tables 2.14 and 2.15). The very young, who also were less likely to be taken to higher level institutions, seemed to be getting less assistance. Even though the slope for getting assistance seems to be negative in 15–54 years range (the years when earning power is increasing), the fact that it becomes positive afterwards

Figure 2.2. Graph of Log of Receiving Support on Age (Spline Function)

$$P_i = \frac{1}{1 + e^y}$$

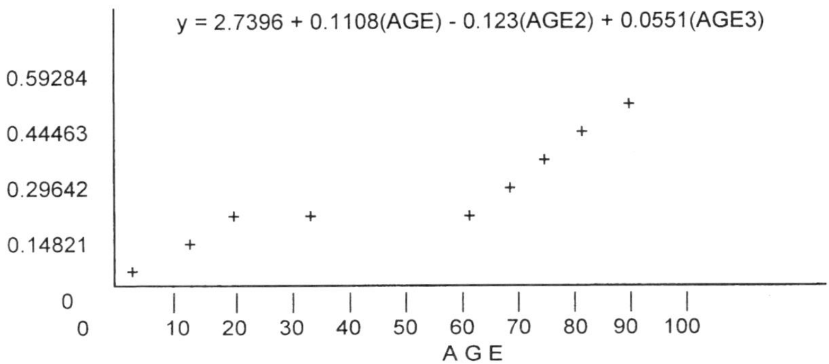

indicates that as one gets older the likelihood of being insured in the system increases. Such a finding is in line with the theory of social exchange, which suggests that the establishment of exchange relations (in this case social insurance) involves making investments that constitute commitments to other parties over time (Blau 1964).

CONCLUSIONS

This study of health care provider choice in Central Ethiopia has sought to identify the factors that influence health care demand. Faced with severe budgetary shortfalls for health care, many developing countries have been looking at alternative ways of generating additional resources. The challenge has been to find ways of increasing resources in such a way as to distribute the burden according to ability of health care users to pay, encourage the provision of appropriate services, and make those services available in accordance with need rather than solely in accordance with willingness to pay (Mills and Lee 1993). In some situations, encouraging private practices has been considered an option to remedy budget constraints in health care, thus also relieving some of the burden on the public sector and increasing interactions between the public and private sectors (Ellis 1993).

This study's findings suggest two important lessons. First, the highest priority for widespread and subsidized services should be given to peripheral units in order to make them more effective in dealing with childhood problems (Vogel 1993; Dor and Van der Gaag 1987; Lavy and Germain 1994). Second, support from extended families, rather than household income, is a crucial factor both in seeking outside medical care and in choosing higher level institutions, and therefore will need to be considered as a means of mobilizing additional resources in well designed cost recovery programs.

The study also shows that severity of illness and proximity to health institutions positively affect the decision to seek outside medical care, as well as the choice of higher level providers. On the other hand, our data did not show gender as a factor in explaining health care seeking behavior. Due to the structure and financing of health services in the study area it was not possible to use health care expenditure or quantity of care consumed as a dependent variable. However, assuming higher level institutions involve higher expenditures on the part of the consumer, the findings of the present study seem to be comparable with other analyses of demand which use standard utility functions.

The local health stations, the study found, seem to be the primary choice for childhood diseases. These local health units are in fact designed to provide Primary Health Care programs. These programs encompass health promotive, preventive and curative activities, with special emphasis on childhood diseases. Given that the social system seemed to be biased toward using higher-level health facilities for adults and the elderly, the local health stations are the appropriate level of focus for programs targeting childhood problems. If this pattern is due to economic bias against children, the local units must be strengthened to accommodate childhood problems, since they are cheaper and relatively easy to access. If instead the epidemiology and nature of childhood diseases are such that they are not amenable to delays and distant travel, the recommendation is nonetheless the same: make the local units more efficient in dealing with these conditions.

The present study shows that extended family support, though understudied, has a significant effect on the health budget constraint. Household income itself is not found to be a factor in affecting health care choice behavior. Potential assistance by relatives as an enabling factor is found to be positive and significant for choices of higher-level health facilities. The study also indicates that extended family support acts as insurance rather than as a credit.

The important implication of the extended family system for health care financing is that it could be a unit to which insurance is sold. Such a shift from household to extended family could help avoid the problem of adverse selection, which is the main anticipated cause of failure in potential insurance markets in developing countries. In addition, Eders may have better information on the level of risk associated with potential clients and more efficient screening techniques, because they are indigenous institutions. Klitgaard (1995) notes that they may also provide a low cost and credible way of pooling transaction costs and risks, taking advantage of economies of scale.

The above findings on health care choice lead to the important conclusion that even in a country with one of the lowest per capita incomes in the world, there is some potential in the community to assist families with their health care problems. This study has attempted to pinpoint other forms of enabling factors and risk sharing opportunities in the community. Theoretically one can assume that the budget constraints for the demand for medical care are multiple, rather than the single budget constraint advanced by standard economic theory. If this is in fact the case, then where the price of a service (or the ability to pay for it) is not rate-limiting due to the multiple budget constraints mentioned above, one can charge fees for services for which people can most easily call upon extended family members to assist in paying. Urban services of a private good nature would be the best candidates for such fees.

In particular, the possibility of levying service charges at the hospital levels should be further investigated. In the context of health care, financing hospitals is viewed with skepticism because they are considered facilities that are not cost effective in the provision of primary health care services. It is also suggested that such institutions should become financially independent from government subsidies and find other ways to finance both their recurrent and capital costs. In this regard, a comparison of fees actually charged at Ethiopian hospitals in 1985 with the computed marginal costs has shown that these fees were generally lower than the marginal cost. Even though this can be justified for maternal and child health services based on positive societal externality, some upward adjustment in fees for the other services is warranted (Bitran, Dicowsky, and Dunlop 1993). If the traditional social insurance systems mentioned in this study can be properly extended to the health care system, there may be a possibility of instituting service charges at urban hospitals, making them more cost effective, and alleviating some of the problems of health financing.

3 The Importance of Proximity, Transport, and Gender as Transaction Costs in the Use of Veterinary Services in Zimbabwe

Pamela S. A. Woods

Subsistence farmers in Zimbabwe rely on livestock for several important functions including draft power, meat and milk production, cash generation from animal sales, and ritual (Cousins *et al.* 1988). Improved animal management including regular deworming, controlled breeding programs, and disease prevention may increase the productivity of both cattle and goats (CARD 1989). The veterinary services could improve animal management by intensifying extension work among farmers living and working on communally owned land, notably by stressing both the importance of health and production management and the increased output expected from investment in these fields.

To this end, in 1987 the Zimbabwe Government Department of Veterinary Services introduced paraprofessionals called Veterinary Livestock Technicians (VLTs).[1] Candidates enter the program with a two-year agricultural certificate and are then given eighteen months of in-service VLT training, including a nine-month intensive theoretical and practical course in livestock production, the recognition, treatment, and prevention of important livestock diseases, and other relevant topics. VLTs operate from 300 Animal Management and Health Centers (AHCs) and their services include aiding animal production— especially of cattle— and extending veterinary expertise to communal area, resettlement, and small-scale farmers. When required, VLTs may request the assistance of Animal Health Inspectors (agriculturale diplomates) or government veterinarians. Despite the introduction of VLTs, several transaction costs have limited the availability of veterinary services for subsistence farmers.

1. From 1987 until 1995, these paraprofessionals were called 'Veterinary Extension Assistants.'

These costs include physical distance to the AHC, uneven VLT access to various modes of transport, social distance (gender, wealth, and educational differences between the VLT and the herder), and a drug sales system that is insensitive to the needs of subsistence farmers.

Livestock owners must often travel a large distance to request the assistance of a VLT for their sick animals. This transaction cost can affect the demand aspect of veterinary services. The supply of veterinary services by the VLTs in turn can be influenced by the VLTs being responsible for relatively large areas. Although some have access to motorcycles, most use bicycles and a few must walk or take public transportation. Transportation costs, in time and money, also affect villagers, who sometimes travel great distances to an AHC only to be told that the VLT is away or has other commitments.

A second transaction cost might be the large 'social distance' between trained VLT personnel, who are mostly male (50 women and 453 men were recorded in the 1995 government veterinary records), and the large portion of their clients who are village women. Together with a paucity of extension services directed toward communal area women, this factor might limit the availability of veterinary services to these women farmers. Policymakers and their advisors have not openly acknowledged the importance of women as livestock producers in communal areas. Yet the fact remains that a woman is the *de facto* head in 41 per cent of households in rural Zimbabwe (Zimbabwe National Report, Census 1992). In addition, while the male head of household might own the cattle, women often manage and care for them (Cousins *et al.* 1988; Amir and Knipscheer 1989). The women's livestock management responsibilities have probably increased because husbands often leave the farm to work in the urban areas and mines.

Our third transaction cost is derived from cost and volume requirements for veterinary drugs. Government VLTs provide their services at no charge, but farmers usually must purchase the drugs required for treatment or prophylaxis. Some commonly used drugs, including anthelmintics and certain antibiotics, are typically available at the AHC or local shopping center, but they are sold only in relatively large, multiple dose volumes that are not suitable for an individual farmer with a small herd. VLTs suggested two possible solutions to this problem: a group of farmers could share the drugs, or an individual could purchase the drug and ask the VLT to direct other potential users to that farmer for private purchase. Cash shortages, absence of credit facilities, and shortages of locally available drugs are additional factors that might prevent the farmer from getting recommended drugs.

This study seeks to establish the major sociodemographic and economic factors affecting the utilization and efficacy of veterinary services—including diagnostic, preventive, and extension services— for subsistence farmers. It will evaluate two transaction costs that might lead to uneven provision of these services. First, social distance between genders is a transaction cost. We hypothesize that this distance exists between male VLTs and female clients and is reduced when the VLT and her client are both women. Second, geographic distance is a transaction cost. We hypothesize that VLTs serve farmers farther from the AHC less well than they serve farmers closer to the AHC. Confirming these hypotheses would have genuine public policy implications because, as we will demonstrate, there is a clear correlation between AHC location and the productivity of livestock herds.

In order to test these hypotheses, we employed a paired sample study designed to investigate the influence of VLT and farmer gender on the utilization and efficacy of the veterinary services. We endeavored to select pairs of areas that are different only in the gender of the VLT serving them. Initially, we obtained details regarding female VLTs from the government provincial veterinary offices. We then matched each selected female VLT with a male VLT located in the same Natural Region (NR) and in an area with similar infrastructure. The matched VLTs had been stationed in their current area for at least two years and were similar in age and number of years out of training college. The proximity of their AHCs to larger commercial centers and to main roads was also similar. Since the study focuses on subsistence farmers, we excluded areas with major cash crops such as tobacco. Also, because our enumerators were Shona speaking and we had translated the questionnaire into Shona, the main language of each selected area is Shona. The Principal Investigator (PI) visited each likely sight before the main survey was conducted and noted the VLT's access to amenities such as transport, water, electricity, telephone, refrigerator, and other equipment. The PI interviewed each VLT before the main survey to assist in the matching process, and each VLT completed a questionnaire about their background, workload, training, and time spent in different activities. After this process, we selected farmers living in the areas served by eight pairs of VLTs for the main survey.

Eight enumerators (four men and four women) were involved in the main survey. Each enumerator performed six interviews for each AHC, two at each distance interval, thus reducing the risk of enumerator bias. A total of 48 interviews were done for each VLT area; a grand total of 768 farmers were interviewed in 16 VLT areas. To examine the influence of farmer gender on transactions with the VLTs, questionnaires were administered to the person actually responsible for the livestock: male head of household (HH), widows or other female HH, or female managers or women who are in charge of the farm but accountable to their husbands who live elsewhere. Care was taken to ensure that at least one farmer in each category had been interviewed per distance zone.

The livestock owner questionnaire contained three sections. Farmers were first asked about household characteristics, livestock owned, whether veterinary assistance had been sought, and the source of that help. They were next asked about management practices such as deworming, vaccination, castration, and nutrition for both cattle and goats. Finally, the enumerator visually assessed the farmer's dwelling place, including building type, and other factors (such as radio, furniture, and vehicles owned) that were later used to calculate a wealth index. Trained enumerators administered the questionnaire at each farmer's homestead, and it took about 45 minutes to ask all the questions if the farmer had both cattle and goats.

The interviews were conducted with farmers situated at three distance zones from the AHC. Zone delineation was based on an earlier study. We hypothesize that these zones represent three levels of transaction cost to reach the AHC. The closest distance, Zone 1, is zero to two kilometers from the AHC, Zone 2 is five to seven kilometers, and Zone 3 is ten to twelve kilometers from the AHC. All distances are direct or 'as the crow flies,' as measured by the Geographical Positioning System (Garmin 95).

The completed questionnaires were checked daily for blanks or inaccuracies; data was entered using EPISTAT and further analyzed with SPSS. The sample was designed to provide a matched evaluation of male and female VLTs, and therefore is not (and is not intended to be) representative of the population of VLTs as a whole. Nevertheless, the sample considers 16 VLTs from four NRs and five provinces. It therefore provides a reasonable sample for evaluating the factors that influence VLT work effectiveness, although it is not suitable for estimation of the exact distribution of effectiveness parameters in the population.

Table 3.1 Zimbabwe: Gender Comparison of Workload-Related Variables

	Female VLT		Male VLT		
	Mean	SEM	Mean	SEM	p value
Total number of cattle in VLT's area	9 777	302.5	8 120	199.2	**
Total number of cattle owners in VLT's area	2 443	76.0	1 542	18.1	**
Total number of Diptanks in VLT's area	7.9	0.1	7.2	0.1	**
Sum of distances: AHC to Diptanks/km	131	3.3	105	1.7	**

SEM = Standard Error of the Mean

PRELIMINARY ANALYSIS: VLT GENDER, WORKLOAD, AND TRANSPORT TYPE

Preliminary analysis indicates two unanticipated correlations that require special attention. First, there is a significant correlation between VLT gender and VLT workload (Table 3.1). Female VLTs have higher mean workload variable values than male VLTs. These workload variables include the total number of cattle, cattle owners, and operating diptanks in each VLT's area, and the sum of the distances from the AHC to each diptank. Variation among AHCs in the number of diptanks increased after the 1992 drought when many cattle died, especially in the drier regions. Consequently, many diptanks were closed. The Provincial Veterinary Officials (PVO) did not mention the possibility of differing VLT workloads; perhaps the PVOs are not aware of the possibly significant relationship between increasing the VLT's workload and decreasing VLT performance. In the regression analyses that follow, workload variance is controlled for by adding a 'VLT workload' variable, which reflects the total number of cattle in each VLT's area.

The second unanticipated correlation is between VLT gender and transport type. The sample includes two female and two male VLTs who have access to motorbikes, three female and six male VLTs on bicycles, and three female VLTs with only foot transport— despite a Government Veterinary Office requirement that all VLTs provide themselves with bicycles. The decision to walk seems to be one of personal choice and appears possibly to be a gender effect rather than due to confounding external influences. Those VLTs without a motorcycle frequently use a bus to get to farms and dips in Zone 3 and often Zone 2 as well. The VLTs must pay these bus fares themselves with no reimbursement. This financial disincentive for VLTs with bicycles or on foot to visit outlying farms is reinforced by time and safety disincentives: the travel time to these farther dips means that VLTs frequently must camp out overnight to be at the dips for the early morning start. These overnight stays are considered uncomfortable and dangerous, especially by the female VLTs.

All VLTs in the sample consider that the lack of a motorbike is an important factor that prevents them from providing services to all the livestock owners. One VLT personally owned his motorbike and the remaining three motorbikes had been provided to the Government as part of an aid package. Government loans to buy motorcycles are available to all VLTs who have been employed longer than two years and have a driver's license. VLTs might be hindered from availing of this loan as a motorbike license must be obtained in Harare, and the cost of lessons, accommodation, and transport to Harare might be prohibitive.

Despite the impression of VLTs who walk or have bicycles, motorcycles bring their own set of difficulties. Those VLTs with motorcycles experience frequent problems when the motorbikes are undergoing repairs and maintenance, which can be for long periods. The subsistence farmers are not charged for the VLT's transport costs, for the Government Veterinary Office (GVO) reimburses the VLTs for petrol used by the motorbike while on official duties. VLTs with motorcycles did not specify that the allocated fuel budget limited their activities, but it is possible that the temporary lack of money to buy fuel prevents VLTs from using their motorbikes as often as duty requires.

RESULTS AND DISCUSSION

Survey results allow us to draw inferences about the effect of transaction costs of distance and gender on each of the VLT's four general tasks: diagnostic services, preventive services, extension activities, and drug sales. We find that female VLTs are as capable and effective as their male counterparts in providing veterinary care. However, farmer's gender bias and distance from the Animal Management and Health Centers both lead to uneven access to and use of VLTs. All correations discussed are significant and positive unless otherwise stated, and (*) indicates significance at 0.05, (**) at 0.01 and (***) at 0.001 or less. For analytic purposes, VLT gender has been coded with male as 1 and female as 0.

Table 3.2 Effect of Dip Location on Frequency of VLT Attendance at Dipping Sessions (as Reported by Cattle Owners)

	Frequency of VLT Attendance at Diptank						
	Weekly		Monthly		Never		Total
Distance from AHC	Farmer Count	%	Farmer Count	%	Farmer Count	%	Farmer Count
Zone 1 (0–2 km)	76	42.9	91	51.4	10	5.6	177
Zone 2 (5–7 km)	54	29.3	100	54.3	30	16.3	184
Zone 3 (10–12 km)	23	13.0	106	59.9	48	27.1	177
Total	153	28.4	297	55.2	88	16.4	538

Diagnostic Services

Diagnostic services include herd inspection for disease surveillance and individual animal diagnostics. VLTs usually conduct livestock inspection during dipping sessions. The purpose of this task, as summarized by the Veterinary Department, is to 'identify diseases, levels of tick infestation, checking brands, and the condition of the cattle' (Department of Veterinary Services 1996). Farmers are legally obliged to take their cattle to the nearest government dip to have acaricide applied to their cattle once a week or once a fortnight, depending on the season of the year. The government recently passed legislation enabling the GVO to charge a small fee per head to start partial cost recovery of this service. However, it has not been strictly enforced and, at this stage, inability to pay this fee does not prevent the farmer from attending the dipping sessions. There is no correlation between the frequency with which farmers dip their cattle and any VLT or farmer characteristics, which we expected because regular dipping of all cattle is a legal obligation and the GVO decides what frequency is suitable for the particular season.

To assess changes in service provision as distance increases, we asked cattle owners how frequently they see the VLT at these regular dipping sessions. The number of farmers who see the VLT at every dipping session, as predicted, decreases with increasing distance from the AHC (Table 3.2). Bicycle possession, however, has a considerable effect on VLT attendance at the dipping sessions, as seen in Table 3.3. Comparing VLTs without or with bicycles for Zone 1 and Zone 2, the percentage of farmers who saw the VLT every week increased from 34 to 50 per cent

Table 3.3 Effect of VLT Transport on Mean Annual Frequency of VLT Attendance at Regular Dipping Sessions, Related to AHC Distance Zone

VLT Transport	VLT diptank attendance (annual)								
	Bicycle			Walking			Motorbike		
	Mean	SEM	Farmer Count	Mean	SEM	Farmer Count	Mean	SEM	Farmer Count
Zone 1 (0–2 km)	16.9	.81	143	15.7	1.38	49	13.8	1.24	63
Zone 2 (5–7)	14.8	.80	146	11.2	1.29	50	9.9	1.31	64
Zone 3 (10-12)	10.4	.66	142	9.5	1.54	48	7.7	1.04	64

and from 19 to 37 per cent respectively. Service in Zone 3 also improves with bicycle availability, but farmers saw the VLT less frequently than in the closer zones regardless of transport type. Still, the percentage of farmers who report seeing the VLT every month increased from 47 per cent to 70 per cent when comparing VLTs without and with bicycles. The 'never seen' category in Zone 3 decreases from 40 per cent to 17 per cent when the VLT has access to a bicycle.

Surprisingly perhaps, the VLTs with motorbikes have the lowest mean attendance rates at the dipping sessions for all three distance zones (Table 3.3). Poor performance in this important aspect of their duties could be due to their motorbikes being non-operational. However, this excuse would not be valid for Zone 1, which is within easy walking distance from the AHC. The VLTs with motorbikes may have been engaged in other aspects of their duties, such as attending to sick cattle; we will evaluate the implications of these service choices in the conclusion. There is a significant correlation between NRs being drier and increased VLT attendance at the diptanks, but this may be due to the significant correlation between NR and VLT workload variables because drier regions have a lower livestock density and fewer dips.

Individual animal diagnostics are the second component in the livestock diagnostics portion of our survey. Farmers report contacting the VLT for a variety of animals including cattle (233 cattle farmers called the VLT), goats (n=54), chickens (n=12), dogs (n=13), donkeys (n=6), pigs (n=3) and sheep (n=2). Cattle and goat owners, who are by far the most important users of the VLT services for animal disease diagnosis and treatment, are discussed below.

Table 3.4 Distribution of Cattle and Goat Ownership by Farmer Category

Manager	Farmer Category						
	Male HH		Widow		Female HH		Total
	Count	%	Count	%	Count	%	
Cattle & Goats	226	59	57	15	101	26	384
Cattle Only	96	52	38	21	50	27	184
Goats Only	97	48	51	25	53	26	201
Total	419	55	146	19	204	27	769

Since we are interested in the effects of gender bias, we ensured that we interviewed a range of farmer households. Male HH comprise 55 per cent of all livestock owners in our survey, 19 per cent of livestock owners are widows or female HH and 26 per cent are female managers whose were not resident on the farm. Since, as noted above, the Zimbabwe census reports that women head 41 per cent of rural households, our sample is reasonably close to the general population. Note that a large minority of animals is owned or managed by women, extending to a slim majority for households with goats only (Table 3.4). Clearly, women form a considerable portion of all livestock managers, so it is important that animal husbandry extension messages be directed toward women.

How frequently do livestock managers use VLT diagnostic services? Approximately the same proportion of cattle and goat owners reported having had a sick animal in the past (45 per cent and 46 per cent respectively), but 30 per cent of owners of sick cattle reported having asked the VLT for assistance, while only 17 per cent of such goat owners had consulted a VLT. Perhaps farmers considered their goats less valuable than cows and not worth the transaction costs entailed in VLT treatment. The low callout rate for sick goats is unlikely to be due to the farmers expecting the VLT to refuse to come for goats, because the percentage of cases that the VLT actually attended to was similar for both cattle and goats (77 per cent and 76 per cent, respectively). The significant partial correlation between farmers who call on the VLT and their distance zone corroborates our hypothesis that the farmer's transaction cost of calling the VLT increases with increasing distance. The vast majority of farmers walk to the AHC to call on the VLT, but some of those living in Zone 3 have to use a bus (Table 3.6).

Table 3.5 Statistical Significance Values from Partial Correlation Analysis on Variables Relating to Demand for or Supply of VLT Services and Area, VLT and Farmer Variables

	Area		VLT Variables			Farmer Variables				Partial	
Demand for VLT Services (Number of Farmers)	Dist. Zone	NR	Sex	Bike	Work Load	MF	HH school	WI	LII	Corr. F sig.	F value
Ever called VLT for any animal (769)	*** (-)		**	.11 (-)		***	0.33	***	*** (-)	***	21.99
Ever called VLT for sick cattle (251)	*** (-)		*			**		0.46	* (-)	***	9.37
Called VLT last 24 mths for sick cattle (565)	*** (-)	.29 (-)	**	.44 (-)	0.11	***		*		***	6.14
Called VLT for last sick cow (235)	*** (-)		0.3		.38 (-)	0.29	0.43	0.45	.09 (-)	***	3.92
Called another about last sick cow (219)	0.19	** (-)	** (-)	*	0.73	.32 (-)			* (-)	***	3.94
Ever called VLT for sick goat (265)	** (-)		0.34		* (-)	.31 (-)	0.07	0.35	0.3	***	3.56
Called VLT last 24 mths for goat (227)	* (-)	.20 (-)			.14 (-)	.31 (-)		0.12	0.13	*	2.22
Called VLT for last sick goat (204)	** (-)				.14 (-)	.08 (-)	0.48	0.34	0.23	**	2.75
Called another about last sick goat (249)		* (-)				.28 (-)			.28 (-)	0.06	2.22
Attend VLT Demonstrations (550)	*** (-)	.21 (-)	0.57	.26 (-)	.23 (-)	***	0.08	-0.74		***	7.23

Supply of VLT Services (Number of Farmers)	Dist. Zone	NR	Sex	Bike	Work Load	MF	HH school	WI	LII	Corr. F sig.	F value
VLT at Dipping Sessions /year (537)	*** (-)	***	0.41	**		0.19	0.21	*	*	***	13.16
VLT examined sick cattle/24 mths (183)	** (-)	0.33		* (-)	.38 (-)	0.42	0.23	0.24		**	2.7
VLT examined last sick cattle (149)	* (-)	*		* (-)		.22 (-)	.23 (-)			**	2.82
VLT attendance sick goat in 24 mths (40)	** (-)	0.32				0.08	.25 (-)		.45 (-)	*	2.68
VLT examined last sick goat (33)	.29 (-)			0.06		** (-)	.26 (-)	.42 (-)		*	3.06

(*) signifies significance at $p = 0.05$, (**) is $p = 0.01$, and (***) is $p < 0.001$, p values in parentheses
Distance Zone from AHC: Direct distance from Animal Health Center to farm, Zone1 = 0–2 km, Zone 2 = 5–7 km, Zone 3 = 10–12 km
VLT Bicycle: Veterinary Extension Agent had a bicycle (= 1) or not (= 0)
VLT Sex: Male VLT =1, Female VLT = 0
VLT Workload: Total Number of Cattle in the area serviced by the VLT, (Range 3606 to 21248)
MF: Member of household had Master Farmer Training, yes = 1 no = 0
HH School: Number of years of schooling for Head of Household
Farmer Wealth Index (WI): Wealth Index calculated from farmer's possessions
NR: Natural Region, based on climatic and geographical features, (2 to 5)
LLI: Livestock Income Importance. Farmer-rated importance of livestock-derived portion of total farm income, (not important = 0, Important = 1, Very Important = 2)
Breeding Index: Percentage of young per adult female animal in farmer's herd

Table 3.6 Farmer Transport to Reach AHC by Distance Zone from AHC

	Farmer Transport Method						
	Bicycle		Walk		Bus		Total
Distance from AHC	Farmer Count	%	Farmer Count	%	Farmer Count	%	Farmer Count
Zone 1	1	1	244	99	2	1	246
Zone 2	1	1	230	92	20	8	251
Zone 3	3	1	164	70	69	29	236
Total	5	1	638	87	88	12	733

Why do some farmers seek VLT assistance, but not others? Those farmers with an increased level of agricultural training from attending master farmer (MF) training or from attendance at VLT demonstrations are more likely to call on the VLT. There are several possible explanations, including increased recognition of disease symptoms, increased confidence in the VLT's abilities after the VLT has taught them, decreased social distance because the farmer has become familiar with the VLT, or the farmer feels that attending demonstrations— which the VLT considers valuable— engenders a reciprocal obligation in the VLT to attend sick animals valued by the farmer. In addition, those farmers who are initially more concerned about their livestock and likely to call the VLT are also more likely to have taken further training.

The wealth index level of the farmer is also positively correlated to whether farmers have called on the VLT. This could be due to farmer realization that the VLT frequently recommends a drug purchase to treat the sick animal. Thus, poorer farmers who cannot afford the anticipated treatment may consider that it is not worth the effort of seeking VLT advice. Poorer farmers might also consider that transport costs, including time and money, to call on the VLT are too great.

Because we are interested in exploring gender bias issues, we asked farmers about the VLT they consulted for a sick animal and why they selected a particular VLT. Each VLT is responsible for a particular area, and only two per cent of farmers went to an alternative VLT. When we asked about VLT response rates, we found that VLTs visit 77 per cent of farmers who seek assistance for sick cattle, and 76 per cent of farmers who call on the VLT about sick goats. The VLTs with motorbikes have the best rate of attending to sick cattle after a farmer's request. This improved rate of attendance by motorcycle-equipped VLTs is especially evident in Zone 3 (Table 3.7).

Table 3.7 Effect of VLT Transport Method on VLT Attending a Sick Cattle after Farmer Request, Related to Distance Zone

	VLT Transport Method							
	Bicycle		Walk		Motorcycle		Total	
Distance from AHC	Farmer Count	VLT Visit	Farmer Count	VLT Visit	Farmer Count	VLT Visit	Farmer Count	VLT Visit
Zone 1	40	83%	9	82%	16	94%	65	85%
Zone 2	28	65%	8	89%	8	73%	44	70%
Zone 3	12	57%	9	81%	11	92%	32	73%
Total	80	71%	26	84%	35	87%	141	77%

Once the VLT diagnoses the condition, he or she recommends treatment or management changes. The VLT did not visit the animal in 36 per cent of the cattle cases (30 per cent of goat cases), but often gave advice and sometimes prescribed costly treatments anyway. This practice is of concern since diagnostic accuracy and validity of the suggested treatment could be doubtful when the VLT bases his or her diagnosis exclusively on a limited history from a messenger. The problem is compounded as, frequently, the person who calls on the VLT is young and not fully aware of the animal's case history (leading to diagnostic difficulties), and might not communicate all of the VLT's instructions to the owner (leading to possible therapeutic failure).

We asked the farmers if the action taken by the VLT had been useful for the bovine's condition. Overall, 77 per cent of the farmers report that the VLT's action 'had helped.' When the farmers' satisfaction levels were separated according to the VLT's action, only 46 per cent of the farmers who received management advice were satisfied, compared with 78 per cent of farmers who were given the name of a suitable medicine and 92 per cent of those who got an injection from the VLT for their sick bovine. This higher satisfaction following administration of an injection, compared with medicine recommendation, could be due to increased drug action following the injection; conversely, it might reflect noncompliance with VLT recommendations. Farmers might not purchase medicine for several reasons: the farmer might lack readily available cash, the drug might not be available locally, or the farmer might decide that the animal's value and chances of recovery are not worth the cost.

We asked the farmers if they had consulted anyone else about their sick bovine. Fifty-two per cent report that they have consulted someone else, usually other farmers (56 per cent) or male relatives (37 per cent). Whether or not the farmer had consulted anyone else is not related to how the VLT responded, but there is a significant gender effect: male farmers in the female VLT serviced areas are the most likely to have consulted others (68 per cent), compared with male farmers in male VLT areas (59 per cent). This gender effect does not appear in the case of goat managers.

Thus, when evaluating VLT diagnostic services overall, we find that farmer distance from the AHC affects provision of virtually every type of service. Transport type is also generally important. VLTs with bicycles appear to be more efficient than both walkers and motorcyclists. Gender also affects service provision in two ways. First, three out of the eight selected female VLTs are dependent on their feet or the bus for transport. This hinders their productivity—especially in Zone 3. Second, some farmers seem hesitant to call on female VLTs to assist with their sick cattle. Most of these asked other farmers for assistance, while a very few were willing to incur additional transaction costs in order to speak with a male VLT from an adjoining area. Possible ways to manage this farmer gender bias will be discussed in the conclusion.

Preventive Services

Preventive services supplied by the VLTs include procedures such as deworming, vaccinations, castrations, and dipping with acaricide. The last of these was discussed above in its context as a diagnostic tool. The use of anthelmintics for deworming is recommended, especially in the wetter areas, and these can be purchased from the VLT or from stores in the business center where the AHC is located. The government views mandatory vaccinations as public goods and supplies them at no charge to the farmers. Other vaccinations are not free. Many AHCs have a refrigerator for storage of heat-labile drugs and are important in the distribution of these vaccines. Castration is another component of basic herd management. As in diagnostic services, we seek to evaluate the effects of gender, distance, and transport type on VLT service requests and provision. We find that distance is a major factor in service provision and that gender also has an effect, especially when female VLTs interact with male cattle managers.

Deworming is important because it increases weight gain and improves the condition and productivity of livestock. Overall, 50 per cent of cattle owners deworm their cattle (15 per cent for goats), and 94 per cent pay for this service. Most (76 per cent for cattle owners, 45 per cent for goat owners) learned of the benefits of deworming from the VLT, with no significant differences between farmer gender and VLT mode of transport or gender. Farmers living farther from the AHC, however, are less likely to have heard about these benefits from their VLT (Table 3.8). In all three distance zones, the largest percentages of farmers who heard about deworming benefits from the VLT are those in areas serviced by VLTs with bicycles (Table 3.9). Only 5 per cent of cattle owners (but 36 per cent of goat owners) have never heard of the benefits of deworming.

We were surprised to find that MF-trained goat owners had learned more of the benefits of general management practices, but HH literacy rather than MF training more closely relates with the actual practice of deworming. This might be because drug companies widely advertise the benefits of deworming goats, and a semi-literate farmer can read of this procedure's benefits. Also, there is a significant negative relationship between the decision to deworm goats and the VLT workload variable of total number of cattle in the area. This could be because VLTs have more time to spend on goats when they have a smaller cattle-related workload; or, perhaps goats are more important to the farmers in areas with fewer cattle and thus goats here receive more farmer as well as VLT attention. Evidence from this survey does not support one of our initial hypotheses: it turns out that decreased social distance between female VLTs and women farmers does not improve communication about goat management techniques.

Vaccinations are perhaps the most widely used preventive measures. Seventy-one per cent of all cattle owners have vaccinated their cattle. There is no correlation between farmers vaccinating their cattle and any VLT or farmer variables, perhaps because many areas included in this survey have mandatory vaccinations against certain diseases of national economic importance. Eighty-seven per cent of all farmers learned of the benefits of cattle vaccination from the VLT. This is related negatively with the distance from the AHC and positively with VLT possession of a bicycle (Table 3.10).

Farmers can choose to purchase vaccines against some commonly occurring diseases. Significantly more farmers in the top third of the wealth index category purchase cattle vaccines (46 per cent), compared with 21 per cent of the farmers in the bottom third wealth index category. However, the interesting point is that as many as 21 per cent of these very poor farmers have been persuaded of the benefits of 'investing' in cattle vaccination. VLTs are deeply involved in telling farmers about the benefits of vaccination, but their role is smaller in promoting

Table 3.8 Statistical Significance Values from Partial Correlation Analysis of Variables Related to Livestock Management Techniques, the VLT's Role, and Area, VLT, and Farmer Variables

Management Procedures (Number of Farmers)	Area Variables		VLT Variables			Farmer Variables				Partial	
	Dist. Zone	NR	Sex	Bike	Work Load	MF	HH School	WI	LLI	corr. F sig.	F value
Cattle Dewormed (517)	.15 (-)	*** (-)		.10 (-)	.18 (-)	**	***	**	*	***	9.63
Cattle Vaccinated (567)	.15 (-)		0.2		0.13	0.1	0.38	0.35	.39 (-)	NS (.19)	1.41
Cattle Castrated (568)		* (-)			***	0.4	0.10	***	**	***	16.11
Cattle Feed Supplementation (565)	0.27	** (-)	.20 (-)	0.4	.29 (-)				*** (-)	***	3.95
Goats Dewormed (586)	.37 (-)	*** (-)			*** (-)		**	*	1	***	6.63
Goats Vaccinated (583)	* (-)		.18 (-)		* (-)	0.4		0.29	**	**	2.85
Cattle Breeding Index (534)			0.2				.48 (-)	*		NS (.12)	1.99
Goat Breeding Index (579)			***	**	0.19	**			0	***	6.90

VLT's Role in Procedure (Number of Farmers)	Dist. Zone	NR	Sex	Bike	Work Load	MF	HH School	WI	LLI	corr. F sig.	F value
Cattle deworming benefits learned from VLT (564)	*** (-)	0.1	0.1		0.1		0.13		0	***	4.96
Cattle vaccination benefits learned from VLT (539)	*** (-)	*					0.44		0	***	6.26
Cattle castrated by VLT (326)	*** (-)	0.4	0.1	0.9	*		0.16		0	***	4.58
Cattle castrated by Govt. Vet. Services (326)	*** (-)		***	* (-)	***		0.34	.29 (-)		***	6.41
Goat deworming benefits learned from VLT (540)	** (-)	.75 (-)		.39 (-)		*	*	**	**	***	6.01
Goat vaccination benefits learned from VLT (544)	** (-)					***	0.2	0.06	0	***	6.64

(*) signifies significance at $p = 0.05$, (**) is $p = 0.01$, and (***) is $p < 0.001$, p values in parentheses
Distance Zone from AHC: Direct distance from Animal Health Center to farm, Zone1 = 0–2 km, Zone 3 = 5–7 km, Zone 3 = 10–12 km
VLT Bicycle: Veterinary Extension Agent had a bicycle (= 1) or not (= 0)
VLT Sex: Male VLT =1, Female VLT = 0
VLT Workload: Total Number of Cattle in the area serviced by the VLT, (Range 3606 to 21248)
MF: Member of household had Master Farmer Training, yes = 1 no = 0
HH School: Number of years of schooling for Head of Household
Farmer Wealth Index (WI): Wealth Index calculated from farmer's possessions
NR: Natural Region, based on climatic and geographical features, (2 to 5)
LLI: Livestock Income Importance. Farmer-rated importance of livestock-derived portion of total farm income, (not important = 0, Important = 1, Very Important = 2)
Breeding Index: Percentage of young per adult female animal in farmer's herd.

Table 3.9 Effect of VLT Transport Method on Percentage Cattle Owners Who Learned about Cattle Deworming from the VLT, Related to Distance Zone

	VLT Transport Method							
	Bicycle		Walking		Motor Bike		Total	
	Farmer Count	%	Farmer Count	%	Farmer Count	%	Farmer Count	%
Zone 1	94	87	24	77	40	89	158	86
Zone 2	87	77	28	74	29	69	144	75
Zone 3	72	71	23	64	31	62	126	67
Total	253	79	75	71	100	73	428	76

Table 3.10 Effect of VLT Transport on the Percentage of Cattle Owners Who Learned the Benefits of Cattle Vaccination from the VLT, Related to Distance Zone

	VLT Transport Method							
	Bicycle		Walking		Motor Bike		Total	
	Farmer Count	%	Farmer Count	%	Farmer Count	%	Farmer Count	%
Zone 1	61	97	13	81	28	97	102	94
Zone 2	74	87.	13	87	25	83	112	86
Zone 3	60	85	15	83	24	75	99	82
Total	195	89	41	84	77	85	313	87

those vaccines that are voluntary and costly than the mandatory vaccines that are free (38 per cent and 62 per cent respectively). Farmers learn about the benefits of purchased vaccines mostly from other farmers.

Only five per cent of goat owners vaccinated their goats. Forty-eight per cent of goat owners report that their VLT explained the benefits of goat vaccination, while 43 per cent have never heard of these benefits. Unlike goat deworming, HH literacy is not related to farmers using goat vaccinations. This could be because drug companies do not widely target subsistence farmers for the sale of goat vaccines, so literature on its benefits is not widely available.

Only 11 per cent of all farmers who were informed of the benefits of goat vaccination actually went on to vaccinate their goats. The farmers generally consider goats to be hardy and almost 'disease resistant.' Monicat *et al.* (1994) reports a similar lack of farmer concern about goat health improvement. Monicat's nationwide survey of goat production reports annual losses of between 11 and 23 per cent of all goats. Diseases and undernourishment resulted in two-thirds of the confirmed deaths. It is plausible that a clearer understanding of goat production economics by the farmers through additional extension and education work would lead to greater farmer investment in these animals. Since farmers, even poor farmers, have been convinced of the value of investing in their cattle, we are confident that intensive extension activities on goat management would yield dividends as well.

Castration is an important management procedure especially for adult draft oxen, and 60 per cent of all cattle owners castrate their cattle. The veterinary services (VLT, including the dip attendant and water carrier) perform 56 per cent of all castrations, and VLTs themselves perform 33 per cent. Expert locals (including male relatives) perform 20 per cent of bovine castrations. The percentage of herds with castrated cattle is constant over the distance zones, and it is interesting that local experts 'fill the gap' if the government veterinary services are unable to cover the distances (Figure 3.1). The procedure is taught during the Master Farmer training, and many VLTs lend out their burdizzos to those Master Farmers. In some areas the VLTs reported that some farmers had purchased their own burdizzos and performed cattle castrations. We were not able to establish the extent of this practice, or if these farmers charged for a castration, but this could indicate an opportunity for 'private practice' of sorts.

Gender is an important factor in bovine castration. Female farmers ($p = 0.069$) and especially widows ($p = 0.012$) are less likely to have their cattle castrated, and female VLTs are less likely to perform castrations. Female VLTs themselves expressed no greater aversion to performing this task than male VLTs, but it is possible that they were speaking hypothetically. It may have been that some felt that the Principal Investigator, a woman, would be critical of their reluctance to perform this procedure which is not without physical work and risk of injury, especially when working on adult bulls. It is likely that some of the female VLTs were in fact hesitant to perform the procedure, and that female farmers were less effective than male farmers at pushing the VLT into action.

Expert locals filled the gap especially in Zone 3 of female VLT areas, but there is no reason to expect that female farmers are any more effective at persuading expert locals to perform this service than they are at persuading female VLTs. Our hypothesis, that decreased social distance between female farmers and female VLTs would lead to improved ser-

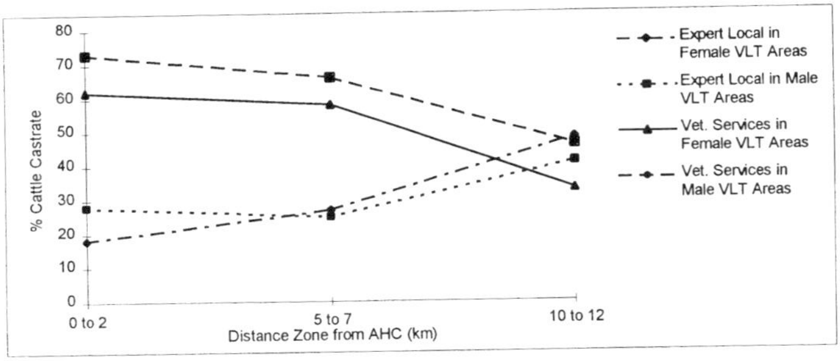

Figure 3.1. Effect of VLT Gender on Percentage of Cattle castrated by Government Veterinary Services and Expert Locals

vice demand and supply, is overwhelmed by another social fact of life: the social status of female HH, and especially widows, is so low that they are unable to influence even female VLTs, who should be relatively sensitive to their needs and position. This gender-based difficulty is not likely to be resolved by the market, so it is incumbent upon policymakers and their advisors to give it their careful consideration.

Extension and Education Services, and Drug Sales

The third set of VLT preventive tasks includes teaching animal production methods in high schools, holding demonstrations about animal husbandry techniques, and holding livestock husbandry training in 'Master Farmer' courses together with crop-focused extension services. During MF training, farmers learn basic information on common livestock diseases and their control, and management techniques such as bovine castration and deworming. Bovine deworming is the only management procedure that correlates with farmers having MF training. Although MF training does not appear to increase the application of cattle management practices, it is significantly related to farmers calling on the VLT to attend to sick cattle. Goat owners, however, are no more likely to call on the VLT for a sick goat after MF training, but they do learn the benefits of various goat management practices from these sessions.

Forty-five per cent of livestock owners are aware that the VLT holds demonstrations on animal husbandry and 36 per cent attend such activities. There is a large drop in attendance with increasing distance from the AHC, from 45 per cent to 32 per cent to 28 per cent in Zones

1, 2, and 3 respectively. Those farmers who have undertaken MF training are also more likely to attend the demonstrations. Farmer attendance at VLT demonstrations on animal husbandry is significantly correlated with their implementation of improved management practices for both cattle and goats. Also, demonstration attendance is significantly correlated both with farmers' requesting assistance from the VLT for sick cattle and goats and with the VLT's actually attending sick animals (Table 3.5).

Drug sales are the final element in a VLT's daily routine, and regulations under the current system generate substantial transaction costs. VLTs may sell anthelmintics, some vaccines, and certain classes of antibiotics. A donor agency subsidizes the sale of common drugs from the AHC and funds from these sales are returned to a revolving fund that subsidizes future sales. The AHC drugs are usually cheaper than similar ones available in the towns. However, VLTs are prohibited from taking drugs with them when they go on farm visits, and the farmers must therefore either purchase the drug before the VLT sees the animal, or they must make an additional trip to the AHC or local market to purchase any recommended drugs. Each of these choices comes with its own set of transaction costs. The farmer may discuss the case with the VLT in the office and, based on a preliminary assessment, purchase in advance the drugs the VLT expects will be appropriate. This choice includes two transaction costs: bearing the risk that the wrong drug was purchased in advance, and bearing the risk that the VLT, knowing that the farmer has a new (and possibly substantial) 'sunk cost,' might not correct an inaccurate preliminary assessment. The VLT could always say that 'we did the best we could' and the farmer often would not have the specialized knowledge needed to refute such a claim.

Alternatively, VLT and farmer could travel to the homestead for a more accurate (and less likely to be biased) assessment of the animal's needs. But the farmer would then incur the huge transaction costs of time and energy required to walk back to town, purchase the appropriate medicine, and finally return to the sick animal. Given the size of this transaction cost and the fact that it must be frustrating for the VLTs to be unresponsive to the farmer's need for convenient drug supplies, we were not surprised to learn that 88 per cent of farmers who had purchased drugs reported that they made their purchase during the initial visit to the AHC. Farmers seldom purchased drugs from other farmers (three per cent) even though VLTs said they usually recommended this practice, and only one per cent of farmers gave nonavailability locally as their reason for failing to purchase the recommended drug. Most reported that either they did not have the money available (48 per cent) or else they did not consider the treatment worth its cost (52 per cent).

CALCULATED BREEDING INDEX

The analysis above emphasized the effect of transaction costs on requests for and provision of veterinary services in Zimbabwe. We now explore the effect of these *services* on the size and productivity of livestock herds through an analysis of herd productivity in relation to distance from the AHC. The degree of success that farmers have achieved in increasing cow fertility and decreasing calf mortality can be observed by creating a breeding index, which compares the percentage of young animals in a farmer's herd with the percentage of adult females. The cattle breeding index shows a significant partial correlation with farmer wealth (Table 3.8). The goat-breeding index shows a significant partial correlation with goat herd size and with both the VLT's gender and transport mode (negative correlation with bicycle-owning VLTs). There is a higher percentage of young goats in herds in the male VLT areas (mean = 0.58) compared with female VLT areas (mean = 0.38) The reasons for this difference are not apparent.

Although the present survey did not observe a significant relationship between the proximity of the AHC and this calculated breeding index, a previous study by CIRAD-EMTV[2] does indicate that VLT services and proximity do positively affect livestock production. The CIRAD-EMVT study classified farming systems in order to evaluate their goat production potential. With the assistance of local government-employed agricultural extension agents, CIRAD-EMVT administered questionnaires to 4161 households in four districts of Masvingo Province. The households were selected by random stratified sampling based on the regions in each district. Subsequently, this author added the distance of each village from the closest AHC and weighted all the data by the number of livestock at the start of the data collection period. We have calculated a productivity index of annual change in herd size after sales and slaughter, but the data does not permit the separation of losses due

---

2. CIRAD-EMVT is Centre de cooperation internationale en recherche agronomique pour le développement, Département d'élevage et de médecine vétérinaire, a French government organization.

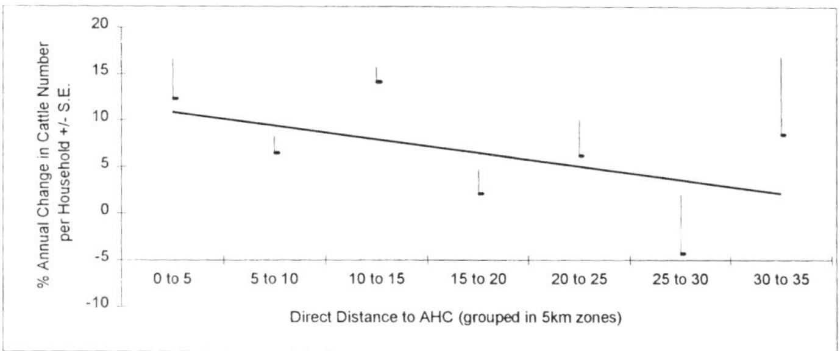

Figure 3.2. Effect of Distance from the AHC on the Percentage Annual Change in Cattle Numbers per Household (Source: CIRAD, 1989)

to death by disease from losses due to disappearance, theft or other causes.

The results clearly indicate the dual value of close proximity to the AHC. First, the relationship between percentage annual change in cattle numbers and increasing distance from the AHC is statistically significant and negative (Figure 3.2). Second, there is a significant, but small, negative relationship between the percentage annual change in goat numbers with increasing distance from the AHC (Figure 3.3). This is unlikely to be due to the typically close proximity of AHCs to the main market as the same study reports that goats are rarely sold at these markets (Gauthier, Pradier and Shumba 1995).

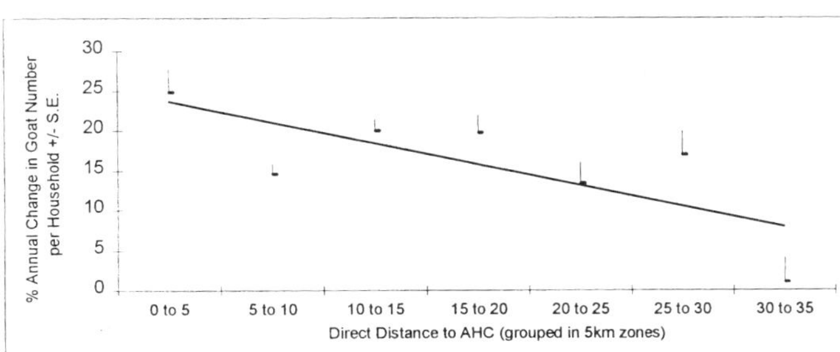

Figure 3.3. Affect of Distance from the AHC on the Percentage Annual Change in Goat Numbers per Household (Source: CIRAD, 1989)

Table 3.11 Percentage Annual Change in Number of Cattle & Goat per Herd Related to Natural Region (NR)

	Per cent Annual Change in Cattle Numbers				Per cent Annual Change in Goat Numbers			
	Mean	Std. Error	Number	p value	Mean	Std. Error	Number	p value
NR 3	1.74	2.24	230		0.1	1.75	1 034	**
NR 4	5.42	0.95	1 446	*	17.2	0.82	5 341	
NR 5	11.79	0.67	3 074	***	19.9	0.47	15 592	**
Total	9.37	0.53	4 750		18.3	0.40	21 967	

Table 3.12 Statistical Significance Values from Partial Correlation Analysis of Productivity Variables for Cattle and Goats against NR and AHC Distance

	Natural Region	Distance to AHC	B Value	Partial Corr. F Sign.	F Value
Per cent Annual Change in Cattle Herd Size	***	*** (-)	-0.47	***	35.51
Per cent Annual Change in Goat Herd Size	***	*** (-)	-0.3	***	52.26

The CIRAD-EMVT study also showed a statistically significant relationship between percentage annual change in cattle numbers and the Natural Region (Table 3.11). This increase in herd growth rates in those NRs with less annual rainfall is probably because the data were collected in the year following a severe drought during which many cattle died, especially in the drier natural regions. Once the rains resumed, grazing pressure would have decreased, especially in the drier zones, allowing greater improvement in livestock nutrition than in those less drought-afflicted areas where more cattle had survived.

After controlling for the effect of natural region, the effect of distance from the AHC on the percentage gain in cattle herd size is more modest but certainly not trivial (Table 3.12). Multiple regression indicates that for every kilometer of distance closer to the AHC, the herd growth rate increases by 0.47 of a percentage point. Thus, by reducing the average distance to an AHC by ten km there would be a 4.7 per cent gain in herd size per household. The average herd size in this data set was eight cattle per household, and the average value for an animal at that time was Z$1500. Thus, the average benefit to a household of decreasing the distance to an AHC by 10km would be equivalent to Z$564 per year, if surplus grazing land is available. However, it would not be easy to provide nearby AHCs for all the subsistence farmers in this province, as the average population density is only 22 persons per square kilometer.

CONCLUSION

The overwhelming importance of distance throughout this survey shows that the transaction costs of time and transport for travel to the AHC consistently reduce both farmers' requests for VLT services and VLT supply of these services. Reducing the travel time to the closest AHC would probably increase both the demand for and supply of veterinary assistance. In turn, livestock size and productivity would probably increase, depending on grazing availability. The supply of VLT services is also related to VLT transport method. None of the modes of transport is consistently better for all the supply variables. Motorbike-equipped VLTs perform better on those variables relating to on-farm attendance for sick cattle. When the VLT has a motorbike, the Government Veterinary Services, including VLTs themselves, also perform more bovine castrations especially in the farther zones. This could indicate improved supervisory abilities in the farther zones when the VLT has easier access with a motorbike. VLTs with bicycles show the best annual attendance rate at regular dipping sessions in all three distance zones. VLTs on foot are the worst performers in all the veterinary services considered in this survey. All of the VLTs who have ignored the Department of Veterinary Services' directive that they provide themselves with a bicycle, and rely instead on their feet, are women; our study does not explore the reasons for this unexpected correlation. We do clearly find, however, that decreased mobility seriously reduces VLT effectiveness in performing both preventive and curative duties.

The trend of VLTs with motorbikes shifting their work from preventive to curative interventions probably reflects farmer demand. Farmers can be expected to put pressure on the VLT to come and help with sick cattle, probably at the expense of performing disease surveillance at dipping sessions. This shift is probably in accordance with the VLTs' own sense of professional satisfaction in their work. It also is consistent with VLT training. One would be naive to think that the pressures applied by the farmers might not also be material (although not necessarily monetary). The finding that there is an unmet demand for assistance with sick cattle and goats reinforces this expectation.

However, this survey found no evidence to suggest that VLTs are accepting any form of reward. Recognizing this shift in service provision by transport type may be a small sign of the direction in which user fees or privatization would shift the system.

Although this survey does not find that female VLTs are more effective in dealing with women farmers because of lower social transaction costs, it does provide evidence that female VLTs generally are as effective as their male counterparts. Despite gender-neutrality in provision of services, there is a definite gender bias in the client population, and farmers do not request the assistance of female VLTs to attend to sick animals as frequently as they do male VLTs. Farmers may not have full confidence in the skills (or in the case of bovine castration, the cultural appropriateness) of female VLTs, and therefore ask less of them. After attending Master Farmer training or the animal husbandry demonstrations held by the VLT, where they presumably are exposed to the VLT's abilities, farmers are more likely to request the assistance of both female and male VLTs. It is likely that, with time and after increased exposure of the farmers to the abilities of the female VLTs, the existing client gender bias will decrease. Female VLTs who are on foot could facilitate this process by to using a bicycle to improve their mobility and provision of services.

4 Incentives in Rural Health Care Delivery: Cameroon I

Kenneth L. Leonard

Patients seek quality health care because it improves not only their experience of visiting a health care provider, but their health as well. We propose that the benefits of health care come not just from the *ability* of a health care provider to produce health but from the provider's *motivation* to do so. We propose that ability and motivation are different because patients cannot perfectly observe or evaluate what is done for their health when they visit a health care provider. Thus rather than assess only the ability of a provider—such as training, experience, or equipment—patients should assess the incentives that practitioners have to direct their ability toward improved health outcomes.

Both practitioners and patients understand and respond to incentives to increase effort. Our examination of the practices of traditional healers, who remain popular among all classes of people in the rural areas, supports this idea.[1] K. Leonard (1998a) shows that traditional healer fee structures provide a direct incentive to exert effort on behalf of their patients. We will argue that the popularity of traditional healers is due in large part to the fact that they have a high incentive to exert effort. Incentives are important to all categories of health practitioners, as our policy simulations near the end of the chapter show clearly.

The exertion of effort in health care is subject to the transaction cost of asymmetric information in which each party does not posses full information about the actions of others. This asymmetry leads to a trans-

1. By traditional healers we mean rural health practitioners whose techniques resemble health practices that existed before the spread of 'western' medicine into the rural areas. We do not imply that all traditional healers use herbal medicines, nor that no non-traditional practitioners use herbal medicines. Our distinction is by method of practice, not by types of medicines used.

action cost because it prevents the formation of a market for medical effort. Patients cannot purchase what they need because they will be unable to evaluate whether or not they have received it. Asymmetric information in particular and transaction costs in general are important concerns of policy makers because they lead to potentially avoidable losses of welfare.

Researchers, like the patients we study, cannot directly observe the motivation of practitioners, but we can examine the incentives to exert medical effort. These incentives derive from the economic relationship practitioners have with their patients and their employers. We develop a theory here regarding patient behavior in the face of the differing incentives for different types of practitioners. This theory—that *patients seek health care as if they were aware of the incentive to exert unobservable effort*—allows us to make hypotheses about the behavior of patients in the search for quality, and can therefore be tested against observed patient behavior.

We interviewed the ill about their choices of providers. To the extent that incentives are important to quality, we can explain why certain providers will be chosen in certain circumstances and others in different circumstances. Thus we use the observed patterns of choices to test and then refine our theory-based predictions. Our results show that patients choose providers as if they were aware of the motivation of various types of practitioners to exert effort on behalf of the patient.

We quantify the diseases from which people suffer according to three types of resources necessary in treatment—medical effort, patient effort, and medical skill—and show that patients choose practitioners in part because of the needs of their diseases. People who suffer from conditions that require a combination of medical effort and patient effort visit traditional healers. Mission facilities (both clinics and hospitals) are visited by people whose conditions require either medical or patient effort alone. People whose conditions require neither significant medical effort nor significant patient effort visit government clinics. Hospitals are visited by people whose conditions respond better to skill and services found in hospitals than to those found in clinics or facilities with other personnel. Thus our results are consistent with patients who evaluate the needs of their conditions and choose the facility that provides the best mix of resources to meet these needs.

Our work has profound policy implications. We not only identify asymmetric information that is present in the market for health care; we go one step further and evaluate the effectiveness of various government policies when there is asymmetric information. Our empirical analysis suggests that the benefit to directly addressing the transaction cost of asymmetric information is huge. The government can significantly increase the quality and benefit derived from its services by exercising its role as regulator of government health care facilities more aggressively. The cost of this additional supervision can be financed by increased drug costs that, our research shows, patients are willing to bear for the superior health services that increased supervision would promote.

This chapter complements a wider African rural health care literature by identifying the health care elements for which people are willing to pay. Many researchers now admit that it has always been culturally acceptable to pay for health care (Van Der Geest 1992), and traditional healing is cited as a health service for which Africans have always paid. We ask how healers are paid and explore the implications of differences between these payment methods and those to modern practitioners. Empirical studies have shown that increasing fees at government-run health facilities leads to a drop in attendance (Waddington and Enyimayew 1989). The usual inference is that patients visit traditional healers because they are less expensive. We find that traditional healers are not less expensive and that healers are popular even among the wealthy. Other studies have established the parameters of the demand for health care in rural Africa (Gertler and Van der Gaag 1990, Dow 1995). We add to the richness of this line of inquiry by exposing the role that characteristics of the illnesses play in the patient's decision.

The next section reports on our interviews with traditional healers. Then, we show how the contractual practice of traditional healers affects the quality of care that is available from those practitioners. Next we present the data collected from randomly chosen households in the South-West Province of Cameroon and use empirical analysis of that data to demonstrate that patient choice of health care is rationally influenced by the incentive structure offered in the traditional healer's contract. Finally, we present the result of policy simulations based on our model. These simulations show the potential for dramatically improved provision in the government health services at manageable cost, even considering Cameroon's difficult economic situation.

TRADITIONAL HEALERS

A random sample of 800 households in South-West Province of Cameroon suggests that patients who visit traditional healers make different payments depending on the success of treatment. Two types of payments were identified in our survey, those made before treatment and those made afterwards. For patients who were cured of their ailments made an average total payment of 6,545 CFA, whereas those not cured paid 3,338 CFA (US$1 = 500 CFA; $p = 0.077$). Payments made after the initial consultation varied even more: 4,990 CFA in successful cases compared to 1,384 CFA in unsuccessful cases ($p = 0.047$). For visits to modern practitioners, payments are higher in unsuccessful cases, though not significantly so. What aspect of traditional instituions explains this result?

We found that this difference in payments was the result of an implicit contract between practitioners and patients that we call a contingent payment scheme. Traditional healers expect to be paid more when the treatment is successful, and less when it is not successful and this expectation is something that the patient agrees to at the beginning of treatment. This is a very different payment scheme than that observed at all other types of health care providers, both in Africa and the rest of the world.

A contingent payment scheme can only work because of the institution of traditional medicine that we claim binds the patient to tell the truth about the result of the treatment. The patient could lie and claim not to be properly cured of her condition. We found, however, that there is a strong belief among patients that if they deceive a traditional healer, some form of magic could be invoked against them that could cause them to become ill again. Many healers told us of patients from far-away villages who were treated and eventually cured, but who did not return to make payment. But the healers added that in all such cases the patient eventually falls sick of something else and then returns to the healer (often years later) begging to be allowed to pay for the previous treatment. The institution of traditional medicine allows for the use of a contingent payment scheme that, as we shall show, gives traditional healers incentives to exercise their skills to the benefit of the patient's health.

INCENTIVES TO PROVIDE EFFORT AND THE BENEFIT OF SKILL

Patients visit a health care provider to benefit from the intervention of health care in the course of an illness. We simplify the intervention of health care into two components: that of effort and that of skill and capacity. Skill and capacity are observable: hospitals have more capacity than clinics, doctors more skill than nurses and clinics more capacity than traditional healers.[2] Effort, on the other hand, cannot be directly observed, but is at least as important as skill and capacity. Being in the best hospital in the world is of no use to a patient if no one will care for her. We advance the idea that it is in the provision of effort that traditional healers are so popular in spite of the intense competition from modern medicine, which is so clearly superior in both skill and capacity.

Effort in health care is a classic example of asymmetric information (Arrow 1963, Arrow 1985, Dranove and White 1987). The patient cannot evaluate what the doctor is doing for her sake. The very reason for going to a doctor is that he has superior knowledge of diseases and treatments. Even after treatment , the patient cannot infer what the doctor did for her sake. It is possible that the doctor exerted all possible effort and the patient remains sick or even dies. It is also possible that the doctor did nothing and the patient recovers naturally. The outcome does teach the patient something about what the doctor probably did, but it does not tell her anything with certainty.

Similarly the practitioner cannot observe the effort exerted by the patient for her own health. Patient effort is a very important component in health, but many health-improving activities cause disutility that the patient would prefer to avoid.

Patients can know the benefit to expect from skill and capacity but they cannot directly know what benefit to expect from effort. Therefore it is important to examine the incentives that each practitioner has to exert the later. When the patient observes that the practitioner has strong incentives to exert effort, she will anticipate greater benefit to her health.

Traditional Healer Incentives to Exert Medical Effort

The contingent payment scheme offered by the traditional healer creates incentives for the practitioner to exert effort. When the payment to the practitioner increases with the success of the treatment and effort increases the probability of success, then the practitioner has a strong incentive to exert effort.

Patient effort is important in a contingent-fee contract. A patient's exertion encourages the practitioner to exert effort as well, because patient effort and medical effort are complementary. For example, if a patient has asthma the doctor can prescribe anti-asthmatics or the patient

2. We group these two ideas together because patients are choosing a combination of skill and capacity when they choose a center. Practitioners (skill) and facilities (capacity) are intimately linked.

can quit smoking. But neither course of action is likely to be as effective as doing both at the same time. Quitting smoking increases the benefit that a visit to a doctor will provide. Since a large portion of the healer's payment is received only if he is successful, his chances of being paid will increase if the patient quits smoking. The healer could refuse to accept the case if the patient does not agree to quit. A fee-for-service provider, if anything, will be paid more if the patient will not quit, while the traditional healer is paid for a cure rather than a shorter or longer succession of treatments. *A practitioner who benefits from the outcome of treatment has an incentive to encourage patient effort as well as to exert medical effort.*

Other Provider Incentives to Exert Medical Effort

This discussion raises two questions. First, why don't other providers (in Africa or the developed world) offer health care on a contingent fee basis? And secondly, given that they do not, must we assume that providers at clinics and hospitals have no economic incentive to provide effort?

A contingent-fee scheme depends on the practitioner's knowing the outcome of the disease. The healer is able to do this because he maintains a cloud of mystery over his practice that encourages people to tell the truth about their condition. Most patients are from his community, where it is easier to track patient's conditions and responses to treatment. But in the end the healer must rely on information from the patient herself about her condition. Traditional medicine is practiced in the context of a very important cultural institution that allows patients and practitioners to interact in a mutually beneficial manner.

If government facilities were to do this they would often be lied to or patients would not return. However modern providers also exist in the context of an institution and it is not true that they have no incentives to provide effort. Rather, the nature of their incentives is different.

Penalties for Sub-standard Performance

For practitioners at clinics and hospitals there is a second client: their employer—the government or the church establishment. Here, effort produces both health for the patient and what we call institutional quality. The employer examines this second output, which correlates with, but is distinct from, the outcome of treatment. Records are kept of the activities that go into producing health, ranging from the mundane (like weighing patients and recording health histories) to the more clinical (like blood tests). The records kept of all such activities are observable to the employer. The information asymmetry between patient and practitioner is based on the patient's ignorance of the practice of medicine, but this asymmetry does not exist between the employer and the practitioner.

Practitioners' employers routinely examine these records. An enormous amount can be learned from these records, or the lack thereof. If a particular record or collection of records is determined to be in violation of standards established for each type of presenting condition, the practitioner can be punished in accordance with the gravity of the deviation. This method of ensuring quality is called a penalty-based scheme. The penalty varies between the two institutions examined in this section. Supervisors at government institutions do not have the power to fire, promote, or demote personnel. The most severe sanction they posses is relocation, albeit a non-trivial sanction. Church-based supervisors, on the other hand, can fire, promote, or demote personnel when justified.

Effort put into institutional quality is also effort put into patient health. Thus the institution that can force a practitioner to produce high institutional quality will simultaneously force the practitioner to exert medical effort, even though the patient's health is rarely observed. Some amount of effort is provided at government and mission clinics and hospitals because if it were not the employers of the practitioners would punish them. However, this system of incentives to provide effort is very different from that of traditional healers. Because the employer does not observe the outcome of the treatment, the decision of whether or not to punish, or by how much, is independent of the effort of the patient. Therefore, *there are no economic incentives for the practitioner to encourage the patient to exert effort for her own health in these types of institutions.*

In a separate empirical investigation, we sat in on consultations by practitioners at government and mission hospitals and clinics in Tanzania.[3] Of 450 consultations observed, the doctor told the patient what medicine was being prescribed or what the diagnosis was in only 71 cases (16 per cent). In only 29 (six per cent) did the doctor inform the patient of any activity that she could undertake to increase the chance of recovery or to avoid a similar illness in the future. Of cases in which a dispensing nurse gave the patient drugs that required that the patient know how or when to take the drug, only 32 per cent checked to see if the patient had any idea how to do so. These observations confirm that patient effort is not a priority in these organizations.

3. The research was sponsored and carried out by Dr. Mpuya under the auspices of the District Medical Office of Iringa, Tanzania, with the support of Centro Universitario Aspiranti Medici Missionari.

Asymmetric Information, Transaction Costs, and Provider Choice

The price at which a standard economic good is supplied will directly affect the quantity demanded. Health care is not such a good. Patients would prefer to purchase the exact quantity of skill and effort—and therefore quality—that they believe is necessary to cure their condition. Since effort is not observable it cannot be directly purchased. There is asymmetric information between patients and providers; providers know how much effort they supply and patients do not. This asymmetric information leads to a loss of utility for both the patient and practitioner. For example, the practitioner might be willing to supply a certain level of quality to the patient in return for a given payment. The patient might in turn be very willing to trade the payment demanded for the quality offered. However, because of the asymmetry of information—the patient cannot be sure she got what she paid for—no trade will take place. This is a significant transaction cost.

Patients cannot choose how much health care to consume but must instead choose a practitioner who will provide a level of health care that is not directly observable. There are, in our sample, five types of practitioners between which the patient can choose: a traditional healer; a government clinic or hospital; or a mission clinic or hospital. When patients choose a particular provider they are choosing a level of skill and capacity as well as an institution and a payment scheme. Though patients cannot observe the effort provided, they can evaluate the incentives that each provider has to provide effort and form an expectation of the effort that would be provided if they were to visit any given practitioner. We show that if incentives come from institutional forms as outlined above, and if patients are aware of the institutions that deliver health care, we can expect predictable patterns of choice between practitioners.

Among the five providers there are three distinct levels of skill and capacity: untrained personnel (traditional healers), trained personnel with limited resources (government clinics and mission clinics), and highly trained personnel with extensive resources (government hospitals and mission hospitals). There are also two types of incentives arising from two different contracts: contingent payment and penalty-based. Only traditional healers use contingent payment schemes. Penalty-based schemes are used by all four modern providers, with government facilities threatening a lower penalty than mission facilities and therefore inducing lower amounts of effort. Thus in all there are three distinct levels of incentives to provide effort.

These combinations of skill and incentives lead people rationally to choose different types of practitioners depending on the disease from which they suffer.[4] When patients suffer from a disease that is very responsive to medical effort, they will seek a practitioner who can provide this effort, even if he is more expensive than other providers are. For such a disease there can be little room for price competition between a provider who supplies effort and one who does not, because the patient would be doing almost nothing for her health by going to the less expensive provider. If the disease requires high levels of skill and capacity, but does not require high levels of effort, the patient will seek out the least expensive hospital. If the patient suffers from a condition that she knows is responsive to a widely available medicine, she does not need to pay for skill and will therefore seek a provider who is inexpensive. In this way the patient first considers what she knows about her condition and then chooses a provider.

This theory leads us to predict the following regarding the practitioners' and patients' rational reactions to the incentives and skills available from these practitioners. Note that we discuss only relative advantage, by which we mean that a patient is likely to visit a provider with a relative advantage when all other factors are the same. Each patient is located at different distances from all of the facilities in question and faces different difficulties in raising cash for travel and fees. These factors can also play a large role in the choice of provider.

When effort is comparable, hospitals do at least as well as clinics and often much better. For example, certain less-accessible drugs or access to an X-ray machine might do a better job of curing or diagnosing a disease than more generally available drugs. For some other diseases such access makes no difference at all. Aspirin for a headache is as effective given at a clinic as at a hospital. Similarly clinics should do at least as well as untrained providers if effort is held constant, because they have use of facilities and drugs to which untrained providers do not have access.[5]

Mission facilities have a comparative advantage in diseases where large amounts of medical effort are required. For modern practitioners fees do not depend on the disease even though the amount of effort provided will vary according to the disease and the protocols for that

4. We refer to the condition from which the patient suffered before they chose a practitioner as a disease although in fact at that time it is only a collection of symptoms.

5. We always assume clinics are at least as skilled as traditional healers because we wish to show that it is not irrationality or an incorrect assessment of skill that leads people to choose healers but rational, correct assessment of incentives.

disease. Thus mission facilities are relatively inexpensive when diseases require large amounts of effort.

Government hospitals have a comparative advantage for diseases that require high levels of skill but less medical effort. Government clinics have the same skills as mission clinics but provide less effort. Government clinics have a comparative advantage when less medical effort is required and the additional benefit to visiting a hospital is low. The additional skill obtained from a visit to a hospital would not be high enough to offset the additional cost of a visit to a government hospital.

Traditional healers have a comparative advantage for diseases in which both patient and medical effort are required. Though traditional healers have an incentive to encourage patient effort it is not generally true that they have a relative advantage in diseases for which patient effort is required. Patients have a natural incentive to exert effort when it, by itself, causes them to get better. Thus if a patient has a condition for which patient effort plays a large role and medical effort does not, they are likely to seek the least expensive practitioner who can provide the necessary skill. Traditional healers do better when both types of effort are required because they have an incentive to take advantage of the complementarity of the efforts. At government and mission facilities both patient and practitioner exert their respective efforts taking into account only the direct effect of their effort; they do not recognize that each actor's efforts are more effective (measured in health outcomes) when the other actor exerts effort as well.

Patients with higher incomes receive more effort from traditional healers because the healer can bargain for a higher payment in the case of success and therefore has more incentive to provide medical effort. We assume that bargaining is based on some measure of the benefit of health to the patient. This measure will vary directly with income— the value of time measured in cash— but it will not vary with wealth.

The contingent payment contract is not better than the fixed payment penalty-based contract. Each contract has circumstances in which it is superior and situations in which it is inferior. These situations will depend in part on the characteristics of the disease.

THE SURVEY DATA

In order to test this theory of choice between practitioners, we collected data on patient behavior in the face of illness in Mbonge subdivision, in

Cameroon's South-West province. Mbonge subdivision is entirely rural. This area was chosen because of the presence of a German aid project that insured a consistent, reasonably priced drug supply in all government health facilities and hospitals. Since drugs are consistently and easily available, we may assert that other factors are driving the patient's choices of health care provider.

Forty villages were randomly chosen and members of 20 randomly selected households from each village were interviewed. Data were collected on all members of the household. There were 681 illness episodes (out of 4,489 individuals) within the previous month represented.[6] Of these, 548 visited one of the five types of providers we are studying. All reported visits are first contacts. Referrals, second opinions, and follow-up visits are not included in this analysis. Normal pregnancy is not considered an illness episode. Other providers included drug peddlers, pharmacists, neighbors, private hospitals and clinics, and parastatal hospitals.

Assuming travel by road, villages sampled were an average of 28 km from a government clinic, 51 km from a government hospital, 87 km from a mission clinic and 212 km from a mission hospital.[7] There was one government hospital and one mission clinic within the sample area. Seventy-nine per cent of all visits were to a provider who was not the closest provider! Of the visits to clinics and hospitals, only 53 per cent were to the closest clinic or hospital. Of visits to hospitals 39 per cent were to hospitals other than the closest hospital. Table 4.1 compares patients by their choice of provider. The average reported family income is equivalent to just over US$ 1,500 per year. Differences in income are very large across different types of providers, with the wealthiest families and individuals visiting mission facilities.

The cost of visiting a clinic or hospital is overwhelmed by the cost of drugs (Table 4.2). Traditional healers are not the least expensive providers, and the reported cost is understated because payments were not completed at the time of the survey. The cost of visiting hospitals is overstated since more severe illnesses require more medication, and people with such illnesses typically visit hospitals rather than clinics.

---

6. We counted illnesses that began earlier, but continued into the recall period.

7. To compensate for vastly different road conditions we use the taxi cost per kilometer to normalize all distances to the distance your taxi fare would take you on the main (paved) road in the sample area.

Table 4.1 Cameroon: Individual Characteristics by Provider Type

ariable	All	Gov't clinic	Mission clinic	Gov't hosp	Mission hosp	Trad healer
Observations	609	158	144	131	58	64
Age	24	18	21	27	41	28
Female (per cent)	49	48	43	50	50	53
Education (years)	2.5	2.3	2.0	2.8	2.3	3.4
Patient income (1,000 CFA/year)	141	65	174	104	448	124
Family income (1,000 CFA/year)	771	605	958	721	1 143	612

1,000 CFA = US$2

Table 4.2 Average Prices by Health Care Providers

Prices	Gov't clinic	Mission clinic	Gov't hosp	Mission hosp	Trad healer
Total cost	4.486	8.153	27.713	29.569	7.812
Drug costs	3.875	7.124	26.530	27.926	(na)
Non-drug costs	0.610	1.028	1.182	1.642	(na)

all prices in 1,000 CFA
1,000 CFA = US$2

We collected information from the respondents on the characteristics of the episode from which they suffered; all of the symptoms they experienced; the self-declared severity of the disease; the number of days sick before seeking care; and the number of those days in which the patient was bedridden. With these characteristics of the disease, plus the age and sex of the individual and information about endemic diseases in the area, we formed an impression for each case using basic medical references (Griffith 1985, Strickland 1984, Werner 1977) and ranked it in the following categories:

Responsiveness to medical effort Is the degree to which outcome depends on the effort of the practitioner. Effort can be time spent investigating or considering diagnoses as well as time spent calculating dosages, treating, or managing the treatment of the patient.

Responsiveness to patient effort Is there a critical role for the patient in her treatment? Examples are keeping follow-up appointments, following dietary or lifestyle proscriptions, or resting adequately. This is especially important for seriously ill children who need to be carefully attended by their parents, since we consider all family effort to be patient effort.

Responsiveness to skill and capacity Though skill and capacity are different concepts, we combine them here because they are correlated—people with higher skill work in institutions with greater resources and capacity. Patients can choose between three levels of skill and capacity. (Skill and capacity is always at least as high at higher level facilities as at lower level facilities.) Informally trained practitioners are health care workers who have never completed a formal medical training program. Their experience can be substantial but it will not be based on a foundation of western medical training. Common drugs are available to them. Formally trained personnel in a clinic have some formal training and work in a facility that has a basic drug supply, beds, IV equipment, and a delivery room, but not much more. Highly trained personnel in a hospital have advanced formal training and practice in a hospital with a much greater supply of drugs and equipment for surgery, long term care, and so on. General practitioners would also be expected to have reasonable access to the services or advice of specialists.

Extremity of Outcomes What is the possibility for a very bad health outcome given the disease from which the patient suffers? This is a measure of risk.

From the three skill and capacity benefit scores we formed two differences—the difference in responsiveness between untrained practitioners and clinics, and the difference between clinics and hospitals. We expect these differences to be more important in the choice of a provider than the scores themselves.

Scores of 0 (low) to 10 (high) were used for all scales. The following are two examples of conditions and their codes. For adults who suffer from a headache and fever for a few days to a week and who did not fear that they might die, the first disease that comes to mind is malaria. For this there is little advantage to skill, since widely available medicines are indicated. Untrained providers score a 4, while providers at clinics or hospitals score 5. The additional benefit to clinic or hospital comes from being able to take a blood test. The responsiveness to medical effort is low, 3, though not zero since it is possible that this condition could indicate something entirely different than malaria. The responsiveness to patient effort is low, 2. The extremity of outcomes is medium, 5.

A second example is a fracture, which responds well to medical effort since it is possible to set a fracture quite poorly. Similarly, it responds to

Table 4.3 Marginal Effects of Independent Variables on the Choice of Provider

Variable	Trad healer		Gov't clinic		Gov't hosp		Mission clinic		Mission hosp	
	coef	z-test	coef	z-test	coef	z-test	coef	z-test	coef	z-test
Disease Characteristics										
resp (medical)	-0.021	-1.28	-0.062	-2.08 *	0.035	1.16	0.014	0.48	0.035	2.27 *
resp (patient)	-0.033	-1.75 **	-0.023	-0.69	0.022	0.66	-0.002	-0.06	0.035	1.74 **
product	0.009	2.33 *	0.005	0.738	-0.008	-1.15	-0.000	-0.06	-0.005	-1.34
skill, hosp	0.005	0.48	0.002	1.21	-0.010	-0.56	-0.012	0.63	-0.006	-0.60
diff in skill (clinic/hosp)	-0.012	-0.66	-0.052	-1.66 **	0.035	1.33	0.019	0.74	0.010	0.89
range of outcomes	-0.041	-2.47 *	-0.011	0.484	0.009	0.43	0.034	1.58	-0.014	-0.92
Individual Characteristics										
family wealth	-0.002	-0.76	-0.001	-0.22	0.007	2.22 *	-0.005	-1.18	0.002	1.44
income	0.006	1.95 **	-0.015	-2.02 *	0.006	0.910	0.001	0.12	0.003	1.02
years of education	0.004	1.09	0.006	0.83	-0.012	-1.78 **	0.006	0.92	-0.004	-1.17
Protestant (yes/no)	0.031	0.98	0.033	0.64	-0.001	-0.02	-0.085	-1.71 **	0.022	0.82

Relative assist	-0.020	-0.70	-0.082	-1.62 **	0.093	1.80 **	-0.003	-0.07	0.011	0.45
polygamous female	-0.094	-0.92	-0.041	-0.27	-0.140	-0.96	0.240	2.10 *	0.031	0.58
child (less than 15)	-0.035	-0.74	0.088	1.0	-0.091	-1.02	0.085	1.00	-0.048	-0.95
elder (over 55)	-0.045	-0.91	0.122	1.18	-0.168	-1.74 **	0.112	1.24	-0.021	-0.64
age (natural logarithm)	0.023	1.18	-0.041	-1.27	-0.051	-1.68 **	0.035	1.10	0.034	1.73 **
adult female (yes/no)	-0.048	-1.26	0.001	0.01	-0.031	-0.43	0.085	1.26	-0.008	-0.25
One-way Taxi Travel Costs										
to gov't clinic	0.105	2.68 *	0.078	1.45	-0.075	-1.31	-0.083	-1.47	-0.024	-0.62
to mission clinic	-0.014	-0.38	0.155	2.240 *	-0.294	-4.20 *	0.068	1.06	0.086	2.27 *
to gov't hospital	0.007	0.24	0.310	5.88 *	-0.036	-0.66	-0.282	-5.00 *	0.001	0.03
to mission hospital	0.008	0.24	-0.058	-0.91	0.154	2.44 *	0.003	0.05	-0.106	-2.84 *

** significant at 90 per cent
* significant at 95 per cent

patient effort (though not to the same degree) because the patient must be careful with the limb for a period of time after it is set. The responsiveness to effort scores are 8 and 6. Untrained providers with experience can offer a medium level of skill and capacity, but hospitals are the only place where an X-ray can be taken. The benefit scores are respectively 5, 6, and 8. The extremity of outcomes is again medium, 5.

Since the analysis is very sensitive to these scores we had two doctors and one nurse (all experienced in rural tropical medicine) validate them by independently scoring all the cases using the definitions above. We found that our scoring correlated better with each of the other three than any of the others cross-correlated. Ours was a median of sorts. Therefore we perform the analysis with our scores, which are justified and documented in K. Leonard (1997). The four sets of scores were not well correlated on the responsiveness to untrained personnel and trained personnel so we have dropped both of these from the analysis. We did find that the difference between the responsivenesses for trained personnel and hospital personnel was well correlated and therefore we kept this difference variable.

EMPIRICAL ANALYSIS

If patients are choosing practitioners based on incentives, then we should find support for our previous predictions. If the contract types we observe exist for other reasons, then patients will choose providers for reasons that are independent of disease characteristics we chose to examine.

We performed a multinomial logit analysis (Greene 1993, p. 666) in which the dependent variable is the choice of provider (five categories) using patient, disease, and provider characteristics as the independent variables. In Table 4.3 we show the marginal effects of the independent variables on the choice of provider that are derived from the four sets of logit coefficients. Thus each element can be read as the percentage change in the probability of visiting a provider given a one per cent change in the variable from its average value.

We use the characteristics of the disease as discussed above as well as the variable *product*, which is a measure of the interaction between the two responsivenesses to effort. Family wealth is an instrumental variable recovered by regressing the reported total family income on the ownership of various durable goods, animals, the condition of the compound and the principal and secondary activities of all members of the house-

Table 4.4 Prediction Success of the Multinomial Logit

	Predicted						
Actual	Trad heal	Gov't clinic	Mis clinic	Gov't hosp	Mis hosp	Total	Per cent correct
Trad heal	19	14	16	10	2	61	31
Gov't clinic	10	101	22	13	8	154	66
Mis clinic	3	29	79	19	10	140	56
Gov't hosp	4	27	35	56	6	128	44
Mis hosp	4	8	15	12	15	54	28
Total	40	179	167	110	41	537	50

hold, using the predicted income rather than actual income. In this way we avoid biases in reported income and the strong correlation, for adult men, between individual reported income and total family income. Personal income is the weekly income reported in 1000's of CFA. We asked heads of households if they thought a close friend or member of the extended family would and could help them if they had a family emergency; a yes answer is recorded in the *friend* or *relative assistance* variable.

The logic of the patient characteristics is as follows. We want to know if patients who visit traditional healers are less educated or older than other patients— variables that could reflect different cultural beliefs. Since both of the nearest mission hospitals are of Protestant denominations we are checking to see if patients visit mission facilities on the basis of religion. It is also possible that children are treated as if their conditions are less serious than adults', and that women are not given the same consideration when it comes to expense that men are. We include the category of women who are in a polygamous marriage since it seems reasonable that if there were any discrimination against women, these women would have even less control over resources than single women or monogamous wives.

Results of Multinomial Logit Analysis

The goodness of fit is represented by the prediction results in Table 4.4. Diagonal elements represent correct predictions. The following is a list of hypotheses and the results.

- Diseases treated by traditional healers are characterized by high levels of responsiveness to both medical and patient effort because the traditional healer recognizes the complementarity of both efforts. This was confirmed. Traditional healers have an increased probability of being chosen when both the responsiveness to medical effort and the responsiveness to patient effort are high, but not otherwise.

- When the responsiveness to medical skill is low, patients will visit the least expensive practitioner who can provide the necessary level of effort. Thus diseases reported at government clinics will have low responsiveness to medical effort and less difference between the responsiveness to skill at hospitals and that of clinics. Both of these hypotheses were confirmed. Government clinics are visited when the responsiveness to medical effort is low.

- Diseases that are highly responsive to either medical effort or patient effort (but not both at the same time) result in visits to mission hospitals and mission clinics. The former is confirmed by the data and the latter is consistent with the data. Visits to mission hospitals are characterized by high responsiveness to either effort, and visits to mission clinics support but do not confirm this same pattern.

- Visits to mission hospitals are characterized by diseases with high additional responsiveness to skill at hospitals over clinics, and visits to mission clinics are characterized by low additional responsiveness to skill. The first was consistent with the data but we found no evidence to support the second. Visits to mission hospitals are characterized by high additional responsiveness to skill at hospitals, but we do not find that visits to mission clinics are characterized by low additional responsiveness to skill, suggesting that patients view mission clinics in this area as hospitals. Almost 30 per cent of all visits to government hospitals (see Table 4.3) were predicted as visits to mission clinics (35 of 128), implying that there is considerable overlap in the function of these two practitioners.[8] The best way to distinguish between visits to these two providers is to look at travel costs, and patient characteristics.

- Diseases characterized by high responsiveness to patient effort and low responsiveness to medical effort result in visits to government hospitals or clinics depending on the requirements of skill and capacity. Note that this hypothesis contrasts with the hypothesis listed third in that medical effort is specifically low. This hypothesis was not confirmed by the data. It appears that such diseases are more commonly treated at mission facilities rather than government facilities. We might have underestimated the incentive that mission facilities have to induce patient effort.

- Visitors to traditional healers have high income levels and they do not necessarily come from wealthy families. This was confirmed.

Of our nine hypotheses, the data confirmed five, was consistent with two, provided no evidence to support two, and rejected none. The two for which we found no evidence concerned patient perception of the role of mission clinics with respect to skill and patient effort. Considering the difficulty of recreating the conditions that the patient faced when she chose a provider, we consider these results to be very exciting. They

8. This could be caused in part by the presence of a very well known, mission-run eye clinic in a town near the sample area.

are particularly strong with respect to the characteristics of diseases reported at traditional healers.

We did not form hypotheses for the other variables but a discussion of some of the findings follows.[9] The range of outcomes is correlated with whether or not the condition represents an emergency. In this case patients with emergencies are visiting mission clinics and government hospitals but not traditional healers, government clinics, or mission hospitals.

Patients of traditional healers are not less educated, older, or poorer than other patients. As individuals they are richer. Visitors to government clinics are poorer, both as individuals and as families, and they are less likely to have a friend or relative who would help them. This implies that government clinics in the sample area are providing a service to the poorer members of the population. It does not appear that there is discrimination within families as to who gets to visit which type of provider, at least when we consider government clinics. Women and children are not significantly more likely to visit government clinics when they are sick. This is a very important implication because the standard caseload at government clinics suggests that women and children are more likely to visit these clinics. By including disease characteristics in the analysis we can conclude— for this sample area— that choices which seem to be driven by access to economic resources are really being driven by the requirements of the disease.

Visitors to mission clinics are from wealthier families, are less educated, are more likely to have a friend or relative who will help them, are younger, and are Protestant. We cannot say for sure why visitors to both mission facility types (clinics and hospitals) are less educated than the rest of the population. A more mathematical model of the demand for health care (Grossman 1975) admits the possibility of an individual-level ability to transform health inputs into health. It is possible that more educated people can transform health care into health better than less educated people, and could therefore consume smaller quantities to the same final effect. More concretely, educated people could know more about what is expected of their practitioners and might be able to induce more effort out of government facilities than the average person.

In order to develop a crude measure of the importance of disease characteristics compared to individual characteristics, we performed a

9. Results of these analyses unrelated to incentives, effort and skill are addressed in Chapter 7 by Ndeso-Atanga.

Figure 4.1 Two Dimensional Projection of Disease Characteristics

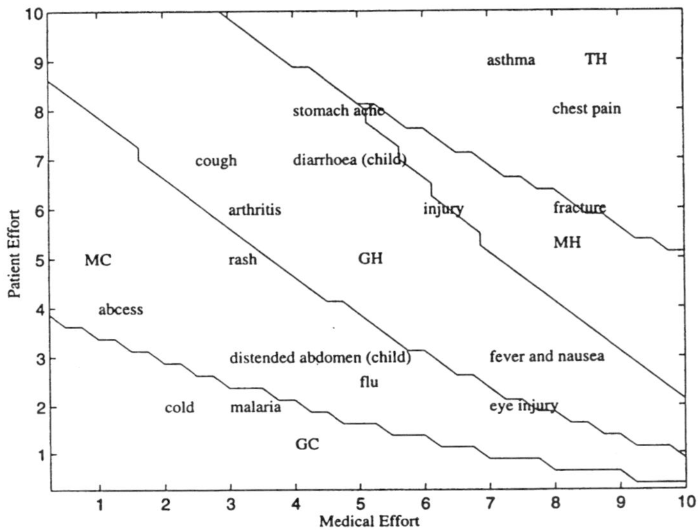

multinomial logit analysis on the same data using only the disease characteristics, and again using only the individual characteristics.[10] The former explained 33 per cent of the data and the latter 34 per cent. We can therefore conclude that both sets of characteristics are equally important in explaining the data. The two together explained 51 per cent of the data.

Structural Estimation

The multinomial logit is good at detecting overall relationships between variables and choices. We can improve on the usefulness of the results if we make some assumptions about the way patients behave and the incentives that practitioners face. In K. Leonard (1998b) we develop a structural model and estimate parameters of the contracts between patients and practitioners, and between practitioners and their employers. The model is useful because we can generate a wide variety of solutions to hypothetical circumstances.

Figure 4.1 is generated by the structural estimation discussed in K. Leonard (1998b). It represents the average individual in our sample who

10. Both included travel costs.

faces the average charges and lives the average distance from all providers. Each point in the two-dimensional projection represents a different disease. Diseases are different according to their responsiveness to medical and patient effort. All diseases in this simulation have the same responsiveness to the skill of hospitals, clinics, and traditional healers. We are examining only the change in responsiveness to effort.

This figure confirms the pattern observed in the multinomial logit. Traditional healers are visited for diseases that have high levels of responsiveness to both medical and patient effort. Mission facilities (both hospitals and clinics) are visited by patients suffering from diseases with high levels of medical and patient effort, though not both at the same time. Government clinics are visited by people suffering from conditions that require low amounts of both patient and medical effort. The results of the two estimations are similar, but this second one allows us to perform policy simulations and make the policy suggestions that follow.

POLICY SIMULATIONS

In this section, we examine a few simple policy measures and their predicted effect on the population of South-West subdivision. The population of the entire sub-division was listed in 1993 as 100,010 people. Our survey reached 4,489 people, or about five per cent of the population. If we weight our interviews according to our sampling method we have interviewed randomly in villages representing 67,527 people, or 67 per cent of the population. To create a sample representative of the subdivision, we weight the survey and then multiply by 1.5. Thus we estimate that 11,817 people were ill in Mbonge subdivision in the month preceding our survey and made first visits to one of the five providers we are studying.

According to our model, all of these ill would have sought some form of health care. We believe they all did so largely on the basis of rational decisions, optimizing expected outcomes. This does not mean, however, that outcomes were efficient. Assuming everyone in our sample behaved rationally there remain two major sources of inefficiency. The first is that travel costs are transaction costs; patients pay these costs, but practitioners do not recuperate them and they purchase no skill, drugs, or effort. For travels to local clinics and hospitals this is a minor consideration, but travel to the more distant mission hospitals is a significant cost. A government policy that increases the probability of visits to local clinics and hospitals over mission hospitals will allow patients to save on travel costs and will increase the net social benefit of health care.[11]

The second source of inefficiency is asymmetric information. At the margin we calculate that 100 CFA worth of effort on the part of a practitioner at government facilities is worth 854 CFA to the patient. In other words it would cost the practitioner 100 CFA to provide effort worth 854 CFA to the patient. Were health care bought and sold on an open market we would expect the marginal benefit and cost to be equal, because the patient could offer the practitioner some amount of money greater than 100 CFA but less that 854 CFA and both would benefit from the transaction. However this cannot happen because the patient has no way of verifying that the practitioner exerted the extra effort because of asymmetric information. If the government could increase the amount of effort supplied the net benefit to society would be quite large.

The structural estimation produces a probability of a visit to any given provider. This is what we refer to as the base run: the predictions given the current data (see Table 4.5). In a sample of 100 people identical to the interviewed individual, the number who are likely to visit any particular provider is equal to the probability of the individual visiting that provider times 100. Thus from the probabilities we can estimate the proportion of the sample who will visit any given provider.

Table 4.5 shows three estimates of the visit patterns for five subgroups of the population. The groups include the entire population, women, infants (under five years of age), the poor (lowest quartile according to household wealth), and the most remote (upper quartile of distance to a modern provider). We chose these groups because they represent potentially targeted populations. Shown in the table are the proportion of visits predicted by the model for the sample, the observed pattern of visits for the sample and the predicted pattern for the subdivision. The sample and subdivision estimates are different because the survey under-sampled residents of big villages, who are more likely to have lower travel costs or have a government clinic or hospital present in the village itself.

The predictions follow the observed data relatively well, though the predictions for infants are disappointing. The model over-predicts visits to traditional healers and mission hospitals and under-predicts visits to

11. Note that policy must encourage the patient to choose willingly a local over distant location; closing the mission hospital would decrease net social benefit.

Table 4.5 Base Run: Pattern of Provider Choice

Population		Healer	Gov't clinic	Gov't hosp	Mission clinic	Mission hosp
Total Visits						
All	sample (observed)	61	154	128	140	54
	sample (predicted)	86	144	117	134	53
	sub-division (predicted)	1 708	3 129	2 559	2 192	1 229
Percentage of Visits						
All	sample (predicted)	16	27	22	25	10
	sample (observed)	11	29	24	26	10
	sub-division (predicted)	14	26	22	27	10
Poorest	sample (predicted)	17	27	22	24	10
	sample (observed)	15	32	24	22	07
	sub-division (predicted)	16	28	20	26	10
Infants	sample (predicted)	16	28	21	25	10
	sample (observed)	05	37	18	37	02
	sub-division (predicted)	16	28	20	26	10
Women	sample (predicted)	15	28	22	25	10
	sample (observed)	13	29	24	24	10
	sub-division (predicted)	14	27	21	27	10
Remote	sample (predicted)	19	25	22	24	10
	sample (observed)	17	32	18	21	11
	sub-division (predicted)	19	25	22	24	10

Table 4.6 Average Net Benefit per Individual

Subgroup	Healer	Gov't clinic	Gov't hosp	Mision clinic	Mission hosp
All	31.31	35.84	45.04	41.22	51.93
Poorest	4.94	5.96	5.32	5.71	3.81
Infants	4.33	7.62	6.61	7.33	4.63
Women	12.83	18.11	18.28	19.63	15.12
Most remote	5.00	3.32	3.69	2.41	5.21

the other providers. Nonetheless the other predictions are close enough to the observed patterns that we can justify the use of the model for policy analysis. [12]

The base run to which we will compare the results of our policy simulations is the predictions for the subdivision. This schema, reported in Table 4.5, reflects the total number of visits expected to any given provider by patients in Mbonge subdivision in a month.[13]

Table 4.6 shows the average utility or net benefit from health care. This measures the increase in health minus any fees paid, drugs purchased, and expenses due to travel. The utility is measured in 1000's of CFA. We are able to report the results in CFA because we know the exact costs that people face and can determine from their willingness to incur these costs, the benefit they expect to receive from health care. The net benefit represents the total utility from health care for an average individual who actually visited the center listed. Thus individuals who visited mission hospitals benefited on average from a net increase in utility of 52,000 CFA.

Table 4.7 shows the average level of effort exerted by each practitioner. The effort is in units of 1000's of CFA in compensation expected for the effort. Traditional healers are compensated by patients for effort; government and mission practitioners are compensated by a reduced probability of being punished. We are able to estimate these rates through making comparisons to the traditional healer, whose compensation we can actually observe. We do not expect these figures to have the same degree of accuracy as the utility figures, yet we believe they are very important to the analysis of policy. The average disease

12. Note that since the model under-predicts visits to government clinics for children and the policies we examine attempt to improve government centers we will be underestimating the benefit to children.

13. Since the survey was taken in the dry season, the results cannot be expected to accurately predict wet-season patterns, when the roads are worse.

Table 4.7 Base Run: Provider Efforts and Expected Compensation

	Healer	Gov't clinic	Gov't hosp	Mission clinic	Mission hosp
Effort for the average visit	5.58	0.83	1.81	1.37	2.36

reported at a government clinic would result in effort on the part of the practitioner for which he would expect about 830 CFA of compensation. The official fee is 100 CFA. At mission clinics practitioners would exert effort expecting about 1,370 CFA of compensation vs. a subsidized charge of about 700 CFA. Though these compensation figures are higher than the fees charged we believe they are relatively accurate. In some areas of Cameroon the practices of health facilities have not been reformed as they were in Mbonge subdivision. Practitioners were not supposed to charge fees at all, but we found that patients were paying substantially higher fees than the ones legally charged in Mbonge subdivision. These illegal fees were much closer to the estimates for compensation that we have obtained above. If a practitioner thinks he can turn away a patient if she does not compensate his effort directly he expects payments much higher than the official government fees. We look at effort in the base run because government policies affect the amount of effort exerted, and this effort must be compensated. For traditional healers effort is compensated by the patient, but for practitioners at government and mission clinics and hospitals the employer must compensate the effort. Thus, although we cannot have high levels of confidence in these figures, they represent an important cost that has not been considered systematically until now. For the policies that we examine, the only relevant change in effort (requiring compensation) is that at government facilities.

Reducing Fees at Government Facilities

The first policy that we examine is that of eliminating the fixed fees at government facilities (clinics and hospitals). Table 4.8 shows the change in the percentage of visits to providers as a result of the policy change. The fees represent a small proportion of the total costs of a visit and therefore the total change in the pattern of visits is very small. Furthermore it does not differ much by subgroup.

Table 4.8 Reduce Fees at Government Facilities by 50 per cent: Visit Pattern

Change in percentage of total visits	Healer	Gov't clinic	Gov't hosp	Mission clinic	Mission hosp
All	-0.14	-0.09	0.70	-0.34	-0.14
Poorest	-0.15	-0.08	0.67	-0.32	-0.12
Infants	-0.14	-0.09	0.69	-0.33	-0.13
Women	-0.14	-0.09	0.69	-0.34	-0.13
Remote	-0.17	-0.09	0.71	-0.30	-0.14

Table 4.9 Halve Drug Prices at Government Facilities: Visit Pattern

Subgroup	Change in percentage of total visits				
	Healer	Gov't clinic	Gov't hosp	Mission clinic	Mission hosp
All	-1.78	0.14	8.13	-4.70	-1.78
Poorest	-2.02	0.24	7.55	-4.36	-1.41
Infants	-1.50	0.25	6.00	-3.47	-1.27
Women	-1.72	0.19	7.58	-4.52	-1.53
Remote	-2.65	0.03	9.13	-4.53	-1.97

Table 4.10 Halve Drug Prices at Government Facilities: Utility

Subgroup	Healer	Gov't clinic	Gov't hosp	Mission clinic	Mission hosp	Total
All						
Total change	-6 509	5 874	69 254	-27 376	-11 745	29 497
Average						2.50
Poorest						
Total change	-981	1 437	9 270	-3 394	-930	5 402
Average						2.24
Infants						
Total change	-514	1 629	8 820	-3 175	-771	5 990
Average						1.74
Women						
Total change	-2 514	3 244	28 486	-12 055	-3 839	13 323
Average						2.24
Most Remote						
Total change	-987	411	6 004	-1 693	-1 329	2 407
Average						2.85

Table 4.11 Halve Drug Prices at Government Facilities: Effort

	Healer	Gov't clinic	Gov't hosp	Mission clinic	Mission hosp	Total
Change in Effort	-954	-13	1 913	-880	-596	
Relevant to gov't		-13	1 913			1 900

Reducing Drug Costs at Government Facilities

The government could also choose to reduce drug costs at its facilities (both clinics and hospitals). This would have the largest effect at hospitals, where the drugs are more expensive to begin with. Reducing the cost by 50 per cent causes an 8 per cent increase in visits to government hospitals. The change in the pattern of visits is similar across groups with the greatest benefit going to the remote (see Table 4.9).

The cost of such a policy is the cost of supplying drugs. If we assume that the price originally charged was equal to the subsidized cost, then the government has to make up the difference in price for every unit sold. The average subsidy at a government clinic would be 2,225 CFA, and we predict 3,207 visits to government clinics with the new policy or a cost of 7,136,000 CFA for clinics. The average subsidy of a visit to a government hospital is 5,981 CFA and we predict 3,560 visits to hospitals for an expected cost of 21,292,000 CFA. The total expected cost to replace drugs is 28,428,000 CFA.

The change in utility per patient is large. The greatest beneficiaries are women and the remote (see Table 4.10). The total benefit to the population is 29,497 CFA. The extra effort exerted by practitioners at government hospitals is quite large because they are seeing so many extra patients. As seen in Table 4.11, the compensation required is on the order of 1,900,000 CFA.

The costs of the policy are conservatively estimated at 30 million CFA and the benefits are estimated at 30 million, or a cost benefit ratio of approximately 1:1. This is not necessarily a bad ratio if the goal is to transfer resources to vulnerable populations, but it must be compared to the cost benefit ratio of other possible polices. Closer examination of this policy alternative reveals that our analysis does not take into account the difficulty of ensuring consistent supply of a subsidized good, especially in the rural areas. If history is a guide, decreasing the cost will simply decrease the supply in clinics and most hospitals.

Quality (Incentive) Based Policies

Reducing costs has a net beneficial effect on the population, and the benefit of health care to the population exceeds the variable cost to the government. The above policies have a large net benefit because they encourage more visits to facilities that are otherwise less expensive in terms of travel and either fixed costs or drug costs. However, they cost

Table 4.12 Increase Penalty at Government Facilities by 40 per cent: Pattern of Visits

Subgroup	Change in percentage of total visits				
	Healer	Gov't clinic	Gov't hosp	Mission clinic	Mission hosp
All	-0.68	2.58	0.91	-1.86	-0.96
Poorest	-0.61	2.08	0.50	-1.37	-0.60
Infants	-0.38	1.50	0.19	-0.94	-0.37
Women	-0.64	2.41	0.61	-1.67	-0.70
Remote	-1.35	2.84	1.51	-1.84	-1.16

Table 4.13 Increase Penalty at Government Facilities by 40 per cent: Utility

Subgroup	Healer	Gov't clinic	Gov't hosp	Mission clinic	Mission hosp	Total
All						
Total change	-3 985	22 288	17 202	-12 811	-11 198	11 496
Average						0.97
Poorest						
Total change	-480	2 845	1 325	-1 240	-653	1 796
Average						0.75
Infants						
Total change	-119	2 295	566	-845	-214	1 681
Average						0.49
Women						
Total change	-1 634	9 911	4 302	-5 319	-2 250	5 009
Average						0.84
Most remote						
Total change	-953	1 662	2 287	-783	-1 247	965
Average						1.14

Table 4.14 Increase Penalty at Government Facilities by 40 per cent: Effort

	Healer	Gov't clinic	Gov't hosp	Mission clinic	Mission hosp	Total
Change in effort	-913	1 465	1 188	-377	-342	1 022
Relevant to gov't		1 465	1 188			1 653

the government money in a time of severe financial constraint. Are there policies that would deliver health benefits without placing such a burden on the exchequer? Indeed there are, and our understanding of incentive patterns enables us to explain them.

Now we consider a policy that changes the manner in which health care is delivered at government facilities, an increase in the penalty at government facilities by 40 per cent. This can be interpreted as an increase by 40 per cent of the probability that a provider will be punished if he is found in violation of accepted standards of medical care. This would bring the expected penalty closer to that of mission centers by 75 per cent.

We assume that the cost of this policy is the increased salary necessary to compensate government employees for the extra effort they are required to exert. It is important to note that in this area of Cameroon the government is already gathering the information required to assess quality. It acts upon this information in a different manner than its mission counterparts. Thus no additional effort is required to gather data about the performance of government practitioners.

Increasing the penalty clearly increases the amount of effort that practitioners at government clinics and hospitals must provide. This increased effort must be compensated. Table 4.14 shows our estimated compensation of 2,653,000 CFA.

Such a policy increases the number of visits to government clinics and hospitals (Table 4.12). The most remote increase their visits to government clinics and hospitals by almost 3 and 1.5 per cent respectively. The utility of all patients increases with the remote and women benefiting the most and infants the least (Table 4.13). The total increase in benefit to the subdivision is 11,496,000 CFA.

The costs of this policy are estimated to be on the order of 2.6 million CFA and the benefits on the order of 11 million CFA, a cost-benefit ratio of approximately 1:4. Though these are rough calculations, the cost-benefit ratio for more effective supervision is far higher than the cost benefit ratio for reducing fees or drug costs. There is an additional effect of increasing quality at government facilities. When quality at a given facility is high, the behavior of patients with respect to fees changes. The following policy simulation shows the effect of increasing quality and increasing fees simultaneously.

Simultaneous Increase in Fees and Penalty

When the government engages in more efficient supervision (increasing the penalty by 40 per cent) and at the same time increases fees (tripling clinic fees and doubling hospital fees) the use of government facilities *increases* (see Table 4.15)! At the same time the utility of the population increases (see Table 4.16). Note that the utility is the net benefit—the benefit of health after taking into account increased fees. We have deliberately chosen these two policies such that the costs of increased effort

Table 4.15 Increase in Penalty and Doubling Fees at Government Facilities: Pattern of Visits

	Change in percentage of total visits				
Subgroup	Healer	Gov't clinic	Gov't hosp	Mission clinic	Mission hosp
All	-0.53	2.48	0.43	-1.55	-0.83
Poorest	-0.45	1.98	0.04	-1.07	-0.49
Infants	-0.21	1.38	-0.27	-0.64	-0.26
Women	-0.49	2.30	0.14	-1.36	-0.58
Remote	-1.17	2.76	1.02	-1.57	-1.04

Table 4.16 50 per cent Increase in Penalty and Doubling Fees at Government Facilities: Utility

Subgroup	Healer	Gov't clinic	Gov't hosp	Mission clinic	Mission hosp	Total
All						
Total change	-3 566	21 371	13 895	-11 452	-10 603	9 645
Average						0.82
Poorest						
Total change	-417	2 658	842	-1 051	-596	1 436
Average						0.60
Infants						
Total change	-84	2 054	51	-655	-181	1 186
Average						0.35
Women						
Total change	-1 422	9 414	2 824	-4 659	-2 053	4 103
Average						0.69
Remote						
Total Change	-891	1 601	2 018	-703	-1 198	827
Average						0.98

on the part of practitioners at government facilities is almost perfectly offset by the increased fees. Thus the government need not increase expenditures. A secondary advantage of pairing these two policies is that it is not necessary that the government collect the increased fees and then disburse them to compensate for increased effort on the part of practitioners. A far better solution would be to allow the increased fees to directly compensate the practitioner by being directly reinvested in the health facilities.

Since the costs of the change are close to zero the cost-benefit ratio of this policy is undetermined, though clearly much higher than the above mentioned policies. This is the singular nature of transaction costs;

if they can be reduced or eliminated all parties to any transaction can gain.

The core message from this model is that people are willing to pay for quality, but that transaction costs are preventing patients from purchasing the desired level of quality from government facilities. When the quality increases at government facilities, patients are more than willing to pay for this increase. Note that this includes even the poorest members of the population.

A student of organization theory might ask whether such increased quality is within the reach of the government. The answer to this question is beyond the scope of this chapter. We do offer, however, the case of mission health facilities as an example of exactly the standard of quality that we propose for government services. Mission facilities deliver quality through increased supervision and they charge high fees that all sections of the population, including the poor, are willing to pay.

CONCLUSIONS

Patients seek quality care but cannot purchase it directly on the market. They must instead choose the practitioner they believe is appropriate from a limited list of possible practitioners. We can learn about the important elements of quality by observing patient behavior in choosing practitioners. Quality clearly is related to the incentives that practitioners have to exert effort on the behalf of the patient. Since mission facilities are more likely to punish practitioners who do not provide high levels of effort, we observe that patients who believe high levels of effort are necessary in order to cure their condition seek mission facilities. Furthermore it appears as if the institution of traditional medicine is designed to insure patients that practitioners have the appropriate incentives to cure their condition.

The structural estimation discussed in this chapter allows us to examine the effect of asymmetric information on different groups within our sample population and to test the effect of different policies on those groups. This chapter should allay the concerns of policy makers that increased fees will disproportionately hurt the poor. It is clear that the current lack of quality has caused great losses to the poor. Concern for the poor could lead to fees differentiated on income, subsidized dispensaries, or fees differentiated on procedures, but it cannot be used to justify inaction on the core question of quality.

Many researchers have suggested that an increase in quality will lead to an increase in attendance; consumers are willing to pay for quality health care. Indeed this is one of the central tenants of the health care reform currently being implemented in Cameroon. Our work confirms the wisdom of this approach while refining the concept of quality. The greatest benefit to increased quality will come in the area that is most plagued by transaction costs: the effort of the practitioner himself. The government has a responsibility to increase the incentives that practitioners have to deliver quality health care by increasing the supervision of medical quality. A government policy that addresses this concern will have a very large benefit to the population and will not require additional outlays from the government.

5 Health Care Quality and the Choice of Care Providers: Cameroon II

Sylvester Ndeso-Atanga

In 1989 the government of Cameroon undertook a series of reforms to improve primary health care delivery in its rural health clinics. A recent review of three such health clinics suggests, however, that patients are bypassing the improved local facilities and are seeking care further afield (Ministry of Health 1994). This study examines the quality considerations that cause patients in rural Cameroon to seek health care outside of their government designated health areas.

Increasing evidence from the literature suggests that quality of care is the most important factor in the choice of health care providers (Larsen 1976; Mwabu 1986; Wong *et al.* 1987; Gilson *et al.* 1994; Tembon 1995). We test this hypothesis by observing the behavior of patients to assess who is seeking quality care and under what conditions. The study examines the importance of quality, along with other factors such as income level, price, and distance, in the choice of health care providers in two types of primary health care delivery—curative and maternity. One of the questions it attempts to answer is whether the same factors determine the choice of providers in these two distinct types of health care.

Previous studies have shown that price, income, and distance are important determinants of the choice of health provider (Heller 1982; Chernichovsky *et al.* 1986). Patients seek inexpensive and physically proximate health providers, and the poor are especially likely to seek less expensive and closer facilities. Empirically, price is often correlated with quality: more expensive facilities tend to have higher quality. Since there are few high quality facilities, on average patients are further away from such providers and have to pay more both for travel and for care. There is therefore a trade-off between quality and cost. An important question the study examines is whether the poor seek quality given its cost.

We suggest that rural poor people often do seek quality care despite the hurdles of price and distance. However, we anticipate that people who fall ill first determine whether or not the quality of treatment is important to the cure of the illness, and then go to the least expensive practitioner who can provide the level of quality necessary (Wouters 1991). Patients may not be perfect judges of medical competence, but they do recognize training and a facility's technical capacity (Hall *et al.* 1988) and they can make subjective judgments about quality. They evaluate the professional qualifications and capabilities of the clinicians based on an image of the provider that reflects the societal definition and subcultural expectations of that role, as well as the conceptions formed by the patient through prior experiences or from hearing about experiences of other people (Mechanic 1968).

To test the hypothesis that despite recent reforms, rural Cameroonians are traveling beyond their local health area because they search for higher quality care, we examine the relationship between the choice of health care provider and cost of care, distance, and patients' income level. We then look at a number of subjective factors that we hypothesize are related to the decision to seek or not to seek quality. These subjective factors—including cost, assessment of their disease, distance, and quality—are the principal reasons the respondents cite for selecting health providers. In the previous chapter, Kenneth Leonard examines objective determinants of patient choice of provider, such as disease characteristics and their relationship to the demand for quality care. In this chapter, we perform similar multinomial logit analyses, but use subjective reasons given by the surveyed population as a predictor of choice. We then proceed to test our ability to predict these subjective reasons from the objective conditions identified by Leonard. We intend that these two studies be read as complements; background material presented in Leonard's chapter is relevant, but not repeated, here.

The study is based on a survey of 800 households in the Mbonge subdivision of South-West Province, Cameroon. Interviews were conducted in households randomly selected from 40 villages that were randomly chosen from the Mbonge subdivision. In each household, information was collected from the head of the household on socioeconomic factors, access to curative and child health services, sickness within the previous four weeks (for curative cases; the survey's 'recall period' for maternity and child health [MCH] care was one year), use of health services, and the reason for the choice of health providers. Of the 4,485 people in the surveyed households, 681 (15 per cent) reported some sickness within the recall period. The choice of health care providers included government health clinics and hospitals, mission health clinics and hospitals, private clinics, and traditional practitioners.

The study has several important findings. First, it confirms my previous observation of low health clinic utilization in Cameroon for curative care, though good use is found for maternal/child care. The most significant findings, however, are related to the importance of the quality of care on patients' choice of provider. We find that when, objectively, high quality care is important to successful treatment of a disease, patients give quality as the primary reason for selecting a health care provider. In addition, the rural poor are willing to pay more for quality care if such care is likely to affect the health outcome. In the case of maternal and child care, quality more subtly dominates the choice of providers, even though there is little use of hospitals or missions for deliveries. We find that many women in rural areas use government prenatal services to discover if they have any complications that would argue against home delivery. We also find that government clinics have an institutional mechanism that enables them to assure quality maternal care at that level.

The majority of patients surveyed sought medical treatment beyond the closest and cheapest government health clinic system. This indicates that distance to quality health care providers is not as important in rural people's choice of health care providers as had been previously believed. In addition, the difference in the choices made by lower and upper income groups was much smaller than expected.

The analysis that follows is divided into two sections. The first section examines the utilization of curative services. The second section analyzes the findings from the maternity component of the study. Finally, the conclusion compares the findings in the choice of providers of curative and maternity care.

QUALITY AND THE CHOICE OF PROVIDERS FOR CURATIVE HEALTH CARE

The survey found that 77.4 per cent of those who reported an illness during the recall period sought care elsewhere than the government health clinic—which is supposed to be the locus of first and primary treatment (see Table 5.1). This finding challenges the results from a study on the effect of user fees on the utilization of health services in the Adamawa province of Cameroon, which showed that improvement of the quality of health services at government rural health clinics mitigated the impact of higher user fees and enhances access to health care in these

Table 5.1 Choice of Health Care Providers by Those Reporting Sickness

Provider Type	Per cent	Frequency
Government health clinic	23.1	154
Mission health clinic	21.3	142
Government hospital	19.7	131
Mission hospital	8.6	57
Private hospital	5.7	38
Traditional healer	9.5	63
Self treatment	12.2	81
Unknown	-----	15
Total	100.0	681

Table 5.2 Choice of More Costly Providers by Income Quartiles

	Annual Family Income in 1,000 CFA				
Provider	Below 240	240–450	450–928	Above 928	Total
	n (%)	n (%)	n (%)	n (%)	n (%)
Inexpensive	66 (40.2)	69 (41.1)	55 (33.3)	42 (25.3)	232 (35)
Expensive	98 (59.8)	99 (58.9)	110 (66.7)	124 (74.7)	431 (65)
Total	164	168	165	166	663

Pearson Chi Square $p < 0.01$

clinics (Litvack *et al.* 1993). To be sure, local health clinics have improved. Yet, the government has not attained its goals of ensuring that most of the symptoms presented by the patients could be treated at local health clinics and essential drugs be readily available. The overwhelming majority of respondents chose to travel to other care providers.

Though income is significantly related to the choice of provider, Tables 5.2 and 5.3 show that low income does not rule out the choice of expensive providers. Government health clinics are inexpensive; all others (including traditional healers) are expensive (see Leonard, *infra* Chapter 4). Sixty per cent of the poorest quartile visited expensive providers (those other than self-treatment and government health clinics), compared to 75 per cent of the wealthiest quartile (65 per cent of the entire sample visited expensive providers). Thus the poor visit expensive providers less than the rich, but still more often than they visit inexpensive providers. Table 5.3 shows that the poor are more likely to self-treat (the cheapest option) than the average patient and the rich are more

Table 5.3 Choice of Provider Type by Income Quartile

Provider	Annual Family Income in 1,000 CFA				
	Below 240 n (%)	240–450 n (%)	450–928 n (%)	Above 928 n (%)	Total n (%)
Government clinic	42 (25.6)	49 (29.2)	33 (20.0)	30 (18.1)	154 (23.2)
Mission clinic	25 (15.2)	34 (20.2)	32 (19.4)	51 (30.7)	142 (21.4)
Government hospital	36 (22.0)	33 (19.6)	30 (18.2)	32 (19.3)	131 (19.8)
Mission hospital	8 (4.9)	9 (2.4)	20 (12.1)	20 (12.0)	57 (8.5)
Private clinic	11 (6.7)	10 (6.0)	8 (4.8)	9 (5.4)	38 (5.7)
Traditional healer	18 (11.0)	13 (7.7)	20 (12.1)	12 (7.2)	63 (9.5)
Self-treatment	24 (14.6)	20 (11.9)	22 (13.3)	12 (7.2)	78 (11.8)
Total	164	168	165	166	663

Pearson chi-square p = 0.01410

likely to go to a mission hospital (the most expensive option). The overall differences, while significant, are quite small. These findings support our hypothesis that even the rural poor look beyond price toward appropriate quality levels when choosing a health care provider. Poor people are willing to pay for quality care. This puts into perspective other findings that suggest public services are more important for the poor and that income matters in the choice of health services (Waddington & Enyimayew 1989; Chernichovsky *et al.* 1986). Though significant, income is not the most important determinant of health care provider choice.

We hypothesized that people were willing to travel long distances to seek health care when high quality is important, despite the fact that transportation in the Mbonge division is precarious. Distance, like income, is significantly related to the choice of a health provider. However, an examination of Table 5.4 shows that of 241 people who had easy access to government health clinics, the closest health care facility (or to a government hospital in cases where the hospital was closer than the nearest clinic), only 26 per cent pursued this option. Of the 100 people who faced a medium level of difficulty of access to government health

Table 5.4 Relationship between Distance and Choice of Provider

	Difficulty of Access to closest Government Practitioner (Clinic or Hospital)			
	Easy	Medium	Difficult	Total
Government health clinic	63 (26.1)	10 (10.0)	81 (27.6)	154 (24.3)
Mission health clinic	58 (24.1)	14 (14.0)	51 (17.4)	123 (19.4)
Government hospital	50 (20.7)	34 (34.0)	41 (14.0)	125 (19.7)
Mission hospital	17 (7.1)	6 (6.0)	34 (11.6)	57 (9.0)
Private clinic	14 (6.6)	16 (16.0)	29 (9.9)	37 (5.8)
Traditional healer	16 (6.6)	16 (16.0)	29 (9.9)	61 (9.6)
Self-treatment	23 (9.5)	12 (12.0)	42 (14.3)	77 (12.1)
Total	241	108	293	634

Pearson chi-square $p < 0.0001$

clinics, only ten per cent went to these clinics. These findings challenge the results of previous studies, which have shown that distance is a major deterrent to health care for the poor (King 1966; Stock 1983; Kloos 1990). For example, proximity to health facilities in Nigeria was rated as the most important factor in determining choice of hospital use (Egunjobi 1983). In our sample, hospitals were the most distant but a significant number of people nonetheless sought care at these facilities. Our results support the conclusion of Akin *et al.*(1986) that, while distance is an important determinant of health provider choice, at least in the Cameroonian dry season, it is not as important as has been believed.

Subjective Preferences for Quality

Respondents were asked to give the most important reasons for selecting the health providers they visited. The proximity of facilities was given as the most important reason for choosing a provider (35.7 per cent, Table 5.5). However, closeness did not deter a majority of people from seeking care from more distant (and expensive) providers, a fact we will examine in more detail below. The second most important factor given for the choice of provider was quality of care (including 'good experience,' 'good reputation,' 'friends or relatives work there,' 'drugs are available,' and 'qualifications of the staff'; a total of 31.8 per cent). Severity of illness (16.9 per cent) and low cost (encompassing 'inexpensiveness' or 'inexpensive drugs'; 7.4 per cent) followed as important factors.

The responses are summarized in Table 5.5. There is a significant association between reasons given and choice of providers. Table 5.6

Table 5.5 Most Important Reason for Choice of Provider
(all visits, not just first)

Reason	Frequency	Percentage
Proximity	222	35.7
Severity of illness	105	16.9
Good reputation	82	13.2
Inexpensive	46	7.4
Good personal experience	40	6.4
Follow-up visit	36	5.8
Qualifications of staff	34	5.5
Availability of drugs	19	3.1
Relative works there	19	3.1
Inexpensive drugs	7	1.1
Referred by first location	6	1.0
Friends work there	3	0.5
Just to see what was there	2	0.3
Total	621	100.0

Table 5.6 Most Important Reasons by Choice of Provider

	Most Important Reason				
Provider	Quality	Inexpensive	Closeness	Severity	Total
Cheap	30 (14.5%)	28 (52.8%)	127 (58.0%)	17 (16.3%)	202
Expensive	177 (85.5%)	25 (47.2%)	92 (42.0%)	87 (83.7%)	381

Pearson chi-square $p \leq 0.0001$

matches the most important reasons given for provider choice with the place they actually sought care (This table reports only those patients who gave one of the four most common reasons for choosing a provider). Those who said their concern was for quality did go to quality providers, and those who said closeness was a factor did go to the least expensive and closest provider, while those who said severity of illness was a factor went to expensive providers where quality care is provided. There is, however, little difference in choice between those who said price was the most important factor and those who did not.

One of the major reasons people gave for choosing a provider was the cost of care. Three elements comprise the cost of health services at different providers: the cost of taxi to the hospital or health clinic, the

Table 5.7 Importance of Price and Type of Health Provider Selected

Type of Provider	Price is Not Important	Price is Important	Total
Cheap	112 (40.6%)	33 (49.3%)	145
Expensive	164 (59.4%)	34 (50.7%)	198
Total	276 (80.5%)	67 (19.5%)	343

Pearson chi-square Statistic $p < 0.2$

cost of consultations, and the cost of drugs. In the Mbonge sub-district, care was most expensive in mission and government hospitals, followed by mission health clinics. Cost of care was least in government health clinics and, of course, in cases of self-treatment. A narrow majority (50.7 per cent) of respondents who said price played a role in their choice of provider nonetheless went to expensive providers (Table 5.7). The difference in choice was relatively small between those who said price was important and those who said price did not matter. Price was not an important factor for 276 people, 59 per cent of whom went to expensive providers. The relationship between the subjective importance of price and choice of provider is therefore weak. This does not mean that price plays no role in the decisions of the people who do not cite it; it may lead them to choose the less expensive of two expensive options. But, contrary to the expectations of many planners, and supporting earlier work by Akin *et al.*(1986), price was not the most important factor even for those who said it mattered.

The nature of the diseases patients present may influence their choice of health care provider. Respondents were asked their own assessment of their condition at the time when the sickness began. From their description of the symptoms three categories of severity of symptoms were derived— potentially fatal, severe, and mild. Indeed, the nature of the complaint was significantly related to the choice of provider. Most potentially fatal complaints were handled by the mission health clinic and government hospital (Table 5.8). An interesting finding is the similarity in the proportions of severe, but not life-threatening, complaints treated by government health clinics, mission health clinics, and government hospitals (21 per cent each). Most of the mild complaints were treated in the government health clinic, the mission health clinic, and by self-treatment. This characterization of diseases is based on each patient's own assessment after treatment. They were asked how severe they had

Table 5.8 Reported Severity of Illness and Choice of Provider

Provider	Severity			
	Fatal	Severe	Mild	Total
Government clinic	31 (16.8%)	63 (22.0%)	59 (31.9%)	153 (23.2%)
Mission clinic	46 (24.9%)	60 (21.0%)	35 (18.9%)	141 (21.5%)
Government hospital	50 (27.0%)	60 (21.0%)	20 (10.8%)	130 (19.8%)
Mission hospital	20 (10.8%)	22 (7.7%)	14 (7.6%)	56 (8.5%)
Private clinic	12 (6.5%)	18 (6.3%)	7 (3.8%)	37 (5.6%)
Traditional healer	18 (9.7%)	32 (11.2%)	12 (6.5%)	62 (9.5%)
Self-treatment	8 (4.3%)	31 (10.8%)	38 (20.5%)	77 (11.7%)
Total	185	286	185	656 (100%)

Pearson chi-square $p \leq 0.0001$

believed their condition was prior to seeking care; their analysis should not be confused with the actual medical conditions of the respondents.

Multivariate Analysis Using Subjective Reasons

The survey results show that quality and severity of illness are significant determinants of the choice of health care providers, and that price and distance matter but are not the most important factors. To what extent can quality and severity predict the choice of health care providers? The analysis has not shown which factors are most significant in the choice of providers when all are considered together. We performed a multinomial logit analysis to test how well the factors mentioned above can predict where rural people will seek care when they fall sick. The analysis sought to establish how well the various factors shown to be related to choice could predict where people went for care. It also tested the extent to which we could predict choice of providers based on the subjective reasons given by respondents.

Table 5.9 shows that the choice of a government health clinic is indeed related to price. An increase in the cost of travel to the government hospital increases the probability of utilizing a government health clinic. Among those who have decided to seek treatment, an increase in the cost of travel to the health clinic also increases the likelihood of going to

Table 5.9 Choice of Provider as Predicted by Subjective Reasons

	Government clinic		Mission clinic		Government hospital		Mission hospital	
Variable	coef	z-test	coef	z-test	coef	z-test	coef	z-test
Constant	-0.139	0.58	0.333	0.36	-0.297	0.36	0.103	0.34
Reasons given								
quality	-0.172	0.00	0.093	0.03	0.075	0.09	0.004	0.97
inexpensive	0.098	0.08	0.104	0.11	-0.200	0.00	-0.002	0.98
close	0.321	0.00	-0.182	0.05	-0.059	0.52	-0.080	0.72
severity	-0.080	0.14	-0.031	0.63	0.097	0.12	0.014	0.78
Demographic								
age	-0.002	0.10	-0.003	0.04	0.005	0.00	0.000	0.62
education	-0.000	0.96	-0.012	0.15	0.012	0.13	0.000	0.61
income	0.002	0.58	0.007	0.09	-0.009	0.09	0.000	0.96
family wealth	-0.009	0.22	0.001	0.89	0.007	0.42	0.001	0.82
Episode severity	-0.013	0.23	-0.015	0.29	0.033	0.016	-0.005	0.57
One-way taxi costs								
Gov't clinic	0.112	0.05	-0.077	0.30	-0.028	0.70	-0.007	0.93
mis clinic	0.184	0.08	-0.253	0.07	0.030	0.81	0.040	0.74
gov't hospital	0.288	0.01	-0.024	0.80	-0.250	0.01	-0.014	0.94
mis hospital	-0.114	0.23	0.083	0.53	0.073	0.53	-0.042	0.56

Statistically significant coefficients have been highlighted.

the government health clinic, rather than elsewhere, because even as the cost to the clinic increases it is still the closest health care facility. As the cost of travel to a mission health clinic falls, the probability of a visit increases. However, people did not often cite closeness as a reason for their choice. This again highlights the distinction between behavior and the reasons given for behavior. Someone who traveled a long distance to their chosen facility might still say they chose it because it was 'close,' meaning that it was the closest facility that offered the required quality of care. An increase in the medically evaluated severity (doctor's diagnosis) of the illness increases the likelihood of going to a government hospital, as does a decrease in the cost of travel, yet hospital patients typically cite quality as a reason and do not mention inexpensiveness. Age also increases the likelihood of going to the government hospital. This is expected because elderly people tend to suffer from chronic diseases that are best handled by the highly qualified staff in government hospitals.

None of the variables included in the analysis could predict mission hospital use. This is not surprising because mission hospitals were very far away from the study area. The fact that patients went there in the numbers observed was also surprising to us. The most singular driving force for these choices was the specialized nature of the care they provide. The hospitals are reputed for good surgery. Demographic variables are not significantly related to the choice of any provider and therefore are not presented in Table 5.9. Both genders use expensive and cheap providers in the same proportions, indicating that there is no gender-based discrimination. This finding is contrary to those of previous studies (Zaidi 1996). Also, ethnic and educational status, which was defined as years of schooling, has no significant relation to choice of provider.

Age, however, is significantly associated with the choice of a government hospital but not with other providers. In all the age groups, the preference was for expensive rather than cheap providers. There is no evidence of discrimination, even when it comes to the care of children. This may be because in the Mbonge sub-district all family members, including children, participate in the cultivation of cocoa plants. A good harvest depends on how well the plants are nurtured, which requires the good health of the entire family because the work is difficult and a collective effort is essential.

Predicting Subjective Preferences

Table 5.9 suggests that most people visited a provider because of quality care. Yet we know that not all providers give the same quality of care. If

Table 5.10 Subjective Reasons for Choice as Predicted by Objective Factors

	Closeness*		Quality**		Inexpensive**		Severity**	
Variable	coef	z-test	coef	z-test	coef	z-test	coef	z-test
Disease characteristics								
responsiveness (medical)	-0.500	0.00	0.011	-0.45	-0.035	0.01	0.036	0.01
responsiveness (patient)	0.006	0.59	-0.009	0.39	0.004	0.72	-0.001	0.90
benefit to clinic skill	-0.010	0.66	-0.045	0.07	0.030	0.21	0.005	0.20
benefit to hospital skill	0.031	0.16	0.046	0.05	-0.003	0.88	-0.030	0.14
Demographic								
age	-0.003	0.00	0.002	0.13	-0.001	0.36	0.001	0.20
sex	-0.004	0.90	0.007	0.86	0.062	0.09	-0.018	0.62
income	-0.000	0.93	0.003	0.31	0.001	0.04	-0.005	0.22
family wealth	-0.013	0.06	0.006	0.23	0.008	0.04	-0.005	0.22
One-way Taxi Costs								
gov't clinic	-0.003	0.94	0.012	0.78	0.046	0.27	-0.050	0.21
mis clinic	-0.051	0.19	0.063	0.10	0.063	0.10	0.009	0.81
gov't hospital	0.048	0.22	0.026	0.52	-0.009	0.83	-0.072	0.07
mis hospital	0.025	0.45	0.033	0.34	0.075	0.03	0.031	0.33

* cited as the most important reason

** cited as at least one reason

Statistically significant coefficients have been highlighted we use objective measures of the characteristics of the disease, such as responsiveness to medical effort and personnel skill, to predict the actual reasons why people choose their providers, we will then know why people give the subjective reasons that predict their choices. To show this, a second multinomial logit analysis was done and the results are reported in Table 5.10. This analysis used respondents' reasons for selecting a provider as dependent variables; responsiveness to medical effort, severity of the disease responsiveness to medical skill, responsiveness to patient effort, age, family, and price were the independent variables. The disease characteristics used in this battery of tests are objective and based on classifications of the symptoms by a team of medical experts (see Leonard, previous chapter). The types of reasons respondents gave for selecting providers were classified as *closeness*, *quality*, *severity* (as described by respondents), and *inexpensiveness*.

The results show that when *closeness* is given as the most important reason for choice of provider, the patient is likely to be suffering from a disease that is not responsive to medical effort (for example, malaria or a common cold), to be younger, and to be from a poorer family. *Quality* is more likely to be cited as an important reason when patients are suffering from diseases that are highly responsive to the medical skills available at a hospital, but not at a clinic. Patients who suffer from diseases that are not highly responsive to medical effort are more likely to cite *inexpensiveness* as a reason for their choice. (This is the same effect as closeness and the opposite effect from quality.)

Patients therefore cite *closeness* and *inexpensiveness* when they are not likely to be concerned about *quality*. Females and those from wealthier families are more likely to visit a provider because they say it is inexpensive. Interestingly, it is the wealthy and not the poor who are more likely to cite inexpensiveness as a reason for choice. Those who are closer to mission hospitals are more likely to cite inexpensiveness as a reason for their choice. Patients cite the *severity* of the disease as a reason for their choice when they are suffering from diseases that require higher levels of medical skill and when they are closer to government hospitals.

The reasons people give for visiting a provider depend in large part on the disease from which the patient suffers. Thus the subjective and objective analyses presented in this section and the preceding chapter by Leonard are similar. The objective analysis is based on a medical evaluation of the symptoms given by the patient, and the subjective analysis relies on the patients' evaluation of that same information. Since the information available to the patient is much richer than that available to the practitioner, we find that the subjective analysis is slightly more successful at predicting the location visited than the objective analysis presented by Leonard in the previous chapter. However, the analysis of factors predictive of choice shows that both the medical evaluators and the patients are using the same basic criterion to determine what care is necessary for any given condition. Thus the search for quality in curative care depends on the *need* for quality. Whether patients seek quality is only slightly affected by the income of the patient, the distance from the quality provider or other demographic characteristics. When asked why they make a particular choice of a health care provider, the reasons or preferences patients give are not fixed; they vary with the diseases from which they suffer.

USE OF MATERNAL AND CHILD HEALTH SERVICES

One of the main objectives of primary health care programs is to make preventive health care services accessible to high-risk populations, including pregnant women and children, in rural areas. There is very little published research on demand and utilization of maternal and child health services in the rural areas. This chapter has so far shown the relative importance of individual and family income, household wealth, distance, price, and above all the quality of services provided in the choice of providers of curative services. It is uncertain, however, how these factors influence the utilization of prenatal and obstetrical services in rural settings. This section analyzes how expectant mothers use prenatal and obstetrical care service in rural areas, and identifies which factors influence their demand for such services.

Among the 403 reported deliveries during the one-year recall period, 288 women reported visiting prenatal services before delivery. Questions on births in the family and use of prenatal clinics were addressed mainly to women, but whenever it was not possible to do so, the questions were addressed to men in their capacity as husbands and as heads of the household. The interviews with heads of households are adequate because the objective was not to elicit detailed descriptions of visits but rather to establish whether or not visits had occurred.

Choice of Prenatal, Maternal and Child Health Services

The choice of maternity services does not follow the pattern of curative services, for government health clinics are the most widely used (Table 5.11). The very high use of the government health clinic may be attri-

Table 5.11 Choice of Delivery Clinic in Mbonge Subdivision, 1995

Location	Count	Percentage
Home and Midwife	110	27.3
Health Clinic	210	52.1
Hospital	70	17.4
Mission Clinic	13	3.2
Total	403	100%

buted to the reform of primary health care, which among other things rehabilitated delivery rooms in health clinics by introducing midwives as staff and improving their equipment. Under the new policy, deliveries that had been free now cost 6,000 CFA (US $12) at health clinics (Owona 1989). The high use of government health clinics thus also could be an indication that rural expectant mothers, for whom 6,000 CFA is a lot of money, are willing to pay for quality. This is further confirmed by the value that women appear to place on certain services at prenatal clinics, notably the obstetrical technique of abdominal palpation to determine fetal presentations and general development of the fetus, and related tests such as checking blood pressure, monitoring of urine for sugar and albumin levels and weight monitoring. The latter tests are necessary to prevent toxemia and eclampsia, a complication in pregnancy that could lead to fetal distress, premature deliveries, and maternal deaths if not controlled.

The number of home deliveries is quite impressive. It is likely that traditional midwives assisted in most of these deliveries, but the way we asked the questions keeps us from confirming it. It is crucial to note that delivery at home does not imply isolation from modern health services. When we asked women whether or not they received such services, 55.4 per cent of those who delivered at home had done so (compared to 76.4 per cent of those who gave birth in various government facilities). While it is clear that many women are giving birth at home because they either cannot afford or do not appreciate the value of the services offered in clinics and hospitals, still more women receive prenatal care and then decide separately whether to deliver at home or not. This is confirmed when we look at women who secured prenatal care for themselves and compare the various prenatal services they reported by their different places of delivery (Table 5.12, 5.13). It is striking that the incidence of specific prenatal services noted by respondents, which is a good indicator of their sophistication in using the medical system, is virtually identical across places of delivery. This is significant because if prenatal services

Table 5.12 Most Important Prenatal Services, Rated by Head of Household, Mbonge Subdivision 1995

Service	Count	Percentage
Physical examination	356	62.6
Checked blood	364	64.0
Checked urine	211	37.1
Checked weight	150	26.4
Health counseling	262	46.1
Total number of households that have used prenatal services	569	100

Table 5.13 Prenatal Services Received Based on Choice Delivery Location

Services Received	Place of Delivery			
	Home	Health Clinic	Hospital	Total
Physical exam	39 (63%)	116 (75%)	47 (75%)	202 (72%)
Checked blood	40 (65%)	92 (59%)	39 (62%)	171 (61%)
Checked urine	17 (27%)	56 (36%)	21 (33%)	94 (34%)
Checked weight	16 (26%)	44 (28%)	14 (22%)	74 (26%)
Health counseling	29 (47%)	85 (55%)	41 (65%)	155 (55%)
Total who received prenatal care	62 (100%)	155 (100%)	63 (100%)	280 (100%)

Pearson's Chi-square p = 0.913

are correctly performed, women will gain very important information about potential complications in their delivery. It also is compatible with the notion that some women decide to deliver at home after they have learned that they are unlikely to have complications with birthing. This information tells many women who make a prenatal visit to government health clinics that they do not need the highest quality of care for their delivery; it helps other women anticipate potential complications and plan accordingly.

Hospital deliveries accounted for 18 per cent of total deliveries. This again is potential evidence for that fact that women who are likely to have complicated deliveries will go to the hospital. This is similar to the skill effect in curative medicine noted in the first part of the chapter. On the other hand, only three per cent of women visited mission clinics. We had expected that mission clinic practitioners would have higher incentives to deliver quality maternity care, though their skills would not necessarily be higher than those of government practitioners. It appears, however, that there is no differential incentive effect. It is possible that the increased cost of delivery at a mission health clinic (9,000 CFA vs. 6,000 CFA) leads women to avoid mission services. We believe, however, that the difference in incentives that appeared to greatly affect choice in curative care is not present in maternal care. Side payments such as cash 'appreciation' are very common after the delivery of a healthy child and we hypothesize that this leads all care providers to provide the highest possibly quality of services. Payment of 'appreciation' cannot provide the same incentives in curative care because the result of treatment is not known until well after the visit to a provider is completed. With the delivery of a child, the success or failure of the delivery is apparent before the mother and child ever leave the hospital.

REASONS FOR CHOICE OF DELIVERY CLINIC

We tested the relationship between income and distance and the choice of provider. Table 5.14 shows that for both lower and upper income groups, more people delivered in the government health clinics than at home or in a hospital. There is a statistically significant difference between lower and upper income groups but the differences are small. The poor deliver more at home and less at hospitals. This suggests that income does have a marginal effect on the choice of provider, but that other factors are more important in determining the choice.

Distance, defined as the relative difficulty of access to facilities, is an important factor in delivery location choice (Table 5.15). Difficulty of access incorporates both cost and difficulty of travel. The vast majority of women with easy access delivered at health care clinics and hospitals; only 18 per cent delivered at home. In contrast, of the women with difficult access to government health clinics almost 34 per cent delivered at home. The choice of a hospital is not influenced by ease of access or by income. We hypothesize that choice of hospital care is influenced by the information that women receive in the process of prenatal care, as well as their own knowledge of the potential for severe complications during delivery. Since this information is available well before the actual delivery

Table 5.14 Relationship between Income and Choice of Delivery Location

Income Group	Home	Health Clinic	Hospital	Total
Lower group	49 (31.2%)	88 (56.1%)	20 (12.7%)	157
Upper group	49 (24.6%)	104 (52.3%)	46 (23.1%)	199
Total	98 (27.5%)	192 (53.9%)	66 (18.5%)	356

Pearson's Chi-square p = 0.03

Table 5.15 Relationship between Choice of Delivery Provider and Distance

	Access to Government Health Clinic			
Place delivered	Easy	Medium	Difficult	Total
Home	22 (18.0%)	22 (33.8%)	52 (33.5%)	96 (28.1%)
Health clinic	76 (62.3%)	29 (44.6%)	76 (49.0%)	181 (52.9%)
Hospital	24 (19.7%)	14 (21.5%)	27 (17.4%)	65 (19.0%)
Total	122	65	155	342

Pearson's Chi-square p = 0.03175

date, travel is possible. The expectant mother could go to town and stay there as the due date approached— though inconvenient and expensive, especially in the rainy season.

MULTIVARIATE ANALYSIS

The relationships between income, distance, price, quality, and the choice of maternal health services observed above do not show us the relative weights of these variables in the choice of a provider of maternal and child health services. We now report on a multinomial logit analysis that tested the collective effects of these variables on the choice of available providers and established the relative importance of each variable. The choice of provider is the dependent variable; distance, quality, and access are the independent variables. The results are reported in Table 5.16.

Women at higher income levels are more likely to choose hospital care and less likely to choose health clinics. Income level, however, does not affect the choice of delivering at home. It is apparent that when women believe they may have a complicated delivery, they take family income into account in making the choice between delivering at a hospital or a health clinic. Under other conditions, however, income level is not an issue.

Table 5.16 Multinomial Logit Analysis of Choice of Delivery Clinic

	Home		Health Clinic		Hospital	
Variable	Coeff	t-test	Coeff	t-test	Coeff	t-test
Constant	0.4240	0.00076	-0.241	0.03110	-0.1830	0.08345
Income	-0.0070	0.79550	-0.040	0.07719	0.0469	0.02016
Access to clinic	-0.1350	0.00207	0.149	0.00072	0.0144	0.66462
Access to hospital	0.0371	0.41370	-0.059	0.19468	0.0220	0.51909
Rainy season	-0.0040	0.95022	0.103	0.03453	-0.0990	0.02688

F-stat significance level ≤ 0.0001

Movement within the subdivision where this study took place is difficult because of the extremely poor state of the roads, and it was therefore hypothesized that distance would prevent women from going very far to deliver. We expected that most deliveries in the rainy season would take place at home, or in health clinics that were close to the sample population. The multinomial analysis shows that women are more likely to deliver at home as the difficulty in access to a health clinic increases, and as difficulty decreases women are more likely to deliver at a health clinic. Distance to the hospitals had no effect on choices. This again is consistent with our hypothesis that hospital visits are affected by other information.

The choice of provider is influenced by income and access. We believe it is also significantly affected by the information a woman possesses about her pregnancy, but unfortunately the study did not collect direct information on this issue. Mission clinics play a very small role in deliveries, which we believe is due to the fact that the payment of 'appreciation' provides a sufficient incentive for government facilities to provide high quality services. Thus quality is a factor in maternity choices (Wong *et al.* 1987), but it is directly visible only in the choice to go to the hospital.

CONCLUSION

This study of health care provider choice found that patients are seeking quality care. This finding holds in both curative and maternal/child care. The finding is not new; however, the study contributes to a better understanding of how patients define what quality care is and how it affects their health care decision-making. Patients, the study found, are aware of the medical skills different providers possess and how these skills apply differently according to the medical conditions from which they suffer. Patients who are seriously ill seek hospitals despite great distances and cost. Many women who face complicated deliveries seek to deliver their children in hospitals, despite great costs. The study therefore finds that patients evaluate the medical needs of their condition in a manner similar to the evaluation of health care professionals. This correspondence is independent of income, age, or sex.

The study has identified an additional component to quality, which becomes apparent in the patients' choice of mission clinics over government health clinics for curative care. This choice is not related to the income of the patient (as might have been believed) but rather to the condition of the patient. The choice of mission over government clinics for curative care is not replicated in the choices made for maternal and child health care. The payment of 'appreciation' is a very important element in childbirth, and it is not an important element of modern curative care. We suggest that since 'appreciation' would increase the direct effort a practitioner would give to one's case, this must be the special component that mission clinics add to curative health care. Medical effort is present in government clinics for deliveries, so maternity patients do not need to go to mission facilities to find it. This finding parallels Leonard's work in the previous chapter; incentives to provide curative medical effort are higher for mission clinics.

Distance, or difficulty of travel, appears to be a minimal factor in the choice of health care provider for curative care, but a much more important factor in the choice of location for delivery. Cost of care is important but is not an overwhelming factor in the choice of provider. Patients say that price is important, but only when they are suffering from diseases they do not believe require high levels of quality. All patients, rich or poor, seek the highest quality of care available when quality is important.

Two concluding observations have great implications for health policy. First, both their values and their medical condition shape patients' statements of the reasons for choosing a particular health provider. They do not represent an invariant or absolute set of preferences. Patients, on average, are making quite rational choices and policy makers need to understand the objective conditions that dictate them. Second, the system of incentives has a tremendous impact on the quality of care provided and should be the first order of attention in setting policy. When incentives are appropriately managed, patient choice will follow.

6 Can Private Veterinarians Survive in Uganda?

Lee M. P. K. Koma

Modern veterinary services were introduced in Uganda by the British colonial government around 1909 (Nsubuga 1993). Since there were only a few foreign personnel and no trained Ugandans, veterinary care was limited to control of major animal epizootics such as Rinderpest and Contagious Bovine Pleuropneumonia (CBPP). The veterinary service also provided for the control of endemic diseases such as trypanosomiasis and tick borne diseases. At that time, livestock production was geared toward the promotion of indigenous breeds of cattle, goats, sheep, pigs, and poultry raised under traditional production systems. By 1950 the Uganda government had adopted a policy of genetic improvement and began to import exotic livestock breeds for multiplication and crossbreeding. During the first post independence decade (1962–72) there was a rapid growth of the livestock industry, driven by government policies that encouraged livestock production. As a result, the cattle population grew to about 5.5 million head of cattle, including 70,000 exotic dairy cattle and their crosses (1.3 per cent of the total population). Uganda became self sufficient in milk production in 1972, when the Dairy Corporation recorded a total collection of 20 million liters for a human population of about ten million.

This progress was possible due to huge investments made in veterinary research into animal production and health, on one hand, and the extension of effective veterinary services to livestock farmers on the other. The range of veterinary services also deepened to include extension advice on pastureland improvement, animal nutrition, and breed improvement, as well as curative services. To facilitate these outreach programs, the Veterinary Department established a unit in each district staffed by at least one veterinarian and several paraprofessionals. The vets headed these units and were mainly involved in administration and supervision of the paraprofessionals, who carried out most of the field work. The number of government employed animal health personnel grew steadily until there were some 500 fully trained veterinarians and 1500 paraprofessionals with two to three years of technical training. After independence, the state continued to fund and directly provide these services satisfactorily until the late 1970s.

Between 1971 and 1985, Uganda experienced waves of political upheaval and civil strife, including several civil wars. In addition to this internal discord, Uganda was buffeted in the 1980s by the faltering global economy, which hit third world countries most severely. The combination of these factors eventually led to a total collapse of the Ugandan economy. Meanwhile the human population steadily increased to about 12 million by 1980 and to approximately 20 million by 1997. The size of the civil service in general and that of the agricultural sector in particular also increased dramatically. Government expenditures soared due to the increasing population and size of the civil service, but revenues could not keep pace. As part of a broad spending reduction policy, the government began to cut the veterinary budget: agricultural supplies and logistics were cut first, making the practice of veterinary medicine more difficult, and then staff salaries themselves were undermined by ever spiraling inflation, leading to loss of morale among the veterinary corps. By the early 1980s, therefore, government could no longer provide veterinary services efficiently and effectively.

These political, economic, and administrative afflictions took their toll on the Ugandan agrarian system. The national cattle herd, as a representative example, declined by 20 per cent between 1972 and 1981, from 5.5 million to 4.4 million head. This nutritive crisis was one among several factors that constrained Uganda to look toward the global financial community for assistance in crafting a firmer national economic foundation. Under International Monetary Fund and World Bank pressure, the Uganda government introduced a variety of structural adjustment programs in the early 1980s. The government was obliged, among other things, to liberalize the economy, reduce public expenditure, and control inflation in exchange for debt relief and funding from international agencies for Uganda's development programs. The government initiated retrenchment of its veterinary staff and ended its policy of automatically hiring new graduates. Veterinary services were then partially privatized, first by introducing cost recovery on such veterinary supplies as pharmaceuticals and agro-chemicals for the control of ticks, and then by identifying services, such as artificial insemination and immunizations against epidemic diseases, to be turned over to the private sector. Still, the government retained its leading role in training, research, policy formulation, regulation, and the provision of services with a pure public goods nature such as extension education, disease surveillance, disease eradication programs, and public health inspections.

There is broad consensus that it is no longer possible or desirable for the African state to finance all animal health services it aspired to provide in the years after independence. There also is a consensus that the state must continue to play a role in the delivery of some veterinary services (FAO 1997). The difficulty has come in defining the appropriate boundary between government and market delivery systems. The distinction made in economics between private and public (or collective) goods was introduced into this debate at a relatively early stage (Leonard 1985, 1987). The proposition was that the private market would optimally provide those goods for which the purchaser enjoys the full benefit and can be made to pay the full price. However, the market will under-provide goods for which nonpurchasers can derive benefit by free riding on the purchases of others, so government intervention will be needed. The World Bank modified this distinction by identifying externalities (costs or benefits that are not borne by the purchaser of a good) as the factor underlying public goods and making the concept a continuum rather than a category. But the proposition that government intervention is required to mitigate the effects of externalities continues to underlie policy thinking (Umali *et al.* 1992). These ideas would lead one to expect that African herders would value private veterinary goods more highly than public ones if they must pay for the services themselves, but that they might be induced to value goods with significantly positive externalities more highly if they could have them paid for collectively rather than individually, thereby avoiding others' free riding off their contributions. No empirical investigation of these assumptions has been made among African herders. One of the purposes of this research project is to fill that gap.

In this context of rapid change many have become concerned about the viability of private veterinary practice and what character it would have if it does survive. In particular there is deep concern that veterinary standards may be damaged as a result of market-induced atomistic behavior that would reshape notions of which veterinary services are 'valuable.' There are also fears that full veterinarians may not be able to earn an adequate income in a market situation, leading to a reduction both in availability of high quality service and in the accompanying professional values. This research seeks to investigate and answer these questions. It concludes that no significant damage to livestock production in Uganda is likely to result from privatization because producers and veterinarians have very similar priorities for animal health. However, full veterinarians will need to adapt their practices to the new realities of privatization if they are to survive in competition with paraprofessional animal health practitioners, because producers will pay extra only for what practitioners actually do, not for their level of training.

Research Method

Two separate surveys were conducted in order to evaluate the current performance of the veterinary service in Uganda. A survey of animal herders was carried out between November 1994 and April 1995. For expository convenience, I refer to all livestock producers as herders despite the fact that many of these people are responsible for small herds and consider farming to be their primary occupation. A second survey of veterinary professionals was carried out between May and June 1996.

Mukono and Mbarara administrative districts were selected for the herder survey. These districts were chosen for two reasons: both districts lie in the high potential zone for privatization of veterinary services as identified by preliminary surveys conducted by the Ministry of Agriculture, Animal Industry and Fisheries; and together, these districts represent nearly the full range of livestock production systems in Uganda. A total of 577 cattle herder-households were interviewed from the two districts, including 276 from Mukono and 301 from Mbarara, drawn from 15 administrative villages (Local Council I) in each case.

Mukono district is adjacent to and east of Kampala, Uganda's capital. It has a population density of 201 persons and 18 head of cattle per square kilometer. Primarily, farmers keep small herds of indigenous cattle breeds as well as exotic dairy cattle and their crosses, but there are some mid-sized producers as well. Mar-kets and veterinary services are relatively accessible to most herders in this district. Five of Mukono district's six counties were selected for this survey. The sixth, Buvuma County, comprises a group of islands in Lake Victoria and was left out due to communication difficulties. A propor-tional number of administrative parishes (Local Council II) were then randomly selected from each of the five counties to give a total of 15 parishes. One village was in turn randomly chosen from each of the 15 parishes. All households that raised cattle in each selected village were then interviewed.

Mbarara district, by contrast, is located in the rural southwestern part of Uganda over 200 km southwest of Kampala. It is largely inhabited by the Banyankole ethnic group, and has a population density of 105 persons and 57 head of cattle per square kilometer. Indigenous, exotic, and mixed breeds of cattle are raised in small, medium, and large herds. The Bahima ethnic subgroup in this district are well known for their traditional lifestyle, in which large herds of Long Horn Ankole (Sanga) cattle continue to play a large role. Pastoralism was practiced among this community, but recently most have adopted a settled life. Because of their long experience with cattle, the Bahima herders possess considerable knowledge about common livestock health problems and practice self-treatment to a far greater degree than do most Ugandan producers. The current President of Uganda, Yoweri Museveni, is from this district.

Three of the Mbarara's seven counties were selected for the herder survey. Nyabushozi County is the traditional Bahima area, characterized by large herds of indigenous cattle, while Kashari and Rwampara counties represent mixed farmers involved both in cultivation and raising livestock. Five parishes were selected at random from each county, and one village was then chosen at random from each parish. All the households that raised cattle in the selected village were interviewed.

As cluster sampling techniques were used, we had intended to weight our results and use statistical techniques that are particularly appropriate to clusters. Unfortunately, we could not make these adjustments and instead use multinomial logit, the analytic method that proved most appropriate. Thus, although we are confident of our analysis of causal relationships in our data, caution should be exercised in using them to estimate precise parameter and population values.

A structured questionnaire was used to generate data on two sets of herder concerns. First, data on the animal health services used by the herder were generated through asking for the kinds of preventive measures taken and not taken for the herd during the preceding year. The herder was asked to present animals that had experienced health problems in the previous year. A maximum of five animals was selected at random and questions were asked about the kind of problems they had and how the herder responded. This provided a clear picture of the nature of the current relationship between herders and professional caregivers. In order to get a sense of how these relations might change in the future, a second set of questions focused on herder priorities for key veterinary services and also on which of these services they were using. In order to test for the effects of free riders and public goods, each was asked to arrange the services in order of preference when he or she had to pay for them, and then if the service was provided free of charge. The services were presented in a set of pictorial illustrations, which were explained to ensure that the herder understood them before making his/her priority selections.

A second survey was intended for vets who are directly involved in the delivery of livestock health services. More than 500 vets are registered with the Uganda Veterinary Board, but reliable information on the number and whereabouts of those actually practicing was not available. In order to quickly and comprehensively canvass vet responses, a notice was placed in the government-controlled newspaper, New Vision, the most widely circulated daily in Uganda. To encourage maximum response, the vets were told that all those who participated in completing and returning the questionnaire would be entered into a raffle with a top prize of U. Shs 300,000 (US $300). The top prize was equivalent to about two months' salary of a young government-employed vet. This was sufficient inducement for 86 vets, who responded and were then provided with a questionnaire, an envelope and stamp for the return mail. Of these, 66 completed and returned their questionnaires. This sample is small and is not based on random selection, so we cannot assume that it is fully representative of the Ugandan veterinarian population. Still, these are the best data available, and they are highly suggestive.

The structured vet questionnaire asked the respondents to indicate their priorities for a list of 14 veterinary services based on the importance of each type of service for livestock production in Uganda. The vet list was similar but not identical to the list in the herder survey. Next, vets were asked about the kinds of activities they were engaged in and how frequently they performed each. Finally, the survey asked about the vet's five most recent treatments each for preventive and curative care, and asked for details regarding the type of disease and fees for service, if any.

RESULTS AND ANALYSIS

Veterinary providers cannot survive in private practice unless there is a demand for their services. What would make a livestock producer more likely to pay a professional to care for their sick animal? Understanding the subtleties underlying this question is crucial if we are to anticipate and avoid friction during the continuing privatization of veterinary service. We address the question in five ways in order to evaluate how a herder sees himself or herself in relation to professional caregivers. First, we examine constraints on demand for professional assistance in general. Second, we evaluate herder priorities for thirteen specific services as reported in our survey. Third, we group these services into five thematic groups and evaluate which herders, and when and why, seek assistance in each of these general categories. We then shift the focus to the vet perspective, first comparing vet priorities with those of the herder, and finally comparing all of these values with actual service provision.

Determinants of Herder Demand for Professional Veterinary Services

The first step in evaluating consumer demand for veterinary service is to place herder and vet in a broad economic and geographic relationship. Tables 6.1 and 6.2 report on the multinomial logit models that we generated to predict the likelihood that a producer will purchase the services of a veterinary provider. We found Mukono and Mbarara Districts are shaped by very different constraints, so we developed a separate model for each. The expected financial cost of treating a disease had an impact on producer demand in both production systems. In Mbarara, where livestock production systems are more extensive and population densities are sparser, the distance to an animal health provider had a large impact on the decision to seek outside care. In Mukono, however, where farming is more intensive and the farm sizes are much smaller, distance to a veterinary provider is much less important and the finer details of the farmer's livestock production system matter more.

Our Mukono model (Table 6.1) contains four independent variables. In the intensive, small-holder systems typical of this district, the willingness to call an animal health provider increased along with two independent variables: the likelihood that the disease might result in loss of the animal's life, and the proportion of the production system comprised of exotic or mixed breeds (as opposed to traditional stock). However, the willingness to call an animal health provider decreased with increasing expected financial cost of the service. Veterinary literature and popular wisdom typically focus on factors like these when anticipating herder behavior in smallholder systems. What is important, however, is that in traditionally pastoral areas like Mbarara such factors are completely overshadowed by the effects of distance. It is important to note also effects that do not significantly affect farmer willingness to call for professional assistance. Farmer income has a very small effect on willingness, and none of the following specific income-related variables were statistically significant in the multinomial logit: external income, a cash crop, education, or size of herd. The presence of exotic or cross-

Table 6.1 Mukono, Uganda: Factors Predicting the Decision to Use a Professional to Treat a Sick Animal

Multinomial Logit Model
Maximum Likelihood Estimates

Number of observations	599
Iterations completed	4
Log likelihood function	-367.6842
Restricted log likelihood	-392.1733
Chi-squared	48.9782
Degrees of freedom	3
Significance level	0

Variable	Coefficient	Standard Error	b/St.Er.	P[|Z|>z]	Mean of X
Constant	1.003200	0.40832	2.457	0.01401	
PREDICTED COST	-5.57E-04	1.24E-04	-4.501	0.00001	3323.0
DANGER OF LIFE LOSS	1.249600	0.21560	5.796	0.00000	1536.0
TRADITIONAL HERD	-0.581970	0.22207	-2.621	0.00877	0.7679

Frequencies of actual & predicted outcomes
(Predicted outcome has maximum probability)

	Predicted		
Actual	NO	YES	Total
NO	51	166	217
YES	42	340	382
Total	93	506	599

bred dairy animals does predict demand and it is related to income. But it is also strongly related to the need for the service and its value.

In the Mbarara model, the dependent variable, likelihood of seeking professional veterinary care, is predicted by only two independent variables: expected financial cost and distance. To properly evaluate financial cost in cases where outside assistance was not demanded, we had to develop a way to predict the amount a herder who used self-treatment would have paid if he had called for outside assistance. We found that the cost of the medicines used and the costs of transport to

Table 6.2 Mbarara, Uganda: Factors Predicting the Decision to Use a Professional to Treat a Sick Animal

Multinomial Logit Model
Maximum Likelihood Estimates

Number of observations	1 090
Iterations completed	6
Log likelihood function	-420.0386
Restricted log likelihood	-471.8774
Chi-squared	103.6776
Degrees of freedom	2
Significance level	0

Variable	Coefficient	Std. Err.	b/St.Er.	P[|Z|>z]	Mean of X
Constant	0.87752	0.32423	2.707	0.00680	
PREDICTED COST	-2.50E-04	7.80E-05	-3.203	0.00136	4 442
EXPECTED DISTANCE	-0.19475	2.57E-02	-7.571	0.00000	8.744

Frequencies of actual & predicted outcomes
Predicted outcome has maximum probability

	Predicted		
Actual	NO	YES	Total
NO	910	10	920
YES	166	4	170
Total	1 076	14	1 090

the farm largely determined the cost of veterinary care. On the basis of my experience as a clinical veterinarian, I assigned each disease or set of symptoms to one of three expense categories. For those farmers who called a vet and paid for this veterinary service, we then calculated the coefficients for the two independent variables of expense and distance between the provider and the farm in a regression equation with actual price paid as the dependent variable. These coefficients enabled us to calculate how much every farmer with a sick animal should expect to pay for service, whether he actually called for it or not. Not surprisingly, livestock producers in both Mukono and Mbarara were less likely to call for an animal health provider the more expensive they expected the treatment to be.

The second variable in the Mbarara model is distance. At first glance it might appear that this factor is incorporated into the financial cost variable since the transport costs of the vet or paraprofessional are reflected in their charges. This variable, however, addresses the distance costs of the herder himself. The herder must pay for his own travel to the animal health provider's office and must absorb the loss of his own labor time while he is away. In Mukono the distances were sufficiently small that these costs were not a significant factor in people's decisions as to whether or not to call for assistance. In Mbarara, however, distance is a large factor in these decisions. Those close to an animal health provider are much more likely to ask for assistance than those who are far away. Our data suggest that for each kilometer closer an animal health provider is to a farm, the probability that he will be called upon to treat a sick animal will increase by 2.23 per cent.

Cost in time and money, of course, is only a part of the demand equation. Even if distance were held constant, we would expect that those Mbarara herders who possess traditional experience in the diseases of their indigenous herds would seek assistance less frequently than Mukono herders who are relatively new to this occupation. We were unable to meaningfully define and measure experience as an independent variable. In any case, our results clearly demonstrate that there is scope for generating a demand increase in the more pastoral areas by bringing professionals closer to the producers. Since it is all but impossible to do this with full vets, the implication is that animal health services in these areas must be provided largely by a denser network of paraprofessionals.

Herder Priorities for Particular Veterinary Services

The second step in our analysis of herder demand for veterinary services is to ask not simply whether Ugandan livestock producers will pay for animal health services but for what types of services. Do their priorities accord with those of veterinary medicine in putting curative measures behind those that promote animal health and prevent disease? These questions were put to the herders in our structured survey and, by and large, the answer is yes. Will they downgrade those aspects of veterinary medicine that provide collective rather than private benefits when they cease to be publicly provided? As it turns out, generally not. And will the loss of public vets pursuing their independent, professionally derived priorities diminish the health of the national herd? Probably not. Herders themselves were surprisingly sensitive to the value of some services with

Table 6.3 Ranking of Average Priorities by Herder for individual veterinary services

Type of Service	Priority No.	Mean	Standard Deviation
Vector (tick) control	1	3.95	3.02
Improvement of pastures and grazing management	2	4.78	3.62
Prophylactic treatment of helminthiasis	3	4.90	2.63
Immunization against prevalent killer diseases for example, CBPP	4	5.48	2.92
Curative care for a seriously sick animal for example, with ECF	5	6.02	3.27
Immunization against non killer diseases, for example, FMD	6	6.47	2.80
Curative care for a mildly sick animal; for example, with lameness	7	6.90	3.27
Extension education on animal husbandry and health	8	7.18	3.79
Improvement of genetic stock for example, by Artificial Insemination	9	7.39	3.33
Herd screening for disease surveillance	10	7.65	3.03
Improvement of housing and sanitary conditions	11	7.71	3.51
Control of livestock movement for animal disease control	12	10.42	2.49
Food hygiene inspection for example, meat inspection	13	11.52	2.41

Analysis of Variance $F = 256.8$ $P > .0001$

collective benefits even when asked explicitly to factor in individual costs in a privatized market environment.

As reported in Table 6.3, when thirteen standard herd concerns were considered individually, the overall average priority of herders placed vector (tick) control top of the priority list, followed by improvement of pastures and grazing management. Prophylactic treatment against helminthiasis was in the third place. Immunizations against killer and non-killer diseases such as CBPP and FMD respectively featured fairly well at the top of the priority list. On the other hand, food hygiene inspection came at the very bottom. Other priority services low in the eyes of herders were the control of livestock movement (quarantine) and improvement of animal housing and hygienic conditions.

When evaluating causes of divergent priorities among herders, geographical location and type of herd are the most important variables; level of education (number school years completed) and membership of a cooperative concerned with livestock matters also correlate with substantial priority differences. We anticipated that the method of financing of the services (whether paid by the herder or provided as a public good) would have a significant effect in determining the choice of herders' priorities. It did not. This suggests major limitations in the private vs. public goods analyses in determining candidates for privatization.

This examination of Ugandan herder priorities with regard to veterinary services leads us to question the simple way in which others have distinguished between public and private goods in animal health. First, it is not true that private goods, ones in which the purchaser can be made to pay the full value of the service and enjoys all of its benefits, receive the highest priority from herders. Curative veterinary services, which are pure private goods, are ranked behind preventive ones among Ugandan livestock producers, even though many of the benefits of preventive treatments, such as immunizations, create positive externalities that are enjoyed by neighboring producers through, for example, herd immunity. One can rescue the original economics proposition by arguing that the reason for the high priority placed on immunizations is that the private benefits to the herder (in reduced mortality in his herd) are so great, relative to the costs, that the fact of uncompensated benefits to one's neighbors (externalities) is overwhelmed. This is perfectly reasonable, but it was not anticipated when the policy analysts first made their deductions from theory.

Second, Ugandan herders appear to attach the same priorities to veterinary services when they pay for services individually as when they pay collectively. Herders seem to evaluate the services solely in terms of their private benefit, with little regard to whether or not they are paying for them. The perceived benefits associated with these services (or the lack thereof) are sufficiently clear, and the non-price costs associated with them (including risk, distance, inconvenience, and others) are strong enough, that payment method does not seem to have the strong effect on herder priorities that standard economic analyses would anticipate. Again, this modification can be accommodated by economic theory, but it was not anticipated at first.

Third, the existence of negative externalities around a service is tremendously important. In our survey, both vets and herders placed a low priority on quarantines and meat inspection, in both of which collective benefits are gained at the cost of private loss. The issue is not simply who is going to pay for these services; it is whether or not their value is recognized at all. As we will see, veterinarians— who are trained to think in terms of the public good— see somewhat greater value to these services than herders do, but the negative evaluation of the public is so strong that vets are wary of them. From the vets' perspective, it seems that because the benefits to the public are diffuse and hard to observe, and the costs to the herder whose animal is condemned are so concrete and visible, severe conflicts and temptations for corruption arise which delegitimize the entire service. Economic theory certainly anticipates these problems, but their effect in Uganda is so great that even effective *governmental* provision of these services is in doubt.

Herder Priorities for Groups of Services

Understanding the individual service priorities of herders is useful not simply to target particular services and regions where enterprising veterinarians and paraprofessionals might effectively carry out specific tasks. It also is a necessary prerequisite to the third component of our analysis of the nature of herder demand for veterinary service: we can now group the services into broader categories and evaluate how, from a public policy perspective, privatization of veterinary service can be effectively pursued. Accordingly, we have grouped the above thirteen specific tasks into five categories. These are, in order of herder priority (see Table 6.4), preventive services with mixed public/private goods attributes, curative services, improvement of animal husbandry, genetic upgrading of stock, and preventive services with pure public goods attributes. It is worth noting that the standard deviation around these five groups is only somewhat higher than the standard deviations for the thirteen individual services. Even when the individual results are aggregated into groups, herder preferences are quite consistent.

It is encouraging that preventive and a number of husbandry measures were placed ahead of curative medicine in the priorities of livestock producers. On the other hand, disease control measures, which can be highly effective and were the historical basis of veterinary interventions in colonial Uganda, are not merely undervalued; they are viewed negatively. In contrast with preventive measures that benefit both private individuals and the public in general, disease control's benefits are all external and in fact impose significant costs on the individual producer. Perhaps as a result, there is a great deal of corrupt evasion of these

Table 6.4 Ranking of Average Priorities by Herder for Groups of Veterinary Services

Type of service	Priority No.	Average (Mean)	Standard Deviation
Preventive Services (mixed public/ private goods attributes): vector control, immunizations, helminthiasis prophylactics	1	5.16	2.97
Curative Services (pure private goods).	2	6.60	3.32
Improvement of Animal Husbandry, Feeding and Extension services	2	6.60	3.87
Upgrading of stock genetically (for example, artificial insemination)	4	7.33	3.37
Preventive Services (pure public goods attributes): herd screening for diseases, control of movement of livestock (quarantine), food hygiene inspection	5	9.80	3.13

Analysis of Variance $F = 931.1$ $P < .0001$

measures in Uganda. As we will see later, unfortunately, professional veterinarians do not value disease control very highly either.

Looking more closely at discrepancies among herder priorities for these groups, and ahead to Table 6.5, it is clear that significant but moderate differences in individual assessments of the aggregate leader, preventive services with mixed private-public goods attributes, are due to the geographical location of herders and type of herd. Herders in Mukono gave this group a higher priority than their counterparts in Mbarara; small traditional herders, who appear to be influenced largely by the type of herd more than its size, favored this service more than other types of herders. As noted above, the small traditional herders are also mainly found in Mukono district, so there is colinearity here.

Preventive services with pure public goods attributes ranked at the bottom in our aggregation. Geographical location of herders again shaped opinions about this group, and members of a cooperative were more likely to value it more highly. Differences were also influenced by the type and size of the cattle herds. Higher priority was given by herders in Mbarara, those with a large herd size, and those with a dairy herd. Not surprisingly, herders with the opposite attributes valued the middle group, curative services, more highly. Non-members of cooperatives ascribed a relatively higher value to curative services, and the less educated gave them a higher relative priority than those who were better educated. Finally, and consistently, traditional herders had a higher relative priority for curative treatment than dairy herders did.

Table 6.5 Explaining Differences in Herder Priorities

Type of service	Mukono	Traditional Herd	Large Herd	Education	Coop Member
Preventive Services (mixed public/private goods)	**	**			(*)
Curative Services	**	**	(*)	(**)	(**)
Improvement of Animal Husbandry, Feeding and Extension services	(*)		(*)	**	**
Upgrading of stock genetically (artificial insemination)		(**)		**	**
Preventive Services (pure public goods attributes)	(**)	(**)	**	(**)	**

* $p = .01 - .05$ (positive correlation) (*) $p = .01 - .05$ (negative correlation)
** $p < .01$ (positive correlation) (**) $p < .01$ (negative correlation)

Genetic improvement of stock is most strongly supported by those who have experience and interest in broadening their horizons in other ways. Cooperative membership, relatively high education, and herding dairy cattle rather than traditional animals all correlate positively among those herders who value genetic improvement. These are the same attributes of herders who valued animal nutrition, husbandry, and extension education more highly than our aggregate herder did.

Analysis of our aggregate herder priority list, as well as discrepancies with the aggregate, leads to two kinds of public policy implications. First, herders value immunizations and curative services the highest; therefore, these are the easiest veterinary services to privatize. Current herder priorities suggest that it is reasonable to expect that private vets and para-professionals will find ready customers for these services. Second, the priorities of herders are likely to shift as other broad social changes like improving education levels and increased cooperative membership take their course. Cooperative members placed higher than average priority on pure public goods types of preventive services, and educated herders were especially interested in genetic upgrading. The latter could be privatized if demand shifts in the expected positive direction.

THE VETERINARIAN SURVEY: PRIORITIES AND PRACTICES

Our emphasis has been on evaluating herder priorities for veterinary service because we anticipate that, in a market environment, supply will follow demand. However, veterinary professionals bring not only skills

Table 6.6 Ranking of Average Priorities by Vets for Individual Services

Type of Service	Vet Priority ranking	Average (Mean)	Standard Deviation
Immunization against prevalent, killer diseases	1	3.09	2.58
Vector (tick) control	2	3.34	2.70
Curative treatment for serious diseases	3	5.17	3.45
Immunization against sporadic killer diseases	4	5.87	3.76
Immunization against non-killer diseases	5	6.75	3.07
Curative Treatment for mildly sick animals	6	7.39	3.58
Improvement of genetic stock (A.I.)	7	7.95	3.31
Extension education: housing and hygiene	7	7.97	3.78
Control of livestock movement (Quarantine)	9	8.09	3.24
Food hygiene Inspection	10	9.16	2.97
Improvement of pastures and grazing mgmt.	10	9.17	3.40
Extension on animal nutrition and health	10	9.20	3.43
Eradication of Vectors (tsetse fly)	13	9.98	3.73
Promotion of purchase of feed supplements	14	11.83	2.62
Prophylactic treatment of helminthiasis	Na	Na	Na
Extension education: husbandry and health	Na	Na	Na
Herd screening for disease surveillance	Na	Na	Na
Improvement of housing and sanitary conditions	Na	Na	Na

Analysis of Variance $F = 36.2991$ $P < .0001$

Table 6.7 Comparison of Ranking of Priorities by Herders and Vets for Service Groups

Type of Service	Ranking by Herder	Ranking by vets
Preventive (private - public nature)	1.0	1.0
Curative	2.5	2.0
Animal husbandry & extension	2.5	5.0
Genetic improvement of stock	4.0	3.0
Preventive (pure public nature)	5.0	4.0

but also values to their clients. Their priorities also figure into our analysis of change in service provision as a result of privatization. The impact of these values is not theoretical; there is a significant and moderately positive correlation between the average priorities and the actual activities of the vets ($r = .22$, $p < .001$). The general pattern of ranking, as shown on Tables 6.6 and 6.7, is similar to that of the herders, but three differences are clearly notable. First, while herders gave very high priority (no. 2) to the issue of animal nutrition, the vets gave it the opposite ranking, at the bottom of their list (nos. 11, 12, and 14). Secondly, food hygiene inspection and restriction of livestock movement for the control of epidemic diseases (quarantine), though not so highly placed by vets, occupied relatively better positions than were given by the herders. Third, immunization against prevalent killer diseases is the first priority of vets but not quite so highly placed for herders.

With respect to the first, vets are wrong to give animal nutrition such a low priority. They appear to value it according to their own skills rather than according to its contribution to animal health. Since feeds are a source of income to private vets, this is a place where the incentives created by privatization would probably lead to more appropriate vet priorities. The second and third points indicate that the vets' professionalism does lead to the kind of increased emphasis on prevention that one would desire. Operationally, however, their differences with herders on these points may not have much significance. The herders give sufficient value to immunizations to lead us to expect these functions to remain relatively secure under privatization. Also, vets do not value government services regarding movement control or food inspection highly enough for us to expect private vets to work actively to promote these activities. These two functions, if they are to be performed, have to remain fully in the public sector.

Participation of Vets in Delivery of Preventive and Curative Services

The final step in our analysis relates herder and vet values with actual private veterinary practice in contemporary Uganda. As Table 6.8 shows, there is a tremendous variety within the population of private veterinarians. Fifty-five of the 66 vets surveyed indicated that they carried out preventive or curative treatments and charged professional fees. When asked about their five most recent *preventive* treatments, some vets said they completed five on the day of the survey, while others took an interval of 740 days. The interval between the first and the fifth most recent *curative* treatments was a (relatively) narrow 1–106 days. Annual incomes estimated from the professional fees, unsurprisingly, showed a similarly broad range, between U.Shs. 67,000 and 25,063,000 (US $ 67–25,000). The estimated average annual income from preventive treatment was about U.Shs. 1,426,000 (US $1,476), with the estimated income of 17 per cent of the vets being equal to or greater than the average. The estimated average annual income for curative treatment was about U.Shs. 1,342,000 (US $1,342), with 29 per cent of the vets receiving equal to or more than this figure.

Table 6.8 Descriptive Data on Vet Respondents

	Interval between five most recent	Average	Standard Deviation
Preventive Treatments	1–740 days	67.7 days	133.5 days
Curative Treatments	1–106 days	19.5 days	19.9 days
Annual Income	\$67–\$25 000	\$2 765	\$4 777

Time allocated to Private Practice		
Full-Time	2	(3%)
50% – 98%	8	(12%)
Less than 50%	42	(64%)
No response	14	(21%)

Nearly all of the vets devoted less than half time to their private practice. Only ten (15 per cent) spent 50 per cent or more of their work time in self-employment and only two vets were engaged in full-time private practice. It was not possible to establish what factors were responsible for the wide variations in annual incomes from charges for professional fees. However, it is clear that fully trained veterinarians can make a career for themselves in the private sector: 16 of the vets (24 per cent) earned more than the \$1,860 annual income of a newly recruited government vet, and some of these earned so much more that the private vet average is \$2,765 (Table 6.8).

Given this clear potential for a lucrative career in the private sector, we must ask why only two vets have chosen to devote their full work day to private practice. We can imagine three possible reasons. First, government employment offers the private vet a measure of legitimacy; herders might be more confident about the skill level of a vet who is regularly monitored by the government. It is plausible that a professional organization could fill this role in the future, but this has not occurred as yet. Second, perhaps vets have developed a synergistic relationship between their public and private practices; they might use government vehicles and other resources to travel into the field on government-sponsored projects and, once in the field, engage in private activities at the end of the official work day. These hypotheses are worthy of careful analysis but are beyond the scope of this chapter. A third hypothesis is that, as presently defined, the market is too small for more full time activity. Understanding these market conditions and how they might be changed

Table 6.9 Preventive Treatments as Reported by Herders (Herder Survey, Mukono and Mbarara Districts)

Not Prevented	2 199	48.70%
Prevented	2 312	51.30%
Professional	1 539	34.10%
Herder	738	16.40%
Unknown	35	0.80%
Total Cases	4 511	100.00%

to public and private benefit has been a focus of this chapter and we return to this subject now.

Producer use of Professionals

What kinds of treatments are most commonly demanded by livestock producers? Herders themselves are actively involved in both preventive and curative care of their animals. As shown above, herders give high priority to immunizations, but that does not necessarily mean that they administer all nine government recommended preventive treatments to all of their livestock. Just over half of the preventive interventions herders *could* have made were not taken. Table 6.9 shows that the herders themselves provided one-third of the immunizations and preventive treatments given.

Table 6.10 provides a rich framework for analysis of where and who performs curative treatments: the herder treated just over half and 16.8 per cent did not receive any treatment. Of those treated by outsiders, vets or paraprofessionals treated more than half and the rest were treated by unqualified providers or by someone of unknown qualification.

Interestingly, there are significant differences in care provision patterns by area and production system. In the small farming area of Mukono over half of the incidents of disease were treated outside the family, and we are confident that 31.5 per cent of all cases in this county were treated by professionals. In Mbarara, a different pattern is seen. In the mixed farming area of Rwampara (but not Kashari), 34 per cent of all cases were treated by someone outside the family and 14 per cent were known to be handled by professionals. But among the traditional large herders of Nyabushozi, 11.7 per cent were treated by outsiders and 6.0 per cent by known professionals. Thus we can see that small farmers with mixed herds are much more likely to use professionals when their animals are sick, while traditional herders are the most likely to rely on self-treatment.

Table 6.10 Curative Treatment by Training/Area
(Herder Survey, Mukono and Mbarara Districts)

Area	Level of Professional Training			Training Level of Service Provider				Total
	Degree	Diploma	Certificate	Total Prof.	Other Outsider	Total Outsider (incl. prof)	Herder or Not Treated*	
Mukono District	7	136	110	253	193	446	357	803
	0.9%	16.9%	13.7%	31.5%	24.0%	55.5%	44.5%	100%
Mbarara District	23	22	40	85	101	186	988	1 174
	2.0%	1.9%	3.4%	7.2%	8.6%	15.8%	84.2%	100%
Nyabushozi	11	21	6	38	36	74	557	631
County	1.7%	3.3%	1.0%	6.0%	5.7%	11.7%	88.3%	100%
Kashari	7	0	6	13	16	29	270	299
County	2.3%	0.0%	2.0%	4.3%	5.4%	9.7%	90.3%	100%
Rwampara	5	1	28	34	49	83	161	244
County	2.0%	0.4%	11.5%	13.9%	20.1%	34.0%	66.0%	100%
TOTAL	30	158	150	338	294	632	1 345	1 977
	1.5%	8.0%	7.6%	17.1%	14.9%	32.0%	68.0%	100%

* Among the population of 1977 cases, Herders treated 1013 cases (51.2%) themselves, and 332 cases (16.8%) were left untreated. Data distinguishing between these two categories at the district and county level does not exist, so they have been presented as a composite figure.

Degree = Full veterinary degree

Diploma = Three year veterinary course

Certificate = Two-year veterinary course

Other = less than two years of formal training

Herders were also asked about the level of formal training received by the professionals they call upon for curative treatments. These results also are reported on Table 6.10. We observe that there is considerable variation in the frequency with which paraprofessionals are sought for treatment. Mukono district herders rely quite strongly on diploma and certificate holders, who treated 16.9 per cent and 13.7 per cent of Mukono's cases respectively. This contrasts with Kashari County in Mbarara district, where there appear to be no diploma holders and where certificate holders were called only two per cent of the time. The remaining Mbarara counties fall between these extremes. Despite wide variation in demands for paraprofessional attention, however, full vets treated a fairly constant proportion of sick animals across the different production systems, despite very great differences in the propensity to seek the services of paraprofessionals. They are called between 0.9 per cent and 2.3 per cent of the time. This suggests that vets are treating conditions that are beyond the capacity of producers, whereas relatively sophisticated traditional herders are often able to do without the services of paraprofessionals. Mukono district's especially low 0.9 per cent vet call rate, especially when we observe Mukono's high volume of paraprofessional service, suggests that paraprofessionals are developing skills and competing with full vets even for some advanced tasks.

The final set of questions regarding herder use of veterinary services addressed the kinds of diseases treated by different categories of professionals. Treatments were provided for a wide range of diseases; helminthiasis (88 cases), East Coast Fever (72), and Trypanosomiasis (69) were the most common. Table 6.10 shows that, in the full range of diseases, vets treated only 30 out of 1977 total cases. The only conditions that were predominantly treated by full vets were Contagious Bovine Pleuropneumonia (CBPP, seven out of eight cases), three out of six cases of wounds or injuries, and both cases of hoof conditions. The remaining 308 curative treatments were provided by three-year diploma holders (158 cases) and two-year certificate holders (150 cases). Although all livestock (except chickens) received some professional attention, cattle were the objects of 97 per cent of the treatments known to be provided by professionals (328 cases).

CONCLUSION

At the time of this survey, very few vets were fully engaged in private veterinary practice in Uganda. Most of the 66 vets surveyed were in government employment as vets, with a few employed by private companies. However, it is clear that the majority of vets were engaged in some part-time private veterinary practice to varying degrees. At least ten of the vets indicated that they spent 50 per cent or more of their work time in self-employment and two vets were in full-time self-employment. The estimated annual income from professional fees of eleven vets, all stationed in the southern part of the country, is substantial and compares favorably with the present annual income of a government employed vet. The fact that this income is based only on professional fees suggests that a private veterinary practitioner would be able to earn a living out of self-employment, especially considering that additional sources of income—from the sale of pharmaceuticals and farm inputs for example— have not been included. An earlier survey identified the southern districts of Uganda as possible areas for viable private veterinary practice, and the results of this study support this view.

This study has shown that, overall, professionals provide for only 44 per cent of the animal health services consumed by livestock herders, who themselves provided 47 per cent of the services. The remaining nine per cent was supplied by persons who are unqualified or whose qualifications could not be determined. Professionals provided two-thirds of preventive services, but only one-fifth of curative services. In Mukono district, animal health professionals of various levels of qualification treated one-third of the sick animals. But in the Mbarara counties, the percentages receiving professional attention ranged from 4–14 per cent. Our analysis suggests that herders would make increased use of paraprofessional providers if distances were reduced, but Mbarara herders are already using full vets at a higher rate than are farmers in Mukono.

Livestock producers in Uganda do not value full vets for their qualifications. Full vets are called and their higher fees are paid only when the herder requires their skill to handle certain types of cases and procedures that are beyond the capabilities of the paraprofessionals. When we analyzed the fees herders paid for curative interventions, we found no relationship with the qualifications of the provider. Instead, higher fees were correlated with the procedure that entailed higher drug costs. For these services they are prepared to pay extra and travel some distance, but they will not absorb the costs for the services of a full vet for more standard treatments. The implications are clear: animal health paraprofessionals have a secure market in southern Uganda, and this market probably can be expanded. But in many areas, veterinarians may be close to the limits of the demand for their high quality services. To expand their practices, vets will have to develop networks with paraprofessionals, so as to get referrals of special cases from them, or will have to sell their services for a similar price and be as accessible to the herders as the paraprofessionals are.

The grouping of preventive services with mixed public-private goods attributes has received top priority from both herders and vets. In the case of vets, the priority given to these services has been shown to have a positive correlation with the activities in which vets were engaged. This survey has also shown that herders consumed just over half of the possible amount of preventive treatment for cattle. Despite the public goods attributes of these services therefore, immunizations, vector control, and the control of helminthiasis are seen to have high private value among the stakeholders in Uganda. This is a clear indication that these services would probably form the heart of private veterinary service in Uganda. Already the control of ticks and helminthiasis is a private sector concern. On the basis of the findings in this study, there is enough evidence to suggest that immunizations against diseases of national concern would be adequately provided under a private delivery system. This is good news because much of the volume of the animal health service in Uganda still consists of immunizations. The high priority given to this service justifies the anticipated government divestment of its provision and funding, at least partially, to the private sector.

This move would be an important step toward ensuring that private veterinary practice takes off. It is expected to provide pioneer veterinary practitioners in Uganda with ready clients and early profits, thus providing the capital required to establish themselves in service areas requiring greater start-up investments. Private veterinarians cooperate with the government by delivering immunizations on a contract basis, contingent on carrying out disease surveillance while in the field. Thus, professional values and priorities would be reinforced with a concrete economic incentive. Although vets have given preventive services of a pure public goods nature the third position in priority, we cannot be confident that their professional commitment is strong enough to withstand the very negative view herders have of these services without firm government support. A very wide difference also exists between herders and vets on the issue of animal nutrition. Whereas livestock farmers gave a high value to animal nutrition, vets gave it the very last priority. However, since the improvement of animal nutrition is a private good and provides profitable opportunities to the vets, it is expected that the market will make private vets responsive to the demands of the herders.

7 Veterinary Professionals in Senegal: Allocation of Priorities and Working Behavior

Cheikh Ly

In 1990, Umali *et al.* concluded that the public sector clearly dominated the livestock service sector in developing countries. After six years of halting privatization, what is the situation in the market for livestock services? The literature on livestock subsector privatization has grown rapidly with the progressive involvement and financial support of international donors. It continues to consist largely of mere descriptions of privatization models, issues, and constraints, or of relatively narrow policy pieces (Akakpo 1992; Cheneau 1985; Leonard 1987; Leonard 1993; Sandford 1983; Umali *et al.* 1992). Sandford (1987) has also raised key issues on organizational ways of improving animal health and husbandry. However, few studies offer complete assessments of the privatization models, especially in French speaking Africa (Akakpo 1992; Toure 1992; Sar 1993; VSF 1994; Zessin 1996; FAO 1997). This study hopes to offer a small corrective.

Senegalese privatization, like all others, has its own permutations. During the colonial and national government eras, government intervention was the leading force in livestock production and marketing systems. Today, however, new organizations and new institutional rules are reshaping incentives for participants in the livestock subsector. Reform of the veterinary profession into a privatized system of animal health and husbandry services has become a major issue, but corporatism and tradition have conspired to limit its progress.

We seek to evaluate the intensity, speed and manner in which veterinary professionals are adapting to the new situation, and how adequately they are intervening in the market for veterinary services. We introduce the subject through an overview of market making efforts in Senegal's veterinary sector, and then place those efforts in a context of theoretical elaboration on professionalism. Next, we present the results of two surveys that elicited the views of Senegalese veterinary caregivers and receivers. Finally, and with the survey results in mind, we explore the case of veterinary medical doctors in a market that resembles the classic 'market for lemons.'

Historical Evolution toward Privatization

As in other parts of Africa, the 'Great Third World Depression' has affected Senegal. Following the oil shocks in the 1970s and early 1980s, tight monetary and fiscal policies in the industrial countries contributed to trigger this recession, which has deepened since then. Senegal was hit both by rising global prices for its imports, especially oil, and falling prices for its commodity exports. After a phase of heavy borrowing and worldwide interest rate increases, the debt service obligations have skyrocketed. A large portion of export earnings is still dedicated to debt service, and the general economic crisis continues.

In the face of sustained and severe imbalances in the economy, Senegal has accepted structural adjustment programs under the advice of the Bretton Woods institutions. After a stabilization program in 1979, the period 1980–84 was one of economic and financial recovery, followed by a long-term program of structural adjustment that ended in 1992. Today, the country is at another turning point since the persisting economic crisis continues to demand radical changes in government interventions and methods.

The first targets of the adjustment efforts, the agricultural sector and its livestock component, have been key areas for policy applications collectively known as Senegal's 'New Agricultural Policy.' In addition, new institutional arrangements reduce direct government involvement while promoting various private sector schemes. Structural adjustment programs to reduce expenditures, combined with a worsening of the economic crisis, are generating pressures for an institutional and economic environment that would dramatically change the nature of public/private interventions that promote agricultural sector development while meeting financing requirements. Since the domestic currency devaluation in January 1994, an entirely new economic setting is generating its own constraints. The specific problems encountered in the livestock subsector consequently have been shaped and aggravated by this broader economic situation.

In Senegal, the delivery of veterinary services was dominated first by the French colonial administration and then by government institutions until 1986. The French colonial legacy has led to a wide range of governmental and parastatal interventions and services from animal health care and the management of prophylactic campaigns against 'exotic pathologies,' to the enforcement of public hygiene regulations and vector controls, to the implementation of livestock development projects and training. So far, performance has been poor and delivery of veterinary services has collapsed for many reasons. On one hand, operational efficiency of government services has decreased, amplified by a general misallocation of scarce human and financial resources; on the other hand, Senegal's fiscal constraints would have challenged even the most efficient of services.

Starting in 1986 with the creation of a special government institution, the *Secrétariat d'Ètat aux Resources Animales*, new rules and institutional reforms dominated efforts for change. Then, from 1987, donor pressures and the structural adjustment agenda have led to a consensus on the need to privatize veterinary service delivery systems. The government publicized this new orientation in its 1987 *Plan d'Actions*. The consensus, renewed in November 1992, is in the mainstream of the new organizational framework favored by donors like the World Bank, the European Economic Community and GTZ, the German development agency. These organizations are in broad agreement that Senegal should set up a new balance between private endeavors and government interventions and should develop new regulatory methods to mediate relations in this new public/private environment.

Today, the structure of the livestock subsector in Senegal is characterized by its broad spectrum of participants. Their objectives and incentives are expressed in various operations of production, consumption, and transaction. The veterinary services, composed of the animal health and animal husbandry services, are essential to the life and the future of the livestock subsector. An estimated 579 veterinary personnel care for Senegal's 4,021,000 Veterinary Livestock Units (VLU),[1] which leaves an average of 7,000 VLU per caregiver. Government veterinary personnel comprise 76 per cent of the registered veterinary workforce.

In 1995, the veterinary public sector was composed of 49 Doctors of Veterinary Medicine (DVM), nine animal scientists, 87 middle level paraprofessionals (ITEs), and 273 low level technicians (ATEs). Laboratories, universities, or training institutions employed a dozen

1. One VLU is equivalent to one cow, one camel, two horses, two pigs, two donkeys, ten mall ruminants, or 100 fowl.

veterinarians. Simultaneously, the private sector was composed of 49 veterinary doctors, 26 middle level technicians, and 61 low level technicians and veterinary nurses. In 1984, only two veterinarians were running private practices in the capital city. Presently, practitioners are starting private businesses because of the recent freeze on government recruiting of young graduates and the squeeze on personnel expenditures required by structural adjustment measures (Toure 1992). About 30 private DVMs were registered in 1996.

A growing number of recently graduated veterinarians are unemployed. They are sometimes involved in various types of private interventions, or have gone on for further training that too often is a disguised unemployed status. With fewer veterinary doctors working in the public sector and a growing number entering the private sector, a more balanced public/private environment is replacing the public sector's traditional dominance. Veterinarians and high level technicians in the private sector have licenses for veterinary care and prevention, excepting vaccinations for Rinderpest and Contagious Bovine Pleuropneumonia (CBPP) that are still under government monopoly[2]. Private veterinarians may also import veterinary drugs and supplies for wholesale distribution and retail sales. Drug imports by private businesses with no government involvement grew from 320 million CFA francs in 1988 to 441 in 1991 and 1.6 billion CFA in 1996 (Toure 1992; US$1 = 500 CFA). Except for twenty-four vaccines produced by the Veterinary Research Laboratory of Dakar, local production of veterinary drugs is absent.

Meanwhile, attempts are being made to create an institutional environment that would promote privatization of the veterinary profession. Before creation of the *Ordre des Docteurs Vétérinaires du Sénégal* in 1993, veterinarians had the opportunity to join the *Association Nationale des Vétérinaires Sénégalais.* The *Association*, however, had no special responsibility in the regulation of a profession that was essentially a government domain. By contrast, the *Ordre* is now expected to exercise regulatory powers on the profession and play a decisive role in the reform of the livestock subsector.

In addition, livestock producers are also creating groups to promote livestock activities. Known collectively as the *Groupements d'inter't Èconomique*, these groups have organized themselves into a federation

2. In the case of the high-level technicians, it is more accurate to consider their licenses as mere administrative authorizations that are transitory since they have to be renewed each year by the government livestock services.

covering the whole country. The *groupements* lobby for improved herder production and marketing opportunities, and this federation is the producer representative in meetings with government and other private institutions. The exponential growth in the number of producer groups underscores the changes occurring in the sector: there were 1,500 registered groups in 1993, against only 100 in 1987 (Sar 1993). Keeping with this trend, the government has privatized its main livestock marketing parastatal organization, the *Société d'Exploitation des Ressources Animales du Sénégal* (SERAS).

Senegal's veterinary sector continues to be dominated by government intervention. Some private sector participation exists in clinical care, delivery of vaccination, vector control and artificial insemination delivery. The private sector dominates only veterinary pharmaceutical marketing and distribution with some government intervention. However, new organizational measures and institutional devices are creating a variety of settings for the pharmaceutical veterinary supply system. Privatization in Senegal is based on an official philosophy of incrementally increasing private sector opportunities. With time, private and village producers' groups, industry branch committees, and private suppliers of veterinary care are expected to become leading forces.

The sequence of events reveals that high-level bureaucrats who have been influenced by ad hoc theories fashionable among international aid and financing institutions have driven the privatization framework. The implications, however, are felt locally by producers and veterinary workers. The acceptance of privatization by local practitioners does not reflect an internalization of the notion that markets outperform hierarchies. Observing that innovative actions often have a high mortality rate in a difficult socioeconomic and institutional environment, veterinarians are skeptical. The experience of veterinarians in sub-Saharan Africa, whose unemployment risks are growing, lends credence to the Senegalese veterinarian's thinly disguised 'wait and see' attitude.

The proposed privatization schemes are often considered unavoidable evils that will only temporarily disrupt the ancient order of things. Veterinarians commonly perceive the new situation as a passing phase in which a few privileged beneficiaries receive special economic opportunities. They do not view it as a new foundation leading to lasting professional reforms and real changes in the livestock subsector. Such an impression is reflected in the warnings for more cautious privatization at a 'homeopathic dosage,' recommended by the 10th Africa Regional Conference of the International Office for Epizootics (IOE) in 1993. It is also reflected in demands for a selective strategy that ensures as its top priority continued job opportunities for veterinarians.

The results presented in this chapter lead to the conclusion that a privatization model appropriate to Senegal's livestock industry would be carried out by government veterinarians in association with private veterinarians who are active members of a professional self-regulatory organization like the *Ordre*. Such an organization would support privatization schemes currently being mooted in consultation with international donors, but urges several new actions that would clarify professional responsibilities of full veterinarians, and would create market and social incentives to promote these responsibilities. To date, paraprofessionals have not received sufficient attention, especially in the starting loan packages. It appears, unfortunately, that the privatization process in most African countries has focused on the DVMs, whereas the real action may be at other levels in the animal health system.

Very much suspected of atavistic conservatism, veterinarians nevertheless have a strategic role to play. Unfortunately, they have not demonstrated that their potential role as driving forces deserves to be strengthened by structural adjustment programs. Moreover, their self-regulatory board continues to struggle under the challenge of conquering and consolidating its role in the regulation of the veterinary profession. In that process, conflicts may arise from the fact that the technicians' organizations are also challenged to ensure that their members will not become victims of new organizational decisions brought with the recent and progressive empowerment of the veterinarians. Despite the lethargy of paraprofessional organizations and their apparent interest only in pre-retirement financial packages, they must be induced to recognize that they have an additional crucial role: ensuring that their members will not be driven out of business or exposed to unfavorable regulations forged by their competitors. A discussion of professionalism and principal/agent theory will provide a framework for analysis of these issues.

Professionalism and Private Veterinary Practice in Senegal

The nature of contractual arrangements and the strength of each actor's incentives shape the dynamics of veterinary service delivery. Senegal's privatization model assumes that markets outperform hierarchies and that potential participants will respond to new financial and administrative policies that promote entry into a more privatized market. The expectations, behaviors, and responses of these potential entrants to the forms, types, and prices of veterinary service delivery are, therefore, shaping the pace and also efficacy of privatization. The actual behavior and priorities of participants shape the distribution of the functions that comprise production, exchange, and consumption of veterinary services. In other words, herders and veterinary professionals alike consider the new institutional and market environment when deciding whether to demand or supply veterinary services. These two actors share a principal/agent relationship, and this relationship is at the core of their supply and demand choices.

Arrow (1985) describes agency as a pervasive fact of economic life. An agency relationship arises when one individual, the principal, delegates to another individual, the agent, authority to take actions that are expected to enhance the well being or utility of each. In the classic example, patients are principals who delegate carefully circumscribed authority to their agents, medical doctors (Dranove and White 1987). Principal/agent theory is a useful analytic tool for situations or organizational arrangements where a principal must act through an agent who has specialized information. The agent is activated by a mechanism Train (1991) calls 'incentive compatibility,' whereby the agent has an incentive make his or her goals consistent with those of the principal. Where goals are consistent, the agent has an incentive to perform effectively and report truthfully to the principal.

Agency relationships are also naturally found in the realm of livestock service provision, for example where veterinarians treat animals or make recommendations for herd management. The principal, who is the herder, does not have his agent's (the veterinarian's) training or skill, so the herder cannot perfectly monitor his veterinarian's actions. Social costs can result from information asymmetries between such principals and agents. Indeed, although the principal can observe the contract's outcome (for example, his cow survives), he cannot determine for sure whether this outcome is the result of his agent's action (the correct medication was provided) or some exogenous uncertainty (the cow was recovering on its own).

The principal/agent problem combines two inextricable elements: risk sharing and differential information (Arrow 1985). Both the principal and agent share a common source of revenue when the contract is fulfilled, but they also share the risk of losing it in case of failure. When the common source is the animal owned by a herder seeking veterinary assistance, the risk of the animal dying if the veterinarian fails to fulfill the contract is therefore shared by the herder (principal) and his or her veterinary agent. The basic hypothesis is that information asymmetries create incentive problems that inhibit the working of firms, markets, and mixed market/hierarchy forms of contracting (Zald 1987). The policymaker's task is to understand the nature of these incentive problems and craft economic institutions that reduce them. Such institutions are considered, in the words of Williamson (1984, 1990), 'evolutionary products of a fascinating series of organizational innovations.'

Thus, the challenge is to maximize efficiency when creating or improving economic mechanisms and arrangements based on agency relationships. The objective is to craft an economic environment, made up of both the market and public or private institutional arrangements, that minimizes agency costs and enhances the creation of contracts that would lead to socially (and individually) optimal outcomes. Reducing transaction costs is fundamental to this process. Of course, ideal outcomes with zero transaction costs are achievable only in the unrealistic world of zero cost information flow and perfect information (Pratt and Zeckhauser 1985). With divergent objectives between the principal and his or her agent, the best we can hope for is an institutional environment that helps to align objectives and match incentives between principal and agent, thereby reducing the principal's monitoring costs and the likelihood of principal/agent conflicts.

This, unfortunately, is easier said than done. Short-term transactions are often replete with uncertain and unpredictable behavior because the contract is similar to a single iteration game. Decision theory shows that punishing an errant agent is very difficult in this situation, so the agent has an incentive to provide defective or low quality services. The honest agent also suffers in such a scenario. Since he cannot credibly convince the principal that in fact he will provide quality service, he must accept a price lowered to reflect the herder's risk that the agent is a crook. However, in the real world case of veterinary personnel, herder and veterinarian are in an iterated game. That is, the veterinarian repeatedly provides services for the same livestock producers or, at least, in the same geographical area. This service delivery repetition often leads to better outcomes— the herder receives higher quality service and the veterinarian receives a higher payment— because agents can be punished in these conditions (or, more positively, because an honest agent's reputation can spread).

Contracts can be expected to yield still more efficient outcomes when competition among agents is added to the mix. Herder interests and priorities are less likely to suffer when the herder can easily replace his agent, his veterinarian. When both competition and reputation are present, agency theory predicts that markets can achieve optimal outcomes without formal regulations or third party intervention. Nevertheless, even in such a scenario, the principal's choice is not automatically optimal because his rationality is bounded and his behavior is 'intendedly rational, but only limitedly so' (Williamson 1990; Simon 1982). Personal judgment shapes behavior, even in iterated games.

The principal/agent relationship in the veterinary services subsector is further complicated when a second principal, with priorities that might differ from those of any given individual herder, enters the mix. This second principal is society, which expects epizootics to be controlled and animal products to be safe (Dranove and White 1987; Pratt and Zeckhauser 1985). Fully trained Doctors of Veterinary Medicine (DVMs) are challenged by this dual principal/agent relationship. A paraprofessional is usually bound solely by a private contract with the herder. However, a second contract binds the professional veterinarian who seeks to provide identical services to the same principal. The second contract is a professional understanding between the veterinarian and society, because society realizes that professional veterinary interventions can dramatically affect society. DVM social functions include controlling diseases that are transmissible between humans and animals, animal product hygiene for human consumption, protection of the national livestock endowment, and ensuring sustainability of livestock products supplies, such as meat, milk, and animal products.

This dual principal/agent relationship is expected to yield specific outcomes. First, because veterinarians are agents for society as well as for herders or other producers in the livestock production system, they have a broader set of obligations and responsibilities than do paraprofessionals. We expect that both values and actual work practices will reflect these differing obligations and responsibilities. Second, since full veterinarians with professional values are expected to deliver public services in fulfillment of their social contract, they can reasonably expect some form of government protection or subsidy. Any veterinary system that envisions wider involvement of private practitioners must ensure both that professional values exist among the veterinary corps, and that they are rewarded.

Historically in Europe and America, the veterinary professions and their regulatory bodies have been important intermediaries in these kinds of agency relationships, assuring that professional values are respected on behalf of both client and society. The question that arises is whether animal health practice in contemporary Senegal reflects these professional values. Evaluating market and institutional incentives that shape the nature and intensity of professional behavior is thus a core issue in an evaluation of the privatization process. The working behavior and the values attached to veterinary tasks by professionals in the public sector, on one hand, and those in the private sector on the other hand, are parameters of their conduct in face of privatization. It is expected that professionals with more rigorous formal qualifications and a stronger relationship to the public sector will emphasize the more publicly oriented aspects of veterinary medicine.

RESEARCH METHOD

A major constraint in the study of sub-Saharan livestock systems is the paucity of quantitative and qualitative information on its structure and operations (Umali *et al.* 1990). This study seeks to begin to fill that gap and offers a more rigorous alternative to the all too common use of simple expert evaluation. Primary data is drawn from two cross-sectional descriptive surveys; one explored the activities and values of veterinary caregivers in Senegal, and the other was directed at livestock herders.

The population of Senegalese veterinary personnel falls into three categories. Veterinary doctors, or DVMs, have six years of specialized training beyond their baccalaureate degree. In addition, there are two paraprofessional categories: *Ingénieurs des Travaux d'Èlevage* (ITEs) who have completed a three-year post-baccalaureate course and are recognized as high level technicians or near professionals, and livestock nurses called *Agents des Travaux d'Èlevage* (ATEs), who have completed three years of training beyond secondary school and reside at lower levels of the technical hierarchy. Our study has not included other auxiliaries such as knowledgeable young herders who, with support from nongovernmental organizations (NGOs), provide some important basic primary animal care and technical support at the village level.

The population of DVMs, ITEs, and ATEs working in the private sector was constructed first by evaluating lists of veterinary doctors and technicians registered with the Department of Livestock Services or the Veterinary Board. Next, non-registered professionals were located by cross checking the official lists with those of the technicians' organizations. Private veterinary practices are new and, as with young businesses in all sectors, there is a high failure rate. Of the 177 names so

Table 7.1 Animal Caregivers in Senegal

Status	Qualification				
	DVM	ITE	ATE	Total	Total (per cent)
PVP	31	10	18	59	44.4
GVP	24	19	31	74	55.6
Total	55	29	49	133	100
Total (%)	41.4	21.8	36.8	100	100

complied, 106[3] (61 per cent) were confirmed to be in effective practice. Of these, 59 (56 per cent) were selected for interviews (Table 7.1). Since privatization is a time of uncertainty and change, a large sub-sample of private sector workers was required to capture divergent trends. The majority of private practitioners work in or around the capital city, Dakar. We selected from those outside the city in order to exclude practices that serve urban family pets.

We determined the population of practicing government professionals and paraprofessionals through a far more straightforward evaluation and confirmation of government lists and selected 74 (17 per cent) for interviews, taking care to ensure a representative distribution of status, qualification and location. Preliminary analysis of government personnel revealed a rather homogeneous population that justified this relatively small sub-sample. Data collection was organized from February through September 1995. Direct and formal interviews were held with most respondents. Mailing was only a last resort when a planned interview was not possible due to time constraints and distance. The questionnaire contained eleven sets of questions that elicited information on three broad topics: self-description, behavior, and values of the practitioner.

Herders comprise the demand side of the market. Understanding their views, we hypothesized, would provide a perspective through which we can evaluate the priorities and behavior of veterinary professionals and paraprofessionals— who comprise the market's supply side. To this end, we interviewed a sample of ordinary herders. The results of this survey are discussed extensively elsewhere in this book. Veterinary auxiliaries have a unique role to play in the privatization process, and they are evaluated in the other chapter. Because they are not major

3. 49 DVMs, 5 ITEs, and 11 ATEs.

players in defining the demand or supply of veterinary services, however, they have not been explicitly included in this analysis.

A major pastoral production zone in Senegal known as *the zone sylvo-pastorale* served as our field area. The pastoralists living in that area mostly belong to the *Fulbe dieri* subgroup of the *Fulani*, and herd cattle and small ruminants (sheep and goats) across natural pastures from one water borehole to the next. Pastoralists must register either as producer groups or as individuals before using the water borehole network. This registration list served as our herder population. Three hundred forty-eight pastoralists who lived in 73 villages around the city of Linguere (Ly 1997) and whose herds traveled among twelve boreholes, were chosen by cluster sampling.

The herder survey elicited herder priorities for a variety of livestock related activities. Each herder was asked to rank ten activities, each depicted pictorially on a card, in order of decreasing importance. Half of the ten activities were government-dominated interventions (government provision of veterinary paraprofessionals, bovine immunizations, genetic improvement, feed and salt lick supplementation, and the Rinderpest-CBPP campaign), and five were private dominated (internal parasites control, external parasites control, literacy training, small ruminants immunizations and provision of veterinary auxiliaries).

RESULTS AND DISCUSSION

The typical veterinary caregiver was forty years old.[4] ITEs were older than ATEs followed by DVMs who, surprisingly and especially in the private sector, were the youngest (34). Among ITEs, those in the private sector were older (45). Public or private status generally is not significantly related to age, but qualification is strongly correlated. There is a dramatic public/private difference in geographic distribution: GVPs are dispersed fairly evenly throughout the country, while the bulk of PVPs work in the densely populated areas of Dakar (45 per cent) and the Peanut Basin (27.5 per cent). Only 7.5 per cent and 12.5 per cent of the PVP and GVP samples respectively occupy the rural pastoral areas of Northern Senegal. Differences in animal health work experience exist, but with low levels of significance and large standard deviations. Professionals as a whole typically have 94 months of experience; disaggregating by status, DVMs, ITEs, and ATEs have 55, 111, and 171 months of

4. Standard Deviation for all age-based means is eight years or fewer.

experience respectively. Government practitioners in general have more work experience than private practitioners, especially when we include the time many private practitioners spent in government service. Duration in public service (including that of those currently in the private sector) is only 90 months for DVMs, compared with 222 for ITEs and 164 for ATEs.

Although the government is trying to encourage public professionals to enter the private sector, only 31 per cent of those in public service planned to leave soon for private practice, and more than half of these (57.9 per cent) were ITEs. Since there are more ITEs than DVMs, however, these statistics veil the aspirations of different categories of caregivers: 72.7 per cent of the ATEs who are GVP are *not* planning to become private against 15.2 per cent of the DVMs. The vast majority of private professionals have their own businesses (83.1 per cent) which, along with NGOs, hire the remainder. The duration in private practice is also a fairly consistent 43 ± 28 months. All of them offer curative assistance and sell medicine and vaccines. Usually, each runs his own clinic with the help of nonspecialized family members, but without other veterinary professionals. For the civil servants, the mean duration of work is 81± 9 months.

Veterinary Values: Herders, Practitioners, and Theoretical Ideals

One way to anticipate which sectors of the market could be effectively privatized is by determining which services are highly valued by service demanders. Understanding how the values of various providers diverge offers one way to anticipate the structure of competition between private and public vets with varying formal qualifications. Comparing the values of service demanders and suppliers with theoretically derived values will help us to anticipate possible friction between the emerging structure of the private veterinary market and society's need for professional veterinary interventions. Senegalese herders' values are discussed briefly (they are examined carefully in Chapter 9), and a set of professional ideals is quickly deduced. In this context, the values and service priorities of professional practitioners are carefully evaluated.

Each herder ranked priorities without influence from interviewers. Individual farmer answers vary considerably from the aggregate list presented in Table 7.2, but when we reduce the list from ten services to two broad categories that reflect private and public needs, variations are substantially reduced. Results show that herders consistently rank their private oriented needs more highly than public oriented needs (Table

Table 7.2 Senegal Herders and Their Priorities

Service	Rank	Mean
Alphabetization	1	4.15 ± 2.84
Small ruminant vaccines	2	4.57 ± 2.73
Auxiliaries	3	4.91 ± 2.40
External parasites	4	4.96 ± 3.00
Bovine vaccines	5	4.97 ± 2.83
Internal parasites	6	5.77 ± 2.48
Feed	7	5.78 ± 2.40
Public veterinary profess.	8	5.83 ± 3.11
Genetics	9	6.32 ± 2.46
Rinderpest/CBPP control	10	7.75 ± 2.69

n = 348 herders; Rank 1 is highest priority

Table 7.3 Herders and Aggregated Needs

Needs aggregated	Sample	
	Rank	Mean
Private-oriented needs, Alphabetization, Small ruminant immunizations, Auxiliaries, External parasites control, Internal parasites control	1	24.35 ± 4.57
Public-oriented needs, Public veterinary profess., Bovine immunizations, Rinderpest/CBPP control, Feed, Genetics	2	30.65 ± 4.56

7.3). Herders did not value government high-input activities highly, especially those that are public goods or have low specificity. This is because service failure in these areas is neither intense nor visible to individual herders (Israel 1987). For example, both CBPP and Rinderpest are considered low-level concerns. However, perceptions of herd immunity are greater than the reality, so the priorities attached to those two traditional inoculations is low. Thus, the low value placed by herders on these bovine preventive health activities reflects the success of government programs rather than indifference by herders. But it also shows that herders will not pay for these services in a privatized market; if these socially (and, in fact, individually) valuable services are to be performed, government must continue to take the lead.

By contrast, those services most highly valued by herders are the ones whose benefits are both visible and clearly accrue to the herder personally. Literacy is the top priority for herders, not only because it facilitates promotion of livestock production but especially because it elevates the herder's social position. Small ruminant immunization and basic services performed by veterinary auxiliaries ranked second and third respectively, are also areas where the benefits can be clearly seen and relative costs easily calculated. Analysis of herder priorities shows that herders have little regard for services that are directed at the population of herders in general rather than each herder in particular. Their consistent preference for services whose benefits are clearly visible also leads them to assign relatively low values to services that are in fact valuable to each individual purchaser but whose effects are more difficult to isolate. A herder's individual, individuated perspective is appropriate for privatization; additional information supplied by a professional organization they respect and trust might engender a change in preferences that conforms more closely to a theoretically deduced social ideal.

In order to deduce such an ideal, we divided veterinary functions into four subtypes: preventive, curative, promotive, and public hygiene functions. Preventive functions are of three categories: immunizations with vaccines and sera, vector control (ticks, *tsetse* flies) and disease control (quarantine, animal transfer surveillance). Curative functions are clinical interventions on already sick animals (inpatient and outpatient visits). Promotive activities allow productivity improvement through interventions and changes into livestock management and production systems. Public hygiene (or public utility) functions include zoonosises prevention, food inspection and public hygiene, and health. Production, training, information and extension for technology transfer are also included, as is livestock inputs marketing (feed, semen, animal health inputs).

Theoretically derived predictions expect that investments in preventive functions will yield the greatest reductions in morbidity or mortality and the biggest increase in productivity, followed in order by promotive, curative and public hygiene functions. This ordering can logically be deduced as the ideal priority ranking from a purely professional point of view. Livestock resources need first to be protected as productive factors, repositories of wealth, mediums of exchange or food. Then, productivity must be improved by promotive functions to the benefit of herders and society. Further, if diseases appear, they will be fought by curative actions. Finally, public hygiene functions aim at a safer environment for livestock resources and human health.

We first asked veterinary practitioners to rank the four functions. The actual priorities of veterinarians are quite similar to the priorities we deduced above. DVMs as a group match this ranking order exactly (Table 7.4). The results, as further disaggregated in Tables 7.5, 7.6, and 7.7, are perhaps most striking for the consistency with which practi-

Table 7.4 Ranking of Veterinary Functions for the Sample and the Different Qualifications

Functions	Sample		DVM		ITE		ATE	
	weight	rank	weight	rank	weight	rank	weight	rank
Preventive	1.6 ± 0.9	1	1.7 ± 0.8	1	1.7 ± 0.9	1	1.6 ± 0.8	1
Curative	2.5 ± 1.1	2	2.8 ± 1.1	3	2.4 ± 0.8	2	2.2 ± 1.1	2
Public utility	2.8 ± 1.0	3	2.9 ± 1.1	4	2.8 ± 1.1	3	3.2 ± 0.8	4
Promotive	3.0 ± 1.0	4	2.5 ± 0.9	2	3.1 ± 1.2	4	3.0 ± 0.9	3

NB: unweighted cases

Table 7.5 Ranking of Preventive Activities

Activities	DVM				ITE				ATE				Total	
	PVP		GVP		PVP		GVP		PVP		GVP			
	w	r	w	r	w	r	w	r	w	r	w	r	w	r
Rinderpest	3.4	2	3.1	1	4.0	4	3.8	2	3.9	3	2.4	1	3.1	2
BCPP	3.8	3	3.5	2	9.0	9	4.5	7	3.9	3	2.6	2	3.6	3
Other diseases	3.0	1	4.5	5	1.0	1	4.2	4	1.2	1	3.4	3	2.9	1
Vector control	3.9	4	6.1	9	3.3	3	5.8	8	3.0	2	5.0	5	4.3	4
Animal move surveillance	4.2	5	5.9	8	6.0	7	4.4	6	5.2	5	6.1	8	5.5	8
Sanitary inspection	5.1	7	4.3	4	4.0	4	3.8	2	6.2	7	4.5	4	4.7	5
Regulation	5.9	9	3.5	2	4.7	5	4.0	4	5.4	6	5.8	7	5.2	6
Relations w/ professionals	5.2	8	5.4	6	6.0	7	6.6	9	6.8	8	6	9	6.1	9
Epidemiological surveillance	5.0	6	5.4	6	2.7	2	3.5	1	8.1	9	5.3	6	5.3	7

w = weight and r = rank

Table 7.6 Ranking of Promotive and Public Utility Activities

	DVM				ITE				ATE				Total	
	PVP		GVP		PVP		GVP		PVP		GVP			
	w	r	W	r	w	R	W	r	W	r	W	r	w	r
Promotive Activities														
Genetic improvement	3.8	5	5.5	10	5.7	10	5.3	9	2.8	2	2.5	2	3.5	4
Biotechnology	5.2	11	3.8	5	1.0	1	5.7	10	3.6	7	2.0	1	3.2	2
Feed inputs trade	2.4	1	4.0	6	1.7	3	3.0	4	2.0	1	2.7	3	2.6	1
Pharmaceutical trade	2.8	2	5.1	8	1.3	2	2.4	2	3.2	6	4.0	5	3.3	3
Vaccines trade	3.5	3	5.0	7	3.0	4	2.4	2	2.8	2	4.1	6	3.5	4
Range management	4.5	8	3.2	4	4.3	5	6.2	11	4.9	8	3.1	4	4.0	7
Feed extension	4.6	6	2.7	2	4.5	6	4.5	5	5.4	9	4.1	6	4.3	9

Hygiene & care extension	4.5	8	5.4	9	5.3	9	4.7	6	7.4	10	5.0	9	5.3	10
Training	4.3	6	2.8	3	4.5	6	4.7	6	7.8	11	7.1	11	6.1	11
Research	4.7	10	6.9	11	4.5	6	2.3	1	2.9	4	5.9	10	3.6	6
Projects	3.5	3	2.6	1	7.0	11	4.8	8	3.0	5	4.2	8	4.1	8
Public Utility Activities														
Sanitary inspection	1.8	1	1.9	1	1.7	1	2.1	1	1.3	1	1.4	1	1.6	1
Regulation enforcement	2.1	2	1.9	1	2.7	2	2.3	2	1.9	2	2.1	2	2.1	2
Regulation improvement	2.5	3	3.1	4	3.0	4	2.7	3	3.3	3	3.0	3	3.0	3
Relations w/ professionals	3.4	4	2.8	3	2.7	2	3.7	4	3.5	4	3.0	3	3.1	4

W = weight and r = rank

Table 7.7 Curative Activities

Activities	DVM				ITE				ATE				Total	
	PVP		GVP		PVP		GVP		PVP		GVP			
	w	r	w	r	w	r	w	r	w	r	w	r	w	r
Acute diseases	2.5	2	2.5	3	2.2	2	3.0	3	1.4	1	2.5	3	2.4	2
Chronic diseases	3.1	4	2.9	4	3.0	4	3.0	3	1.5	2	2.8	4	2.8	4
Parasites	1.7	1	2.1	1	1.2	1	2.0	1	3.2	3	2.4	2	2.2	1
Diagnosis	2.5	2	2.4	2	2.8	3	2.3	2	3.5	4	2.2	1	2.5	3

w = weight and r = rank

Table 7.8 Ranking of Veterinary Functions by Public, Private Professionals

Functions	Government veterinary professionals		Private veterinary professionals	
	weight	rank	weight	rank
Curative	2.5 ± 1.1	2	2.1 ± 1.0	2
Preventive	1.6 ± 0.9	1	1.7 ± 0.8	1
Public utility	2.8 ± 0.9	3	3.3 ± 0.9	4
Promotive	3.0 ± 1.0	4	2.9 ± 0.9	3

NB: unweighted cases (n = 127)

tioners, whether public or private and with different levels of training, ranked each intervention or service. Our interest is in evaluating differences among categories of caregivers. This analysis, however, should be understood in the context of broad homogeneity.

Public and private professionals agreed that preventive and curative functions are the top two veterinary priorities (Table 7.8). GVPs placed public hygiene functions third, which is consistent with government's emphasis on public hygiene issues since colonial times. By contrast, and perhaps *because* of governmental emphasis on public hygiene issues, PVPs assigned promotive activities the third position. This perhaps shows how interest in filling a market niche can shape professional values. Within the GVP category, DVMs so consistently ranked curative activities as the least important task that their aggregate ranking for each of the other three other tasks is higher than the ITE or ATE rankings for those tasks (Table 7.9). Among private professionals, ATEs value curative functions far more highly than DVMs, and DVMs place a much greater value on promotive activities than ITEs. Across the public/private divide, those with lower formal qualifications consider curative functions more important than do DVMs.

Caregivers were also asked about the relative importance of specific interventions within each of the four broad veterinary services. Again, the most notable result is homogeneity of preferences among public and private practitioners, and independent of training level, regarding particular interventions in three out of the four services. The exception is promotive activities, in which each category of provider by status and public/private sector ranked the eleven promotive activities quite differently (Table 7.6). To the extent that differences exist, the GVP rankings tend to favor public goods and those of PVP private goods.

One explanation for this unanticipated homogeneity of values is that the same set of ancient views, in which government is solely responsible for activities with a public goods character, shapes the outlook of all

Table 7.9 Ranking of Veterinary Functions According to Status

Qualification Status	Government Veterinary Professionals	Private Veterinary Professionals	Total
Preventive Activities[1]			
DVM	1.35	1.87	1.67
ITE	1.92	1.40	1.70
ATE	1.56	1.73	1.61
Total	1.60	1.70	1.64
Curative Activities[2]			
DVM	3.45	2.42	2.82
ITE	2.46	2.20	2.35
ATE	2.33	1.73	2.16
Total	2.54	2.10	2.36
Promotive Activities[1]			
DVM	2.70	2.45	2.55
ITE	2.92	3.40	3.13
ATE	3.11	2.91	3.05
Total	3.01	2.87	2.95
Public Utility Activities[2]			
DVM	2.40	3.27	2.92
ITE	2.69	3.00	2.83
ATE	3.00	3.64	3.18
Total	2.84	3.35	3.04

Weighted cases (n = 211)
[1] no statistical difference in ranking for main effect of status
[2] statistical difference in ranking ($p < 0.001$)

caregivers. In Senegal, the veterinary hierarchy has been clear-cut since the colonial period. Technical and administrative roles, domains of interventions, and contracts with herders have been cast in and distributed through this rigid hierarchical mold, and in important ways the activities and priorities of caregivers continue to reflect this traditional ideology. However, the broad category 'curative services' and (among the components of promotive interventions) areas valued differently by different professional status groups, are areas in which the traditional veterinary corps either has not been actively engaged or has not taken a consistent position. Therefore, it is in these areas especially that other sources of value formation, such as professional training, might generate the greatest difference among different categories of service providers. A second source of values includes the pressures, incentives, and opportunities that exist on the job.

When analyzing service provision in relation with training levels, DVMs clearly have lower volumes for all activities. ITEs and ATEs have similar volumes and, like DVMs, give much more attention to prevention than to curative interventions (Table 7.12). So, DVMs do not stand out in their attention to prevention. In the curative area we see clearly the effect of price upon demand: the fact that DVM attention and private services are more expensive than their competitors' shows up in how little work they receive. Some public DVMs are local government representatives and explain that their lower treatment rate is due to other activities including administrative duties, meetings, policy designing, supervision, and extension.

Skills vs. Behaviors: Analyzing Incentive Structures

When we look more carefully at the details of various activities and apply institutional economic reasoning, a different set of explanations emerges for the low number of treatments performed by DVMs compared with paraprofessionals. DVMs choose to engage in activities that do not exploit their professional skills, they choose not to engage in activities that do exploit their professional skills, and market imperfections inhibit the DVM from effectively communicating the value of his superior skills.

Working Behavior of Animal Health Practitioners

Working behavior has been evaluated with respect to three domains: animal health, food hygiene and public health, and related veterinary activities. Interview questions referred to actual work done in the preceding year and the extent to which practitioners used their full professional skills while performing these activities. As Tables 7.10 and 7.11 show, some activities were performed by more practitioners than others were; this might reflect an emerging division of labor between private and public professionals and among status groups.

GVPs and PVPs were asked about the frequency of various activities during the week before the survey, which was conducted at a time when government personnel were engaged in inoculation campaigns. The quantifiable interventions on weekly activities show that small ruminants, cattle and horses are the animals that receive most curative as well as

Table 7.10 Veterinarian Activities

	Response Relative Frequencies (%)		
Animal Health Activities	Government	Private	Sample
Veterinary activity planning	21.6	11.9	17.3
Animal diseases control	75.7	32.2	56.4
Coordination of animal diseases control	56.8	16.9	39.1
Voluntary collective vaccinations	78.4	86.4	82.0
Compulsory collective vaccinations	77.0	15.3	49.6
Animal health clinics	79.7	89.8	84.2
Epidemiological surveillance	60.8	8.5	37.6
Health certificate for international trade	16.2	6.8	12.0
Health certificate for domestic trade	58.1	3.4	33.8
Vaccination certificate delivery	67.6	23.7	48.1
Laboratory diagnosis	12.2	8.5	10.5
Laboratory work for regulation	2.7	5.1	3.8
Laboratory work for inspection	5.4	6.8	6.0
Research	31.1	13.6	23.3
Public Health Activities			
Food inspection for livestock products	82.4	10.2	50.4
Food processing inspection	10.8	8.5	9.8
Quality control			
Veterinary pharmaceutical	10.8	3.4	7.5
Food	21.6	8.5	15.8
Trade inspection			
Import	5.4	18.6	11.3
Export	8.1	1.7	5.3
International cooperation	16.2	15.3	15.8
Relations with professional organizations	44.6	25.4	36.1
Rules and regulations	21.6	8.5	15.8

Table 7.11 Other Veterinary Activities

	Response Relative Frequencies (%)		
Veterinary pharmaceutical marketing	Government	Private	Sample
Regulation	1.4	5.1	3.0
Import	0.0	22.0	9.8
Export	0.0	11.9	5.3
Processing	0.0	10.2	4.5
Direct distrib.	6.8	79.7	39.1
Network distrib.	5.4	37.3	19.5
Regulation	6.8	3.4	5.3
Quality Control	6.8	0.0	3.8
Biotechnology			
Embryo transfer	0.0	3.4	1.5
Artificial Insemination	0.0	0.0	0.0
Veterinary training	13.5	5.1	9.8
Animal protection	14.9	5.1	10.5
Environment	17.6	8.5	13.5
Research	8.1	5.1	6.8
Aquaculture	4.1	3.4	3.8
Fisheries	6.8	5.1	6.0
Livestock studies	45.9	57.6	51.1
Veterinary auxiliaries training	43.2	40.7	42.1
Counseling in husbandry-extension	77.0	76.3	76.7
Administrative meetings			
Region level	13.5	10.2	12.0
subregion level	21.6	0.0	12.0
local level	27.0	0.0	15.0
Production			
Poultry	1.4	28.8	13.5
Beef fattening	12.5	15.3	13.5
Sheep fattening	13.5	8.5	11.3

Table 7.12 Frequencies of Activities According to Training Levels

Activities	Sample		DVM (1)		ITE (2)		ATE (3)		Sig*
	Mean ± sd	n	Mean ± sd	n	Mean ± sd	n	Mean ± sd	N	
Curative activities	23.7 ± 41.3	3 150	12.5 ± 21.3	689	38.6 ± 59.4	1 120	27.4 ± 42.8	1 341	0.01* (1,2)
Small ruminants	10.7 ± 16.1	1 430	7.5 ± 10.8	414	15.8 ± 19.1	458	11.4 ± 8.4	558	0.07 (1,2)
Cattle	4.9 ± 12.6	655	1.5 ± 4.9	81	7.6 ± 15.4	220	7.2 ± 15.7	354	0.03* (1,3) (1,2)
Food animals	15.7 ± 26.5	2 085	9 ± 13.4	495	23.4 ± 30.8	678	18.6 ± 32.9	912	0.04* (1,2)
Horses	3.9 ± 9.8	524	1.5 ± 5.5	85	7.7 ± 15.4	222	4.4 ± 8.7	217	0.02* (1,2)
Pets	4.1 ± 10.0	541	2.0 ± 5.8	109	7.6 ± 15.4	220	4.3 ± 9.4	212	0.05* (1,2)

Preventive activities	45.5 ± 100.6	6 047	30.7 ± 80.4	1 688	42.7 ± 89.9	1 240	63.6 ± 123.5	3 119	0.04* (1,3)
Small ruminants	17.9 ± 39.1	2 382	12.4 ± 28.5	681	22.1 ± 48.3	640	21.7 ± 43.3	1 061	0.07 (1,2)
Cattle	15.2 ± 35.7	2 017	9.4 ± 26.0	515	13.8 ± 35.1	400	22.5 ± 43.9	1 102	0.04* (1,3)
Food animals	33.1 ± 69.4	4 399	21.7 ± 52.5	1 196	35.9 ± 71.3	1 040	44.1 ± 83.3	2 163	0.03* (1,2)
Horses	10.6 ± 32.2	1 410	7.7 ± 26.0	421	6.9 ± 25.8	200	16.1 ± 40.6	789	0.1 (NS)
Pets	1.8 ± 6.2	238	1.3 ± 4.6	71	-	0	3.4 ± 8.8	167	0.05* (2,3)

* N.B.: * Groups with a statistical difference, (< or = 0.05)

Table 7.13 Frequencies of Activities of Private and Government Professionals

Activities	Private professionals		Government professionals		Significance level
	Mean ± sd	n	Mean ± sd	n	
Curative activities	15.2 ± 20.9	898	30.4 ± 51.3	2 252	0.03 *
Small ruminants	9.5 ± 10.2	560	11.7 ± 19.5	870	0.42
Cattle	2.0 ± 5.4	119	7.2 ± 15.9	536	0.02*
Food animals	11.5 ± 13	679	19 ± 33	1 406	0.11
Horses	2.2 ± 5.8	128	5.4 ± 119	396	0.06
Pets	1.5 ± 5.5	91	6.1 ± 12.2	450	0.009*
Preventive activities	30.9 ± 66.0	1 821	57.1 ± 120.6	4 226	0.14
Small ruminants	16.1 ± 35.9	952	19.3 ± 41.6	1 430	0.64
Cattle	9.3 ± 25.8	550	19.8 ± 41.5	1 467	0.09
Food animals	25.5 ± 51.0	1 502	39.1 ± 81.0	2 897	0.26
Horses	4.5 ± 18.3	266	15.5 ± 39.4	1 144	0.05*
Pets	0.9 ± 4.2	53	2.5 ± 7.4	185	0.14

NB: * is significant (< or = 0.05)

preventive interventions (Table 7.13). If we discount meat inspection in the months when government vets are engaged in inoculation campaigns, public and private practitioners engage in similar activities. Although each government practitioner does a much larger volume of curative work than private ones, government and private practitioners do similar volumes of preventive work outside the campaigns. GVPs do more curative work partly because herders demand their cheaper services. Another explanation, however, is that GVPs can capitalize on opportunities to perform curative services on the side while on government subsidized field trips for mandatory preventive activities. If private vets were officially enfranchised— through the sanitary mandate[5]— to participate in vaccination and food hygiene campaigns, the volume of their curative and preventive work would increase.

There are two important types of veterinary services that DVMs are uniquely qualified to perform which either are performed by others or are not performed at all. The first is public health inspections of meat and fish. These inspections for spoiled produce represent perhaps the greatest divergence between individual herder priorities and those of society, and one should not be surprised to hear that herders might offer private inducements in return for a 'satisfactory' rating. Although this is an area where professional values are most clearly necessary, it is the area where those most expected to possess such values, the DVMs, are most conspicuously absent.

The second activity, which is currently performed by few technicians of any qualification, is laboratory diagnostics (Table 7.10). DVMs are the professionals qualified to perform sophisticated diagnostic activities, yet experimental or laboratory diagnoses are activities that are no longer practiced. As laboratory diagnosis is one visible area in which DVMs possess more skill, promotion of this activity will lead not only to healthier livestock but also to DVM competitive advantage.

Rather than devoting time to (and being rewarded financially and professionally for) activities that take advantage of the DVMs professional and technical skills, many DVMs in the private sector are engaged

---

5. A sanitary mandate is an official agreement between the Department of Livestock Services and a private DVM, such that the DVM may perform a specific service in a particular geographic area on either a contract or a franchise basis. Sanitary mandates are granted for services with a public good component and, in addition to being given the right to perform the service, the DVM is given a government subsidy. Presently, sanitary mandates are granted for some immunizations, and some food hygiene and inspection services are expected to be considered in the near future.

in pharmaceutical sales— an important activity to be sure, but one that does not exploit the DVMs special competence. Government is officially out of the veterinary pharmaceutical marketing business, and has given DVMs a legal monopoly on the sale of drugs. This monopoly right creates a negative side effect: it is creating market incentives that deprive livestock producers of access to the superior veterinary skills of the DVMs. If DVMs concentration on pharmaceuticals led to better drug usage or quicker reporting of epizootic outbreaks, this might be an acceptable tradeoff. But the pharmacies often employ untrained people to work at the counters, leaving the DVMs free to concentrate on business matters elsewhere on the premises. Thus, DVMs' interest in pharmaceutical business activities should be analyzed as a major concern in the privatization process since it appears to be hindering private DVMs from assuming their role as leading forces in the improvement of production systems following government divestiture. If pharmaceutical activities keep private vets from playing their role as *cadres de développement* involved in technology transfer, extension, and improvement of production systems, then the policy of granting this monopoly should be reconsidered.

This monopoly discussion is perhaps more hypothetical than real since laws are not enforced. More commonly used drugs are sold everywhere without prescription; further, DVMs even consider paraprofessionals as legitimate drug sellers authorized to buy from them since they are part of the technical veterinary community. DVMs are reluctant, however, to sell wholesale stocks— especially antibiotics— directly to herders. The monopoly issue may become more salient after sanitary mandates have been granted to DVMs by the government. Private DVMs will then have a vaccine supply monopoly in their designated areas, and the monopoly issue will develop a new dimension.

Economic theory recognizes that markets are imperfect and that market shortcomings create suboptimal outcomes. For our purposes, the 'lemons' model elaborated by Akerlof (1970) is useful because it shows how quality and uncertainty interact with the market mechanism. In a hypothetical market for veterinary services, the 'lemons' principle predicts that bad veterinary services will tend to drive good services out of the market when buyers (herders) are unable to evaluate service quality. Good quality service is more expensive to provide, and if the provider is not compensated for this additional cost, he will stop offering his superior service. This tendency is very important when considering the nature of competition expected to develop between veterinary professionals and their paraprofessional competitors. If herders cannot evaluate quality differences, paraprofessional competition might lead to either of two socially suboptimal outcomes: veterinary doctors capable of higher quality veterinary service provision might be driven out of the market, or full veterinarians might lower their own standards so that their quality matches the new market standard. In either case, full veterinarians face a clear private cost: they would have to be satisfied with a lower income than someone with their skill level could reasonably expect.

Data reported from the herders survey suggests that herders do not recognize any qualitative difference among caregivers; they are not willing to pay a premium just for extra qualifications. Clearly, the veterinary care market is vulnerable to penetration of less qualified 'lemons.' Thus, we need to evaluate the challenges faced by veterinary professionals more closely, and take a closer look at the ability of DVMs to remain leading forces in Senegal's privatization scheme. At least part of the problem is that private sector DVMs choose activities that do not require their superior technical skills. It therefore is not surprising these skills do not enhance their income levels.

The DVM's choice to engage in activities that do not exploit his skills hinders the creation of markets that enhance both livestock health and the DVM's security. More than that, this choice *facilitates* the creation of market norms that *endanger* those public and private goals. One such norm is the absence of social differentiation by herders of members of different professional status groups. Analysis of payment levels reported by the interviewed professionals shows that payments rarely dissociate products used and services offered. Unless the herder brings his animal to the office (which is a rare case), the professional determines his price based on the cost of medicine and a flexible formula relating the type of service and distance to the client. Only two per cent of the professionals interviewed dissociated products and services. Professionals act mostly as mere pharmaceutical merchants instead of veterinary service providers.

A second market failure with which policymakers must come to terms is more straightforward: genuine competition does not exist in many parts of Senegal. Sixty-nine per cent of the responses show that herders and animal owners come after their animal's sickness is quite advanced, but once they arrive they cooperate with professionals, and 65 per cent always accept the recommended treatment and buy any necessary prescriptions. When explaining this seemingly high acceptance rate, only 37 per cent of professionals suggest 'confidence in the caregiver.' More often, the principal cooperates with his agent because there is no alternative. Theoretical notions of replacing one agent with another simply do not apply.

Important lessons can be drawn from the above analysis of the patterns of professional activities. First, private practice is viable, but competition from the public sector still impedes its full realization. Second, it does not appear that reliance on private practice for preventive interventions would have negative effects. Finally, herders are not willing to pay private DVMs more than paraprofessionals and auxiliaries for the same procedures. They are, however, willing to pay more for the specialized procedures that only DVMs have the skills to perform. Therefore, it is proposed that if veterinarians rely only on their traditional services, which do not require their superior abilities, they will be poorly positioned to take advantage of new economic opportunities created by privatization schemes. It is consequently strategic for them to diversify quickly, to stress more high skill promotive actions in their marketing strategies, and to emphasize special technical attributes in their services delivery. Differentiation in proven and effective practical skills is vital to DVMs' survival in a market characterized by competition with paraprofessionals.

Increased competition would be a benefit to herders as well. They would be able to choose from a portfolio of services and providers, ranging from basic veterinary care to highly specialized advice. Asset specificity, especially its human component, is going to be a crucial factor in the supply of veterinary services and their sustainability. The promotion of clear and high standards and diversification of services offered by veterinarians will help to modernize the livestock subsector.

Professional responsibility would help still more. In 1993, as noted above, the government approved the creation of a professional self-regulatory organization called the *Ordre des Docteurs Vétérinaires du Sénégal*. The *Ordre* is expected to exert professional self-regulation on the veterinarians and be their sole representative. To fulfill its self-regulatory role effectively, the *Ordre* needs to develop a sustainable organizational form and become a more efficient organizational entrepreneur. Unfortunately, the *Ordre* is not yet effective, and has not developed the reputation needed to solve the 'market for lemons' problem. That is, it is currently unable to assure herders credibly that DVM products are indeed superior.

The Challenges of Veterinary Professional Self-Regulation. The veterinary profession has to undergo dramatic changes in both orientation and organization if it is to make the most of the new types of institutional relations introduced by privatization. These institutions will have to recognize and mediate among divergent interests and agendas of the subsector's participants. So, policymakers observing the intensity of externalities and moral hazard problems in animal health and public hygiene will need to recognize both the general limitations of direct government intervention and the need for new organizational reforms.

Leonard (1993) notes that external donors have been the only venture capitalists in African organizational reform. Since privatization is an externally generated reform, structural adjustments nurtured by incremental changes will lead to patterns of exchange that have not yet been internalized. Better results would be obtained if a local organizational entrepreneur were involved, so that the institutionalization of the reform would be in harmony with the local details of the livestock subsector and the veterinary profession. Even when the market works properly, a strategic aspect of the privatization process is the orientation and choices of the veterinary professional body in charge of securing, self-policing, and contributing to an efficient and sustainable involvement of more professionals.

In the spectrum of institutions present in the livestock subsector, the *Ordre* is the self-regulatory association that occupies the strategic position to fill the gap and to provide a focused impetus for a successful privatization without sacrificing the needs of society—the second principal. However, professional participation is low. Eighty-eight per cent of the professionals interviewed knew about the *Ordre* and 46 per cent have read some of its publications. However, two years after the creation the *Ordre*'s creation, only 35 per cent of DVMs have registered themselves and, partly due to distance and transport difficulties, most DVMs have attended fewer than three meetings.

Despite the strategic role of the *Ordre*, as yet there is no underlying framework for its role and actions. The *Ordre* is only starting to be operational: its board has now been elected and it plans to be progressively involved in the veterinary sector. The present regulatory activities of the *Ordre* are not well developed, but DVMs and technicians know and seem to accept its authority. During the study period, the *Ordre* did not attempt any clear-cut interventions and its activities are still focused on official representation, professional lobbying, and registration of participants. The challenges of a self-regulating, self-policing professional organization in a privatizing environment are, as yet, far from being matched.

As a part of its mission, the *Ordre* has to play a prominent role in enforcing high quality standards among its members. Furthermore, since the propensity for lemons to force out quality diminishes as the ability to evaluate quality improves, one of the *Ordre's* key interventions would be to enhance the information level of herders and other producers. Additional information would help herders understand when the superior quality of full veterinarians really does add value, and when it does not. The result would be a more rational division of the veterinary services market among professionals and paraprofessionals. Diversifying quickly into areas that exploit their abilities is strategic for them, leading us to propose more promotive actions in their marketing strategies and more special technical attributes, such as laboratory diagnostic activities, in their services delivery.

Unless DVMs start building a market niche that exploits their superior training, there is no reason to expect or hope that they remain in existence— save for a few policy and regulatory positions in government. Policies and efforts that are dominated by actions intended only to keep DVMs alive commercially without addressing why DVMs *should* survive are counterproductive. The provision of certain special privileges in the trade of veterinary pharmaceuticals and drugs has encouraged DVMs to use their elite networks to focus on business purposes rather than using their elite training to do specialist veterinary services. This drives them away from the market niches in which they would be socially useful.

New institutional economic theory predicts that professional self-regulation will emerge in this kind of market. The *Ordre* is optimally placed to help avoid the negative course of DVMs activities as well as the predicted market distortions caused by collective action problems (Williamson 1994; Zald 1987). The proposed *Ordre* intervention, however, is not one of market regulation or direct intervention. Although good government interventions are not the only possible response to market failure, a realistic conceptual framework recognizes that, often, free competition alone cannot be relied on to achieve socially desirable outcomes. Mediating policies and effective regulation should replace the invisible hand of competition so that the very visible hand of direct intervention can be avoided (Train 1991).

The theory of contestable markets opposes all interventions (Coase 1982). In fact, in the face of market inadequacies like veterinary monopolies, potential competitors do create strong tendencies for efficient pricing and output decisions even by monopolists (Wolf 1988). Such a competitive threat leads to strong discipline on service delivery and high levels of effort to improve services retaining or attracting potential agents (Israel 1987). However, this model requires the existence of competitors as the disciplining agent, and this condition does not exist in remote areas or in areas characterized by a low veterinarian-to-livestock ratio. Such situations could be managed under a framework in which second best choices reduce the expected market shortcomings. If necessary, government or professional self-regulation, mandatory or supervised fee scheduling, or price discrimination could be used for this purpose.

A new structure of the veterinary services market is ineluctably evolving, and policy guidance is very much needed for better performance in economic efficiency and distribution equity. Since the development hypothesis at the foundation of the privatization scheme is that improved access to veterinary services is optimally attainable through user fee recovery and private practice, the outcome of such a scheme would be to the advantage of the veterinary profession and all of its members only if the challenges of professionalism are addressed directly.

Thus, it is important that the *Ordre* finds institutional design and governance arrangements so that veterinary professionals capitalize on their skills and on the special privilege of freedom from the control of outsiders. As somewhat controversially stated by Freidson (1970), professional privilege is explained and justified by three claims: their technical skills defined as their technical knowledge acquired in formal training; their set of professional norms guiding ethical behavior and producing conscientious work without supervision; [6] and their trust in proper self-regulatory actions by the profession. The aim is not to legalize market failures such as monopoly. Rather, the *Ordre* is charged with mediating the healthy tension between the veterinarian's need for a reasonable salary, the herder's need for healthy livestock, and society's need for safe animal products.

CONCLUSION

The situation in Senegal is one of structural reform in the livestock subsector with a major emphasis on selective privatization of veterinary services combined with rehabilitation of public veterinary organizations to help them regain operational efficiency. Despite the importance of a strategic role for a self-regulatory institution, there is as yet no underlying framework for its role and actions. Since it lacks experience in wide rural private practice, the *Ordre* needs to take an entrepreneurial approach and

6. Leonard (1991) refers to the concept of 'institutional altruism' to describe the same criteria.

implement innovative policies in the livestock subsector.

The structure of the subsector generates specific responses from all participants, who decide under a variety of constraints that often are exacerbated by privatization requisites and their outcomes. The transition is still difficult, and discrepancies continue to persist between the new environment and professional behavior that remains very much inspired by traditional views. The market alone is not yet the more efficient organizer, although it is quite clear that top-down government procedures are outmoded. Consequently, a veterinary self-regulatory institution like the *Ordre* could play a strategic role and validate its mandate and responsibilities if it reshapes its orientation and organization to match the new types of relationships forged by the privatization process.

The analyses lead us to conclude that the solution to efficient privatization of the Senegal veterinary subsector has to be sought in policy designs and procedures that help local actors to internalize the incentives created by the new public/private relationship. The veterinary professionals' institution can play a leading role in this internalization by harnessing market forces to promote higher standards for veterinary service delivery. Its agenda should be directed toward institution building and professionalism in an emerging free market of veterinary services. Most important, good participatory governance by its members is essential for well-balanced veterinary services regulations that are consistent with professional values. With these requisites, startup or expansion loans will then be better designed and more sustainable. Such an institutional package would successfully invert the current top-down change forced by insensitive outsiders and outmoded policymakers. It is also a basis for internalizing the new market incentives, which is required if the privatization of veterinary services delivery and structural reform of the livestock sector, so much desired by everyone, will be successful.

8 Decentralization and the Quality of Health Care in Tanzania

Gilbert R. Mliga

It is often claimed that the quality of health care provided by church health facilities is superior to that provided by government health facilities in Tanzania. A study by Kanji, Kilima, and Munishi (1992), for example, found that Protestant health facilities performed much better than government facilities in providing quality health care, measured by technical criteria. Gilson, Alilio, and Heggenhougen (1994) found that clients' evaluation of care also favored church health facilities, because of the availability of medicines and the good attitude of personnel.

This study examines the relationship between the quality of health care and the organizational structure of the services. It compares four types of health providers using both technically derived scores of quality (based on professional observation) and client evaluations of quality. The four service providers are the Tanzanian government and three different church denominations— Lutheran, Seventh Day Adventist, and Roman Catholic. The differences in the scores between health services are explained by their distinct organizational structures. This investigation, undertaken in the Iringa and Arusha regions of Tanzania, demonstrates that quality generally follows from local incentives and decentralized administration.

While the Ministry of Health tightly controls government health services (at least nominally), church denominations provide a variety of governance mechanisms. Since their entry into Tanzania in the late nineteenth century, church missionaries have established health facilities in the rural areas. Today, church health services contribute an almost equal number of hospital beds as the government. Church facilities are predominantly in rural areas, although in recent years churches have also opened dispensaries in urban centers. Tanzania provides one of the best examples in the world of collaboration between the church and government in the provision of health care. Some church hospitals are Designated District Hospitals—that is, the Tanzanian government contracts with churches to provide the services of a district hospital. The hospital remains under the administrative control of the churches, which receive a grant from the government. The government also contributes personnel and pays their salaries; the church is responsible for the purchase of medicines and other operating expenses. Churches are likely to play an even greater role in health delivery in the future because the government now supports the privatization of health services. Some church services that had been nationalized, such as the Kilimanjaro Christian Medical Center in Moshi and Bugando Medical Center in Mwanza, have now been returned to church control.

Churches in Tanzania make a significant contribution to the training of nurses. Out of 30 certificate and diploma nursing schools, churches own 20, nine are government-run, and one is private. The training of clinical officers and clinical assistants (the personnel who form the majority of the clinicians observed in this study), on the other hand, all takes place in government institutions. The training is standardized and clinicians have to pass examinations set by the Tanganyika Medical Training Board. External examiners are normally involved to ensure that regulations and standards set by the Board are followed. Therefore the training background of all clinical officers and clinical assistants surveyed in this study is the same, although some work for the government and others are employed in church facilities.

This study identifies the organizational level at which important decisions governing human and material resources management take place within the health services and relates this to the quality of care, as determined by both technical criteria and by client assessment. We then examine two hypotheses that relate the quality of health care delivery to the organizational structure of health services. First, church incentives to staff for quality assurance may be greater than government's, because (a) firing is easier and a more credible sanction, (b) disciplinary penalties are more easily assessed, (c) discretionary bonuses are tied to performance and easier to administer, and (d) care is taken to select personnel whose values drive them to quality assurance (that is, they do not rely only on formal qualifications). The second hypothesis holds that facilities that are financially independent can charge fees that enable them to maintain a more reliable supply of medicines, compared to facilities that depend on higher organizational levels for their budgets. However, services pro-

Table 8.1 Distribution of Facilities by Region, Facility Level and Provider Type

	GOVT	ELCT	RC	SDA	Total
ARUSHA					
Hospitals	2 (3)	2 (4)	2 (3)	0 (0)	6 (10)
Health Centers, Dispensaries	6 (131)	6 (23)	5 (20)	5 (5)	22 (179)
IRINGA					
Hospitals	2 (4)	0 (2)	1 (3)	0 (0)	3 (9)
Health Centers, Dispensaries		7 (26)	7 (24)	0 (0)	20 (213)
Total	16 (301)	15 (55)	15 (50)	5 (5)	51 (411)

Total population in parentheses.

vided by these facilities will be found to be more expensive than those provided by facilities that are not financially independent.

METHODOLOGY

The study was carried out in Iringa and Arusha regions during March through July 1996. Fifty-one health facilities owned by the government, Lutheran, Roman Catholic (RC), and the Seventh Day Adventist (SDA) church denominations were surveyed. Table 8.1 shows the distribution of facilities studied by type of provider.

Diocesan Medical Secretaries and Medical Directors were interviewed to obtain information on the organizational structure of the services in their respective dioceses. They were also asked questions on how health services are managed, and particularly at which organizational level decisions are made regarding staff recruitment, staff development and firing, and purchase of medicines and other medical supplies. Similar interviews were conducted with at least two health facility chiefs for each diocese to elaborate on the structure and management of health services and how these relate to the health facilities. Information from all sources was consistent, thus improving our confidence in the reliability of the information obtained in these interviews.

In health care, quality is understood as the degree to which the resources for health care, or the services included in health care, correspond to specified standards. It is generally expected that if those standards are met, a sick client is more likely to return to good health (Roemer and Montoya-Aguilar 1988). Quality in this study was assessed from both a professional perspective and the clients' perception. Due to the severe information asymmetry in this principal/agent relationship—

that is, the client-clinician relationship— the profession has set standards of health care to safeguard the principal.

The professional role lies in the exercise of decision-making authority, based upon specialized knowledge, on behalf of the client. The client delegates to a professional the authority to bring specialized knowledge to bear in making practical decisions on the client's behalf and in the client's interest. The professional, in short, acts as his client's agent (Tuohy and Wolfson 1978).

We call the quality assessment by professionals 'technical quality' and it is based on standard procedures and disease management protocols. Clients' assessment of quality is as important as technical quality because clients will only utilize services they believe are efficacious (Waddington and Enyimayew 1989). Technical quality and what clients perceive as quality need not be different. However, because of the information asymmetry inherent in this relationship, the expectations of service by professionals and clients normally differ.

Technical assessment of the quality of care was undertaken through observation of consultations by doctors, clinical officers and clinical assistants. Trained clinical officers using a prepared checklist adapted from the one prepared by the Aga Khan Foundation (1990) conducted these observations. The officer indicated whether a specific question was asked or a procedure was performed by the attending clinician, as a minimal requirement in order to diagnose the presenting condition correctly.

Observations were made on all clients with fever, cough, diarrhea, and sexually transmitted diseases during the normal Monday to Friday working hours (8.00 am to 3.00 pm). These are top priority conditions because they appear frequently in the out-patient department and clinicians are supposed to be well versed in their management. They can therefore be used as tracer conditions for assessing quality (Kessner 1973). The main performances that we assessed are:

- Completeness of history and physical examination.
- Requests for examination of blood slides for malaria parasites in cases of feverish clients.
- Health education for clients: explaining the diagnosis, treatment, whether and when to return for treatment, and how to prevent the condition.
- Attentiveness, that is welcoming and ensuring the client is comfortably seated, patience and active listening while making the necessary clarification, and politeness.

Table 8.2 Distribution of Consultations Observed by Region, Level of Facility and Type of Provider

	Government	Lutheran	RC	SDA	Total
ARUSHA					
Hospitals	24	38	39	0	101
Health Centers, Dispensaries	83	75	47	50	255
IRINGA					
Hospitals	53	0	25	0	78
Health Centers, Dispensaries	90	71	154	0	315
Total	250	184	265	50	749

Table 8.3 Distribution of Consultations Observed by Disease and Type of Provider

	Government	Lutheran	RC	SDA	Total
Fever	103	86	125	24	338
Cough	83	59	81	14	237
Diarrhea	41	30	45	9	125
STD	18	9	14	3	44
Total	245	184	265	50	744

Five Missing Cases (0.67%).

After the consultation and having received the service, clients on their way out of the facility were interviewed by other research assistants. They were asked whether they received the medicines that were prescribed and whether they would come back to the facility if they developed the same or other conditions, how much they paid for the services, and how they valued the services relative to what they were charged. Notes were taken on the clinician's diagnosis and the prescribed list of medicines: dosage, frequency, and duration. The medication was assessed on the basis of standard treatment for the diagnosis and on whether there was under or over-prescription.

A total of 749 consultations were observed; their distribution by disease and type of provider is shown in Tables 8.2 and 8.3. Of the 763 clients interviewed, 242 were male with a mean age of 32 years (range 10 to 85), and 469 were females with a mean age of 29 years (range 11 to 85). In this chapter, 'client' refers either to the patient or, in the case of

Table 8.4 Measures of Health Care Quality

DIAGNOSIS Measures completeness of history taking and physical examination for the four conditions that were being observed. This measure assesses the performance of an entire facility in eliciting important information from clients and performing a clinical examination that will result in a correct diagnosis. To compute diagnosis, the scores for the different conditions were standardized such that they all have a mean score of zero and a standard deviation of 1. Thus some scores had to assume a negative value. This was a necessary procedure to make the scores comparable across presenting conditions.

LAB Measures frequency with which a request for laboratory examination of blood slides for malaria parasites was made when it was warranted. Laboratory examination for malaria parasites is important to reach a correct diagnosis in clients presenting with fever. Without laboratory examination, many clients end up being treated for malaria when they could be suffering from other conditions for which malaria treatment is ineffective. Lack of examination often leads to over-diagnosis of malaria, over-use of chloroquine, and delayed treatment of other conditions presenting with fever.

ATTENTIVENESS Measures a combination of activities including welcoming and greeting the client, having the client comfortably seated, looking at the client while talking, active listening and asking questions for clarification. The maximum possible score was 7.

EDUCATION Measures the extent to which clients were given health education, which includes explaining the diagnosis, the treatment given, whether or when to return for treatment, and how to prevent the disease. The maximum possible score was 4.

PRESCRIPTION The list of medicines clinicians prescribed for their diagnosis was measured to determine the appropriateness of the combination of medicines, to check for over-prescription (poly-pharmacy) or under-prescription, accuracy of the dosage, frequency of administration, and duration of treatment. A correct combination of medicines, dosage, frequency, and duration was given a score of 1; if an error was committed in any of these a score of 0 was given.

PHARMACY Measures the availability of medicines at a facility. For all medicines prescribed, the client was asked to confirm that they got the medicines from the facility. If all medicines were obtained a score of 2 was given, if only some medicines were received 1, and 0 if no medicines were obtained.

DEMAND Level of attendance at each facility was a measure of demand for service.

SATISFACTION Clients were asked if they would ever come back to the facility if they developed a similar condition, an acute condition, or a chronic condition requiring keen follow-up. A 'yes' response to these questions earned a facility a score of 1, a 'no' answer 0. Answers to these questions indicate clients' confidence in their being properly managed if they develop these conditions.

VALUE Measure of the value of the services clients received at a facility in relation to what they paid. Possible scores were: too expensive 1, somewhat expensive 2, reasonable 3, inexpensive 4, and very inexpensive 5.

Table 8.5 Mean Scores on Performance Measures by Type of Provider

	GOVT	ELCT	RC	SDA
DIAGNOSIS	-0.1830	0.1232	0.1246	-0.2236
LABORATORY	0.2857	0.2281	0.5463	0.2941
EDUCATION	1.4756	1.8418	2.0570	2.4167
ATTENTIVENESS	6.0174	6.6369	6.7500	6.5510
PRESCRIPTION	3.6102	3.3058	3.3602	3.4706
PHARMACY	1.2213	1.9569	1.9102	1.8824
SATISFACTION	2.5103	2.6377	2.2607	2.4314
VALUE	3.3214	2.8221	2.9522	2.7000
Total	18.2589	19.5483	19.9612	19.5226

All differences between types of facility on performance measures are statistically significant at p < .01.

children, to the person who brought in a sick child. Fifty-one clients (6.8 per cent of all observations) did not give their age.

Measures of Quality and a Preliminary Analysis

We computed nine measures of quality to assess technical performance and client's assessment of the service. The measures of technical performance were DIAGNOSIS, LAB, EDUCATION, ATTENTIVENESS, and PRESCRIPTION. In these indices we gave a score of 1 when a relevant question or procedure was asked or performed, and 0 when it was not asked or performed. Adding up the scores gave the total score for each consultation. We also assessed the PRESCRIPTION, PHARMACY, and facility DEMAND, for which a different scoring system was used. Two indices were used to measure clients' assessment of quality of services: SATISFACTION and VALUE. These nine measures are summarized in Table 8.4.

Qualitative Results

We found that church facilities typically performed better than government facilities on technical measures. In particular, the churches excelled in DIAGNOSIS, LAB, ATTENTIVENESS, EDUCATION and PHARMACY. Government facilities scored higher than all three church denominations in PRESCRIPTION—the appropriateness of treatment. Table 8.5 summarizes the findings.

Among the churches, the RC facilities outperformed the others in history taking and clinical examination (DIAGNOSIS), as well as in LAB and ATTENTIVENESS. It also was second in EDUCATION. They performed more laboratory investigations for malaria parasites (both in hospitals and in smaller facilities), followed in order, by SDA, government facilities, and the Lutherans. RC facilities were the most ATTENTIVE, followed by Lutheran and SDA facilities. Treatment (PRESCRIPTION), however, was the most appropriate in government health facilities, then at SDA and RC, and least so in Lutheran facilities. It is interesting to note that while church health facilities provided more health education in hospitals than in health centers and dispensaries, the reverse occurred in government facilities.

Most clients visiting government health facilities did not receive the medicines that were prescribed to them (PHARMACY). This problem was more severe in hospitals than in health centers and dispensaries because health centers and dispensaries were supplied with medicines through the Essential Drugs Program, funded by DANIDA and UNICEF. Church health facilities seem to have been better stocked with medicines than government facilities. Clients experienced the least difficulties in getting medicines at Lutheran facilities, then RC followed by SDA. The general trend that clients missed medicines more in hospitals than health centers and dispensaries is reversed only in the case of Lutheran health facilities.

In terms of client SATISFACTION with the health services, most clients of Lutheran facilities asserted that they would come back to the facility if they developed the same or different conditions. Government facilities came in second, followed by SDA facilities. Roman Catholic facilities, in contrast to the favorable technical measures of quality, were least favored for a return visit for a similar or different condition.

Clients valued the service provided by government facilities relative to the cost of those services, most highly. Roman Catholic services were second and Lutherans third. SDA services were thought to be too expensive. Hospital services were accorded more value than services provided by health centers and dispensaries. It appears, however, that clients may not have been comparing quality with what they paid, but simply saying whether they found the services inexpensive or not. This is evident when we analyze what they paid on average for consultation and medicines in the different facilities. Government facilities were found to be the least expensive (Tshs 58, US$ 0.11), followed by RC (Tshs 860, US$ 1.62) and Lutheran (Tshs 1,097, US$ 2.07). SDA services were found to be the most expensive (Tshs 1,458, US$ 2.75). The differences are statistically significant ($p = 0.00$), as are all of the differences between types of facility on performance measures ($p < 0.01$).

Overall, hospitals performed better than smaller facilities (health centers and dispensaries). Hospitals in general performed better on the

Table 8.6 Average Number of Observations or Attendance by Provider Type

	GOVT	ELCT	RC	SDA	Total
Hospitals	19.25 (77/4)	19.00 (38/2)	21.33 (64/3)	-- --	19.89 (179/9)
Health Centers and Dispensaries	14.42 (173/12)	11.23 (146/13)	16.75 (201/12)	10 (50/5)	13.57 (570/42)
Total	15.62 (250/16)	12.27 (184/15)	17.67 (265/15)	10 (50/5)	14.67 (749/51)

NB: ratio in parentheses reports cases per facility

LAB, PRESCRIPTION, SATISFACTION, and VALUE variables. Hospitals were also better in DIAGNOSIS, except for the RC hospitals, and better in EDUCATION, except in government facilities. Smaller facilities were found to be more ATTENTIVE in all cases. Availability of medicines was poorer in hospitals than in smaller facilities, except for the Lutheran ones. Availability of medicines was most assured in Lutheran health facilities, but the Lutherans' overall performance was relatively low because their health centers and dispensaries performed poorly. The RC facilities were the exception in these comparisons; RC health centers and dispensaries performed slightly better than their hospitals on tasks that were commonly performed by all three types of facility.

Demand for Services

The demand for services provided by facilities was determined by the number of clients that we observed during the working hours of each facility. We found that RC facilities received the most visits, followed by government, Lutheran, and SDA facilities (see Table 8.6). When we compare the prices that people pay with the facilities they utilize, we find that cost is not the most important decision making factor. Clients do not just go to the least expensive place. Quality seems to be the more important decision factor.

ORGANIZATION OF HEALTH SERVICES AND DEGREE OF DECENTRALIZATION

In order to explain the above findings, we sought to relate the performance of the four health service providers to their respective organizational structures. Particular attention went to assessing the impact of organizational decentralization across and within the services. There was some variation in the degree of decentralization within denominations.

Table 8.7 Decentralization Variables

FIRE = Ability to fire staff at local or regional level. No = 0; Yes = 1.

FNCL IND = Financial independence, the ability of a facility to pay salaries and buy essential medical supplies to run the facility. Low = 1; Medium = 2; High = 3.

SALARY = Level at which salaries are set. National = 1; Regional = 2; Local = 3.

STAFF DECN = Location at which medical staffing decisions occur. National = 1; Regional = 2; Regional and Local = 3; Local = 4.

ADMIN CON = Location of administrative control. National = 1; Regional = 2; Local and Regional = 3; Local = 4.

DRUG PRCH = Level at which decisions to buy medicines and where to buy them from takes place. Regional = 1; Local = 2.

For example, among RC facilities, those that were run by religious orders were more decentralized than those under the control of bishops. Decentralization in this study is defined with regard to the level in organizational hierarchy at which important decisions governing provision of health care take place. Of particular concern is where decisions are made on the management of human and material resources. We distinguished between three organizational decision levels: national, regional, and local (facility). The human and material resources decisions that we considered important in determining the degree of decentralization, and their corresponding variables, are given in Table 8.7. Facilities were classified according to the organizational level at which decisions related to the control of human and material resources take place (Table 8.8). These variables correlate significantly with each other. Table 8.9 shows this correlation. In order to better interpret these results, a brief description of the organizational structure of the health services (government, Lutheran, SDA, and RC) follows.

Government Health Services. Government health services are highly centralized. The district hospital, led by the District Medical Officer (DMO), is the administrative center for all health services in the district. However, the supervision of health services in most cases leaves much to be desired because staffing, lack of managerial skills, and unreliable means of transport all militate against the DMO fulfilling his or her mandate. The power to hire and fire staff is vested at the national level, though there is some administrative control over staff at the local level. Government health facilities are totally dependent on the centrally allocated government budget, and regional and district hospitals have only recently started charging some user fees. Revenue from user fees is still negligible

Table 8.8 Classification of Facilities According to Decentralization Measures

	STAFF CONTROL				RESOURCE CONTROL	
Type of Center	FIRE	SALARY	FCNL IND	STAFF DECN	ADMIN	DRUG PRCH
Gov. HC & Disp	no	national	low	national	regional	regional
Gov. Hosp.	no	national	low	national	local	local
SDA	yes	national	high	regional	regional	regional
Luth. HC & DISP	yes	regional	medium	regional	regional	regional
Luth. Hosp. Arusha	yes	regional	high	local	loc & reg	local
Luth. Hosp. Meru	yes	regional	high	local	local	local
RC HC & Disp. Arusha	yes	local	high	regional	local	local
RC HC & Disp. Iringa	yes	local	high	local	local	local
RC Hosp. Arusha	yes	local	high	loc & reg	local	local
RC Hosp. Iringa	yes	local	high	local	local	local
RC Order related	yes	local	high	local	local	local

Table 8.9 Correlation Between Decentralization Variables

	FNCL IND	ADMIN	DRUG PRCH	STAFF DECN
FIRE	0.9081	-0.2615	0.2860	0.7708
SALARY	0.8150	0.6475	0.6356	0.8790
FNCL IND		0.4961	0.5267	0.8870
ADMIN			0.0979	0.6257
DRUG PRCH				0.6658

All correlations $p < 0.01$

and its use remains under central regulation due to guidelines governing its use set by the Ministry of Health. Health centers and dispensaries have no control over what medicines and supplies they buy; they have to address their needs to the district level.

District and regional government hospitals, however, can make budgeting decisions on purchases. The district hospital also acts as a referral center for health centers and dispensaries in the district. All except the few newly formed districts have a district hospital. The regional hospital often acts as a district hospital for the district in which it is located. This is the case for both Iringa and Arusha. The study, however, also included two district hospitals (Mafinga in Iringa and Arumeru in Arusha).

Lutheran Health Services. Lutheran health facilities surveyed fall under the Evangelical Lutheran Church of Tanzania (ELCT) dioceses of Iringa, Arusha, and Meru. The manner in which health services in these dioceses are organized is quite similar. The center of power is at the diocese level, exercised through the Diocesan Medical Director. It is the diocese level (comparable to 'region') that makes decisions on recruitment and personnel, coordinates logistics to health facilities, and provides technical support. Hospitals are capable of handling their own day-to-day staff decisions, while smaller facilities refer to the diocese.

The revenue that facilities generate through fees charged for health services is pooled at the diocese and each facility maintains its account there for supply purchases and salary payments. Facilities are expected to run themselves financially, but the diocese occasionally subsidizes health centers and dispensaries. An important exception to this structure is the diocese of Iringa, which does not have a hospital to operate from. The Meru Diocese Medical Director, himself a medical officer, operates from the diocese headquarters at Usa River and not from Nkoaranga Hospital, while the Medical Director of Arusha diocese operates within Selian

Hospital. Thus, there is more administrative control of the diocese in running the Selian Hospital than Nkoaranga hospital, though both of them have a medical officer in charge of the hospital other than the diocesan medical director.

SDA Health Services. All SDA health facilities in the country are under the Union Medical Director based at Arusha, the headquarters of the SDA Tanzania Union. The Union is divided into Conferences and Fields, which are at the same organizational level except that conferences are more established and are financially independent of the Union. The Associate Medical Director is in charge of health services in the Conference. The SDA facilities studied are in Arusha under the North-Eastern Conference and consist of only dispensaries, as the SDA has no hospital there. The national SDA Union directs staff recruitment and sets the salary scale according to level of education and professional training. Regular staff decisions and administration are made at the Conference level. The Conference assists in the process of procurement of medicines and other medical supplies. Each facility is expected to generate its own income and does not receive subsidies from the Conference. No significant staff or supply decisions are made at the local (Field) level.

The Roman Catholic Health Services The organization of health services in Roman Catholic facilities is the most heterogeneous. In general they are the most decentralized, but the degree of decentralization varies greatly. In fact, the heterogeneity itself is an indication of their decentralization. The diocese exercises much less influence in running the health services compared to other denominations, and in some cases there is almost none at all.

Facilities recruit their own staff and salaries are set locally. Administrative control is localized and staff decisions are made locally, except those involving the staff seconded by the government, which are referred to the diocese. Drugs and medical supplies are purchased locally and facilities are financially independent. Non-health personnel, often a nun who is affiliated to a RC Order, are in charge at some health centers and dispensaries. The nun reports to the local parish priest. RC Orders do run some hospitals, but in these cases the person in charge is a doctor. These Order-run facilities have the greatest autonomy from the diocese and have links abroad that provide some financial support as well as drug donations.

The Correlation between Decentralization and Performance

We created two summary variables to measure personnel and resources

Table 8.10 Correlation of Performance Measures, Decentralization and the Presence of a Doctor

	RESOURCE CON.	MD PRESENT	DIAGNOSIS	EDUCATION	ATTENTIVE	LAB
STAFF CONTROL	0.593	0.036	0.150	0.203	0.366	0.240
p-value	0.000	0.324	0.000	0.000	0.000	0.000
RESOURCE CON.		0.490	0.108	0.080	0.668	0.417
p-value		0.000	0.090	0.033	0.740	0.000
MD PRESENT			0.032	-0.004	-0.192	0.348
p-value			0.437	0.925	0.000	0.000
DIAGNOSIS				0.234	0.243	0.056
p-value				0.000	0.000	0.369
EDUCATION					0.260	0.132
p-value					0.000	0.032
ATTENTIVE						-0.108
p-value						0.085

decentralization, and correlated these to our performance indicators. Personnel are the most important resource of an organization. Health institutions are estimated to spend up to 60 per cent of their budgets on personnel (World Bank 1994) and their proper management is therefore crucial to organizational success. The level at which control of recruitment, deployment, development, motivation, incentives, and firing lies is very important. The control of all these depends on the financial capability of that level. We therefore created a variable representing the ability of the *local facility* to exert control over staff and a second variable for resource decentralization, representing the ability of the local facility to exert control over material resources:

staff control = fire + salary + fncl ind + staff decn.

resource control = admin + drug prch.

Variables related to the ability to exert control over human resources correlate much more among themselves than with those that constitute the ability to control material resources and vice versa (Table 8.9). Table 8.10 shows the correlation between the performance indicators and the independent variables— ability to exert control over staff and ability to exert control over material resources. We also included another variable, the presence of a medical doctor, for reasons that will be explained later.

Table 8.11 Correlation of Client Assessment, Prescription Practice and Decentralization

	SATISFACTION	PRESCRIPTION	VALUE	STAFF CONTROL	RESOURCE CON.
PHARMACY	-0.026	-0.068	-0.032	0.457	0.070
p-value	0.474	0.069	0.455	0.000	0.054
SATISFACTION		0.054	0.063	-0.121	-0.026
p-value		0.145	0.135	0.001	0.473
PRESCRIPTION			0.266	-0.115	0.003
p-value			0.538	0.002	0.928
VALUE				0.001	0.081
p-value				0.991	0.055
STAFF CONTROL					0.576
p-value					0.000

Table 8.12 Regression on Performance Measures of Decentralization and the Presence of a Doctor

Dependent Variable:	DIAGN.	LAB	EDUC.	ATTENTIVE	PRESCRIP.	VALUE
Independent Variable:						
MD PRESENT		0.329**		-0.206**	0.086*	0.090
STAFF CONTROL	0.150**	0.208**	0.203**	0.373**	- 0.117**	
RESOURCE CON.				-0.129**		
DEMAND	0.135**	0.166	-0.127**	0.108**	- 0.216**	0.142**

* $p < 0.051$
** $p < 0.011$
Independent variables:
STAFF CONTROL = decentralization of human resource management
RESOURCE CONTROL = decentralization of material resource management
MD PRESENCE = presence of a doctor at a facility
DEMAND = number of clients that were attended

There is a significant positive correlation between each of the performance variables DIAGNOSIS, LAB, ATTENTIVENESS, EDUCATION, and both ability to exert control over human resources (STAFF CONTROL) and ability to exert control over material resources (RESOURCE CONTROL). Thus compared to facilities that are more strongly controlled by higher organizational levels, decentralized facilities perform better in history taking and clinical examination, provide more laboratory examinations for malaria parasites, are more ATTENTIVE to the clients, care more to educate their clients, and dispense more medicines. However, these more careful diagnoses at decentralized facilities are undercut because these facilities prescribe inappropriate medicines more frequently than centralized facilities (see Table 8.11). Clients are also less satisfied with decentralized facilities.

Regression analysis determined the strength of the independent variables in influencing the dependent variables. The independent variables and regressions are shown in Table 8.12.

DISCUSSION OF RESULTS

Some defenders of government health facilities claim that these facilities provide better technical quality care than church or private health facilities, but that the government falls short on the availability of medicines. Hence, they argue, people prefer to go to government health facilities to get free or inexpensive consultation and get the prescribed medicines elsewhere. Our results demonstrate the contrary— clients get medication appropriate to their diagnosis at government facilities, but these diagnoses are more frequently suspect. Government facilities perform more poorly in taking history and performing clinical examination, and they take fewer blood slides for examination of malaria parasites (especially in health centers and dispensaries). Getting a proper diagnosis is an important step in achieving a cure. Church health facilities are more likely to arrive at a correct diagnosis than government facilities due to their good histories and clinical examination as well as their reliance on the laboratory to rule out malaria.

Church pharmacies are better stocked than are those at government facilities. However, clinicians in most church health facilities prescribe inappropriate medications more often. Inappropriate prescriptions included giving too many medications (for example too many antibiotics), use of multi-vitamins and combinations of antibiotics and antimalarial drugs, or inappropriate use of injections. The incentive to prescribe too many drugs most likely comes from the facilities' increased revenue if they sell more medicines.

The problem of inappropriate treatment, in terms of using too many medicines or inappropriate injections, was greater in decentralized facilities than in those that are less decentralized. The most frequent form of inappropriate treatment was poly-pharmacy, which occurred in 34.8 per cent of the cases in RC facilities, 34.0 per cent in Lutheran, 34.0 per cent in SDA, and 14.8 per cent in government facilities ($p = 0.0000$). Excessive use of injections also occurred frequently: Lutheran (18.0 per cent), RC (12.0 per cent), SDA (9.8 per cent) and government (9.3 per cent) ($p = 0.05$). The frequency of prescribing the wrong dosage and duration of treatment was low and the difference between care providers was not significant. Considering that the poly-pharmacy was mainly due to the use of vitamin supplements and, less frequently antibiotics, mission facilities can be considered to deliver better care because they also provide health education and are more attentive to their clients.

The number of clients seen by each type of provider correlates significantly with the way they were attended technically and the attitude of the clinicians in welcoming clients, keeping them comfortable, and listening to them. It also correlates significantly with the availability of medicines. Since the completeness of history-taking and clinical examination does not correlate with clients' appreciation of the services when they were interviewed (SATISFACTION), it is reasonable to conclude here that they choose locations where medicines are available and where the clinicians are attentive. Though they may not be aware of it when using these two criteria, they are also choosing locations where they are being well attended technically, because technical quality seems to correlate with availability of medicines and attentiveness of clinicians.

It is interesting to note that hospitals seem to have less medicine than smaller facilities. It is possible that operating in larger institutions makes it difficult for clinicians in hospitals to know what is available in the pharmacy. What they prescribe may not in fact be available, with the result that clients miss their medication. It could also be that hospital clinicians know the medicines are not there but they prescribe what the clients need in the hope that they will get them elsewhere. Hospitals are mainly located in large towns and the opportunity for clients to get medicines in other pharmacies is high. Clinicians in health centers and dispensaries quite likely know what is available and avoid prescribing medicines that are not there, for they will not have private pharmacies nearby.

SDA facilities were the best at educating their clients. This is what was expected given their philosophy. They often promote healthy living behavior and address such issues as proper nutrition. Facilities that are more decentralized— those that have more power to make decisions on the allocation of human and material resources— displayed better performance than those with less power to make such decisions. Government facilities, which are the most centralized, perform most poorly.

Why do we have these differences in performance? The principal issue here is decentralization. Better performance is associated with decentralization, and more so when facilities are able to exert control over staff and are made financially independent than when they are able only to control material resources. Performance of clinicians is better when staff and resources are controlled locally or regionally. Where there is a full doctor, the administrative decisions and management of human and material resources will tend to be more localized at the facility level than the regional level. This is part of the reason a doctor's presence increases lab use. But MDs also impose higher professional standards, as can be seen as well in the way in which they reduce poly-pharmacy (PRESCRIPTION).

Hospitals perform significantly ($p < 0.01$) better than smaller facilities in laboratory examinations for malaria parasites and giving proper prescriptions. They are, however, worse than smaller facilities in being attentive to people and having adequate medicines ($p < 0.01$). There is no significant difference between them in completeness of history-taking and clinical examination, yet clients significantly prefer hospitals, and claim that hospitals provide the best value for their money.

CONCLUSIONS AND POLICY IMPLICATIONS

This study found that decentralization improves the quality of health care. Local control of personnel, along with staff salaries linked to facility revenues, gives health care providers the incentive to provide quality service and to attract clients. Decentralization of resource management is closely associated with staff but is a less powerful contributor to quality. The presence of a doctor at the facility contributes to quality both directly through higher professional standards and indirectly by increasing resource decentralization.

We also found that hospitals are superior to smaller facilities in appropriateness of prescription and laboratory examination, and were more appreciated by clients. But these factors are influenced by the greater presence of doctors at hospitals. Smaller facilities scored better in availability of medicines and their clinicians were more attentive. There was no significant difference in history taking and clinical examination. Thus from a technical point of view, smaller facilities need only to improve on laboratory examination and their prescriptions to compete with hospitals. Taking into account that most of the improper prescriptions were somewhat trivial, the effort that is needed to improve them may be much less than the cost of having more hospitals to please clients. We know that clinicians in small health facilities do not request laboratory tests because the laboratory does not exist. The problem would have been much more complex if a laboratory existed but was not used. Services in small facilities can therefore be improved if they are provided with laboratories that are appropriately equipped. If this is done, appropriate health care can be provided to the majority of the population at an affordable cost at health centers and dispensaries, and there would be no justification to bypass the referral system and go to a hospital for simple ailments. The same logic leads us to conclude that it would be legitimate to charge a bypass fee to those who wish to go to the hospitals for simple out-patient care.

Something needs to be done to improve the performance of clinical officers and clinical assistants of Tanzania's government health centers and dispensaries, where most people receive health services. This study suggests that health care outcomes would improve if health personnel decisions were placed under local control. The Ministry of Health has proposed the formation of District Health Boards, which will look after the affairs of health in the district. The Boards will be answerable to the District Councils. Health Facility Boards will also be formed to govern health facilities, and each hospital, health center, and dispensary will have its own board. It is not enough, however, if personnel remain under central government control. If the boards are to function effectively they should control not only the cost-sharing money from fees, but the entire budget and personnel matters as well. Most important, the boards should be able to give discretionary bonuses to health personnel when their performance merits it *and* their facilities generate sufficient income to finance it. This would provide the incentives from which quality emerges, and they should be able to take disciplinary measures if staff do not perform as expected. The chief-of-post should also be given more authority to govern the health facility, under the guidance of the facility's board.

The Ministry of Health has been hesitant to devolve control of health care to local authorities. This has been due to the frequent experience that the DMO has had no control over district health funds, which are sometimes used to fund other projects by the authority of the District Executive Director (the top local government authority in the district). From this study we find that even if the DMO is given financial autonomy, health care provision might not improve until such autonomy finds its way to the facility level. We therefore propose that with the formation of Hospital Boards that is underway, autonomy should reach the facility level as well. If these boards are to be formed and legally empowered to govern health facilities, they should be given the authority to hire and fire and have financial resources that they can control to remunerate and provide bonuses to those who perform well.

We also recommend that church denominations grant more authority over their health personnel and material resources to their health facilities. It will be easier for church denominations to grant this autonomy to their health facilities than it is for the government. As noted earlier, the involvement of the church in provision of health in Tanzania is very significant and there is a close collaboration between the government and the Church. We think that more opportunity exists for expanding this collaboration. The government could contract with churches to administer and manage some health facilities, particularly health centers and dispensaries in the rural areas. Since churches have less qualified staff, the existing arrangement by which some government employees are seconded to work in the church should be continued.

The study also indicates that the church facilities' decentralization, and their need to survive and sustain themselves financially, acts as an incentive to engage in poly-pharmacy. This makes medical care expensive and sometimes unaffordable. But private for-profit health care would be even more expensive, and the study shows that financial incentives do work to improve the quality of care. The impact of fiscal incentives on quality may be different for private practitioners, because the churches provide a value context in which the *health* of the client has a special importance. This value context substitutes for the weakness of professional self-regulation in Tanzania and helps to solve the principal/agent problem we have observed of imperfect client evaluation of technical quality.

The problem of poly-pharmacy in the more decentralized facilities nonetheless shows the need for regulation even among the churches. State regulatory mechanisms have to provide clients with some form of protection from paying excessively for medical care. The state does not need to do this itself. Since all church health facilities are coordinated by the Christian Social Services Commission (CSSC), successor to the defunct Christian Medical Board of Tanzania (CMBT), the CSSC can assist the government in its function of regulating services provided by church health facilities.

If facilities are to become independent, financing mechanisms need to be established that enable people to meet the cost of medical care.

The state needs to create an enabling environment for the creation of insurance schemes and to protect other stakeholders like the companies that have to pay hospital fees for employees. We encountered a number of clients whose hospital expenses are met by the companies for which they worked. The Ministry of Health is piloting a Community Health Fund Scheme in Igunga District, Tabora region, where each household is contributing an agreed amount of money during the harvest season to meet medical expenses for the family for the whole year. Such a scheme may provide an alternative health care financing mechanism for rural areas.

In this study, when we compared the prices people paid and where they go for service we found that they do not simply go to the least expensive place; they go where the service is of high quality, but where it is also not too expensive. This seems an obvious observation but it has far reaching policy implications. Service of poor quality will not be utilized, and thus a facility providing such care will have no impact on improving the health of the people in its catchment area. Similarly, a facility that is too expensive will not be utilized and will fail to sustain itself financially. Facilities that rely too heavily on diminishing government subsidies also will have to restrict access. The challenge is to provide widely available services of high quality at low cost. All efforts and innovations need to be employed to cut the cost of providing good quality care. Decentralization and reliance on the professional mission of the churches, combined with higher level regulation, subsidies and supports (such as the common purchase of medicines at the regional level) seem most likely to achieve this result.

9 Management and the Impact of Auxiliaries on Pastoral Production and Veterinary Services Delivery in Senegal

Cheikh Ly

Senegal's government decision-makers and private professionals are facing many challenges as they develop new models for delivering animal health services and husbandry inputs. Official policy statements have emphasized privatization since 1987, but achievements are lagging. Many supportive interventions, such as start-up loans, sanitary mandates,[1] and legal and institution-building measures are yet to be developed. However, a new veterinary service market structure is emerging and policy guidance is very much needed to ensure superior levels of both economic efficiency and distributional equity.

Policy guidance must be based on an understanding of the privatization process at the herders' micro-level and in their dealings with the veterinary systems offered to them. In this respect, veterinary auxiliaries—local herders with rudimentary training in basic animal husbandry practices—and village veterinary pharmacies (VVPs) have become crucial yet controversial components of privatization design (FAO 1997; Zessin 1996). For example, it is important to know when and how auxiliaries and VVPs improve livestock health outcomes, and whether their performance is shaped by the kind of supervision they receive. This study focuses on how herders in one of Senegal's major livestock production zones fit into the current transition toward privatization. It attempts to describe a veterinary matrix in which principal/agent relations exist and herders are individual decision makers with individual needs. Understanding how herders choose providers, and how the auxiliary-VVP coupling shapes these choices, is crucial for the effective implementation of and adjustment to veterinary service privatization.

---

1. Public contracting of mandatory immunizations to private practitioners.

In the 1970s and even the 1980s, governments in sub-Saharan Africa were skeptical of the notion that the market could be used to improve livestock production; they were concerned that equity distortions resulting from market imperfections would outweigh any market-based efficiency gains. In consequence, the livestock subsector was heavily assisted through government-led programs and projects. Today, with the collapse of traditional government interventions and public veterinary health and production systems, new challenges are faced within the livestock subsector (Akakpo 1992; Cheneau 1985; Leonard 1987; Leonard 1993; Ly 1989; Sar 1993; Touré 1987; Sandford 1983; Umali *et al.* 1992; VSF 1996).

All of the actors in the livestock subsector comprise a veterinary matrix. In such a matrix, the market combines livestock needs with products that are either concrete (drugs, vaccines) or intangible (veterinary diagnoses). The structure and strength of each participant's incentives generates complex and competing behaviors. Thus, a veterinary matrix is understood here as the particular set of permutations under which the various participants operate in the veterinary domain of the livestock subsector. The framework of the matrix results from privatization initiatives and their consequences regarding three issues: the supply of veterinary drugs and other inputs; the nature of the curative, promotive, and preventive functions executed using the available veterinary inputs and services; and the distribution of those veterinary inputs and services among the beneficiaries, the different levels of veterinary staff, and the different types of organizations (private, public, projects, nongovernmental organizations (NGOs), producers' groups, and the informal sector).

The types of contractual arrangements used and the strength of each participant's economic incentives combine to shape the dynamics of the veterinary matrix. This is especially true when traditional herders deal with veterinary auxiliaries, village veterinary pharmacies, and government veterinary paraprofessionals. Variation in the types of interventions or responsibilities offered by each veterinary service provider shapes these relations. Therefore, in each emerging or persisting veterinary system, herders' expectations, behaviors, and responses to the forms, types, and prices of veterinary service delivery determine the pace of the privatization process and its outcome—especially at the lower levels of the veterinary hierarchy.

The dynamics of the veterinary matrix are shaped by the types of contractual arrangements used and the strength of each participant's economic incentives. This is especially true when traditional herders are dealing with veterinary auxiliaries, village veterinary pharmacies, and government veterinary paraprofessionals. Their relations are shaped by variation in the types of interventions or responsibilities each veterinary service provider offers. Therefore, in each emerging or persisting system, herders' expectations, behaviors and responses to the forms, types and prices of veterinary service delivery determine the pace of the privatization process and its outcomes, especially at the lower levels of the veterinary hierarchy.

Restructuring in the Senegalese livestock subsector is based on the implementation of new organizational arrangements using a privatization model in which markets are set free in the expectation that they will outperform hierarchies. The formerly dominant public sector is ceding responsibility for several important interventions (such as immunizations, diagnostic support, vector control, drugs, and vaccine sales) to private veterinarians, NGOs and veterinary auxiliaries. Public goods management and delivery, externalities, and moral hazard problems are still at stake, as are general aspects of public monitoring and regulation of livestock development policy, which is recognized as a core component of national food policy. These issues have particular sets of consequences for the privatization process (Ly 1997).

Different organizational innovations have been implemented, notably including government divestiture from livestock economics operations, movement toward contracting of sanitary mandates, the creation of village veterinary pharmacies with their locally trained auxiliaries, greater involvement of NGOs, and decentralization in favor of local producers' groups. The path and rate of herders' adoption and participation in these new innovations are fundamental issues, yet the little information that exists has been barely analyzed. Therefore, herders' willingness to participate in the new veterinary matrix needs to be assessed, and innovations need to be reshaped according to that assessment, before we may conclude with confidence that the Senegalese veterinary service system is efficient, effective and sustainable.

As we will explain below, there exist three distinct yet related systems within Senegal's veterinary matrix (Figure 9.1). First, the traditional system (TRA) was established during the colonial period. Government veterinarians and paraprofessionals dominate supply and thereby shape demand for veterinary systems. Next, the first level transformation (FLT) was the result of a 1989 government policy of creating government-supervised village veterinary pharmacies (VVPs). This was followed in

1992 by a second level transformation (SLT) in which VVPs have been created and managed by NGOs. All three systems exist today, sometimes in a single geographic area. After considering the features and outcomes of the veterinary matrix as it operates at the macro level, we will explore its functioning at the micro level where herders are in daily confrontation or cooperation with veterinary service providers and are shaping demand for veterinary services.

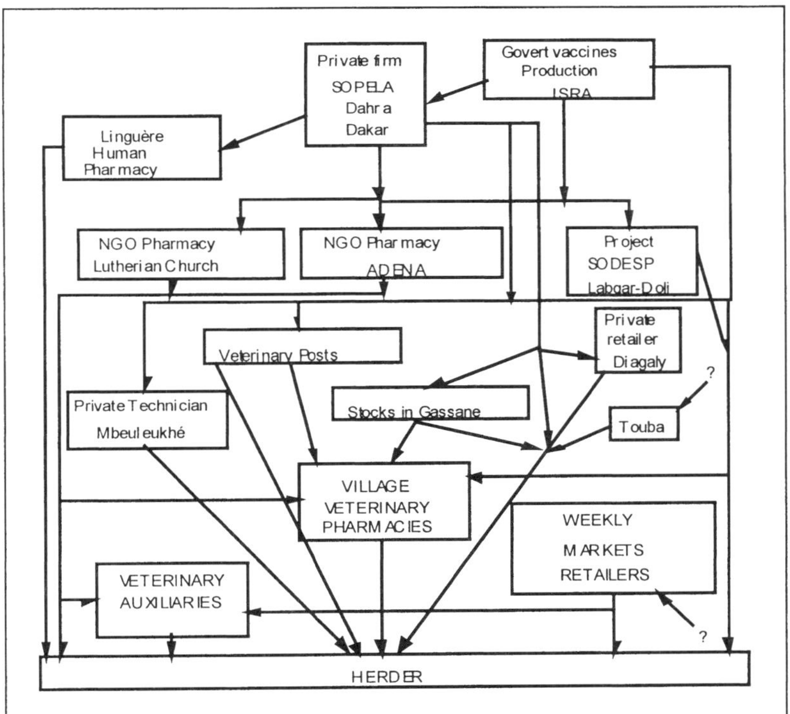

Figure 9.1. Ferlo Area Veterinary Matrix

Principal/Agent Theory and Herders' Choice

The privatization process at the herder level can be better understood through the principal/agent framework. Principal/agent theory is in the mainstream of the New Institutional Economics, a framework that has been expanding exponentially since the 1980's and is devoted to explanations of microanalytic organizational details (Leonard 1993; Williamson 1990; Williamson 1993). The New Institutional Economics explains social organizational phenomena by using assumptions deriving from transaction cost economics. The literature describes it as an analytical tool joining aspects of law, economics, and organization theory to observe and understand the organizational variety involved in economic activity. Williamson (1984) summarizes this approach as one that recognizes the human behavioral attributes of an 'organizational man' who is assumed to be cognitively less competent but motivationally more complex than his 'economic man' counterpart; describes the microanalytic detail of transactions with dimensions such as asset specificity, uncertainty, and frequency; and uses a transaction cost economizing criterion to evaluate alternative modes of organization.

The pertinence of this approach is reinforced by the limitations of pre-transaction cost reasoning, which views the organization of economic activity as given and takes firms as production functions to which a profit maximization principle can easily be applied. However, although it can be said that the ideas of transaction cost economics have made it into the mainstream of neoclassical economics, it is clearly only part of that mainstream (Williamson 1990; Zald 1987).

Principal/agent theory is the part of the New Institutional Economics that is especially concerned with those situations in which there is a severe imbalance (asymmetry) in information between the buyer and the seller. In both human and veterinary medicine, clients (patients or herders) are at a disadvantage in dealing with health practitioners (MDs, veterinarians, and their associated paraprofessionals): practitioners are consulted because they have specialized knowledge, but clients, who know less, cannot be sure that the practitioner's skills are appropriate to the problem or that they will be fully used. Unless this problem is solved and the clients can gain confidence in the quality of the services offered by practitioners, clients either will reduce their consumption of the services or will be prepared to pay no more than the value of the lowest quality service available in the market because they fear that this is the service level they *might* receive. When this information asymmetry problem between the principal (the client) and her agent (the practitioner) is not resolved, we have what Akerlof refers to as a 'market for lemons:' a situation in which transactions are dominated by inferior products (1970). Possible mechanisms for assuring principals (clients and patients) that they are getting good quality service from their agents (health practitioners) are incentive systems, including professional supervision and regulation (Arrow 1985) that maximize agent effort (Leonard, Chapter 5).

The Management Issue

If left alone, the market for veterinary services in Senegal would evolve toward a typical lemons market where only low quality services would be demanded. This would create a suboptimal situation for herders, providers, and society. This may be avoided if the work of veterinary professional associations, as elaborated by Ly (Chapter 7), is complemented by effective veterinary service management at the herders' micro level. This is especially true during the current transition phase of the veterinary market. Once a well functioning market is established, the immediate incentives generated by the interplay of demand and supply competition and market flexibility could manage people's behavior to both individual and social advantage. In the meantime, however, distortions and inelasticities as much as opportunistic behavior needs to be tackled. Organizational alternatives to classical hierarchies such as government can have strategic and facilitating roles in consolidating workable principal/agent relations.

In Senegal, while divesting from direct control of the livestock subsector, the government has supported a national extension agency, the *Programme Nationale de Vulgarisation Agricole* (PVNA). This is what we refer to as the first level transformation (FLT). It became part of the veterinary matrix both by creating VVPs with startup stocks and by training local auxiliaries who would be integrated into VVP activities. Its interventions were accompanied by a training and visit system (T&V) aimed at improving livestock producers' awareness, animal health, and production with the help of government veterinary staff. This approach raises important questions about the sustainability and efficiency of the PNVA in the animal health and production domains. Because T&V was a quintessentially top down model for managing staff behavior, it is very likely that programming supervision and support for the highly variable needs of livestock producers would be more difficult and less detailed than for crop based agricultural extension. Therefore, PNVA's T&V is expected quickly to become rigid and nonadaptive, and its results are expected to be only minimally superior to those of the traditional governmental system it replaced.

The second level transformation occurred in 1992 when, in addition to PNVA, NGOs such as OXFAM, Association Française des Volontaires du Progrès (AFVP), Vétérinaires sans frontières (VSF), Aide Action, and Èglise Èvangèlique Luthérienne du Sénégal (EELS) created VVPs and trained auxiliaries. We hypothesize that these NGOs have provided better supervisory management and have induced stronger participation from beneficiaries. Questions are then raised about their real capacity to offer an appropriate management strategy for curative, preventive, and promotive interventions in the livestock sector. Consequently, NGOs can be described as organizational hybrids that are better models of horizontal management veterinary systems. They are expected to consolidate workable principal/agent relations by taking advantage of the herders' participation and employing supervision patterns based on priorities and incentives coming from internal and professional values. However, a quantitative assessment of comparative service efficiency, outreach, and production or producer benefits for these systems is yet to appear and is the purpose of this study.

Since the veterinary matrix is prone to distortions and inelasticities as much as opportunistic behavior of the participants, market incentives could usefully be accompanied with better management of the way herders interact with auxiliaries and veterinary technicians at the micro level. Consequently management, a very scarce resource in Africa, is a core issue in the privatization of animal health and production systems. The strategic combination of supervision, professionalism, and participation will strengthen the current transition toward privatization.

We hope to enhance the prospect that appropriate contracts or models leading to superior outcomes will become a defining feature of Senegal's privatization process. To this end, we will analyze the results of three surveys that elicited information from herders, auxiliaries, and VVP managers on both specific choices and expected tendencies regarding demand for various veterinary services. Armed with this data, an agency theoretical framework will help us to anticipate institutional changes that would increase the likelihood of a superior outcome, and also changes that could help herders to cope with the type of veterinary service delivery system they are likely to face in a more open environment. Therefore, more specifically, one needs to know how well herders respond to the particular veterinary system they face and how well that system responds to herder demands and expectations.

METHODOLOGY

Research Area and Context

The Ferlo, a major pastoral production zone in Senegal, is our research area. Its ecology is typical of the Sahel region and annual rainfall is between 250 and 650 mm. There have been three droughts in the last twenty-five years. The French colonial administration introduced water boreholes in the 1950s, and these boreholes have transformed agricultural organization and management in this region. Social relations also changed as individuals left their ancestral homes to go to new villages and encampments that emerged near the boreholes. The pastoralists living in the area are mostly *Fulani*, precisely *Fulbe dieri*, who take their cattle and small ruminants (sheep and goats) on seasonal transhumant treks from one natural pasture and water borehole to the next. After the 1973 drought, important pastoral development projects were initiated to stabilize the traditional production systems. Today, those projects are practically defunct, yet the zone sylvo-pastorale remains Senegal's major supplier of cattle and sheep.

Throughout the Sahel, a great variety of diseases challenge animal herders. Botulism-pica, Black Leg, Anthrax, *la Peste des Petits Ruminants*, sheep pox, and pasteurellosis are the most common. Internal parasites also constitute a major constraint, as are blood parasites found especially on herds coming back from transhumance in the south. Controlling Rinderpest after its first appearance in 1915 was a major challenge, but after the pan-African Campaign in 1964 and an annual mandatory immunization campaign by government veterinary institutions, the disease seems to be eradicated. The last appearance was in 1972–73. Contagious Bovine Pleuropneumonia (CBPP) is the second major threat for which a mandatory immunization campaign has been conducted since 1969. It is commonly accepted that the disease map is stable in the area, and our research corroborated this impression.

With the collapse of government livestock development projects, new types of herders' organizations have sprouted since the end of the 1980s. With the assistance of NGOs and also government (PNVA) extension activities, these new organizations are becoming the local level veterinary service centers. They combine two activities: selling drugs at VVPs and training local herders to perform basic veterinary tasks for other herders in the village. Now that the government has decided not to take such a direct role either in providing veterinary services or in selling

Table 9.1 Veterinary Delivery System, VVPs and Sampled Herders

Veterinary System	Traditional		First level Transformation		Second level Transformation		Total	
Village Veterinary Pharmacies	n	%	n	%	n	%	n	%
Presence	-	-	85	24.4	94	27.0	179	51.4
Absence	117	33.6	33	9.5	19	5.5	169	48.6
Total	117	33.6	118	33.9	113	32.5	348	100.0

drugs, these local level ventures are at the core of Senegal's veterinary market expansion. The effects of this institutional shift are especially clear in the Ferlo area, whose privatization measures are the focus of this study.

Sampling and Data Collection

A team of four interviewers conducted three surveys in the 1995 dry season (February through May). All interviews were based on structured questionnaires and conducted in villages or herders' encampments in the language chosen by the interviewee (generally *Fulani*) and without translation. For the first survey, we selected all 32 VVPs that were operating in the Ferlo area at the time (25 additional VVPs were closed for one reason or another). Each manager was asked about infrastructure, drug and vaccine availability, finance and management issues, and constraints on supply, storage, and distribution. The second survey sampled 63 auxiliaries (out 93 officially registered), who were asked about their personal characteristics, training, activities, relations with herders, and relations with more highly trained paraprofessionals and full veterinarians. The third survey identified 348 pastoralist households by cluster sampling based on the water borehole network and access to VVPs, auxiliaries, and government paraprofessionals. Of these, 169 households were in subzones without any VVP and 179 were in subzones with a VVP (Table 9.1). The sampling area for all three surveys was stratified into three different zones with respect to the type of veterinary service delivery systems found in the study area— TRA, FLT, and SLT (Table 9.1).

The herder's survey elicited information on the herder and his management of animal health. Progeny and health history were drawn by referring explicitly to four named cows chosen by the herder. For each cow, mortality, reproduction, and sale parameters were collected. In addition, immunization and treatment records for cattle and small ruminants were assembled by recall. Questions were also addressed to the utilization of traditional treatment and self-treatment. Next, the herder was asked about VVP membership and views on the veterinary services delivery system. Except for records on numbers and price, questions were open ended. Finally, a set of ten pre-defined cards were used to determine by decreasing importance the herders demand for a variety of government and private services (See Chapter 7). An extensive coding procedure was used to compare answers and derive the appropriate coding for data handling.

Data analysis was conducted in two steps, aiming first at describing the veterinary matrix components with a focus on VVPs and auxiliaries. Characteristics of VVPs were targeted to show how they function within the veterinary matrix and as sites of exchange or contact between herders and auxiliaries or government veterinary paraprofessionals. This allowed us to evaluate the relative effectiveness of the TRA, FLT, and SLT systems and draw conclusions about the efficacy of the three management styles. Auxiliaries are then described as participants in the veterinary matrix whose position and role are essential in understanding the context and nature of their principal/agent relations with herders. In a second step, herder data were used to evaluate the availability and quality of the actual conduits for livestock services and to compare the performance of the three systems of veterinary services distribution. Comparisons were made and statistically tested by analysis of variance (ANOVA). The Least Significant Difference (LSD) multiple range test was then conducted to sort out the effect of the factors studied. The herders' own ranking from the ten-card sets was summarized for the sample as a whole and also for the three different systems. By transformation, a new proxy variable was computed to represent the aggregated weight of the ten cards chosen by coding the five private interventions as (1) and government dominated interventions as (0). Analysis of this variable led to the conclusion that herders tend to value private interventions more highly.

RESULTS AND DISCUSSION

Descriptive statistics are used to characterize the veterinary matrix components, which were focused on the VVPs, the auxiliaries, and the herders. Information available from VVP managers confirms that the

Table 9.2 Membership in VPPs

Range of members	mean	standard deviation	min	max	herders/ members	cases	herders %
< 200	53	43	12	200	1 603	30	83
< 100	45	27	12	100	1 253	28	65
Sample	62	64	12	320	1 923	31	100

presence of VVPs enhances the operation of the veterinary matrix. However, management issues lead to a tremendous variation in the effectiveness of individual VVPs. Sustainability—especially of government managed (PVNA) pharmacies—is a genuine concern.

Village Veterinary Pharmacies

The first VVPs were established in 1989 and new ones have been created at the slow rate of 11 per year ever since. VVPs are cooperative ventures and must be started with their own funds, which are provided initially by their members. Most VVPs have fewer than 150 members, who are pastoralists, farmers, or petty traders (Table 9.2). The average starting capital for a VVP was 56,000 CFA francs, although some were opened with as little as 20,000 CFA francs and six opened with an initial investment of 150,000 CFA francs or more. Twenty-one VVPs (66 per cent) have agreed to supply products on a credit basis. They report net gains of an average of seven per cent of investments.

VVPs supply drugs, vaccines, and animal feed. Naturally, the products we found on the shelf at the time of our survey were shaped by the season of the year (the dry season). The most common drugs were antiparasites, antibiotics, and anti-inflammatory products. There is some brand competition for antiparasites and antibiotics. All VVPs supplied the four major domestically produced vaccines that are directed against the major diseases. Notably, these vaccines are all nonmandatory, so their universal presence shows that they are really used at the local level. Feed supplies are mostly mineral licks, cotton seed cake, pellets, and bone meal (Table 9.3). Products available in the pharmacies are sold only on a retail basis and products in solutions are even pumped into syringes to be sold in unit doses. Occasionally, auxiliaries are allowed to buy small stocks when they have to practice on large herds, but this situation is rare since capital is usually too low to permit it. Indeed, a continuing problem is anticipating demand and providing additional stocks at the time of year when they are demanded. Vaccines and antibacterials are both used differently according to the season.

Table 9.3 VVPs and Drugs

Types of products	March 95			July 94			
	n1	% PVV	% occurrences	n2	% PVV	% occurrences	Evolution in stocks
		(n = 32)	(n = 310)		(n = 31)	(n=295)	(n1-n2)
Vaccines:							
anabot	32	100	10	26	84	9	6
pasteurellad	23	72	7	23	74	8	0
pasteurellox	29	91	9	26	84	9	3
carbosympto	20	63	6	21	68	7	-1
Total vaccines	104	na	34	96	na	33	8
Antiparasites:							
ivomex	21	66	7	25	81	8	-4
exhelm	13	41	4	19	61	6	-6
trypamidium	10	31	3	18	58	6	-8
berenyl	3	9	1	8	26	3	-5
bayticol	12	38	4	3	10	1	9
rental	7	22	2	8	26	3	-1
cydectin	7	22	2	0	0	0	7
ticide	7	22	2	6	19	2	1
g. antiparasites . (injection)	28	88	9	25	78	8	3
g. antiparasites . (external)	19	59	6	9	28	3	10
g. antitryps	13	41	4	26	81	8	-13
g. antiparasites . (pills)	20		6	27		9	-7
Total Antiparasites	80	na	26	87	na	28	-7
Antibiotics:							
TLA	13	41	4	16	52	5	-3
septotryl	5	16	2	14	45	5	-9
oxytetracycline	2	6	1	2	6	1	0
Total antibiotics	20	na	6	32	na	11	-12

Types of products	March 95			July 94			
Feed:							
pellets	11	34	4	4	13	1	7
licks	15	47	5	11	35	4	4
cotton seeds	11	34	4	8	26	3	3
Total feed	37	na	12	23		8	14
Products listed	241	na	78	238	na	81	3
Others	69	na	22	57	na	19	12
Total for occurrences	310	na	100	295	na	100	15

NB: Data was collected in March 1995 stocks found at that time are primary data; data on stock on hand in July 1994 (period before the last rainy season) come from secondary sources obtained from VVPs managers.
n1 = number of VVPs considered and n2 = number of types of products in each VVP considered; na = not applicable. 'Others' refers to all products present in stocks but not listed separately (Antibiotics: Tenalon Sulfametox; Antiparasites: Dysto-5, Sinantic, Diamil; Anti-inflammatories: Phenylarthrite, Tifáne; Feed: Groundnut cake, bone meal, Multiphos; Miscellaneous: Fercobsang, Stress Vitam, Veto-antidiar, Alcohol, Calmalgine, Theracalcium, Meteoroquinol, Olivitasol).

One reason for this inventory problem is that VVPs, including NGO VVPs, tend not to be carefully monitored. After startup there are virtually no follow-up activities (with the exception of VVPs that are monitored by the Lutheran Church). The only link with the veterinary matrix is the local veterinary auxiliary, who is a crucial animal caregiver but still is at the bottom of the human capital chain in terms of both skills and status. Even if this is the only link, it is still a strong one; 16 VVPs (47 per cent) had an auxiliary as either president or vice president, and an auxiliary was manager at 24 VVPs (72 per cent). These managers appeared to be truly alone in terms of making management decisions; eleven managers wrote regular reports, but only one passed reports on to the official government paraprofessional responsible for the area.

This management as well as geographic distance from the veterinary caregiving hierarchy led two-thirds of managers to view their VVPs as simple drug selling places rather than the link between pastoralists and the higher levels of the veterinary service hierarchy. Indeed, information is usually not shared between managers, their VVPs, and the officially supervisory NGOs or government authority (typically PNVA) and rivalry is common. Also, if a manager is not able to account for missing stocks or financial losses, the VVP and the official supervisor have no recourse beyond social pressure. In such a situation, it is clear that sustainability is an issue and it should come as no surprise to learn that 25 of the study area's 57 officially recognized VVPs were nonfunctional at the time of the survey. One of our main tasks is to evaluate the institutional reasons for this less than stellar record. To this end, we move on to an analysis of the veterinary auxiliaries and the herders.

The Veterinary Auxiliaries

Ninety-seven per cent of the auxiliaries interviewed hailed from the Ferlo and were *Fulani*. Their average age was 33, and ranged between 18 and 56 years. Nearly half were heads of their household and could be considered as stable. Only eight per cent were women. Most of the auxiliaries were herders and the others were involved in petty trade and rain fed agriculture. Half had lived in the city for educational purposes or job search, and the vast majority was literate in *Fulani* (86 per cent), Arabic (25 per cent), or French (16 per cent). Auxiliary training sessions were organized by the institutions associated with the VVP where the auxiliary was registered. Forty-four per cent had taken the opportunity to update their knowledge since their initial auxiliary training session.

The activities described by auxiliaries include supporting the official veterinary technicians (11 per cent of answers), performing nonmandatory immunizations (21 per cent) and curative interventions (51 per cent), and counseling herders (16 per cent). Only 14 per cent of the interviewees admitted that they merely sell pharmaceuticals. During the immunization periods, 60 per cent of the auxiliaries declare being in contact and working with government technicians. Fifty-seven per cent of them never worked with other auxiliaries either because they did not need assistance or did not want to share their fees with another auxiliary. Nearly half of the auxiliaries acknowledged that they are working beyond the area of their village and thus do not respect the basic principle of their recruitment. Several explanations were offered, the most common being financial opportunity (30 per cent) and following nomads or transhumants from their own area (31 per cent). The vast majority does not consider that competition is present in their village surroundings.

The instruments used by auxiliaries are very simple and common: all had at least one syringe but only 38 per cent had a thermometer. Ten per cent had a castration clip, six per cent had a device to introduce pills or bolus, five per cent had a marking device and only two per cent had scissors. Sixty-three per cent of the auxiliaries waited until a pastoralist came to their office before going to the herds, 18 per cent operated on the basis of appointments, and 19 per cent proceeded both ways. Ninety-one per cent of the auxiliaries report being paid regularly by herders, although 43 per cent said that payment is usually delayed. The problem, rather, is with the price they could ask; only 35 per cent of the auxiliaries are satisfied with their gains. Eighty-six per cent charged a common price for product and service; the remainder used a sliding scale. Only five per cent differentiated between the payment of products and services.

Auxiliaries are present in the veterinary matrix and play important roles both through VVPs and independently of them. Auxiliaries are always well identified and accepted willingly as service providers by the herders, who clearly differentiate them from the veterinary paraprofessionals. The syringe, the symbol of the auxiliary status, is linked with the capacity to give curative injections and vaccinations. The absence of other veterinary instruments shows that their technical activities are not diversified and remain limited to three simple types: drug sales, pellet distribution, and injection services.

Auxiliaries are members of the community they serve, and this adds a level of social complexity to their interaction. Social criteria and hierarchical considerations that could be constraints on the efficiency of a system frequently influence herders' choices of auxiliaries. The combination of social and professional obligation also affects the repayment rate, since arrangements are more easily determined and enforced between principals and agents who are not only dealing with economic matters but are also interrelated socially.

Relations with their paraprofessional superiors are also complex. Only 60 per cent of the auxiliaries declared that they are in contact with paraprofessionals, although the auxiliary system is supposed to be completely controlled by them. The 40 per cent gap reveals how far the government structures are from satisfying herders' demand for veterinary services and how important auxiliaries are for the herders. There is, to be sure, a geographical component to this monitoring problem: VVPs were an average of 49 kilometers from the nearest large town (either Lingerie or Dhaka). Onsite supervision by a city-based paraprofessional would require substantial time and travel costs. The efficacy of auxiliaries and the problems their presence might create appear to be rather dependent on the specific situation of the herder and on the opportunities available to him in terms of veterinary services and supply systems.

Table 9.4 Bovine Immunization Rates

Types of vaccines	Mean of vaccinated heads	Standard deviation	Min.	Max.	Sum	% of cattle	% of herders
Anthrax	1	4	0	40	454	39	19
Pasteur-ellosis	7	17	0	133	2 445	21	40
Botulism	14	21	0	133	4 843	42	13
Total	34	18	6	133	11 564	100	100

Table 9.5 Treatments and Veterinary System Delivery

System delivery	Treatments on cattle (%)*	Treatments on small ruminants (%)*
TRA	8	9
FLT	3	10
SLT	6	16
Sample	17	34

*% of responses

The Herders

The vast majority of herder households (92 per cent) interviewed were *Fulani*; a few were *Wolof*, *Serere* or *More*. The dominant production system is pastoralism and the population sampled has been sedentarized for a long time. Eighty-four per cent considered that they were not nomadic and 67 per cent had been present in the area for more than thirty years. The mean age is 45. The vaccination data collected for each herder shows an average herd size of 34 head of cattle, including 22 breeding cows (68 per cent of the total number), for a total of 11, 564 head owned by 336 herders. Small ruminants in the sample are estimated at 34,700 head with the ratio of one bovine for three small ruminants (mostly sheep). This leads to an average of 100 small ruminants per herder. All interviewees said that they and their families alone managed their herds. Many herders derive all of their income solely from livestock production and sales; 51 per cent practiced rain fed agriculture, but this was commonly limited to millet production for household consumption. Only 14 per cent of interviewees were involved in petty trade.

Among the herders interviewed, only 33 per cent were members of their area's VVP and 28 per cent participated in other types of rural organizations. These data confirm the well-known weak organization of herders, especially in the pastoral area due to transhumant constraints but also atavistic attitudes with respect to individual autonomy. A significant difference was observed between systems: herders tended to be better organized in the second level transformation (SLT) system.

All herders declared that their herds had received mandatory immunizations, but only 43 per cent of them had vaccinated at least some of their herd against all three major prevalent bovine diseases during the year prior to the survey (Table 9.4). Frequency of immunization is statistically related to the type of delivery system; SLT herds (24 per cent) were immunized at twice the rate of both FLT (ten per cent) and TRA (nine per cent). The same is true for botulism. Despite these dangerously low bovine vaccination levels, 45 per cent of the herders vaccinated their small ruminants, thus explaining the importance of Anabot in VVPs stocks as shown earlier.

The frequency of curative treatments is also very low: 17 per cent of the herders recalled a treatment on their bovine herd during the last year. Only 150 head (from among 368 herders) had been treated in the previous year, but herders in the SLT system had significantly more animals treated (Table 9.5). As with preventive services, herders (34 per cent) gave a curative priority to small ruminants. Eleven different products were also reported used by herders. All of them are commonly seen in the area.

One has to note that the wide use of *Ivomec*™ before fattening creates an overestimation of sick small ruminants. The low general frequency of treatment cannot be linked, however, with known alternative means of treatments such as self-treatment or referral to witch doctors. Surprisingly, very few herders talked about specific traditional treatments. Besides a few references to treatment of lameness and mystic or religious invocations, the herders interviewed seem in practice to be fully dependent on modern treatments. This is confirmed by their wide utilization of injectable antiparasites and antibiotics, albeit at a low incidence. Also, the average herder age of 45 years reveals that a new generation is heading households and providing herd management. It seems that old, close relationships with livestock development projects and extension have created a relative decrease in traditional treatment.

A fairly homogenous pricing system for drugs and vaccines was observed throughout the study area. Vaccine prices per bovine dose were consistently in the 50–70 CFA franc range.[2] Anabot, which is the most

2. Exchange rate: US$ 1 = 500 CFA francs

Table 9.6 Herders and Their Priorities

Needs Ranked[1]	Sample			Traditional system		First level transformation system		Second level transformation system	
	Rank	Mean	Signif.	Rank	Mean	Rank	Mean	Rank	Mean
Alphabetization	1	4.04	0.0447	2	4.54a	1	3.81a	2	4.10
Small ruminant vaccines	2	4.37	0.0000	4	5.04a	2	4.66b	1	3.97ab
Auxiliaries	3	4.94	0.0000	3	4.63a	5	5.46ab	3	4.62ab
Bovine vaccines	4	4.96	0.0863	5	5.06	3	4.71a	4	5.13a
External parasites	5	5.19	0.0000	1	4.44a	4	4.75b	6	5.72ab
Internal parasites	6	5.76	ns	7	5.79	6	5.78	7	5.73
Public veterinary profess.	7	5.78	ns	8	5.97	7	5.87	5	5.65
Feed	8	5.87	0.0243	6	5.44a	9	6.09a	8	5.81
Genetics	9	6.25	0.1719	9	6.61a	8	6.03a	9	6.32
Rinderpest	10	7.84	ns	10	7.47	10	7.83	10	7.95

[1] Descending importance from 1 to 10

All computations after weighting cases

a and b show the means statistically different with the Least Significant Difference multiple range test with $\alpha = 0.05$

Table 9.7 Herders and Aggregated Needs

Needs aggregated	Sample			Traditional system		First level transformation system		Second level transformation system	
	Rank	Average	Signif	Rank	Average	Rank	Average	Rank	Average
Private-oriented needs: Alphabetization Small ruminant vaccines Auxiliaries	1	13.4	0.0001	1	14.2a	1	13.9b	1	12.7ab
Public-oriented needs: Public veterinary profess. Rinderpest control Feed	2	19.5	0.078[1]	2	18.9a	2	19.8a	2	19.4

[1] Least significant difference (LSD) procedure for the multiple range test

All computations after weighting cases

a and b show the averages statistically different with the LSD multiple range test with $\alpha = 0.05$

widely sought, is the most expensive vaccine (70 CFA francs). For small ruminants, vaccine prices range from 35–50 CFA francs per dose. The homogeneity is explained by the fact that comparative price information is easily available to herders who discuss these issues at weekly markets and are willing to travel farther to get lower priced goods.

Herders were asked about the importance of ten veterinary services, and they ranked their priorities without any influence from interviewers. Literacy in native languages, auxiliaries, feed, and internal parasites control were highly valued; public service technicians and major vaccinations (Rinderpest and CBPP) were consistently at the bottom of the list. The analysis of variance made for the different types of veterinary delivery system shows statistically significant differences in expressed needs. Expectations appear to be different among herders according to the veterinary system in their area (Table 9.6).

To reduce the dispersion in group answers, two proxy variables were computed as private oriented needs and public oriented needs after excluding parasite controls and bovine vaccines that are provided equally well by all three systems. Results show that the private oriented needs are valued much more highly than public oriented needs. After weighting data with the type of delivery system, statistical differences are found between herder values in the three systems: herders in SLT are most interested in private interventions, followed respectively by FLT and TRA herders (Table 9.7).

When SLT and FLT herders are put in the same group, a statistical difference is also present and shows that herders expressed more clearly needs related to private interventions. From this we can conclude that herders already view themselves as members of a privatized system and seek to make the most of it.

Animal health history for breeding cows

A total of 1,265 breeding cows were evaluated from among the 7,950 cows registered by the herders in our sample. Each herder for this evaluation chose four cows, and questions were focused on animal health history and the destination of their progeny. Among these 1,265 cows, herders described 3686 live births over the lifetimes of the presented cows (11 per herder on average), 152 stillbirths, and 174 abortions. This amounts to 326 negative health events and a total of 515 reported deaths and negatives (1.4 per herder, 0.4 per evaluated breeding cow). The sex ratio for calves is one female for 1.13 males. Based on the primary data collected, variables were created to characterize reproduction, mortality,

Table 9.8 Aggregated Cow Progeny Health and Production History Data (sample data)

Parameters	Mean	Standard Dev.	Range	Min.	Max.	Sum	Herders
Cow age	9.1	1.8	8.7	5	13.7	n.a	277
Cow breeding life	6.1	1.8	6.7	2	10.7	n.a	277
Calves/breeding year	1.83	0.80	3.2	0.8	4	479	262
Fecundity/cow	2.57	0.79	4.25	0.5	4.75	784	305
Negatives	0.94	1.34	5	0	5	326	348
Mortalities	1.73	1.81	6	0	6	515	298
Males	5.72	2.45	11	1	12	1 763	308
Females	4.84	2.24	11	0	11	1 480	306
Σ Products /herder	10.28	3.14	17	2	19	3 135	305
Sales	1.16	1.21	7	0	7	402	348
Gains from sales	60 673	74 251	443 000	0	443 000	21 114 000	348
Gains/product sold	54 270	39 292	310 000	0	310 000	12 699 086	234
Females/males	1.13	0.97	--	--	--	--	306

NB: all events are for the interviewed herder, that is, his four cows;
cow breeding life is the cow's age minus three years; negatives refers to abortions and declared stillbirths; products stand for calves; units for gains and gain/product are in CFA francs; na: not applicable.

and production parameters. Data were aggregated for each cow and then, since the sampling unit for the survey in general is the herder, the data were aggregated for the herders as well (Table 9.8).

Appreciation of veterinary services delivery

Contacts with veterinary service providers depend on the type of system dominating a herder's area. Although some veterinary professionals claim that auxiliaries invade areas beyond their official territory, neither observations by our survey team nor herder responses confirmed such tendencies. When herders have a sick animal, they contact the veterinary provider they met previously. This person might be an auxiliary or a public paraprofessional; the first meeting typically occurs during a mandatory vaccination campaign. It is clear that decades of these meetings have fostered a precise understanding of the veterinary hierarchy. In times of emergency, herders use this prior knowledge to evaluate both their needs and the skills of available practitioners.

While auxiliaries usually give only the specifically demanded curative or preventive services, herders explain that paraprofessionals give additional promotive assistance during their visit. This practice is considered a tradition, which indicates that professional values have been internalized and are expected by both herder and paraprofessional. There appears to be no additional financial reward for these services, as payments are usually given for the specific service offered with a lump sum for products and labor, and the bulk of the cost is for the vaccines or drugs actually used. Especially for drugs but also for labor, money is the dominant medium of exchange. The labor cost is negotiated individually, and service payment is understood more as a voluntary gift, the *botari*, which strengthens social relationships and enhances the prospect that a particular provider will be called on and will respond when the herder or other herders in the same village have future needs.

EVALUATING ALTERNATIVE SYSTEMS: TRA, FLT, AND SLT

An important goal of the study is to evaluate the effect of modern organizational innovations, and especially the presence of NGO supervision, on herder acceptance of veterinary services and animal health performances. Tables 9.9 and 9.10 show the results of this analysis and demonstrate clearly that appropriate supervision does bring its rewards. Not all results are statistically significant, but results in virtually every category suggest the value of FLT and especially SLT systems. Negative

Table 9.9 Significant Differences Between Veterinary Systems

Variables	Sample	TRA	FLT	SLT	Signif. level*
Herd size	34 ± 18	35 ± 19a	36 ± 17b	32 ± 19ab	0.0010
Total products per herder	10.1 ± 3.2	10.7 ± 2.8a	10.1 ± 3.3	9.9 ± 3.1a	0.070
Fecundity/cow	2.5 ± 0.8	2.7 ± 0.7a	2.5 ± 0.8	2.4 ± 0.7a	0.07
Calves/breeding year	1.7 ± 0.6	1.9 ± 0.6a	1.8 ± 0.6	1.7 ± 0.6a	0.05
Small ruminants treated	16.5 ± 22.3	12.3 ± 21.9a	11.8 ± 19.7b	21.3 ± 23.3ab	0.000
Pasteurellosis doses	8.4 ± 18.3	4.4 ± 13.2a	3.3 ± 12.4b	13.6 ± 21.6ab	0.000
Anabot doses	16.0 ± 21.8	9.5 ± 17.6a	10.0 ± 20.3b	22.6 ± 22ab	0.000
Carbosympto doses	1.8 ± 4.8	0.4 ± 2.2a	0.3 ± 2.0b	3.3 ± 6.2ab	0.000
Price for past. Doses	65 ± 13	69 ± 14a	67 ± 11	63 ± 14a	0.0098
Price for anabot doses	70 ± 11	68 ± 16	69 ± 10	71 ± 11	0.033
Price for Carbosym. doses	51 ± 14	nc	58 ± 18	47±9	0.000

ANOVA with $\alpha = 0.05$ with Least Significant Difference method;
data with same letters (a, b) are statistically different;
data weighted by systems;
n.c. = no case;

Table 9.10 Differences between veterinary systems (non-significant)

Variables	Sample*	TRA	FLT	SLT
Cow age	9.1±1.8	9.0±1.8	9.2±1.7	9.1±1.8
Negatives	7.8±3.8	8.3±4.1	7.7±4.0	7.7±3.6
Mortalities	1.7±1.8	1.8±1.7	1.7±2.0	1.6±1.7
Sales	1.16±1.2	1.14±1.2	1.15±1.2	1.17±1.3
Gains from sales	61,380±75,128	58,756±74,662	60,835±65,614	62,487±82,050
Gains/sale	54,253±36,120	53,745±48,377	55,894±33,272	53,022±34,691
Bovines treated	0.47±1.5	0.35±1.1	0.37±1.5	0.6±1.6

* data weighted by systems

Table 9.11 Acceptance of Veterinary Services in the Veterinary Systems

Systems:	TRA	FLT	SLT	Sample	Ass'n Strength
Acceptance variables	%	%	%	%	Cramer's v
Bovine immunization	29	27	74	50	0.46
Pasteurellosis control	12	7	39	23	0.36
Botulism control	26	30	73	48	0.49
Anthrax control	4	4	31	13	0.35
Small ruminants immunization	26	42	68	53	0.31
Bovine treatments	23	10	19	16	0.13
Small ruminant treatments	26	29	48	38	0.20

% = proportion of herders in the particular system to participate in the treatment
All findings have significant Chi square level of less than 0.001, computed from Pearson method.
Cramer's V: measure of association between variable and systems varying between 0 and 1.0

events[3] and mortalities tend to be higher in TRA systems and, not surprisingly, vaccinations are lower despite the fact that (with the exception of pasteurellosis) vaccine prices are similar. The effect of the SLT, especially for small ruminants, is extraordinary: the herder acceptance rate for some services is double the rate in FLT and TRA (Table 9.11). Globally, the SLT system is clearly better at providing accepted bovine and small ruminants immunizations and treatments and more vaccine doses at the same or cheaper prices.

Interestingly, though, reproductive performances when measured as total products *per herder*,[4] fecundity, and number of calves per breeding year are better for the TRA system. Perhaps this is because herd size is smaller in SLT system. Even apparently superior production results *per cow* in TRA areas could be explained by the emphasis in TRA areas on herd size while herders in SLT areas focus more on the quality of each animal and may incorporate more intensive destocking strategies.

Statistically speaking, it is very difficult to isolate the variables responsible for the generally positive animal health and reproductive performance in TRA areas. The dominant husbandry activities are based on ancestral knowledge, which is supplemented by the veterinary matrix when such services are clearly complementary. There is some reason for concern: although (or perhaps because) the animal health situation appears to be so stable, immunization rates are maintained at danger-

3 Abortions and stillbirths.
4 Histories were taken of four cows per herder.

Table 9.12 Aggregated Cow Progeny Health and Production History in FLT and SLT Systems

Variables/herder	VVP member		VVP non member		Sign. Level
	mean	s.d.	mean	s.d.	
Negatives	0.8	1.3	1.2	1.6	0.0086
Mortalities	1.6	1.7	2.1	2.0	0.0038
Calves/breeding year	1.7	0.5	1.9	0.7	0.0000
Fecundity/cow	2.5	0.8	2.6	0.8	0.0000
Products	9.9	3.3	10.6	3.2	0.0172
Sales	1.2	1.2	1.2	1.2	0.8744
Gains from sales (CFA francs)	62 969	77 495	57 077	61 367	0.3116
Gains/product (CFA francs)	55 617	33 657	50 778	22 465	0.0962
Herd size	34	19	34	15	0.5736
Bovine treated	0.6	1.7	0.1	0.7	0.0000
Small ruminant treated	20	23	5	15	0.0000
Price for pasteurellosis (CFA)	63	13	74	3	0.0000
Vaccinated for Pasteurellosis	10	20	2	11	0.0000
Price for anabot*	70	11	71	7	0.4207
Vaccinated for Botulism	19	23	4	14	0.0000
Herder age (years)	46	13	46	13	0.8907
Distance to gov't post (km)	12.8	9.0	7.7	7.8	0.0000
Distance to VVP (km)	5.9	8.6	6.4	7.0	0.6017

ously low levels of 20–40 per cent for nonmandatory vaccinations. Treatment incidence is also low, especially for cattle. However, the relative increase in the number of small ruminants, especially in conjunction with their heightened market importance, maintains the incidence of their higher level of treatments (34 per cent) compared with cattle (17 per cent). Despite their economic importance, horses are not yet included in the health strategies. It seems that the known rusticity of the more widely used donkey is attributed to horses; extension work to correct this mistaken impression has been minimal.

Evaluating VVP membership alternatives

The above analysis addressed general effects of livestock production in a system that has undergone a first or second transformation. This section brings the analysis down to the individual level by exploring the effect of an individual herder's decision to join a VVP on that herder's livestock. Table 9.12 clearly shows a simple correlation between VVP membership and positive herd attributes in nearly all categories. VVP members have treated and vaccinated more animals at cheaper prices, and they have higher treatment rates as well; we expect that this explains and does not

Table 9.13 Acceptance of Veterinary Services in the Veterinary FLT and SLT Systems

Acceptance variables	% in the System			Association Strength
	VVP member	VVP non-member	Sample	Cramer's v
Bovine immunization	61.5	11.5	25.3	0.51
Pasteurellosis control	27.4	5.8	11.7	0.30
Botulism control	57.5	11.5	24.3	0.48
Anthrax control	22.3	0	6.2	0.41
Small ruminant immunization	51.4	65.4	61.5	0.12
Bovine treatments	17.3	3.8	7.6	0.22
Small ruminant treatments	45.3	13.5	22.3	0.34

All findings have statistically significant Chi squared values of less than 0.001, computed from Pearson method.

If $p < 0.05$, variable considered and systems are not independent

Cramer's V measures the association between variable and systems varying between 0 and 1.0

merely coincide with the VVP members' experience of fewer negative events and mortalities. The important exception, reproduction, has also been explained above as potentially a modern management choice. A second exception is the superior rate of small ruminants' immunization acceptance (65.4 per cent vs. 51.4 per cent) by VVP nonmembers (Table 9.13).

There is a potential flaw in the use of such simple comparisons to establish the value of membership in a VVP. Those who have chosen to join a VVP are different from their neighbors who have not. It could well be that the cause of their superior livestock management is not the VVP but the distinguishing characteristics that led them to join. To solve this causal puzzle we proceed in two steps. We first establish the various factors that are associated with the decision to join a VVP in the FLT and SLT areas where they are available. Second, through the use of multiple regression we can create statistical controls for the impact of those factors on our performance indicators and see the residual effect of VVP membership itself. This exercise strengthens the preceding findings of a positive impact from the VVP.

For the first step—which establishes the factors associated with the decision to join a VVP—we use logistic regression. We created a model that integrates herders' attributes that influence the odds of choosing a VVP, including age, membership in other associations, duration of presence in the area, practice of transhumance, size of herd, sales, and

Table 9.14 Odds on herders' choice of VVP membership: Logistic regression results

Variables	Estimate of B[1]	Exp.B[2]	R[3]	p values	- 2 Log-likelihood	$\chi2$	Model signif.
Age of herder	-0.033	0.97	-0.11	0.0000			
Participation in group[4]	-0.998	.369	0.12	0.0000			
Year of presence	-0.012	1.01	0.04	0.0225			
Herd size	-0.009	1.01	0.04	0.0264	1163	513	0.000
Distance to official post	0.033	1.03	0.08	0.0006			
Importance of public needs	0.073	1.08	0.09	0.0002			
Practice of transhumance[4]	-0.170	1.19	0.00	0.3443			
Sales	-0.014	0.99	0.00	0.8200			
VVP type[4]	9.581	.0001	0.02	0.0838			
Constant	9.967			0.0732			

1. B is the magnitude of the influence of the predictor variable and gives the sign of that influence on the choice; it shows the change in the log odds associated with one unit change in the Xs. If X increases one unit, the log odds of the event increase with the value equal to B.

2. Exp. (B) is the value by which the odds change when the *i*th independent variable increases by one unit. It is used when we prefer to think in terms of odds and not in terms of log odds. eBi is the factor by which the odds change when the ith X increases one unit. If Bi < 0, the factor is <1 and the odds are decreased. If Bi = 0, factor = 1, the odds are unchanged. If Bi > 0, factor > 1, the odds are increased. If Xi increases from 0 to 1 or 1 unit, the odds increase by factor eBi.

3. R = partial correlation between each independent variable and the dependent it goes from -1 to 1. When R>0, if X increases, the likelihood of the event occurring increases. If R<O, if X increases, we have the opposite.

4. B shows the sign and influence on the odds of the variable in the yes situation = 1. (No situation = 0.)

Table 9.15 Effect of VVP Membership on Aggregated Cow Progeny Health and Production History in FLT and SLT Systems when Controlled for the Effect of Variables Associated with the Decision to Join a VVP.

Herder Variables	Partial Regression Coefficient for VVP Membership		Significance level	
	VVP membership	NGO VVP membership	VVP membership	NGO VVP membership
Negatives	-.329112	-.047084	.0000	.4610
Mortalities	-.298781	-.111331	.0120	.1519
Products	-.329910	-.598317	.0470	.0000
Calves per breeding year	-.007656	-.018715	.0352	.0000
Fecundity/cow	-.082478	-.149579	.0470	.0000
Gains from sales	8 645	-1 008	.0008	.6421
Gains/product*	6 201	-3 486	.0001	.0083
Bovine treated	.247092	.318182	.0011	.0000
Small ruminant treated	7.097	4.522	.0000	.0000

expressed priority for government related services. Attributes of the veterinary services provider, including distance to the nearest government veterinary post and the existence of an NGO VVP, were also incorporated. The three categorical variables (membership in other associations, practice of transhumance and VVP management) were coded as indicator variables with the value for the yes situation (1) as the reference for the internal parameter coding realized by the statistical software used for modeling.[5] The coefficients for the three new variables represent therefore the effect of the no situation compared to the no (0) condition (Table 9.14).

Table 9.14 shows the logistic regression statistic of the odds between the choice of being VVP member or not; that is, the odds of choosing a VVP with improved management as in SLT veterinary systems that are offered to herders by NGOs as in the Ferlo. The model is specified with eight variables as:

$$\frac{\text{Prob (choosing VVP)}}{\text{Prob (not choosing VVP)}} = Y$$

$$Y = e^{0} * e^{1\ \text{AGE}} * e^{2\ \text{PRESENCE}} * e^{3\ \text{HERD SIZE}} * e^{4\ \text{PUBLIC NEEDS}} * e^{5\ \text{SALES}} * e^{6\ \text{OTHER ASSOCIATIONS}} * e^{8\ \text{DISTANCE}} * e^{9\ \text{VVP MANAGEMENT}}$$

5. Statistical Package for the Social Sciences (SPSS)

Table 9.16 Acceptance of Veterinary Services in the Veterinary FLT and SLT Systems

Systems	VVP non member	PNVA VVP	NGO VVP	Sample		Sign. Level	Ass'n Strength
Acceptance variables	%	%	%	N	%	Chi sq.	Cramer's V
Bovine immunization	11.5	36.5	84.0	34.2	50.2	0.000	0.59
Pasteurellosis control	5.8	9.4	43.6	17.7	22.5	0.000	0.42
Botulism control	11.5	30.6	81.9	33.3	47.2	0.000	0.59
Anthrax control	0.0	5.9	37.2	15.2	17.3	0.000	0.43
Small ruminant immunization	65.4	36.5	64.9	26.4	54.5	0.000	0.27
Bovine treatments	3.8	11.8	22.3	9.1	14.3	0.007	0.21
Small ruminant treatments	13.5	35.3	54.3	22.1	38.1	0.000	0.32

c.% = % in the system; s.% = % for the whole sample

Significance level for test of independence with Chi-square computed from Pearson method.

If $p < 0.05$, variable considered and systems are not independent

Cramer's V measures the association between variable and systems varying between 0 and 1.0

Only 49 per cent (172) of the herders sampled were used because of the exclusion caused by missing values in each variable used, so the outcome does not allow us to infer strong statistically significant conclusions and recommend precautions. However, the magnitude of predictors allows us to infer the general trend, and this trend confirms our general expectation. Herders are more likely to join a VVP if they belong to other associations ($p < 0.000$), if the VVP has been in the area for a relatively long time ($p < 0.02$), the herd size is larger ($p < 0.03$), if the government veterinary post is more distant ($p < 0.0006$), if the herder is relatively young ($p < 0.000$) and if the herder sees private veterinary services as more important than public ones ($p < 0.0002$). There is some

Table 9.17 Aggregated cow progeny health and production history in FLT and SLT systems with VVPs differentiation according to type

Herder Variables	Sample	Not VVP member	PNVA VVP member	NGO VVP member	Sign. level
	mean ± s.d.	Mean ± s.d.	mean ± s.d.	Mean ± s.d.	
Negatives	0.9 ± 1.4	1.2 ± 1.6	0.9 ± 1.3	0.9 ± 1.3	0.280
Mortalities	1.6 ± 1.8	2.1 ± 2.1	1.7 ± 1.9	1.5 ± 1.6	0.170
Mortalities (weighted)	1.6 ± 1.7	2.1 ± 2.1a	1.6 ± 1.9	1.5 ± 1.5a	0.050
Products	10 ± 3	11 ± 3	10 ± 3	10 ± 3	0.280
Calf per breeding year	1.8 ± 0.6	1.9 ± 0.7a	1.8 ± 0.6ab	1.7 ± 0.4ab	0.000
Fecundity/cow	2.5 ± 0.8	2.6 ± 0.8a	2.5 ± 0.8ab	2.4 ± 0.8ab	0.000
Sales	1.2 ± 1.2	1.2 ± 1.2	1.1 ± 1.1	1.2 ± 1.3	0.980
Gains from Sales*	61647 ± 74185	57077 ± 61899	62647 ± 66385	63260 ± 86681	0.800
Gains/product*	54532 ± 34029	50779 ± 22756	58083 ± 36783	53110 ± 36666	0.600
Herd size	34 ± 18	35 ± 15	37 ± 18a	31 ± 19a	0.050
Bovine treated	0.5 ± 1.5	0.1 ± 0.7a	0.4 ± 1.6ab	0.7 ± 1.7ab	0.000
Small ruminant treated	16 ± 22	5 ± 15a	15 ± 21ab	24 ± 23ab	0.000
Price for pasteurellosis*	65 ± 13	74 ± 3a	65 ± 12	62 ± 15a	0.030
Vaccinated for Pasteurellosis	8 ± 18	2 ± 11a	5 ± 14b	15 ± 22ab	0.000
Price for anabot*	70 ± 11	71 ± 8	68 ± 11	71 ± 11	0.310
Vaccinated for Botulism	16 ± 22	4 ± 14a	13 ± 23ab	25 ± 22ab	0.000

Price for Carbosympto*	51 ± 14	0 ± 0a	58 ± 19a	47 ± 9a	0.020
Vaccinated for Anthrax	2 ± 5	0 ± 0a	0.4 ± 2b	4 ± 7ab	0.000
Age of herder**	46 ± 13	46 ± 13	44 ± 13a	48 ± 12a	0.140
Dist. to govern. post.***	11.6 ± 9.1	7.7 ± 7.9a	12.4 ± 8.3a	13.1 ± 9.7a	0.001
Distance to VVP***	5.9 ± 8.4	6.4 ± 7.3	8.7 ± 9.9	3.8 ± 6.8	0.280
Number of herders	231	52	85	94	n.a

*: ANOVA with $\alpha = 0.05$ with Least Significant Difference method;
data with same letters (a, b) are statistically different
CFA francs; ** year; *** km; n.a. = not applicable; s.d. = standard deviation;
weight with VP membership

increase in the likelihood of joining a VVP if it is an NGO one, but this difference is not statistically significant. (Table 9.14.)

The second step, then, was to do multiple regression analyses on the various performance indicators, using both the variables that predict VVP membership and the fact of VVP membership itself. In this way we can abstract the effects of the VVP itself from that of the factors that led the herder to join it. The partial regression coefficients for VVP membership and their degree of statistical significance are presented in Table 9.15. In all cases, the statistically significant findings in the simple, uncontrolled analyses are sustained (compare Table 9.12). Access to and use of a VVP clearly increases the treatment of sick cattle and small ruminants, reduces failed pregnancies and deaths, and leads to augmented returns from livestock sales. Once again, however, VVP membership is associated with reduced fecundity for cows. We interpret this as a consequence of these herders' stressing herd profitability (hence increased net income from livestock) over a simple increase in herd size. It is unfortunate that we did not collect more information on small ruminant productivity and income, as it is evident that this is a major focus of VVP activity.

Overall, it is clear that VVPs provide positive health benefits, but how does performance change when supervision of VVPs changes? To answer this question, we disaggregated VVPs into those supervised by the government (PNVA VVPs) and those supervised by NGOs (NGO VVPs). These results, reproduced in Tables 9.16 and 9.17, show clearly that supervision type does matter. As the NGO VVP columns in Table 9.15 demonstrate, the *additional* effects of NGO supervision on their VVPs generally are confirmed, even when we control for the variables that lead herders to join the VVPs. The healthiest herds, on average, belong to members of NGO VVPs. This is true whether one is measuring in terms of veterinary service demand and provision or more direct animal reproductive and health parameters. Again, we suspect that this is not a coincidence. All VVPs are institutional settings that were created on the same basis and with the same goals. Management is the difference, and the difference shows most strongly in the follow-up and supervision systems. It can be hypothesized that the PNVA system has not been very efficient, so that the SLT is often markedly better than the TRA and FLT systems. The closer supervision, periodic follow-ups, counseling, and organizational backup we observed help to explain the SLT's superior results.

Auxiliaries can have an impact on the utilization of animal health services but only under the right management conditions. The *Peul* of the Ferlo are well known for their skills as herders and are widely assumed to be able to make diagnoses and provide treatments by themselves in many circumstances. But our data lead us to argue that shortages of personnel with basic skills, rather than the more commonly heard need for readily available veterinary supplies, might reasonably be considered as the major constraint on animal health practice in a region such as the Ferlo. Supplies in the Ferlo are privately available in reasonable quantities and at known prices. Availability is also ameliorated since the travel distances needed to acquire these supplies on the private market do not have much effect on behavior. People travel to markets regularly anyway, so buying drugs does not require extraordinary travel costs.

The major inference to be drawn is that the more privatized veterinary delivery system, which includes operating VVPs and acting auxiliaries, is far and away superior to its governmental and traditional counterparts. Differentiation between the traditional veterinary system that includes a paraprofessional and the first level transformation implemented by the government extension program agency, however, is not clear-cut.

CONCLUSIONS: THE VETERINARY MATRIX IN OPERATION

In the Ferlo, the channels for livestock services at the herder micro level are diverse and include VVPs, auxiliaries, veterinary public paraprofessionals, and private formal and informal drug and vaccine sellers. Sales take place either at weekly or occasional markets, and retailers are often from unknown origin. So, the market is quite open and herders have many opportunities to get drugs or information on pharmaceutical supplies and prices. But the market may not be characterized as perfect. This is due to the low density of producers and a low effective demand for vaccinations and treatments. Product differentiation is also poor due to the stable health situation and the short list of products used in the area (Figure 9.2). The administrative delimitation of the veterinary systems and the relative stability of the auxiliaries lead us to predict the presence of effective local monopolies for animal health service providers or even oligopolies involving paraprofessionals and auxiliaries or full vets with other veterinary workers.

Village veterinary pharmacies are important components of the veterinary matrix since they offer collective action opportunities and can be intermediate actors for the availability, assurance, management, and the diversification of veterinary services in the absence of government financing. NGOs also have filled a crucial need. Management, training and support of the work of the auxiliaries themselves as animal health practitioners seem to outbalance management and support of the supplies for the VVPs. Therefore, content of the training and its frequency, combined with the provision of better regulation of defective effort through NGO supervisory work are strategic issues in the transformation of the veterinary systems the herders are facing.

Finally, the NGO auxiliaries are doing more veterinary work than their government PNVA counterparts and also the government paraprofessionals, because they are operating under more high powered incentives: they are paid in accordance with the services provided. Price charges are quite homogeneous but, given so much better access to a volume of supplies, auxiliaries in NGO VVPs are in a position to make attractive returns out of quantity. Improved services are linked with improved profits/incentives.

We would like to suggest that the increased volume of veterinary services being provided by the NGO VVPs and auxiliaries is due to their successful contribution to the resolution of the principal/agent problem in the Ferlo. As we noted in the introduction, the relationships between a herder and an animal health provider are hampered by an asymmetry in information— the very reason the herder needs help is that he knows less about what might be done for his animals health that the paraprofessional or auxiliary does. Faced with uncertainty as to whether or not he is receiving good service, the herder tends to be unwilling to pay for quality service or reduces his consumption of the animal health products offered. This principal/agent problem is largely solved for curative treatments by the repeated use of the same practitioners. The outcome of any single treatment is inconclusive as to the quality of the service provided, but the pattern of outcomes across many treatments to one's own animals and one's neighbor's establishes a basis for inferring quality.

The principal/agent problem is harder to solve for preventive treatments, particularly in a region such as the Ferlo where disease incidence is very low anyway. One has to observe the benefits of immunizations for an exceptionally large number of animals over a long period of time to make an accurate judgment as to their appropriateness. In this situation the herder needs to be able to rely on the recommendation of his animal health provider, not just on his own assessment. If a herder has a high degree of confidence in the quality and professionalism of his provider, he is more likely to follow that advice and use more preventive measures. We believe that the superior supervision provided by the EELS NGO to its VVPs and auxiliaries gives herders such an assurance of professionalism, lessens the principal/agent problem, and increases herder use of immunizations for their livestock. NGOs with a strong set of client oriented, professional values therefore have an extremely important role to play in the market for veterinary services.

At the herders' level, the privatization process depends as well on herders' organizations to counter the power of other actors and demand improvements. These organizations can also be seen as an alternative, decentralized supervisory force, contributing to regulation of the market and to tackling the moral hazard aspects of veterinary markets. Policy makers need to recognize the role such organizations can play, especially their roles in counteracting local informal hierarchies, balancing market distortions and improving contractual arrangements between herders as principals and their veterinary agents.

Professional associations, especially the veterinary association, should also have a sustained interest in strengthening their links with herders' associations. Both sets of organizations can complement market forces with disciplining forces. This would help in tackling privatization issues at both macro and micro levels so that the current transition phase could move quickly toward a stable and structured system.

To conclude, the challenge faced by the privatization of veterinary services delivery systems in Senegal is in the urgency of strengthening the transformation process in the subsector so that livestock production and productivity is higher and the veterinary inputs marketing systems are more efficient. Among the prerequisites are the creation of more suitable and workable organizational and institutional arrangements, leading to a new shape of veterinary input and service delivery with respect to structure, form, quality and prices. Such 'institutional and management packages' combined with the necessary 'technical packages' will hopefully lead to strong growth in the production systems, help the small producers to secure their herds, and create revenues for reaching food security and greater well-being.

10 Lessons from the New Institutional Economics for the Structural Reform of Human Health Services in Africa

David K. Leonard

Curative medical care in Africa has become increasingly commercialized. By and large, however, the market has not yet worked any miracles. Instead, the expansion of markets has exposed the absence or weakness of the institutions required for their efficient operation. Among the important institutional issues that need to be addressed are three on which the New Institutional Economics and the research presented in this book cast considerable light. (i) An institutional mechanism for providing some kind of insurance against catastrophic medical expenses must be crafted. In the context of economies dominated by the informal sector and peasant agriculture, our research suggests that the extended family is the most viable base for such an insurance system. (ii) The organizations providing curative care need to be restructured so that the increasing fees and charges paid by patients unlock improved supply rather than simply reduce demand. Our work suggests the benefits of extending the role of decentralized nongovernmental organizations (NGOs) that manage their own resources and depend on them for their survival. (iii) Mechanisms that reduce the serious imperfect information problems in medical transactions must be found if markets are to prosper and patients are to find quality care. Our research leads us to give particular attention to two institutional solutions that are particularly important in contemporary Africa: the contingent contract and church missions.

THE CONTEXT

The 'Great African Depression' of the 1980s and 90s has had profound but subtle effects on the continent's health services. Certainly health has fared better than most other sectors of the economy. The overwhelming majority of countries continued to show improvements in basic indicators of public health during 1980s: infant and child mortality declined, while the coverage of childhood and maternal immunizations increased (Vogel 1993, pp. 41, 44; World Bank 1994, Tables A–4 and A–10). Similarly, the share of health in government budgets generally has been protected, although there is substantial inter-country variation (Sahn and Bernier 1995, pp. 251–2). Even real per capita government expenditures on health have been sustained—particularly in countries that adopted structural adjustment programs—thanks in part to the response of the World Bank to early UNICEF criticisms that its policies neglected the human dimensions of development (Van der Gaag and Barham 1998; Vogel 1993, p. 29; Jorgensen 1995, p. 23).

Nonetheless, one would be hard pressed to find someone associated with a ministry of health in Africa who did not feel that the system was in crisis. Questions have been raised about the methodology underlying the preceding statistics and there is concern that some immunization rates may have declined in the 1990s (Bijlmakers and Harnmeijer 1995, pp. 130–31). Even if the patterns described in the preceding paragraph are valid, however, there are areas of concern. First, pharmaceutical supplies which must be imported were particularly hard hit by the major devaluations dictated by structural adjustment. Increases in government expenditures well above the general rate of inflation would have been necessary to maintain constant levels of supply (Jorgensen 1995, p. 26); Vogel's data show declines between 1981 and 1989 in real pharmaceutical expenditures in 16 out of the 21 sub-Saharan African countries for which data is available (1993, pp. 30–36). As the economic crisis deepened, most African governments protected personnel numbers (although not always salaries) at the expense of pharmaceuticals and the other materiel needed to make productive use of these staff. Private and mission health facilities in Africa spend between 45 and 55 per cent of their budgets on staff. In contrast, the average for governments in the 25 countries on which Vogel was able to obtain data was 63 per cent and for seven countries exceeded 80 per cent (1993, p. 74). Shortages of essential drugs, which had begun to be a problem even before the economic crisis, became pervasive in government facilities in the 1980s. African health ministers gathered at Bamako (Mali) in 1987 decided to increase user fees in order to enable local health facilities to increase their purchase of drug supplies (MacPake 1993).

A second problem concerns dependence of the health sector on donor finance. African countries spend only a marginally smaller percentage of their gross national products on health than the average less developed country (4.5 per cent vs. 4.7 per cent). Government spending is significantly less, however (1.5 per cent vs. 2.1 per cent) and the gap is filled by very substantial aid flows (0.9 per cent vs. 0.1 per cent), averaging US$2.50 per capita (World Bank 1994, pp. 153, 210–11). The usual worry of donors about the sustainability of their initiatives adds to the pressure for increased long-term reliance on user fees.

The third problem, inherently harder to document, concerns the growing informal market in health services. As economic crisis and then structural adjustment effectively reduced real government salaries, health sector personnel sought supplementary strategies to assure their 'survival.' In a variety of ingenious ways, they found informal strategies to charge for their services and the drugs they dispensed, adding still another dimension to the increase in user fees at government facilities (Van der Geest 1982). As a consequence, government curative services in many African countries have been transformed informally from public services into publicly-subsidized commercial ones. Even where these practices are pervasive and accepted, they still are technically illegal, so we have no statistics on their extent; African consumers probably are experiencing health costs that are imperfectly reflected in official data.

From the point of view of the African consumer of health services, a great deal has changed. The post-independence commitment of most African states to provide free medical services to their populations is a thing of the past and is unlikely to be revived. Curative care is particularly unlikely to receive priority for new subventions. From the point of view of improving the health of the population, investments of new government funds in prevention and nutrition are far more cost effective. To the extent that the health status of Africans has suffered, disruptions in immunizations and problems with food supply are the most important causes (World Bank 1994, Table A–8; Bijlmakers and Harnmeijer 1995, pp. 122–24). Real cuts in government social spending have had a limited impact on the health status of African populations because preventive work has been largely spared from the budgeter's knife. Also, the state's curative services historically had been inefficient, which makes the health impact of their decline more modest (Sahn and Bernier 1995, pp. 247, 253).

The great change in the *price* of curative services has not been accompanied by the kinds of changes that have affected other sectors of African economies, however. For example, in most African countries above the southern cone, curative veterinary services have been effectively privatized and significantly reorganized (for example, see Chapters 6 and 7). The pre-crisis organizational structure of human health care has remained largely intact, however. It is true that mission facilities account for as much as half the total in many countries and that private health expenditures often exceed public ones (Sahn and Bernier 1995, pp. 250, 263). But the mission health systems are frequently subsidized by the government; the only significant policy shift toward nongovernmental providers has been to open up the possibilities for an expanded small private practice in the urban areas.

Because most of the real changes have been in prices and not institutions, the major impact of crisis and adjustment has been on consumer demand, and it is upon this that studies have focused. Curative care in Africa is nowhere near the point of diminishing marginal returns for health (as some suggest it is in the United States; Cutler *et al.*, 1998) and Africans value it as much as peoples do elsewhere. Changes in prices have shifted patients away from government facilities and toward mission and other providers, but the differences in numbers of cases treated have been modest. Of greatest concern have been the signs that the very poorest African families are sometimes forgoing medical care as a result of the increased prices (for example, Gertler and van der Gaag 1990; Mbugua *et al.* 1995; Russell 1996). There are legitimate concerns as to how to target subsidies to the poorest of the poor (Gilson, Russell, and Buse 1995) and how to insure the individual against large, unexpected expenditures (Chapter 2). From an economic theory point of view, however, the finding that an increase in price leads to a decrease in demand for an unchanged product is trivially obvious.

The very fact that the great changes in Africa's health care systems have been so concentrated on prices and consumer demand has deprived the sector of the deep and positive institutional restructuring that otherwise might have occurred. An increase in prices normally not only restricts consumer demand but also induces increased supply. Since the recipient of these increased revenues has been the government, however, very little change on the supply side— either in terms of the nature of the providers or in reforms to their methods of 'production'— has been forthcoming. With the set of studies presented in this volume we hope to begin a shift in focus, leading to an examination of the rich potential incentive effects that can follow from consumer-producer interactions.

Our analyses center on curative services in Africa because these are the part of the health sector that is most subject to change and that would most benefit from restructuring. We have already cited the evidence that preventive medicine and nutrition are more important than curative services to health status in Africa. Nontheless, curative services are vital to the analysis of government health systems in Africa because the sick give them high priority and because they consume 70 to 87 per cent of the public sector budgets for health in developing countries (Vogel 1993, p. 62). Thus unless satisfactory curative options are available to the general public, governments are likely to have difficulty adequately financing the preventive and nutritional work which should be their first priority.

INSURANCE

Insurance must feature prominently in any consideration of medical markets in Africa. The largest proportion of an individual's curative care costs are associated with major health events, which occur infrequently and unpredictably. When misfortune affects a productive adult, maximum stress is placed on the family's finances precisely at the time when the family's capacity to respond is weakened. Without some kind of insurance, private sector involvement in health services provision will be severely restricted, particularly in the area of inpatient hospital care (Griffin 1989). As a consequence health care features prominently in the history of insurance. It lays the groundwork for a viable hospital market.

Formal insurance systems are notably small in Africa. Coverage of even one in nine families is rare and those are the better-off in any case (Vogel 1993, pp. 103–05). If we assumed that such miniscule coverage reflects Africans' own assessments of their best welfare, we would have to conclude that Africans are not risk averse (Berman 1995, p. 49). The consensus is exactly the opposite, however (for example, Hyden 1980). In fact, the level of medical expenditure that would be considered catastrophic, and against which the typical family would therefore want to insure, is much lower for Africa than it is in developed societies. The shortage of individually purchasable insurance systems on the continent, then, is not a consequence of preferences but of market failure. This failure is produced by adverse selection, high transaction costs in a peasant society, and a poor fit of formal insurance offerings with the financial structure of most African families.

Adverse selection is a frequent problem in insurance because of *imperfect information.* The purchaser of an insurance contract knows more about her likely future health needs than the seller does. Individuals who know they are unhealthy are more likely to purchase health insurance than are those who believe themselves to be fit. As a result, most of those who purchase insurance at any given price will be sicker than the actuarial projections, making the insurance contract unprofitable to the seller and driving him to a higher price. This vicious circle continues until the insurance is inordinately expensive and almost no one buys it (Berman 1995, p. 48). The usual solution to this problem is to offer insurance to larger *groups* of people that were formed for purposes other than health care, so that the group's average will come closer to the actuarial projection for the population as a whole.

The second problem is a transaction cost one. The costs of collecting premiums from peasants are steep, as cash is available at only certain seasons and the price of treatment and the amounts of money available for health care are modest. The administrative costs of handling a large number of small accounts can be high even when confined to those in formal sector employment. Not much is known about administrative costs of formal insurance systems in Africa, but they range from as much as 50 per cent in Mali to as low as 10 per cent in Zimbabwe (Vogel 1993, p. 146). These percentages would shift upward if insurance systems were extended to cover peasants.

The third issue concerns the way in which the insurance is sold. Formal sector systems are based on the assumption that nuclear families buy insurance for themselves and hence that there is a balance between a family's demand for health care and its capacity to purchase insurance. The research reported in this volume, however, makes it clear that the *extended* family, not the nuclear one, is the unit that budgets for health care in Africa. In Ethiopia, differences in individual family income are insignificant in the choice of health care provider once extended family support is taken into account (Chapter 2). Both sources of health finance are important in Cameroon (Chapter 4). Since formal insurance systems assume that nuclear families purchase the care they use, these systems are misfits in African social structures.

For these three reasons, then, formal insurance systems are of marginal significance in African health finance and real insurance is provided through the extended family and other informal structures. The extended family is a large group in which one has involuntary membership and it thereby mitigates the adverse selection problem. The transaction costs of maintaining a family system are certainly high, but they are a part of people's expected social intercourse and have modest cash costs. Thus the *marginal* transaction costs of the extended family as an insurer are very low. Finally, the extended family system is able to tax its better-off, employed, urban members for the benefit of their poor rural kin.

In addition, informal insurance systems based on the extended family solve the moral hazard problem for medical insurance, to the extent that it is a real issue in Africa. In industrial countries a 'moral hazard' is created by the fact that, once an individual has medical insurance and if the copayments are small, she has an incentive to 'overconsume' medical treatment, since it comes at insignificant marginal cost to her. The travel costs and times involved in getting to medical care in Africa generally are high enough that 'overconsumption' of treatment is a minor problem. In effect these costs play the same role as a large 'deductible' on insurance payments. To the extent that the threat of overconsumption is or becomes an issue, however, informal insurance through the extended family deals with it effectively. A poor person who receives extended family assistance may never be able to pay for the care of another family member, but she does incur social obligations for deference and non-monetary assistance. Hence the aid she receives is not costless to her and she will not be likely to 'overconsume' medical care. (Of course, family obligations work in this way only as long as the family self-insures; a different set of incentives would be in place if the extended family bought a formal insurance policy for all its members and moral hazard would then be a somewhat greater concern.)

Since the extended family already is the real unit of medical insurance in contemporary Africa, it makes sense to build on it. Most studies of 'ability to pay' for health care in Africa have ignored the extended family; Ronald Vogel's discussion of health insurance in his definitive book on *Financing Health Care in Sub-Saharan Africa* (1993) does not even mention it. Such neglect by policy analysts has perpetuated an unnecessary weakness in an institution that is key to medical markets.

Nonetheless, the institution of the extended family will need support if it is to bear the full burden of medical insurance for African populations. Damen Haile Mariam found that 58 per cent of his survey respondents in central Ethiopia had a relative on whom they could rely for help with major health expenditures (Chapter 2). The amounts of family support he documents are impressive and they probably would be even more extensive in a wealthier African country. But what of those who cannot rely effectively on relatives? Such families are widely spread and are not concentrated in poor regions. These families would not benefit from subsidizes targeted on poor regions. The AIDS epidemic has put even more pressure on the extended family insurance system. Not only has it created a new category of demand for medical care, but it has also struck most fiercely at the employed urban dwellers who traditionally have been the source, not the recipients, of extended family assistance.

Ghana recently decided to expand its reliance on the extended family for insurance in its restructured health system. It has given the rural chiefs a monitoring role, apparently both to enforce family obligations on those who might wish to evade them and to identify those individuals who do indeed lack extended family support and merit government assistance with medical bills (Lauren Morris MacLean, personal communication). Such a system has to be rurally based to collect accurate information efficiently and function effectively. In Ethiopia, where local officials have the authority to grant exemptions from medical fees, Damen Haile Mariam found that the incidence of forgiveness was much higher in the cities than in the countryside, even though the pattern of real need would be the reverse.

Damen Haile Mariam has identified another informal sector institution on which African health insurance can be built, one that generally overlaps with kinship networks. Ninety-two per cent of adults in central Ethiopia contribute an average of $11 a year to burial societies (or *Eders*). This sum exceeds the estimate of per capita health expenditure from all sources for the country. Such organizations are pervasive in Africa. As they already have developed their own mechanisms for collecting and administering monies and for enforcing obligations, they are an ideal base on which to further build medical insurance. Already, 21 per cent of the Ethiopian *Eders* provide some form of assistance with medical emergencies. The Friendly Societies which provided English workers with their earliest medical insurance, grew out of burial societies in the late 19th century as well (Hollingsworth 1986, pp. 12–13). The state can facilitate the development of such societies and assist families that are too poor to join them, but it probably should not attempt to make membership in them mandatory. Doing so might risk development of the same problems that plagued mandatory agricultural cooperatives: people would lose their exit option and the corrupt and incompetent societies would persist, damaging the welfare of their members (Peterson 1982).

Finally, it would be desirable if extended families and burial societies began to develop relationships with particular medical facilities and invested directly in their facility's improvement in return for discounts in serving their members. Damen Haile Mariam found in Ethiopia that a high percentage of extended family assistance was spent on transporting the sick from the villages to the towns and putting them up while they awaited admittance at the better urban hospitals. Such expenditures represent 'dead losses' in that they neither improved the facilities nor benefited the medical practitioners. There are substantial efficiency gains available if and when these informal organizations undertake to invest in the quality of the facilities that are closer to the homes of most of their members. Furthermore, they may have the local presence to enforce good management of those facilities. Urban elites in Africa already frequently contribute generously to the capital costs of developing new health facilities in their villages of origin. It is a modest extension to involve them in recurrent expenditures and their management as well, as a way of providing medical assistance to their relatives more efficiently.

Support from extended families and burial societies therefore represent an important way in which the demand side of medical markets in Africa can be strengthened and poor families can become better able to purchase appropriate care when a catastrophic health event occurs.

THE DECENTRALIZATION OF INCENTIVES

The most serious institutional problems and the greatest opportunities for major improvements in African health care systems are to be found on the supply side of the market equation. In a well functioning, uncorrupt government agency, supply remains fixed in response to excess demand and services are allocated by some nonmarket mechanism— which may or may not be more equitable than the market. When curative veterinary medicine in Kenya was free, the ratio of services received by the advantaged, compared to the poor, was 6.4:1. But when the integrity of the government system began to break down and veterinary staff began to charge informally for their assistance, the ratio of inequality decreased to 3.6:1 and the total amount of work done by the staff increased, so that unmet demand diminished. In this instance, when formal bureaucracy was supplanted by an informal market, a mechanism for a supply response was created and farmers actually were better served. (Leonard 1977, Chap. 9; Leonard 1987.)

From the point of view of neoclassical economic theory, we would *expect* an increase in price for an unchanged product to lead to a decrease in demand for it; there is ample empirical evidence that this has occurred as fees for government medical services have increased during the restructuring of African economies. We also observe an interesting and important asymmetry, however, as discussed in Chapter 4. When prices for government medical care decrease, there is only a *small* increase in demand; but when they increase there is a *large* decrease in patient load. This imbalance arises because government facilities represent the low-quality, last-resort part of the African medical market. So there are not that many more who would want to purchase government services when their prices decline, but when government prices increase, higher quality medical options become much more attractive and patients flee to them. Price in African medical markets does not so much determine *whether* people are getting care when they need it as influence *where* they get it.

These observations suggest that there is an unsatisfied demand for medical quality in Africa and that institutional failings on the supply side are inhibiting this demand from being met. In Chapter 4, Kenneth Leonard analyzes the benefits that would accrue to the general population if various health financing options were adopted in South-Western Cameroon. Just as critics of structural adjustment have suggested, reducing either treatment fees or drug costs would create more benefit for society than would be paid out in the raised taxes necessary to finance them. But, as the World Bank might hope to respond, the ratio of social benefits to increased expenditures would be *even greater* if fees were increased and the resulting income were used to create a disciplined system of bonuses and sanctions for government medical staff that created quality similar to that found in the mission facilities. All social groups, including the most vulnerable, would gain in net welfare from such a change. The absence of an institutional mechanism for enforcing quality in government medical facilities prevents people from purchasing a higher price medical product from which even the poorest would benefit.

Gilbert Mliga's research in Tanzania (Chapter 8) takes a different route to the same conclusion. He compares the quality of medical care provided under various management regimes in government and mission clinics and hospitals. He finds that the greater the degree to which control over personnel is decentralized and the health facility is financially independent, the higher the quality of care provided. Clinics and hospitals that must balance their income and expenditures in order to remain open have a much stronger incentive to provide good quality care to their patients. Facilities that may hire, fire, discipline, and reward their own staff have the tools with which to pass these incentives on to their employees.

The finding that decentralization in church medical facilities leads to high powered incentives that in turn provide high quality service nonetheless does not mean that quality will necessarily result from *any* kind of decentralization. Reorganizations generally lead to a shift in the relative power of the parties involved in a service delivery system, and a primary question always ought to be what the values of these new powerholders will be. Decentralization moves operational control closer to those who actually receive and deliver day-to-day services and thus amplifies the incentives experienced in the facility. But different types of decentralization allocate power among those at the local level in quite dissimilar ways. And the local institutional context may cause incentive 'messages' to be heard quite differently. When power changes hands, we must remember to ask about the new purposes to which it will be put. (Leonard and Marshall 1982, Chaps 1 and 6.)

There is a general enthusiasm about decentralization at the moment. But the failure to conceive of it as a political process can lead to serious naivete about its likely impacts (Bossert 1998). The crisis in African health care is due to a breakdown in the functioning of the state on the continent. This comes in part from the corrosive effects of patronage on governmental institutions (Chapter 1). If control over health institutions is being decentralized from the national government to elected local governments (devolution) or field branches of the central government (deconcentration), is there good reason to expect that patronage will be less present at these levels? Patronage and corruption are somewhat less likely in highly professionalized settings, and professionalism tends to be diminished with devolution (Leonard 1991, Chap. 12). It may well be true that elected municipal and district government officers are more directly responsive to their constituents than appointed central government officials are. But which pressures do local politicians feel most acutely: those for better service and lower costs, or those for more jobs and generous contracts for their supporters? Unless the institutional setting of local politics in Africa were to be quite different from the national one, it would be naïve to expect anything other than the latter (Gilson and Mills 1995, p. 293).

The lessons of the cooperative movement in Africa are an important caution in this regard. When agricultural producers' cooperatives were government-supported and a farmer's membership in his local primary society was mandatory, the problems of corruption and mismanagement frequently were quite severe (Hyden 1973; Peterson 1982). These primary societies were effective local democracies, but they were dominated by a politics of patronage. Thus 'voice' was not as effective an instrument of discipline over the managers of these institutions as 'exit'— the ability to leave and use another more effective cooperative, thereby threatening the continued existence of the unsatisfactory co-ops and assuring the survival of only the fittest (Hirschman 1970). Mandatory membership had removed the 'exit' option. When a local government health facility looses its clients because of its poor performance, its survival is not necessarily threatened; in fact fewer patients may enable it to bring its expenditures and tax revenues into better balance and make it a more effective patronage operation.

Deconcentration may not work any better. If local employees of the national government are given autonomy to make operational decisions and manage tax and fee resources but are constrained by civil service regulations, facility managers will be unable to exercise the discipline over personnel that improved quality requires. In these circumstances, deconcentration may mean only that the facility is run for the benefit of its employees, with little in the way of improved service for the public.

Delegation of authority to autonomous government corporations is more promising. (The distinctions between the different forms of decentralization— devolution, deconcentration, delegation, and privatization— are further explained in Leonard and Marshall 1981, Chap. 1.) Autonomy means that these organizations will be jeopardized if their accounts do not balance (even if they receive certain subsidies for the public services they provide). It also means that they are free of civil service regulations and can run a more disciplined personnel system. If each government facility were a professionally controlled corporation subject to national regulation, it would look more like the decentralized mission facilities that Mliga found worked so well in rural Tanzania. They would have the incentives to provide quality service to attract patients and the mechanisms to enforce the discipline needed to assure it.

Our analysis so far has left out the form of decentralization most often promoted by neoliberals: reliance upon private, profit-seeking firms. Such an alternative certainly produces high powered incentives, but without an appropriate institutional setting it actually leads to a deterioration in quality, not its enhancement. In the same Tanzanian setting in which Mliga finds that the decentralization of financial responsibility produces high quality in *church* health facilities (Chapter 8), Gwatkin (1997) reports that it induced inferior performance in profit-making ones. The difference is in the institutionl context in which the 'message of the market' was delivered; in effect, 'client demand' means something quite different to a mission facility than it does to a profit-making one. Facilities that were subject to active church management responded to market pressures by improving the quality of the product they were offering in order to gain an increased share of the clientele. Profit-making clinics and hospitals engaged in a 'rush to the bottom' and often became little more than pharmaceutical suppliers, with very poor medical supervision.

Thus privatization to NGOs has worked very well in Africa, whereas privatization to profit-driven firms has had negative effects for health care. Why should this be so? It is quite unsatisfactory to stop with the implication that churches simply have more ethical people. We have already seen that church facilities differed in their quality according to the degree of decentralization in their management. In a similar manner, we want to understand the institutional mechanisms that enable mission health facilities to respond more appropriately to market demands. To do so, we will have to take a lengthy excursion into institutional economic theory.

REDUCING THE PRINCIPAL/AGENT PROBLEM

It is widely acknowledged that the markets for health everywhere fail to meet a condition of neoclassical economics for fully competitive transactions.[1] They are troubled with imperfect information, in that someone who is sick and contracts for medical treatment (the *principal*) will have a great deal of difficulty knowing the appropriateness and quality of the efforts the health practitioner (her *agent*) is making on her behalf. Without some institutional mechanism to overcome this principal/agent problem (which was explained more fully in Chapter 1), the market for health will not operate in an economically optimal manner. In the United States, medical practitioners overcome agency loss through the institution of professional self-regulation (Arrow 1963, 1985; Pratt and Zeckhauser 1985). In Africa, however, such self-regulation by professional organizations is absent or weak, and Cheikh Ly's research (Chapter 7) suggests that it is unlikely to emerge. There are two related aspects of this principal/agent problem—'moral hazard' and 'adverse selection'—and both offer insights into the kinds of institutions that could overcome the imperfect information problem in the African medical context. As we will see, the first, 'moral hazard', addresses the issue of how the patient can assure herself that she is receiving quality care when she has an im-

1. This section draws on work done collaboratively with K.L. Leonard (Leonard and Leonard, 1998)

perfect understanding of what is being done on her behalf. The second, 'adverse selection', concerns the issue of how quality health care providers can continue to survive in a market in which their patients have an imperfect grasp of the nature of the treatments they are receiving.

Differentiating Demand

Much of the discussion of health policy for Africa implies that medical treatment is an undifferentiated product, at least from the point of view of the consumer. Implicitly, most economic theorizing about health derives from the 'medical model' of Talcott Parsons (1951, Chap. 10). Parsons saw the patient as an inadequately informed and hence passive recipient of care from an omniscient physician. To the extent that legitimate distinctions were to be made in the quality of medical treatment offered to patients, they emerged from the insight of the (informed) practitioner, not from the (ill-informed) consumer. But is this model of medical demand valid empirically? Our research leads us to the conviction that the African consumer seeks to purchase different *qualities* of medical treatment which vary according to her medical condition. Furthermore, these choices are exercised in ways that are more consistent with the medical professional's understanding of treatment effectiveness than is generally believed (Chapters 4 and 5). The ability to make these choices well is shaped by the institutional environment, however, and better institutions would lead to choices that were still more effective medically.

The empirical literature on health care in Africa demonstrates quite conclusively that the sick are not passively pliable in their use of the health care system but instead actively make choices among a wide array of options. Babies in Burkina Faso may be delivered by professionals at dispensaries, traditional birth attendants, or the 'old woman of the village' (Nougtara *et al.* 1989). When the sick make health care choices, they actively consider attributes of their illness as well as government clinics and hospitals, mission facilities, private-for-profit practitioners, and traditional healers. Their choices often are explained by factors unrelated to medicine, such as price and distance, or by static attributes of the facilities such as availability of drugs or perceived quality (Cameroun: Litvack and Bodart 1993; Ghana: Waddington and Enyimayew 1989; Nigeria: Omorodion 1993 and Stock 1983; Swaziland: Yoder 1989; and Tanzania: Abel-Smith and Rawal 1992). None of these factors contradict the image of the sick as passive recipients of health care from providers whose methods of operation are obscured in a 'black box.' Another group of studies, however, indicates that choice is guided by the character or severity of the illness (Benin: Bichmann *et al.* 1991; Burkina Faso: Sauerborn *et al.* 1989; and Kenya: Mwabu 1986). Sometimes these studies cast doubt on the appropriateness of the patients' judgements (Mali: Coppo *et al.* 1992). But as a group, this body of research suggests that the sick may be less ignorant about the kinds of medical treatment they require than the traditional medical model has implied.

Despite these intimations that the sick may know something important about their conditions and the providers that are appropriate to them, health policy makers persist in treating them as ill-informed and driven by unhelpful perceptions. Self-referral by the sick directly to higher-order medical facilities is seen as a serious problem, and administrative mechanisms and differential fees are imposed to force them to enter the system at the bottom of the referral hierarchy (Vogel 1993, p. 93).

If the sick in Africa match their conditions to the providers they go to, on what rational basis could they be making those choices? The classic principal/agent model for health suggests that they are guided by professionals whose quality is assured through self-regulation. Self-regulation by professional associations is essentially absent in Africa north of Zimbabwe, however. (We will see below that emergence of such associations is impeded by collective action problems.) The alternative, referral networks, also are missing, because there is no incentive to providers for them in large, subsidized organizational networks.

The imperfect information problem is therefore seen as being resolved by government (and mission) services as organizations that act as the regulator for the principal to assure that she receives health care of a minimum quality. (We will later refer to the organizations that fulfill this function as 'super-principals.') Professionals in these organizations (and especially the state) see themselves as the sole legitimate allocators of access to various types of health care.

In practice, however, the empirical research done in Africa shows that individual choice continues to be exercised against the wishes of the organizational professionals. What is the basis on which that choice is made, and do economic/market institutions exist that can make it more efficient?

MORAL HAZARD

Moral hazard in principal/agent relationships arises when one or both of the parties to a transaction is unable to effectively monitor the effort the other devotes to the production of the contracted good (Chapter 1). If a principal is unable to observe the quality of the agent's work on her behalf, she may have difficulty providing adequate incentives to induce the quality she requires. If this problem is unresolved, the principal will be willing to pay only the value of inferior quality work, for that is all she can be sure she is getting.

Capacity vs. Effort

In thinking about these issues it is helpful to make a distinction between the capacity a medical provider has and the effort he (or it) exerts in actually using that capability. We will follow this up by making further distinctions between observable and unobservable effort and verifiable and unverifiable outcomes. All of these are important to the extent to which the patient knows what she has bought and the institutional mechanisms necessary for effective markets. It is much easier for the patient/principal to ascertain medical capacity than effort. The medical equipment that is available at different types of facilities can be directly observed. If a patient can't find an x-ray machine in a hospital, she knows that an x-ray won't be provided even if it is needed, for the capacity doesn't exist. If a machine is availiable but not used in her case, she cannot know for sure whether x-rays were unnecessary for her diagnosis or if the doctor, for some other reason, chose not to bother with x-rays. And even if the machine is present and used, she will have difficulty knowing if the effort has been exerted to maintain it properly and to interpret its photographs correctly.

In principle, the patient/principal also can ascertain the qualifications of medical practitioners, thus establishing their basic technical capacities. She may have to be diligent to obtain this information in Africa, however, for both government and mission organizations historically have tried to obscure from patients the distinctions between professional qualifications. Given that their services were subsidized, state and church had an incentive to not alert patients to the distinctions between staff, so as to be able to treat them more cheaply and with less work for the most qualified practitioners. Hence the term 'doctor' was applied to staff who would never have been allowed to bear that title in the north. This contributes to the adverse selection problem to which we will return below. Nonetheless, even if the patient does determine the technical capacity of the practitioners, she still knows very little about the degree of effort that is likely to be made on her behalf.

Observable Effort. Some features of a health facility and its clinicians do indicate that effort and are visible even to the untrained observer: (i) the degree to which adequate quantities of pharmaceuticals are maintained in stock; (ii) the propensity to prescribe treatment and the quantity of drugs given; (iii) the frequency with which prescriptions are given by injection rather than orally; (iv) the 'clinical manner' (also known as 'bedside manner') of the attending practitioners; and (v) the adequacy of instruction given to patients as to how to use their prescriptions and how to prevent recurrence of the problem.

The first four items on the preceding list are acknowledged in the literature as influential in patient choice and satisfaction in Africa (Bichman *et al.* 1991; Litvack and Bodart 1993; Omorodion 1993; Stock 1983; Waddington and Enimayew 1990). Adequate pharmaceutical supplies obviously are closely related to the quality of medical care provided. In Chapter 8, G.M. Mliga found that in practice health education (the fifth item), 'clinical manner' (the fourth) and the accuracy of diagnosis (which the patient is *not* able to observe) are all related to one another (with r-values between .23 and .26 and $p < .001$). So the patient is able to observe some important aspects of medical effort and incorporate that information into her choice of health care facility.

On the other hand, Africans value poly-pharmacy and injections, both of which are negative for medical quality (Chapter 8; Holdswoth *et al.* 1993). All of the above observables also leave the patient ignorant or with nothing but inferences about the quality of the diagnosis, the relevance of any prescriptions, and the skill and care exercised in medical procedures.

Unobservable Effort. The patient is not necessarily helpless, however, if she can select practitioners who are subject to institutional mechanisms that assure effort and the presence of which are observable. There are two broad classes of such mechanisms: those which are and those which are not based on the ability to verify objectively that the outcome of a medical intervention has been desirable. After all, there is a substantial stochastic element in the relation between health and medical treatment. A patient might well recover even if the medical intervention provided is defective, and there is a similar possibility that illness will persist even if medical effort is first-rate. Thus generally neither the patient nor the provider can be certain from what they know of themselves what is going on with the other. It is not enough that the patient says she has been cured or not, for she might wish to deny the success of a treatment in order to avoid payment.

Verifiable Outcomes

In Africa, we observe two types of medical transactions that are based on verifiable outcomes, both of which are varieties of contingent contracts. In both of these sets of transactions the bulk of the payment is made only if the outcome of the medical intervention is successful, which of course greatly increases the incentive for the practitioner to exert maximum effort on his patient's behalf. The advantage of these contracts from the point of view of the patient/principal is that she knows what these incentives are and can proceed to purchase health care based on the knowledge that the medical effort of the practitioner/agent will be working fully to her advantage, even though she can't observe it.

Numerous anthropological studies have observed that traditional healers in the rural areas of central and eastern Africa charge only a nominal initial fee and expect the bulk of their income to come from 'appreciation' payments by the patient over several years after successful treatment. In Chapter 4 K.L. Leonard demonstrates that the character of this contract decisively influenced the types of cases people brought to traditional healers. Under this kind of retrospective payment system, the healer has the maximum incentive both to provide effort himself and to encourage the patient to take all the steps necessary to assure her full recovery. The patient would know that these are the kinds of incentives created by this type of contract, and the study demonstrates that the kinds of cases people take to traditional healers generally are precisely those that respond best to joint healer-patient effort. For example, success with broken bones requires both that the healer take great care in the initial setting and that the patient not put strain on the set limb. To assure the latter, healers often have the patient stay with them during recovery.

The success of the traditional healer contract, however, depends on the fact that the success of the outcome is effectively verifiable. The patient could deny that she had been successfully treated and refuse to make the contingent payments. However, most Africans believe that the healer has the spiritual powers to know the true outcome of the treatment and to invoke supernatural punishment on those who seek to cheat him. Since the patient is virtually certain to get sick again with something in the next several years, she will have reason to believe these sanctions are being invoked against her if she has not fulfilled her obligations under the contingent contract and will return to the healer begging him to accept her payment. Thus, although the contingent contract is highly functional for a whole range of medical conditions, science-based practitioners usually lack the traditional healer's ability to produce verifiable outcomes and are unable to transact business in this way. Traditional healers' ability to create (ironically unverifiable) supernatural payment incentives keeps their practices in business.

A 'modern' medicine variant of the contingent contract is reported for maternity by S. Ndeso-Atanga in Chapter 5. With the severe decline in real government salaries from Africa's prolonged economic crisis, an informal convention has developed in Cameroon that the family pay a substantial 'appreciation' to the government clinic midwife after the delivery of a healthy child. This outcome is readily observable and hence verifiable among all the parties to the transaction, and the payment is expected before the mother and child leave the clinic, so the contract is more enforceable than usual in modern medical matters. The existence of such a contract, which creates strong incentives for maximum effort on the part of the midwife, has quite dramatic effects. There is no doubt that government hospitals and clinics in Cameroon have staff and facilities with a medical capacity equal to or greater than that of the missions. For a whole range of illnesses, however, many people go to missions because they believe that the quality of effort exerted by their staff will be superior to that of their government counterparts. Since the contingent contract induces that effort in government clinics, however, the proportion of people going to missions for deliveries is dramatically lower (3 per cent for maternities vs. 30 per cent for other conditions).

Unverifiable Outcomes

We have distinguished medical capacity and effort and argued that patients must know what they are buying of both if medical markets are to function effectively. Having discussed the easier situations in which effort is either observable or its outcomes verifiable, we now turn to circumstances in which medical effort is unobservable and outcomes cannot be easily verified. In most types of medical transactions, neither are the outcomes as verifiable nor are the contracts as easily enforced, as discussed in the preceding section. Which institutional mechanisms can assure effort in more typical circumstances? We examine three here: repeated interactions, contingent contracts, and organizational sanctions.

Unavoidable Repeated Interactions. The first class of solutions involves unavoidable repeated interactions between the principal and her agent. If both parties know that they will have an ongoing set of transactions of indefinite duration, both the verification and enforcement problems are easier to solve. We noted above that there is only a probabilistic relation between medical effort and health outcome. Thus in any one-off transaction neither can the patient be sure of the effort of the medical practitioner nor can the latter be sure of the resulting health condition of the former. As the number of transactions increases, however, the underlying patterns emerge: the patient will be able to judge the quality of medical effort from the average changes in her health condition, and the practitioner will be able to assess the patient's typical effort in her own recovery and her veracity about her health outcome. Similarly, contracts based on nothing but mutual trust are more likely to function well if they are based on repeated interactions. The patient can reduce her use of a practitioner who is not making a quality effort on her behalf and the practitioner can decline the custom of patients who haven't paid their bills and effectively increase charges to those who do not make a good effort in their own recovery. (For a game theory demonstration that repeated play with a tit-for-tat strategy creates a mutually cooperative environment, see Axelrod 1985).

Note, however, that the repeated interaction solution depends on *both* the patient/principal and the provider/agent developing reputations with one another. Each must know the past behavior of the other and be able to adjust their current behavior in response. For the threat of sanctions to be meaningful, each party must have *some* alternative partner for the transaction, but the reputational and sanctioning effects are stronger if this choice is costly. In medicine, this is more likely to occur in the rural than in the urban areas and in veterinary than in human health. Distances to alternate medical providers for humans are smaller in the towns, and the more remote the area the more costly it is for a patient to bypass a local clinician. As it is more difficult and costly to move large animals than humans to non-local practitioners, travel looms even larger as a transaction cost in veterinary medicine (Chapter 3). Thus livestock owners find it somewhat easier to induce effort on their behalf from vets, and the latter are more likely to be able to trust the former to settle their accounts, for both know they will be seeing one another again. One sign of this local monopoly effect in Africa is that private vets can be observed charging lower prices to poor owners. (That is, they engage in price discrimination against the rich, charging both poor and rich what they are willing to pay.) (Cameroon: Gros 1993; Kenya: D.K. Leonard 1987). Another sign is George Njiru's observation in Kenya for this project that private veterinary practitioners in Central Kenya do half their business with livestock owners who call on them for assistance *once they are already in the neighborhood* at another farmer's request, for this eliminates the transport charge (1996, personal communication). The point is that practitioners who enjoy a degree of local monopoly (even if only in their skill class) have more stable clienteles and are more likely to be able to form mutually beneficial contracts with their clients. Thus breaking an imperfect local monopoly without introducing another form of institutional guarantee of quality could hurt, rather than benefit clients.

Contingent Contracts. An extension of the repeated interaction solution is an attenuated version of the contingent payment that we discussed above. It is extremely rare (and generally considered unethical) for science-based medical practitioners to make their fee contingent on the outcome of their treatment. On the other hand, when fees are billed after the service is provided, implicitly or explicitly there is a loan. If the practitioner knows that his chances of collecting the fees are small if the outcome of the treatment is a failure, the contract informally becomes a contingent payment one, complete with the implied incentive effects to medical effort. With the exceptions noted above we do not find this form of contract among human health care providers in Africa. But we do find it in private veterinary practice, where deferred fees are granted to livestock owners who have no liquidity problems and clearly are using them to gain the incentive effects of a contingent contract (Kenya: D.K. Leonard, personal observation and G. Njiru, personal communication). This form of implicit contract is possible in veterinary medicine in Africa while it is not in human health care precisely because of the higher transaction costs to transporting animals than humans.

Having observed this phenomenon and its incentive effects in Africa, we then realized that a similar informal contract existed in U.S. private practice before health insurance became pervasive. In the 1950s, physicians reported very substantial amounts of uncollectable fees (a third of gross was not uncommon). And if the patient died, it would have been considered ghoulish to press the family for payment, an inhibition that did not exist when the insurance company could be billed. Implicitly, then, the development of insurance removed from the American health system one of the institutions providing incentives for medical effort. Since the U.S. had other institutions in place that could achieve this incentive effect, the change may have had only minor consequences there. (It probably did contribute to the decline in personal attention from physicians.) Its absence in Africa— where the anonymous character of most human health care and the weak loyalty of families to particular medical providers make credit impossible— is much more consequential for practitioner effort.

The Organization of 'Budget-Breaking' Incentives. When the payoffs (and thus the incentives) to one party are independent of those of the other, we have what is alternatively called a 'budget-breaking' or 'nonconservative' institution. If the penalty for poor performance by the practitioner/agent is revocation of the right to practice or of access to patients/clients, a powerful incentive to medical effort is created. This penalty is 'nonconservative,' since the patient/principal does not gain from the loss of the practitioner/agent. Only organizations have the capacity to be 'budget-breaking' in this way (that is, not to balance losses with gains). One of the advantages of such an institution is that it renders the testimony of the patient/principal about the success of treatment more reliable by removing a major incentive for her to be biased. But it may also create an institutional setting in which the principal/patient doesn't have to play any role in the monitoring of the quality of effort, by instead assigning that role to a group of fellow professionals who make independent observations of the practitioner's work. Such an institution can be much more efficient than individual, 'conservative' (or 'budget-keeping') efforts to monitor and enforce quality of effort, such as lawsuits or even money-back guarantees. Professional observers can make accurate judgements on a much smaller sample of cases than the individual patient would have to use. And by imposing a penalty that doesn't have to be paid to the past clients of the practitioner, as is the case in class action lawsuits, it saves the money of finding and paying a dispersed and perhaps itinerant group. Both of these factors reduce transaction costs and therefore make medical practice under these conditions more efficient and cheaper. When an organization assumes the role of regulation *on behalf of* the patient/principal, we can refer to it as a 'super-principal.' In other words, it too becomes a part of the principal-agent relationship with the medical practitioner/agent.

Regulation of the right to practice is 'nonconservative' and depends on the existence of a body that will monitor and enforce professional standards. The state plays this function in France and large parts of Africa. As we noted in Chapter 1, however, the same governmental incompetence and corruption that makes privatization attractive to Africa renders the state unreliable as a regulator. Anglo-Saxon countries instead have relied upon self-regulation by professional associations, which not only control licenses but hospital privileges as well. Due in part to very small private markets and in part to statist traditions, professional self-regulation has been quite weak in Africa north of Zimbabwe. The agency literature would lead one to predict that, as private medical markets emerge, professional associations would become strong regulators so as to enable their members to collect the higher prices the market would pay for the assurance of quality effort. Cheikh Ly examined this hypothesis in Senegal (Chapter 7). He found a strong reason to expect that professional self-regulation would emerge for full doctors of veterinary medicine (DVMs) in that country: the downsizing of the state had forced large numbers of veterinary practitioners into the market and the political power of the union representing veterinary paraprofessionals had won them the legal right to practice in competition with DVMs. Full vets therefore had a particularly strong need to convince the livestock producer that paying a premium for their services would purchase higher quality. DVMs did create a professional body that gained state recognition, but it has not made a meaningful effort to regulate its members. Ly concludes that the agency literature underestimated the collective action problem of such regulation. Rigorous self-regulation increases reputation and therefore improves income. But the creation and operation of the necessary mechanism requires an extra level of effort from leading DVMs that would exceed the benefits they would personally obtain.

Most of Africa therefore lacks institutional structures that would solve the imperfect information problem for medical markets *as a whole*. The problem can be and is resolved *within* the context of specific organizations, however, where hierarchical supervision can take the place of open market contracts and professional regulation. Organizations can apply 'nonconservative' penalties internally and in this way become 'super-principals' on behalf of their clients. Observation, cajoling, fines, and firing are all tools of the supervisor, even though none of these costs directly benefits the patient. In theory government health systems could apply these incentives, but in practice they do not. Hierarchical supervision in government does not function effectively because it is too difficult to fire practitioners for deficiencies, the personnel systems are either too bureaucratic or too politicized to reward staff for good performance, and supervisors have too little incentive to overcome the inertia of the system.

Hierarchical supervision does effectively assure quality effort in the health facilities of NGOs, most of which are run by churches or missions. Service tends to feature prominently among the preferences of the leadership of NGOs, so it derives satisfaction from exercising the strong supervision needed to elicit staff effort. These general NGO motives for quality are even stronger for church-related facilities, for their leadership expects to derive the tangible and intangible benefits of increased church membership from having a strong service reputation and interacting with the clienteles that use their facilities. These incentives and the supervision that follows from them assure (an otherwise unobservable) quality medical effort on the part of mission medical staff, which then interacts with the observable capacity of these facilities. Note, however, that because mission supervision concentrates on the quality of effort made by the medical staff and because these staff alone gain or lose (the 'budget breaking' benefits) from these assessments, no incentives are created for patient effort. In that area, the contingent contract of the traditional healer is still superior.

It is very clear that mission health facilities have a strong market position in most African countries and that many people are prepared to pay a premium over government facility charges in order to use them. This quality premium cannot be due to superior mission capacity, for staff qualifications and equipment in NGO facilities typically are equal to or worse than those in their government counterparts (Chapters 4 and 8). It could be due, however, to aspects of observable effort such as better drug supplies and superior 'clinical manner' (Chapter 8; Bichmann *et al.* 1991; Litvack and Bodart 1993; Omorodion 1993; Stock 1983; Waddington and Enimayew 1990). To demonstrate that mission facilities also are attractive because they help to solve the moral hazard problem, we need to show that a patient/principal is most likely to chose a mission-based practitioner as her agent when she knows that unobservable dimensions of quality of medical effort (and not just capacity and observable aspects of effort) are desirable for her particular medical condition. To prove that missions, as an institution, serve to reduce the imperfect information problem we must now return to the examination of the extent to which African patients have knowledge of their medical needs.

Preliminary Self-Diagnosis. The first point is to note again that the medical model almost certainly overstates the extent of the imperfect information problem; even in Africa the patient does know something about her condition and what is appropriate to it. Research throughout this volume confirms that Africans make choices between medical providers based on their own understanding of their illnesses. The question is not whether these choices are being exercised but whether they are based on some real knowledge and therefore are good choices.

In the literature on insurance, some self-knowledge on the part of the insured (the principal) is seen as the primary source of the moral hazard problem. Those who are more likely to get sick or die are more likely to buy insurance, invalidating the actuarial tables on which the premiums are based. There is no reason to believe that consumers of medical interventions are any less knowledgeable than those who purchase insurance.

In fact, prospective patients/principals do have some useful insight into the severity and symptomology of their illness. They use their perceptions to guide their choice of health care providers/agents. K.L. Leonard's research in Cameroon demonstrates that there is an important overlap between patient perceptions and the objectively appropriate medical arena for their treatment, and that their choices hence are generally functional (Chapter 4). He examined a sample of 700 illness episodes and used professional medical expertise to classify the patients' report of their symptoms according to how sensitive the illness was likely to be to variations in medical capacity and effort and in patient effort. He found that he could explain 50 per cent of the choices made between five different types of medical providers (government hospitals and clinics, mission hospitals and clinics, and traditional healers) using a model with these criteria. In other words, the patient was heavily influenced in her choice of medical practitioners by the extent to which the incentive systems governing them would deliver the kinds of capacity and effort most appropriate to her condition.

This is not to suggest that poor, uneducated patients unfailingly choose the appropriate place to go for medical treatment. The African literature does suggest that self-referrals to hospitals, bypassing primary care facilities, are often wasteful. But the same literature also can be read as suggesting that self-referrals often are appropriate, that both the preferences of the health providers and the behavior of the patients can be wrong (Vogel 1993, p. 93; Mwabu 1986.) The fact that hospitals generally are more distant than clinics means that self-referrals are costly in time and transport for the sick, and therefore unlikely to be chosen if they are believed to be unnecessary. The existence of some poor self-referrals would suggest a need for institutions that will help to filter out the inappropriate from the appropriate more often, not to deny the possibility of patient choice altogether.

Summing Up Moral Hazard.

Moral hazard in the provision of health services creates agency costs for both the client and the practitioner. When this problem is not resolved by either institution or contract, we find practitioners who specialize in the (observable) sale of pharmaceuticals but do not use their (unobservable) skills as diagnosticians. This phenomenon is widespead in the privatization of both veterinary and human health services in Africa. There exist solutions to this problem that do not require institutions or for which viable institutions have long existed. The credit/contingent contract system of veterinarians with local monopolies and the contingent contract of traditional healers stand as examples. There are, as well, many organizations that independently make use of the institution of hierarchical supervision to resolve these issues. However the extension of good private health care (or veterinary) services in Africa will rely on the existence of pervasive institutions that allow modern practitioners to be paid for the skills they possess. We have shown that government supervision has been ineffective and that it is unlikely to become more effective (Chapters 1 and 8). Self-regulation by professional associations has not become an effective institution and we see little reason to believe that it will become so (Chapter 7). The other major alternatives are NGOs and referral networks, which we will discuss below.

ADVERSE SELECTION

We shift now from the moral hazard problem to one that is related, especially in African practice: adverse selection. In markets with imperfect information, higher-cost quality providers have difficulty surviving. If they are unable to demonstrate the superior quality of their capacity and effort and to persuade patients of its relevance to their conditions, a 'market for lemons' will exist in which lower price, low-quality practitioners will compete them out of existence (Akerloff 1970).

Currently in rural Africa, where the presence of private human medical practitioners is small, clients tend to associate skill levels with the facility in which one practices. Hospitals and their staff are differentiated from clinics and their staff. For private practitioners to succeed, however, patients must be able to discern their skill without the aid of an established organizational setting. Whether this is the only block to the establishment of more extensive private medical practice is not clear, but resolving this issue has already become a top priority of private veterinary medicine.

Unlike practitioners in human health, veterinarians either visit herders in the field or work on their own away from physical facilities that might suggest skill levels. Our project's studies of the emerging private veterinary markets in Senegal and Uganda show that full vets (DVMs) must struggle to compete effectively against their paraprofessional counterparts (Ly 1999a; Koma 1999). In Uganda DVMs enjoyed no price premium over paravets when they performed the same procedures; their sole market advantage came when they did procedures of which their less qualified competitors were incapable (Chapter 6).

Science-based human health facilities certainly are not threatened with survival in Africa, even though the reduction of their subsidies causes them to compete more vigorously. It is interesting that mission facilities do not have difficulty prospering in competition with government facilities that cost less and are often closer to the patient. Modern practitioners are distressed, however, that traditional practitioners and drug merchants continue to capture as large a market share as they do. We submit that the very same regulatory institutions that solve the moral hazard/unobservable effort problem for the missions are central to the solution of the adverse selection one as well.

If clients can correctly identify the skill level of a given practitioner and *that additional skill is worth its extra cost*, both the practitioner and the client will gain from its identification. The returns to skill appear to be high enough in human health care to justify its widespread use. The value of skill in veterinary medicine does differ from region to region (with varying market prices for meat and dairy products and the type of animals). Nontheless, even in the areas with the highest value for animals, when appropriate institutional guarantees of skill are absent, more highly skilled professionals suffer, whereas even in areas with lower-value animals the existence of institutions that solve the problem of adverse selection lead to higher use of professionals (Chapters 6 and 9). In this section we discuss some possible institutional solutions to the adverse selection problem and discuss their potential in the African context.

Labeling

The most common way in which quality providers seek to prevent adverse selection and establish a market share for themselves is through the way in which they present themselves to the public. Professional associations publicize the value of certain kinds of qualifications, certify those who possess them, prosecute those who falsely claim them, while the individual practitioner advertises that he is so qualified. This version of labeling has not worked well in Africa, for subsidized medical organizations have had a motive to obscure these distinctions. This deficiency is reversible, but only with considerable effort by professional associations, which we have already characterized as suffering from collective action problems. Even if the public better knew differences in medical qualifications, however, they would signal only differences in capacity, not the medical effort to utilize the capacity fully, which we have argued is so important. Much more common on the continent is 'brand name' labeling, whereby certain missions and denominations become known for high quality medical care in their facilities. Missions can be quite deliberate in the way they use their names in medical markets and the better ones are able to create instant customer demand for facilities in new locations through this device (K.L. Leonard, personal observation). Mission 'brand' advertising has the advantage of signaling not only capacity but medical effort as well. As we argued in the discussion of moral hazard, missions have incentives to provide a governance system that assures such effort. The inverse side of this coin is that government facilities are 'branded' with having a governance system that is ineffective at assuring medical effort. Note, however, that both systems label their facilities, not the differences between their practitioners.

Signaling

A second way in which providers can counter the tendency toward adverse selection in markets characterized by imperfect information is by 'signaling' their higher quality. This mechanism involves doing or showing things that 'good' practitioners find easy or inexpensive and inferior ones find difficult or expensive. The use of procedures that are associated only with higher levels of training and expertise, such as surgery, is one example. It would be difficult for a paraprofessional to open and close an incision successfully in the presence of witnesses, whereas a full medical professional could do so easily. Koma (Chapter 6) finds that as private veterinary practice emerged in Uganda full vets would develop reputations for their ability to do surgery, even among livestock owners who could not distinguish full vet credentials from those of paraprofessionals. Medical practitioners who want to establish a reputation for quality therefore would find it desirable to occasionally perform surgery in a highly visible setting. To do so on humans (but not animals) requires access to a hospital, and thus hospital privileges become another signaling device. Another example of signaling is the public use of expensive pieces of medical equipment, such as microscopes to examine blood slides. This mechanism is visible in the de facto privatization of the Chinese medical system, where county hospitals that are financially hard pressed have been observed to invest in expensive new equipment in order to attract patients away from other facilities (Chen 1997; Tang 1997). Some Kenyan vets are sought out by pastoralists because of their use of sophisticated diagnostic procedures (D.K. Leonard, personal observation). Koma (Chapter 6) concluded that the failure of full vets in Uganda to purchase and use the expensive diagnostic tools in which they had been trained was one of the sources of their difficulty in establishing market position and avoiding adverse selection.

Referral Networks

The third solution to the adverse selection problem involves the development of meaningful referral networks. These do not function effectively in Africa at present. Nonetheless, they are the mechanism whereby most real professional self-regulation and enhancement of the quality of practice takes place in the United States (Freidson 1970; Savage 1997). Since they are networks of participating professionals rather than organizations, their creation can be more decentralized and accomplished at lower cost than many of the other moral hazard and adverse selection solutions we have discussed in this chapter. It therefore is worth exploring further how professional referral networks work and what the prospects may be for their emergence in Africa.

Freidson (1970) found in the U.S. that physicians tend to develop networks of relations with others who perform their different specialist functions with similar medical capacity and effort. Because medical personnel are better trained to understand the nature of one another's work and because they see many more examples of the outcomes of their colleagues' treatments, they are in a much better position to overcome the imperfect information problem of medicine than is the average patient and to evaluate accurately the technical capacity and quality of effort of their fellow practitioners. Thus if frequent interaction teaches the patient that their primary care physician provides a quality of care they regard as satisfactory, they can use that MD's referrals to find other specialist medical providers of similar quality.

Savage (1997) shows that these networks perform functions for professionals beyond providing mutual referrals of business. Professionals learn from one another in their network relationships and through their interactions collectively become more competent by testing insights and learning new procedures and developments in the field. She calls this creation of new knowledge 'professional coproduction' and argues that it represents one of the distinct advantages of professional knowledge systems.

These self-organizing referral networks are rarely visible in African health and veterinary systems. There seem to be several reasons why this is so. (a) Historically, veterinary systems were subsidized and human health systems still are. This created excess demand for the more highly qualified practitioners. The response was to blur distinctions among personnel, so that the cheaper staff with lower qualifications could take up the slack. There also is an attempt to get patients to enter these systems at the level of the cheaper providers, where the simpler cases can be filtered out. The function being fulfilled here is an efficiency, not a quality enhancing one (Vogel 1993, p. 93). When referrals are made they are made to *facilities*, not to particular practitioners. Given the depersonalized character of these relationships, there is very little personal interaction or even communication among medical practitioners about the cases they have shared (Sauerborn *et al.* 1989; K.L. Leonard, personal observation). Thus there is no learning, no 'professional co-production' of knowledge, and little information generated that might teach personnel about one another's quality. (b) To the extent that referrals take place across levels in the government and mission systems (health and veterinary) they are between subordinates and those who are their supervisors or are closely connected to them. It is a well established principle of organizational behavior that communication takes place more readily and accurately between peers than up a hierarchy (Blau 1955). (c) The sharing of knowledge (both about medicine and about one another) takes places most effectively through informal and frequent personal interactions. Such an interactive environment is rare in the African health and veterinary systems, where large numbers of the professional staff work in isolation. Hospitals don't exist for veterinary medicine, (human) health practitioners in clinics don't have hospital privileges, and rural hospitals tend to have very small professional staffs.

Until medical professionals in Africa interact more with one another in non-hierarchical settings and with the possibility of personalized referrals, professional networks that recognize, reward, and encourage quality are not likely to emerge. It does seem possible that increased commercialization of African medical systems may cause this to occur. Since such networks can be organized in decentralized, low cost ways, they seem more likely to emerge than self-regulation by professional associations, which is troubled with collective action problems. Particularly in veterinary medicine, where both DVMs and paravets have been thrown into the private market, it seems reasonable to hope that such networks will be created. DVMs already find it difficult to compete with paravets, for it is irrational for the livestock owner to pay them extra to do something a paravet can do. DVMs need paravets to refer to them the cases that need higher order skills, and the paraprofessionals will want to serve their clients with better quality referrals. DVMs will eventually realize that they cannot make a living by doing procedures that are appropriate to paravets and will want to have a set of these paraprofessionals to whom they can recommend their clients as well. Indeed, they might become sufficiently busy that they don't have time to perform less-remunerative paravet procedures; they will still benefit from an extended mutual-referral relationship with paravets that will ensure customer satisfaction with service at both levels. As time progresses, the isolated paravets will begin to suffer from being cut off from further developments in their fields and would benefit from the opportunity to advance themselves professionally by learning from DVMs. Thus mutually symbiotic relationships that enhance quality should and could emerge at low cost. They have not yet done so in Uganda (Chapter 6), but the evolution of the veterinary market there is still young.

It will be harder for the same spontaneous development of referral networks to take place in human health, where large, subsidized organizations dominate medical provision. More organizational effort will be required in these settings, but we believe that, as the subsidy element of these systems declines—particularly in the mission ones—the competitive pressures to provide quality service to one's clientele will make them increasingly likely.

CONCLUSIONS

Medical markets have the potential for significantly improving the quality, reach, and efficiency of health services in Africa. This potential will be realized, however, only if both the full power of market incentives is released and the institutional mechanisms necessary to correct market failures are put in place. The full extent of African demand for health services cannot be felt until some kind of medical insurance system is functioning effectively on the continent. We suggest that this requires building on the informal insurance of the extended family and providing it, rather than the individual or nuclear family, with assistance when it is unable to cope.

We further have observed that markets are not just about demand but about supply responses as well. Most health sector reforms that have taken place in Africa to date have inhibited supply responses by confining the changes to traditional government health bureaucracies. Fee increases may help to relieve resource problems for ministries of health but they do little to unleash the power of the market on the forces of supply. When, as in Tanzania, decentralization passes market incentives directly on to the operatives of medical facilities, staff effort and quality result. High-powered market incentives and decentralization will not be positive in just any setting, however. Success depends on the form of decentralization and it depends on the institutional mechanisms that govern market exchanges. Those empowered by decentralization must be responding to demands for medical service, not patronage. The forms of decentralization most likely to be effective are delegation to professionally controlled autonomous government corporations and privatization to nongovernmental organizations.

Imperfect information in the provision of health services creates agency costs for both the client and the practitioner. When this problem is not resolved by either institution or contract we find that many practitioners specialize in the sale of pharmaceuticals (observables) and do not use their skills as diagnosticians (unobservable). Autonomous and idiosyncratic solutions to the agency problem in the provision of professional medical services abound in rural Africa. Some do not require institutions (the credit/contingent-contract system of veterinarians with local monopolies) and others are built on viable institutions that have long existed (the contingent contract of traditional healers). However, they depend in large part on the existence of a particular exogenous technological or institutional environment and therefore are difficult to replicate.

We identified, through theory and comparison with the west, four institutions that in principle might do a better job of solving the agency problem. We dismissed government regulation because adequate regulatory capacity does not exist in most African countries. Self-regulation, by professional bodies, is a very attractive option and theory suggests that such regulation should arise as privatization continues. The empirical evidence, however, suggests that this conclusion is overly optimistic. There are significant collective action problems to the formation of self-regulatory bodies and since these organizations require centralized control, we are pessimistic that these problems can be overcome in the present African context. On the other hand, referral networks perform much the same function but do not require centralized control. For this reason, we hold out the hope that they can be coaxed into existence.

The Role of NonGovernmental Organizations

The most successful institution for the delivery of quality medical care in Africa is that of independent, pre-existing value-based organizations that use the institution of hierarchical supervision to ensure quality. This result parallels a large body of empirical and theoretical work on health care in the U.S., where nonprofit hospitals frequently arise in discussions of quality. Many authors have suggested that nonprofit administrators direct supervisory control toward different ends than for-profit ones do (Newhouse 1970; Pauly and Redisch 1973). We certainly believe that the bishop of a church does not operate health services with the simple goal of earning profits.

Mission hospitals and health services are invaluable resources that should be tapped to their fullest extent and encouraged to grow. Many African governments implicitly or explicitly block the expansion of these services, policies that should be reconsidered. Other countries, such as Tanzania, effectively subcontract government-subsidized care to missions, which are permitted to charge fees but sell their services at below market prices. This arrangement makes effective use of the missions' ability to supervise their staff more effectively than government does its. It also takes advantage of the fact that the less-bureaucritized targeting procedures of the NGOs reach the poor more effectively and at less expense than governments do. The prevalence, effectiveness, and positive 'brand' image of mission health facilities are unusually great in Africa. The challenges of transition to market-based health care are much more likely to be successfully surmounted if African countries build on this part of their institutional heritage. Expanded contracts by African governments to established, value-based, competitive NGOs to provide health care for the poor would provide higher-quality, more equitable service at lower cost.

Consolidated Bibliography

Abel-Smith, B. (1991) 'Financing Health For All,' *World Health Forum* 12:2, pp. 191–200.

Abel-Smith, B. and P. Rawal (1992) 'Can the Poor Afford 'Free' Health Services? A Case Study of Tanzania,' *Health Policy and Planning* 7:4, pp. 329–41.

Acton, J.P. (1975) 'Nonmonetary Factors in the Demand for Medical Services: Some Empirical Evidence,' *Journal of Political Economy* 83:3, pp. 595–614.

Afrique Agriculture (1993) no. 204 (May) pp. 13–15.

Aga Khan Foundation (1990) 'MAP Series on Quality Assessment,' mimeo.

Akakpo, A.J. (1992) 'La privatisation des activites veterinaires en Afrique: A quel prix?' in *Production et sante tropicales. actes de la 7e conference internationale des institutions de medecine veterinaire tropicale* Yamoussoukro, Cote d'Ivoire, CIRA.

Akerlof, G. (1970) 'The Market for 'Lemons': Quality, Uncertainty, and the Market Mechanism,' *Quarterly Journal of Economics* 8:3, pp. 408–500.

Akin, J.S. *et al.* (1986) 'The Demand for Adult Outpatient Services in the Bicol Region of the Philippines,' *Social Science & Medicine* 22:3, pp. 321–8.

Alubo, S.O. (1990) 'Debt Crisis, Health, and Health Services in Africa,' *Social Science & Medicine* 31:6, pp. 639–48.

Amir, P. and H.C. Knipscheer (1989) 'Conducting On-Farm Research: Procedures and Economic Analysis,' Morrilton, Arkansas: Winrock International Institute for Agricultural Development and International Research Center.

Andersen, R. (1968) 'Behavioral Model of Family's Use of Health Services,' Center for Health Administrative Studies Research Series no. 25, Chicago: University of Chicago Press.

Anteneh, H.A. (1984) 'Financing Animal Health Services in Some African Countries,' Pastoral Development Network Paper 176, London: Overseas Development Institute.

___________. (1989) 'Elevage et production alimentaire en afrique: une chance et un défi pour les services de l'élevage et les services vétérinaires nationaux,' *Revue Scientifique et Technique* (Office International des Epizooties) 8:3, pp. 607–23.

Arrow, K.J. (1963) 'Uncertainty and the Welfare Economics of Medical Care,' *American Economic Review* 53:1–2, pp. 941–73.

___________. (1985) 'The Economics of Agency,' in J. Pratt and R. Zeckhauser, eds., *Principals and Agents: The Structure of Business* Boston: Harvard Business School Press, pp. 37–51.

Bates, R. (1981) *Markets and States in Tropical Africa: The Political Basis of Agricultural Policies* Berkeley: University of California Press.

Benyoussef, A. and A.F. Wessen (1974) 'Utilization of Health Services in Developing Countries: Tunisia,' *Social Science & Medicine* 8:5, pp. 287–304.

Berman, P., ed. (1995) *Health Sector Reform in Developing Countries: Making Health Development Sustainable* Boston: Harvard School of Public Health.

Bichman, W., H. Diesfeld, Y. Agboton, E. Gbaguida, and U. Simshauser (1991) 'District Health Systems: Users' Preferences for Services in Benin,' *Health Policy and Planning* 6:4, pp. 361–70.

Bijlmakers, L. and J-W. Harnmeijer (1995) 'Discussion and Conclusions,' in Chabot *et al.* 1995, pp. 119–48.

Bitran-Dicowsky, R. and D.W. Dunlop (1993) 'The Determinants of Hospital Costs: An Analysis of Ethiopia,' in A. Mills and K. Lee, eds., *Health Economics Research in Developing Countries* Oxford: Oxford University Press.

Blau, P.M. (1955) *The Dynamics of Bureaucracy.* Chicago: University of Chicago Press.

__________. (1964) *Exchange and Power in Social Life* New York: J. Wiley.

Bossert, T. (1998) 'Analyzing the Decentralization of Health Systems in Developing Countries: Decision Space, Innovation and Performance,' *Social Science & Medicine* 47:10, pp. 1513–27.

Burrows, G.E., A. Mauromoustakos *et al.* (1995) 'MIC's for selected antimicrobials against Escherichia coli. Recovered from various animal species in Zimbabwe compared with isolates from Australia and the United States,' *The Bovine Practitioner* 29 (September) pp. 110–113

Buschkens, W.F.L. and L.J. Slikkerveer (1982) 'Health Care in East Africa: Illness Behaviour of the Eastern Oromo in Hararghe

(Ethiopia)' *Studies of Developing Countries* no. 28. Assen, Netherlands: Van Gorcum.

Caiden, N. and A. Wildavsky (1974) *Planning and Budgeting in Poor Counties*. New York: Wiley.

CARD (Coordinated Agricultural and Rural Development) (1989) 'Small Ruminants in Zimbabwe, A Review on Functions, Research and Proposals for Communal Lands,' Discussion paper, Masvingo, Zimbabwe: Belmont Press.

Central Statistical Office (1992) *Zimbabwe National Report, Census 1992* Harare, Zimbabwe: Central Statistical Office.

Centre de Suivi Ecologique (CSE) (1992) 'Estimation des effectifs du bétail par vol systémique de reconnaissance dans la moitié nord du Sénégal,' *Rapport de Campagne* Document NT 92.

Chabot, J., J.W. Harnmeijer, and P.H. Streefland (1995) *African Primary Health Care in Times of Turbulence* Amsterdam: Royal Tropical Institute.

Chen J. (1997) 'The Impact of Health Sector Reform on County Hospitals,' in G. Bloom and A. Wilkes, *Health in Transition: Transforming China's Rural Health Services. IDS Bulletin* 28:1, pp. 48–52.

Cheneau, Y. (1985) 'L'Organisation des services vétérinaires en Afrique,' *Revue Scientifique et Technique* (Office International des Epizooties) 5:1, pp. 57–105.

Chernichovsky, D. and A.O. Meesock (1986) 'Utilisation Of Health Services In Indonesia,' *Social Science & Medicine* 23:6, pp. 611–20.

Christianson, J.B. (1976) 'Evaluating Locations for Outpatient Medical Care Facilities,' *Land Economics* 11, pp. 298–313.

Clark, R.C. (1985) 'Agency Cost versus Fiduciary Duties,' in J.W. Pratt and R.J. Zeckhauser (eds.) *Principals and Agents: The Structure of Business*, pp. 55–79. Boston: The Harvard Business School Press.

Coase, R.H. (1964) 'The Regulated Industries: Discussion,' *American Economic Review* 54(3) pp. 194–97.

__________. (1974) 'The Lighthouse in Economics,' *The Journal of Law and Economics* 17(2) pp. 357–76.

Coppo, P., L. Pisani, and A. Keita (1992) 'Perceived Morbidity and Health Behavior in a Dogon Community,' *Social Science & Medicine* 34:11, pp. 1227–35.

Cousins, B., C. Jackson, and I. Scoones (1988) 'Socioeconomic Dimensions of Livestock Production in the Communal Lands of Zimbabwe,' Report and Recommendations of a Workshop held under the auspices of the Center for Applied Social Sciences, University of Zimbabwe.

Cutler, D., M. McClellan, and J. Newhouse (1998) 'What Has Increased Medical Spending Bought?' *American Economic Review* 88, pp. 132–35.

Demsetz, H. (1968) 'Why Regulate Utilities?,' *Journal of Law and Economics* 11, pp. 55–66.

Department of Veterinary Services, Zimbabwe (1994) 'Animal Disease Control in Zimbabwe,' Report from Department of Veterinary Services. Ministry of Lands, Agriculture and Water Development, Government of Zimbabwe.

____________. (1996) Internal Communication on VLT Work Evaluation, April 1996.

Dor, A. and J. Van der Gaag (1987) 'The Demand for Medical Care in Developing Countries: Quantity Rationing in Rural Cote d'Ivoire,' Development Research Department, LSM Working Paper no. 35. Washington: World Bank.

Dow, W.H. (1995) 'Discrete Choice Estimation of Price-Elasticities: The Benefits of a Flexible Behavioral Model of Health Care Demand,' Technical Report 739, New Haven: Yale University.

Dranove, D. and W.D. White (1987) 'Agency and the Organization of Health Care Delivery,' *Inquiry* 24 (Winter) pp. 405–15.

Duan, N. *et al.* (1983) 'A Comparison of Alternative Models For the Demand For Medical Care,' *Journal of Business and Economic Statistics* 1:2, pp. 115–26.

Ehui, S. and M.E. Lipner, eds. (1993) *Livestock and Resource Management Policy: Issues and Priorities for Research* Proceedings of the Research Planning Workshop held at ILCA, Addis Ababa, Ethiopia, 24–27 March 1992. ILCA (International Livestock Center)

Ellis, R. (1993) 'Public and Private Interactions in Health Sector in Developing Countries,' Health Financing and Sustainability Project, paper no. 5.

Elster, J. (1989) 'Social Norms and Economic Theory,' *Journal of Economic Perspectives* 3(4) pp. 99–117.

Egunjobi, L. (1983) 'Factors Influencing Choice of Hospitals: A Case Study of the Northern Part of Oyo State, Nigeria,' *Social Science & Medicine* 17:9, pp. 585–8.

Ethiopian Central Statistical Authority (1991) 'Population Size for Shoa Region by Awraja, Wereda, Town, Farmers' Association, and Urban Dwellers' Association,' mimeo.

Ethiopian Ministry of Health (1991) 'Strategies for the Implementation of the National Population Program,' mimeo, Maternal and Child Health Department.

__________. (1992) 'Health Manpower Study: Staffing Pattern in Health Institutions in Ethiopia,' mimeo, Planning and Programming Department with Health Professional Training Department.

__________. (1993) 'Guidelines for the Organization of Private Health Institutions,' mimeo, Health Institutions and Training Department.

Ethiopian Office of the Council of Ministers (1993) 'Health Policy of the Transitional Government of Ethiopia,' mimeo, Office of the Council of Ministers.

Evans, R.G. (1984) Strained Mercy: The Economics of Canadian Health Care. Toronto: Butterworths.

Feldstein, P. (1993) *Health Care Economics* Albany, NY: Delmar.

FAO/OIE/WHO (1992) *Annuaire de la sante animale* Rome: Food and Agriculture Organization, pp. 185–95.

Food and Agricultural Organization (1997b) 'Summary Report of Technical Consultation on the Principles for Rational Delivery of Public and Private Veterinary Services,' (Rome, Italy, 25–27 March 1997) Rome: Food and Agricultural Organization.

__________. (1997) Principles for Rational Delivery of Public and Private Veterinary Services with Reference to Africa Rome: FAO, 25–27 March 1993.

Freidson, E. (1970) Profession of Medicine. A Study of the Sociology of Applied Knowledge New York: Harper & Row.

Friedman, M. (1962) *Capitalism and Freedom*. Chicago: University of Chicago Press.

Fuchs, V.R. (1968) 'The Growing Demand for Medical Care,' *New England Journal of Medicine* 279:4, pp. 190–5.

Gauthier, J., A. Pradier, and A. Shumba (1995) 'Main Results of the Survey on Goat Marketing in Masvingo Province,' Agritex French goat project. Centre de coopération internationale en recherche agronomique pour le développement. Département d'élevage .

George, D. and P. Mallery (1995) *SPSS/PC+ - Step by Step* Belmont, CA: Wadsworth Publishing Company.

Gertler, P., and J. Van der Gaag (1990) *The Willingness to Pay for Medical Care: Evidence from Two Developing Countries* Baltimore: Johns Hopkins University Press.

Gilson, L., M. Alilio, and K. Heggenhougen (1994) 'Community Satisfaction with Primary Health Care Services: An Evaluation Undertaken in the Morogoro Region of Tanzania,' *Social Science & Medicine* 39:6, pp. 767–80.

Gilson, L. and A. Mills (1995) 'Health Sector Reforms in Sub-Saharan Africa,' in Berman (1995) pp. 277–316.

Gilson, L., S. Russell, and K. Buse (1995) 'The Political Economy of User Fees with Targeting: Developing Equitable Health Financing Policy,' *Journal of Intrnational Development* 7:3, pp. 369–401.

Goode, W.J. (1960) 'Encroachment, Charlatanism and the Emerging Profession: Psychology, Sociology, and Medicine,' *American Sociological Review* 25(6) pp. 902–14.

Gould, D.J. (1980) Bureaucratic Corruption in the Third World: The Administration of Underdevelopment in Zaire. New York: Pergamon-Maxwell.

Gould, D.J. and J.A. Amaoro-Reyes (1983) 'The Effects of Corruption on Administrative Performance: Illustrations from Developing Countries,' Staff Working Paper No. 580. Washington, D.C.: The World Bank.

Greene, W.H. (1993) *Econometric Analysis*. 2nd edition. Englewood Cliffs, NJ: Prentice Hall.

Gros, J-G. (1993) *The Privatization of Livestock Services in Cameroun: A Study in the Feasibility of State* and *Market Participation in Economic Restructuring*. Ph.D. dissertation submitted to the Department of Political Science, University of California, Berkeley.

____________. (1994) 'Of Cattle, Farmers, Veterinarians, and the World Bank: The Political Economy of Veterinary Services in Cameroun,' *Public Administration and Development* 14:1, pp. 37–52.

Griffin, C.C. (1989) 'Strengthening Health Services in Developing Countries Through the Private Sector,' Discussion Paper no. 4. Washington: World Bank.

Griffith, H.W. (1985) The Complete Guide to Symptoms, Illness and Surgery Los Angeles, CA: Body Press.

Grossman, M. (1972) 'On the Concept of Health Capital and the Demand for Health,' *Journal of Political Economy*, 80:2, pp. 223–55.

Gwatkin, D.R. (1997) 'Private Health Care in Tanzania: Guiding Its Development,' IHPP Policy Brief, Washington, D.C.: International Health Policy Program.

de Haan, C. and S. Bekure (1989) 'Animal Health Services in Sub-Saharan Africa: Initial Experience with New Approaches,' Washington, D.C.: World Bank.

Hall J.A., D.L. Roter, and N.R. Katz (1988) 'Meta-Analysis of Satisfaction with Medical Care: Description of Research Domain and

Analysis of Overall Satisfaction Levels,' *Social Science & Medicine* 27:6, pp. 637–44.

Hardin, R. (1982) *Collective Action*. Baltimore: Johns Hopkins University Press.

Hargreaves, S.K. (1987) 'The Animal Disease Situation in Zimbabwe,' Proceedings of a conference on co-operation in the diagnosis of animal diseases. *SADCC Conference* Harare, Republic of Zimbabwe, 6–9 October 1987, pp. 49–54.

Hayek, F.A. (1945) 'The Use of Knowledge in Society,' *American Economic Review* 35(4) pp. 519–30.

__________. (1966) *The Road to Serfdom*. Chicago: University of Chicago Press.

Hellberg, I. (1990) 'The Swedish Veterinary Profession and the Swedish State,' in R. Torstendahl and M. Burrage (eds.) *The Formation of Professions: Knowledge, State and Society* pp. 174–85. London: Sage.

Heller P.S. (1982) 'A Model Of The Demand For Medical And Health Services In Peninsular Malaysia' *Social Science & Medicine* 16:3, pp. 267–84.

Hirschman, A. (1970) *Exit, Voice and Loyalty: Responses to Decline in Firms, Organizations and States* Cambridge: Harvard University Press.

Hoare, G. (1987) 'Policies for Financing the Health Sector,' *Health Policy and Planning* 2:1, pp. 1–16.

Holdsworth, G., P.A. Garner, and T. Harpham (1993) 'Crowded Outpatient Departments in City Hospitals of Developing Countries: A Case Study from Lesthoto,' *International Journal of Health Planning and Management* 8:4, pp. 315–24.

Hollingsworth, J.R. (1986) *A Political Economy of Medicine: Great Britain and the United States*. Baltimore: Johns Hopkins University Press.

Honhold, N. *et al.* (1987) 'Production and Disease in Communal Land Goats,' *Proceedings* Zimbabwe Annual Veterinary Congress 1987.

Hosmer, D.W. and S. Lemeshow (1989) *Applied Logistic Regression* New York: John Wiley and Sons.

Hughes, E.C. (1958) *Men and Their Work*. New York: The Free Press of Glencoe.

Hyden, G. (1973) *Efficiency versus Distribution in East African Cooperatives: A Study in Organizational Conflicts* Nairobi: East African Literature Bureau.

__________. (1980) *Beyond Ujamaa in Tanzania: Underdevelopment and an Uncaptured Peasantry* Berkeley: University of California Press.

____________. (1983) *No Shortcuts to Progress: African Development Management in Perspective* Berkeley: University of California Press.

Institut d'Èlevage et de Médecine Vétérinaire des Pays Tropicaux (IEMVT) (1988) 'Vers Une Nouvelle Structure Pour La Santé Animale en Afrique,' Rapport de synthèse d'un atelier tenu à Bangui (République Centraficaine) du 22 au 27 février 1988. Maisons Alfort, France.

Israel, A. (1987) *Institutional Development: Incentives to Performance* Baltimore: John Hopkins University Press.

Jackson, R. and C. Rosberg (1982) *Personal Rule in Black Africa: Prince, Autocrat, Prophet, Tyrant* Berkeley: University of California Press.

Janzen, J.M. (1978) *The Quest for Therapy in Lower Zaire* Berkeley: University of California Press.

Johnson, B. and W. Clark (1982) *Redesigning Rural Development* Baltimore: Johns Hopkins University Press.

Johnson, C. (1982) MITI and the Japanese Miracle: The Growth of Industrial Policy 1925–1975. Stanford: Stanford University Press.

Jorgensen, S.L. (1995) 'Health Reforms as a Complement to Structural Adjustment,' in Chabot *et al.*, eds., *African Primary Health Care in Times of Turbulence* Amsterdam: Royal Tropical Institute, pp. 19–30.

Joseph, R.A. (1987) Democracy and Prebendal Politics in Nigeria: The Rise and Fall of the Second Republic. Cambridge: Cambridge University Press.

Joseph, R.A., F. Hayashi, and L. Kotlikoff (1989) 'Is the Extended Family Altruistically Linked: Direct Tests Using Micro Data,' National Bureau of Economic Research Working Paper no. 3046, pp. 1–57.

Juul, K. (1996) 'Migration et innovations technologiques chez les peuls du Sénégal suite aux sécheresses: le triomphe de la chambre ‡ air,' IIED, Programme Zones Arides, Dossier no. 64.

Kanji, N., P.M. Kilima, and G.M. Munishi (1992) 'Quality of Primary Curative Care in Dar-es-Salaam,' Unpublished paper, Dar-es-Salaam, Tanzania.

Kennedy, P.A. (1992) *Guide to Econometrics* 3rd edition. Cambridge: MIT Press.

Kessner, D.M., C.E. Kalk, and J. Singer (1973) 'Assessing Health Quality: The Case of Tracers,' *New England Journal of Medicine* 288:4, pp. 189–94.

King, M., ed. (1966) *Medical Care in Developing Countries* Nairobi: Oxford University Press.

Kish, L. (1965) *Survey Sampling* New York: John Wiley and Sons.

Klitgaard, R. (1990) *Tropical Gangsters* New York: Basic Books.

___________. (1995) 'Including Culture in Evaluation Research,' in R. Picciotto and R.C. Rist, eds., *Evaluating Country Development Policies and Processes* San Francisco: Jossey-Bass.

Kloos, H. (1990) 'Utilisation of Selected Hospitals, Health Centres, and Health Stations in Central, Southern and Western Ethiopia,' *Social Science & Medicine* 31:2, pp. 101–14.

Korte, R. *et al.* (1992) 'Financing Health Services in Sub-Saharan Africa: Options For Decision Makers During Adjustment,' *Social Science & Medicine* 34:1, pp. 1–9.

Larsen, D.E. and R. Irving (1976) 'Physician Role Performance and Patient Satisfaction,' *Social Science & Medicine* 10:32, pp. 29–32.

Lavy, V., and J.M. Germain (1994) 'Quality and Cost in Health Care Choice in Developing Countries,' Living Standards Measurement Survey Working Paper no. 105. Washington: World Bank.

Lavy, V., and J.M. Quigley (1993) 'Willingness to Pay For the Quality and Intensity of Medical Care: Low Income Households in Ghana,' Living Standards Measurement Survey Working Paper no. 94. Washington: World Bank.

Leonard, D.K. (1977) *Reaching the Peasant Farmer: Organization Theory and Practice in Kenya* Chicago: University of Chicago Press.

___________. (1983) 'Appropriate User Fees for the Ministry of Livestock Development and New Systems for Their Collection,' Unpublished report submitted to the Ministry of Livestock Development. Nairobi, Kenya.

___________. (1985) 'African Practice and the Theory of User Fees,' *Agricultural Administration* 18:3, pp. 137–58.

___________. (1987) 'The Supply of Veterinary Services: Kenyan Lessons,' *Agricultural Administration and Extension* 26:4, pp. 219–36.

___________. (1991) African Successes: Four Public Managers of Kenyan Rural Development. Berkeley: University of California Press.

___________. (1991) 'The Organizational Dilemmas of Non-Professional Work in Professional Domains,' Unpublished paper. Sussex: Institute of Development Studies.

___________. (1993) 'Structural Reform of the Veterinary Profession in Africa and the New Institutional Economics,' *Development and Change* 24:2, pp. 227–67.

Leonard, D.K. and D.R Marshall, eds. (1982) *Institutions of Rural Development for the Poor* Berkeley: Institute of International Studies, University of California.

Leonard, K.L. (1997) *Contractual Structure of Health Care in Rural Cameroun* Ph. D. Dissertation, Department of Agricultural and Resource Economics, University of California, Berkeley.

__________. (1998a) 'African Traditional Healers: Incentives and Skill in Health Care Delivery,' Columbia University, Department of Economics Discussion Paper Series No 9798-13.

Leonard, K.L. "Institutional Structure of Health Care in Rural Cameroun: Structural Estimation of Production in Teams with Unobservable Effort," Department of Economics Discussion Paper No. 9798-16. New York: Columbia University.

Leonard, K.L. and D.K. Leonard (1998) 'Institutional Solutions to the Principal-Agent Problem in African Health Care,' Department of Economics Discussion Paper No. 9899-02. New York: Columbia University.

Litvack, J. and C. Bodart (1993) 'User Fees Plus Quality Equals Improved Access to Health Care: Results of a Field Experiment in Cameroon,' *Social Science & Medicine* 37:3, pp. 369–83.

Ly, C. (1989) 'La politique de développement de l'élevage au Sénégal. Repères sur l'évolution, les réalités et les perspectives de l'élevage des bovinés et petits ruminants, 1960–1986,' *CRDI - ISRA, Série Réflexions et Perspectives*, 1:1.

__________. (1997) 'Veterinary Professionals in Senegal: Working Behavior and Values,' Working paper for Dutch – IDRC Conference, Nairobi, July 1997.

Madala, G.S. (1983) *Limited-Dependent and Qualitative Variables in Econometrics* New York: Cambridge University Press.

March, J.G. and J.P. Olsen (1989) *Rediscovering Institutions: The Organizational Basis of Politics* New York: The Free Press.

March, J.G. and Simon, H.A. (1958) *Organizations* New York: John Wiley.

Mbugua, J.K., G. Bloom, and M. Segall (1995) 'Impact of User Charges on Vulnerable Groups: The Case of Kibwezi in Rural Kenya,' *Social Science & Medicine* 41:6, pp. 829–35.

McCorkle, C.M. and E. Mathias (1995) 'Paraveterinary Health Care Programs: a Global Overview,' in K.H. Zessin, ed., *Livestock Production and Diseases in the Tropics: Livestock Production and Human Welfare* Proceedings of the VIIIth International Conference of Institutions of Tropical Veterinary Medicine, 25–29 September.

McCrindle, C.M.E. *et al.* (1994) 'An Investigation into the Potential Veterinary Needs of a Semi-rural, Low-income Community,' *South African Veterinary Journal* 65:3, pp. 90–6.

McKelvey, R.D. and W. Zavonya (1975) 'A Statistical Model For the Analysis of Ordinal Level Dependent Variables,' *Journal of Mathematical Sociology* 4:2, pp. 103–20.

McPake, B. (1993) 'User Charges For Health Services in Developing Countries: A Review of the Economic Literature,' *Social Science & Medicine* 16:11, pp. 1397–1405.

McPake, B., K. Hanson, and A. Mills (1993) 'Community Financing of Health Care in Africa: An Evaluation of the Bamako Initiative,' *Social Science & Medicine* 36:11, pp. 1385–95.

Mechanic, D. (1968) *Medical Sociology* New York: Free Press.

Merton, R.K. with T.F. Gieryn (1982) 'Institutionalized Altruism: The Case of the Professions,' in R. K. Merton, A. Rosenblatt, and T.F. Gieryn (eds.) *Social Research and the Practicing Professions* Cambridge, Massachusetts: Abt Books, pp. 109–34.

Mills, A. and K. Lee (1993) *Health Economics Research in Developing Countries* Oxford: Oxford University Press.

Ministry of Public Health (1994) 'Report of the Divisional Health Centres Supervisory Team,' Divisional Service of Public Health, Meme Division-Kumba, South-West Province, Republic of Cameroon.

Mintzberg, H. (1979) *The Structuring of Organizations: A Synthesis of Research* Englewood Cliffs, N.J.: Prentice-Hall.

Moe, T.M. (1987) 'The New Economics of Organization,' *American Journal of Political Science* 28, pp. 739–77.

__________. (1990) 'The Politics of Structural Choice: Toward a Theory of Public Bureaucracy,' in O. Williamson (ed.) *Organization Theory: From Chester Barnard to the Present and Beyond*. New York: Oxford.

Monicat, F., *et al.* (1994) *Goat Production in Zimbabwe* Centre de cooperation internationale en recherche agronomique pour le développement. Département d'élevage et de médecine vétérinaire. Harare, Zimbabwe.

Monicat, F., P.M. Borne, and J. Keravec (1991) Structures et méthodes associées a une enquête multifactorielle sur la mortalité des chevreaux dans les zones communales du Zimbabwe Veterinary Research Laboratory, P. O. Box 8101, Harare, Zimbabwe.

Montgomery, J.D. (1987) 'Probing Managerial Behavior: Image and Reality in Southern Africa,' *World Development* 15(7) pp. 911–29.

Moris, J. (1977) 'The Transferability of Western Management Concepts and Programs, an East African Perspective,' in L.D. Stifel, J.S. Coleman, and J.E. Black (eds.) *Education and Training for Public Sector Management in Developing Countries*, pp. 73–83. New York: The Rockefeller Foundation.

Munroe B.H. and E.B. Page (1993) *Statistical Methods for Health Care Research* 2nd edition. Philadelphia: J.B. Lippincott Company.

Mwabu, G.M. (1986) 'Health Care Decisions at the Household Level: Results of a Rural Health Survey in Kenya,' *Social Science & Medicine* 22:3, pp. 315–19.

Mwabu, G., M. Ainsworth, and A. Nyamete (1993) 'Quality of Medical Care and Choice of Medical Treatment in Kenya: An Empirical Analysis,' African Technical Department, Human Resources and Poverty Division, Technical Working Paper no. 9. Washington: World Bank.

Newhouse, J.P. (1981) 'The Demand For Medical Care Services: A Retrospect and Prospect,' mimeo, prepared for the US Department of Health, Rand Corporation, Santa Monica, California.

____________. (1978) *Economics of Medical Care: A Policy Perspective* Reading, Mass: Addison-Wesley.

____________. (1970) 'Toward a Theory of Nonprofit Institutions: An Economic Model of a Hospital,' *American Economic Review* 60, pp. 64–74.

North, D.C. (1990) Institutions, Institutional Change and Economic Performance. New York: Cambridge University Press.

Norusis, M.J. (1994) *SPSS Advanced Statistics 6.1* Chicago: SPSS Inc.

Nougtara, A., R. Sauerborn, C. Oepen, and H.J. Diesfeld (1989) 'Assessment of MCH Services Offered by Professional and Community Health Workers in the District of Solenzo, Burkina Faso. 1 Utilization of MCH Services,' *Journal of Tropical Pediatrics* 35 (suppl. 1, pp. 2–9.

Nsubunga, H.S.K. (1993) 'History of Veterinary Services in Uganda,' *Uganda Veterinary Journal* 1:5–6.

Olson, M. (1965) *The Logic of Collective Action*. Cambridge: Harvard University Press.

Omorodion, F.I. (1993) 'The Socio-Cultural Context of Health Behavior Among Esan Communities, Edo State, Nigeria,' *Health Transition Review* 3:2, pp. 125–36.

Pankhurst, R. and E. Eshete (1958) 'Self-Help in Ethiopia,' *Ethiopia Observer* 2:11, pp. 354–64.
Parsons, T. (1951) *The Social System*. Glencoe, Illinois: The Free Press of Glencoe.
Pauly, M. and M. Redisch (1973) 'The Not-For-Profit Hospital as a Physicians' Cooperative,' *American Economic Review* 63, pp. 87–99.
Peterson, S.B. (1982) 'Government, Cooperatives and the Private Sector in Peasant Agriculture,' in Leonard and Marshall (1982) Chapter 3.
Pindyck, R.S. and D.L. Rubinfeld (1991) *Econometric Models and Econometric Forecasts* 3rd Edition. New York: McGraw-Hill.
Posner, R.A. (1972) 'The Appropriate Scope of Regulation in the Cable Television Industry,' *The Bell Journal of Economics and Management Science* 3, pp. 98–129.
Pratt, J. and R. Zeckhauser, eds. (1985) *Principals and Agents. The Structure of Business* Boston: Harvard Business School Press.
Pudney, S. (1989) Modeling Individual Choice: The Economics of Corners, Kinks and Holes New York: Basil Blackwell.
Republic of Kenya, Ministry of Livestock Development (1982) 'Submission by the Ministry of Livestock Development to the Working Party on Government Expenditure,' Nairobi: Republic of Kenya.
Roemer, M.I. and C. Montoya-Aguilar (1988) 'Quality Assessment and Assurance in Primary Health Care,' Technical Report 105, Geneva: World Health Organization.
Russell, S. (1996) 'Ability to Pay for Health Care: Concepts and Evidence,' *Health Policy and Planning* 11:3, pp. 219–37.
Sahn, D. and R. Bernier (1995) 'Has Structural Adjustment Led to Health Sector Reform in Africa?' in Berman (1995) pp. 245–75.
Samuelson, P. (1954) 'The Pure Theory of Public Expenditure,' *Review of Economics and Statistics* 36(1) pp. 387–89.
Sandford, S. (1983) *Management of Pastoral Development in the Third World* New York: John Wiley & Sons.
Sar, S.C. (1993) 'Etude de la relance du sous-secteur de l'élevage par la libéralisation et la privatisation,' République du Sénégal, Ministere du développement rural et de l'hydraulique.
Sauerborn, R., A. Nougtara, and H.J. Diesfeld (1989) 'Low Utilization of Community Health Workers: Results from a Household Interview Survey in Burkina Faso,' *Social Science & Medicine* 29:10, pp. 1163–74.
Savage, D.A (1997) *Self-Regulation and the Professions* New Haven: Institution for Social and Policy Studies, Yale University.

Savage, D.A. and P.L. Robertson (forthcoming) 'The Maintenance of Professional Authority: The Case of Physicians and Hospitals in the United States,' in P.L. Robertson, ed., *Authority and Control in Modern Industry* London: Routledge.
Schmidt, P. and R.P. Strauss (1975) 'The Prediction of Occupation Using Multiple Logit Models,' *International Economic Review* 16:2, pp. 471–86.
Seifu, A. (1968) 'Eder in Addis Ababa: A Sociological Study,' *Ethiopia Observer* 12:1, pp. 8–33.
Selden, T.M. (1993) 'Uncertainty and Health Care Spending by the Poor: The Health Capital Model Revisited,' *Journal of Health Economics* 12:1, pp. 109–15.
Sere, C. (1979) 'Towards an Economic Assessment of Veterinary Inputs in Tropical Africa,' Working Document No. 1. Addis Ababa: International Livestock Centre for Africa.
Shimkin, D.B., E.M Shimkin, and D.A. Frate (1978) *The Extended Family in Black Societies* The Hague: Mouton.
Simon, H.A. (1982) 'Theories of Bounded Rationality,' in Herbert Simon, ed., *Models of Bounded Rationality* Cambridge: MIT Press.
Simpson, J.R. and Evangelou, P. eds. (1984) *Livestock Development in Sub-Saharan Africa* Boulder: Westview Press.
Slikkerveer, L.J. (1982) 'Rural Health Development in Ethiopia: Problems of Utilization of Traditional Healers,' *Social Science & Medicine* 16:21, pp. 1859–72.
____________. (1990) Plural Medical Systems in the Horn of Africa: The Legacy of 'Sheikh' Hippocrates London: Kegan Paul.
Stanton, B. and J. Clemens (1989) 'User Fees For Health Care in Developing Countries: A Case Study of Bangladesh,' *Social Science & Medicine* 29:10, pp. 1199–205.
Stigler, G.J. (1968) *The Organization of Industry*. Homewood, Ill.: Richard D. Irwin.
Stinchecombe, A. (1968) *Constructing Social Theories*. New York: Harcourt, Brace and World.
Strickland, G. Thomas, ed. (1984) *Hunters' Tropical Medicine* 6th edition. Philadelphia: W.B. Saunders Co.
Stock, R. (1983) 'Distance and the Utilisation of Health Facilities in Rural Nigeria' *Social Science & Medicine* 17:9, pp. 563–70.
Sutter, J.W. (1987) 'Cattle and Inequality: Herd Size Differences and Pastoral Production Among the Fulani of Northeastern Senegal,' *Africa* 57:2.

Tacher, G. (1986) 'Projet de Développement de l'Èlevage dans l'Ouest de la République Centrafricaine: Evaluation Ex Post'. Maisons-Alfort, France: Institut d'Èlevage et de Médecine Vétérinaire des Pays Tropicaux.

Tang, S. (1997) 'The Changing Role of Township Health Centres,' in G. Bloom and A. Wilkes, *Health in Transition: Transforming China's Rural Health Services. IDS Bulletin*, 28:1, pp. 39–47.

Tembon, A. (1995) *A Study of Community Demand and Utilisation of Health Care Services in Ndop District Health Service in North West Cameroon* Unpublished Doctoral Thesis, London School of Hygiene and Tropical Medicine, University of London.

Thebaud, B. (1994) 'Exploitation agro-sylvo-pastorale des sols dans le nord du Sénégal: GTZ: Bilan et identification d'un nouveau projet,' Rapport de mission 28 mars au 5 mai 1994.

Theil, H. (1969) 'A Multinomial Extension of the Linear Logit Model,' *International Economic Review* 10, pp. 251–59.

Thonnat, J. (1993) *Formation des promoteurs d'élevage: Guide méthodologique* C.T.A., Wageningen.

Tipping, G. and M. Segall (1995) *Health Care Seeking in Developing Countries: An Annotated Bibliography and Literature Review* Development Bibliography 12. Brighton: Institute of Development Studies.

Touré, A.M. (1992) 'Strategies a adopter pour la privatisation,' in Production et Sante Tropicales.' Actes de la 7e *Conférence Internationale des Institutions de Médecine Vétérinaire Tropicale* Yamoussoukro, Côte d'Ivoire, CIRAD–EMVT, pp. 145–53.

Toye, J. (1995) 'The New Institutional Economics and Its Implications for Development Theory,' in J. Harriss, J. Hunter, and C.M. Lewis, eds., *The New Institutional Economics and Third World Development* London: Routledge, pp. 49–68.

Train, K.E. (1991) Optimal Regulation: The Economic Theory of Natural Monopoly Cambridge: MIT Press.

Transitional Government of Ethiopia (1995) 'Health Care Strategy,' mimeo, Addis Ababa (April).

Tuohy, C.J. and A.D. Wolfson (1978) 'Self-Regulation: Who Qualifies,' in P. Slayton and M.J. Trebilock, eds., *The Professions and Public Policy* Toronto: University of Toronto Press.

Umali, D.L., G. Feder and C. de Haan (1992) 'The Balance between Public and Private Sector Activities in the Delivery of Livestock Services,' World Bank Discussion Papers 163, Washington: World Bank.

Vétérinaires Sans Frontières (1994) 'Actes du colloque de bamako sur la privatisation des services vétérinaires,' Vétérinaires Sans Frontières.
Van der Gaag, J. and T. Barham (1998) 'Health and Health Expenditures in Adjusting and Non-Adjusting Countries,' *Social Science & Medicine* 46:8, pp. 995–1009.
Van der Geest, S. (1982) 'The Efficiency of Inefficiency: Medicine Distribution in Southern Cameroon,' *Social Science & Medicine* 16: 2145–53.
___________. (1992) 'The Cultural Acceptability of Paying for Health Care,' *Social Science & Medicine* 34:6, pp. 667–73.
Vogel, R.J. (1993) *Financing Health Care in Sub-Saharan Africa* Westport, Conn: Greenwood Press.
Waddington, C.J., and K.A. Enyimayew (1989) 'A Price to Pay: The Impact of User Charges in Ashanti-Akim District, Ghana,' *International Journal of Health Planning and Management* 31, pp. 17–47.
Wade, R. (1990) Governing the Market: Economic Theory and the Role of Government in East Asian Industrialization. Princeton: Princeton University Press.
Wamukoya, J.P.O., J.W. Gathuma, and E.R. Mutiga (1995) 'Spontaneous Private Veterinary Practices Evolved in Kenya Since 1988,' Rome: Food and Agricultural Organization.
Weber, M. (1978) *Economy and Society* (G. Roth and C. Wittich, eds.) Berkeley: University of California Press.
Werner, D. (1977) *Where There is No Doctor; A Village Health Care Handbook* Palo Alto, CA: Hesperian Foundation.
Wilensky, H.L. (1964) 'The Professionalization of Everyone?' *American Journal of Sociology* 70, pp. 137–58.
Williamson, O.E. (1975) Markets and Hierarchies: Analysis and Antitrust Implications: A Study in the Economics of Internal Organization New York: The Free Press.
___________. (1984) 'The Economics of Governance: Framework and Implications,' *Journal of Institutional and Theoretical Economics* 140, pp. 195–223.
___________. (1985) The Economic Institutions of Capitalism: Firms, Markets, and Relational Contracting New York: Free Press.
___________. (1990) 'A Comparison of Alternative Approaches to Economic Organization,' *Journal of Institutional and Theoretical Economics* 146:1, pp. 61–71.
___________. (1993) *Les Institutions de l'Economie* Paris: InterEditions.
Wilson, J.Q. (1980) *The Politics of Regulation* New York: Basic Books.

Wilson. R.T. *et al.* (1985) 'Preweaning Kid and Lamb Losses in Traditional African Management Systems,' 6th Conference OIE Regional Commission for Africa. Harare, 22–25 January 1985.

Wolf, C. (1988) *Markets or Governments: Choosing Between Imperfect Alternatives* Cambridge: MIT Press.

Wong, E.L. *et al.* (1987) 'Accessibility, Quality of Care and Prenatal Care Use in the Philippines,' *Social Science & Medicine* 24:11, pp. 927–944.

Wonnacot, T.H. and R.J. Wonnacot (1991) *Statistique* 4e Èdition, Paris, Economica.

World Bank (1981) *Accelerated Development in Sub-Saharan Africa: An Agenda for Action* Washington, D.C.: The World Bank.

World Bank (1989) *Sub-Saharan Africa: From Crisis to Sustainable Growth* Washington, D.C.: World Bank.

World Bank (1994) *Adjustment in Africa: Reform, Results and the Role Ahead* Oxford: Oxford University Press.

World Bank (1994) 'Better Health in Africa: Experience and Lessons Learned,' Technical Report, Washington: World Bank.

World Bank (1997) *World Development Report: 1997: The State in a Changing World* Washington, D.C.: World Bank.

World Health Organization (1993) 'Health Sector Financing and Budgeting in Ethiopia,' Unpublished report, Office for International Cooperation, WHO, Geneva.

Wouters, A.V. (1991) 'Essential National Health Research in Developing Countries: Health Care Financing and the Quality of Care,' *International Journal of Health Planning and Management* 6, pp. 253–71.

Yoder, R.A. (1989) 'Are People Willing and Able to Pay for Health Services?' *Social Science & Medicine* 29:1, pp. 35–42.

Zaidi, A.S. (1996) 'Gender Perspectives And Quality Of Care In Underdeveloped Countries: Disease, Gender And Contextuality,' *Social Science & Medicine* 43:5, pp. 721–30.

Zald, M. (1987) 'Review Essay: The New Institutional Economics,' *American Journal of Sociology* 93:3, pp. 701–8.

Zessin, K.H. ed. (1995) Livestock Production and Diseases in the Tropics: Livestock Production and Human Welfare. Proceedings of the VIII International Conference of Institutions of Tropical Veterinary Medicine, held from 25–29 September 1995.

Index of Persons

Index of Subjects